P9-DOG-469

# GOLF
# RESORTS
# OF THE
# WORLD

# GOLF RESORTS
## OF THE WORLD

# THE BEST PLACES TO STAY AND PLAY

BY BRIAN MCCALLEN
PHOTOGRAPHS BY MIKE KLEMME
A GOLF MAGAZINE BOOK

HARRY N. ABRAMS, INC., PUBLISHERS

*To golfers everywhere who believe that a golf trip is the best vacation of all, this book is dedicated*

Project Director: Margaret L. Kaplan
Copy Editor: Pauline Crammer
Designer: Robert McKee
Photo Editor: John K. Crowley

Library of Congress Cataloging-in-Publication Data
McCallen, Brian
    Golf resorts of the world: the best places to stay and play: a Golf
Magazine book / by Brian McCallen; photographs by Mike Klemme.
        p.   cm.
    ISBN 0–8109–3372–1
    1. Golf resorts—Directories.  2. Golf resorts—United States—
Directories.   I. Golf Magazine  (New York, N.Y., 1993)  II. Title.
    GV962.M33    1993          796.352 ' 06—dc20          93–21854
Text and, unless otherwise noted, all photographs
copyright © 1993 Harry N. Abrams, Inc.

Published in 1993 by Harry N. Abrams, Incorporated
All rights reserved. No part of the contents of this book may be
reproduced without the written permisssion of the publisher
Printed and bound in Hong Kong

Harry N. Abrams, Inc.
100 Fifth Avenue
New York, N.Y. 10011
www.abramsbooks.com

Endpapers: Hyatt Regency Sanctuary Cove, Australia
Page 1: Bali Handara Country Club, Indonesia
Pages 2,3: Awana Golf & Country Club, Malaysia
Pages 4,5: The Rose Garden, Thailand
Pages 6,7: Tryall Golf, Tennis & Beach Resort

# CONTENTS

# INTRODUCTION AND ACKNOWLEDGMENTS

In the fall of 1987, I was hired by *GOLF Magazine* to expand its travel section. The first task at hand was the establishment of a resort awards program. The idea was to tread where no golf publication had gone before—into the land of objectivity. Correspondents would be dispatched to resorts anonymously at the magazine's expense to play golf, dine, and enjoy the good life the way a typical paying guest would. (Members of the press normally receive gratis accommodations and other perks when traveling on assignment.) At the conclusion of the survey, the finest properties would be awarded gold or silver medals. Citations would be made without regard to current or future advertisers. Our aim was to establish standards of excellence and a voice of authority that readers could rely upon to make educated travel choices.

To that end, selected subscribers were asked to rate the most important elements of a golf vacation. Based on their responses, a detailed questionnaire was drafted. Sixty percent of the questions were devoted to the resort's golf experience, from quality of course design (including balance and variety of holes, memorability, aesthetics, and tradition), to speed of play, friendliness of pro shop staff, and, most important of all to the sampled readers, course condition.

The second part of our survey was devoted to the quality and comfort of a resort's accommodations, overall service, availability of nongolf activities, and quality of food in the dining rooms. A splendid meal at day's end was considered indispensable to the resort experience. According to those surveyed, the dining category was exceeded in importance only by course condition.

And so the standards were set: peerless golf in a beautiful setting, a friendly, welcoming staff, and superior dining with service to match. Those closest to perfection would be golds, those one rung below would be silvers.

It remained only to draw up a roster of properties to be visited, choosing from among more than 600 resorts nationwide. With the list pared down to slightly more than 100 resorts, a group of well-traveled golf writers, golf officials, and assorted golf nuts with good taste and spare time were instructed to purchase a golf package for a minimum of two nights, play the golf course(s), order room service, eat a variety of meals at different on-site restaurants, and take note of how the staff treated them. There was also the resort's ambiance to consider, that often intangible sense of place that separates the superior from the pedestrian. And people. In the final analysis, it was people, not fantastic scenery or spouting fountains or great par fives, who separated the gold medal winners from the silvers and the silvers from those that didn't make the cut. Consequently, the magazine's roving band of correspondents and I took note of how we were treated from check-in to check-out by the front desk personnel, pro shop staff, maitre d', and waiters.

In addition to filling out the questionnaire, each correspondent was also asked to submit an essay detailing his or her impressions and opinions of each property. Outspokenness and honesty were encouraged. The questionnaire enabled us to assign a numerical value to each resort, while the essay provided us with subjective insight. The combination of the two gave us a clear picture of a resort's merits—or lack thereof. I myself racked up nearly 100,000 miles in air travel between November 1987 and June 1988, an ordeal that quickened my backswing, expanded my waistline, and left me with a fabulous collection of small shampoo bottles. The October 1988 issue of *GOLF Magazine* published a list of America's best resorts: twelve gold medal and thirty-two silver medal winners.

The following year, we set our sights on the world, a far more daunting (and costly) enterprise. Nearly 100 resorts in forty countries were visited and evaluated. It was a logistical nightmare, both for me and for our far-flung correspondents, many of them British journalists whose droll, witty essays about nine-hole goat pastures with pup tents pitched near the smoking ruins of a hotel could qualify as chapters of their own. My own experiences abroad were mixed. The French police at Orly Airport in Paris blew up my (momentarily unattended) luggage. I was passed counterfeit money in Spain. When I tried to exchange it for lira in Italy, bank officers threatened to have me arrested. I ate meals that tied my stomach into knots for weeks. I watched the glamour of international travel fade with each canceled flight. About every other time zone, a medalist would leap to the fore. Nine gold medal and twenty-four silver medal winners were identified in the November 1989 issue. (One medalist sustained major hurricane damage in 1990 and lost its standing.)

Now that my passport has had a chance to cool off, I can honestly say that nothing matches the excitement and adventure of an overseas golf trip. Golfers as a tribe are a friendly lot. They speak a universal language. The passion for the game is shared from Turnberry to Tryall. And while foreign courses aren't always as well-manicured as the home-bred variety, neither are they as "designed" as stateside layouts. Natural contours, not artificial hazards, usually provide the challenge. For a sport that evolved on sandy deposits along the seashores of Scotland, the game has adapted amazingly well to other environments.

Imposing the American concept of a resort (by our definition, a jointly owned and physically proximate golf course and lodging entity) on the international scene eliminated many contenders. A classic example is the Old Course Golf & Country Club in St. Andrews, Scotland. Although situated alongside the infamous Road Hole of the Old Course, hotel guests are not guaranteed a chance to play the storied links, but must apply to the Links Management Committee for a tee time like everyone else.

In 1990, we took a second look at the leading domestic resorts to update our list of medalists. Newcomers with high standards were welcomed to the fold, but we also identified casualties (of both natural disasters and financial calamities) from the 1988 resort list. By this time, *GOLF Magazine*'s gold and silver medals were as coveted among golf resorts as the Mobil and AAA awards are among all lodging establishments.

In 1992, our anonymous visitors were armed with a reconstituted questionnaire. The American Hotel & Motel Association, a respected federation of hoteliers with more than 10,000 members, helped us to broaden the survey's golf categories—and bolster its lodging, dining, and service aspects. More scientific in scope than previous rating sheets, the questionnaire required correspondents to evaluate everything from the texture of the sand in the traps to the quality of the furniture in the guest rooms. Five resorts made the necessary self-improvements to move up in class from silver to gold. In addition, two properties that had fallen from grace in 1990 were reinstated. Finally, eight new resorts earned a medal, pushing the number of domestic award winners to sixty-four. This book is the fruit of those five years of research, travel, and evaluations.

Each chapter in this book is organized geographically. Descriptions of the properties are followed by a golf tip from a resort pro, often with specific application to the region. A "Side Trips" section describes natural wonders, cultural attractions, places of historic interest, family-oriented amusements, scenic drives, and other activities within the vicinity of each resort. There is, after all, life beyond the golf course, especially for nongolfers traveling in the company of the committed.

Unless otherwise noted, all yardages given are from the regular men's tees. (The average handicap of a GOLF Magazine subscriber is 16. Enough said.)

A few tips for the traveling golfer. Lay out all the items you plan to bring, divide the pile, and pack half. Club rentals have improved dramatically at most resorts—consider renting clubs instead of lugging your own. A comfortable pair of golf shoes is indispensable to an enjoyable golf holiday. Personally, I travel with spikeless golf shoes, a golf glove, a packet of tees, and a dozen balls. I'm not that particular about equipment—I usually shoot the same 82 (or 94) with or without my own sticks. If you insist on traveling with your clubs, invest in a canvas cover for your golf bag and stuff a couple of towels into the bag to protect your clubs en route.

Be a smart traveler. Call the resort's pro shop ahead of time for their course maintenance schedule. Recently aerated or top-dressed greens can take the fun out of a golf holiday. Check with the concierge about proper dress: Many of the older, more traditional resorts require a jacket and tie at dinner. (A few, like The Greenbrier and The Cloister, encourage black tie on selected nights.) Those seeking good value for dollar should inquire about shoulder season packages. (Each resort's address is listed in the back of the book.) Resorts discount their rates dramatically before and after peak seasons, though it should be noted that in travel, as in everything else, you get what you pay for. The Arizona desert in July isn't nearly as inviting as it is in January. Tariffs reflect seasonal desirability.

No book is the work of one person. In the case of Golf Resorts of the World that statement is doubly true. My first thanks go to George Peper, who hired me for the job and who gave me full rein and liberty to shape the magazine's travel section. His ideas, contacts, and support were responsible for bringing the medalist program to fruition. Not many editors are given carte blanche by a publishing company to run up a six-figure bill in the name of "research." I am indebted both to George for his confidence in my ability to organize the resort evaluations, and to the Times Mirror Company for its faith and trust in a project that has cost more than $400,000 to date. Thanks, too, to Jim Frank, an early booster of expanded travel coverage in the magazine. George, Jim, and I serve as the magazine's travel roundtable. It is we who sort through the questionnaires and essays to determine each year's list of medalists.

My sincere thanks to GOLF Magazine publisher Peter Bonanni and the advertising staff, who turned their collective cheek when a resort that believed it was slighted (either by omission or by the awarding of a silver rather than a gold medal) withdrew advertising. Never once was I asked to change a single word to placate a current or potential advertiser. No journalist could ask for more. My thanks go as well to my fellow staff members at GOLF Magazine, whose good cheer carried me through many a long day spent in the office hunched over my resort files.

As for the book itself, my thanks to photographer Mike Klemme for putting his life and family on hold for a year while he globetrotted to nearly all of the ninety-six medalists. He could have written a book himself about his experiences. Instead, he contributed his superb photographs to this one.

I owe a large debt of gratitude to Margaret L. Kaplan, executive editor at Harry N. Abrams, who demonstrated unfailing enthusiasm for this book from day one and who skillfully edited my weighty manuscript. Thanks as well to photo editor John Crowley, for his fine eye and organizational skills, and to Bob McKee, for his superb design of the book. Special thanks to Polly Crammer, whose deft copy editing and professionalism buoyed my spirits when the task seemed endless.

Though their anonymity has remained intact till now, I would be remiss not to mention by name the correspondents whose reports shaped this book. They are: Eliot Asinof, Dave Baldridge, Michael Bamberger, Jim Bartlett, Matthew Bell, Furman Bisher, Andy Brummer, Rob Buchanan, Sam Cantor, Mike Cox, Ron Crowley, Tom Doak, Jim Dodson, Joann Dost, David Earl, George Eberl, Jim Finegan, William Price Fox, Stephen Goodwin, Frank Hannigan, John Harbottle, Red Hoffman, Teague Jackson, Jacob Kamhis, Brad Klein, Arnold Langer, Robert Laubach, Marshall Lewis, Robert MacDonald, John Paul Newport, Jr., Jack O'Leary, James Olman, Lee Pace, Herb Partridge, Russ Pate, T. R. Reinman, Dave Richards, W. Lynn Seldon, Jr., Loran Smith, Parker Smith, Robert Sommers, Art Spander, Walt Spitzmiller, Pat Sullivan, John Veracka, Glen Waggoner, and Jeff Wallach. Their fair and timely reports opened a window on each resort's quality and ambiance.

On the international side, a thousand blessings on our stalwart correspondents: John Barnes, Derek Collier, Dudley Doust, Brad Ewart, Jim Fitchette, Mark Garrod, Colin Hastings, Robin Knight, Derek Lawrenson, Michael McDonnell, Terry McLean, Phillip Morrice, Charles Mulqueen, Nick Pitt, Chris Plumridge, Tom Ramsey, Lorne Rubenstein, Bob Weeks, and Keith Wheatley.

Public relations departments at resorts were prompt and helpful in their provision of facts and vital statistics. So were the many directors of golf who shared with me the particulars of their operation.

Two reference books served me well during the course of my research: The Golf Course, by Geoffrey Cornish and Ronald Whitten; and The World Atlas of Golf, by Pat Ward-Thomas, Herbert Warren Wind, Charles Price, and Peter Thomson.

To friends and family members whose patience and understanding sustained me through many long days and nights of research and writing, my heartfelt thanks. A tip of the hat to computer whiz Martin Weinberg, who guided me through the minefield of word processing; to my golf buddies, especially my dad and my brother David, who often played without me and were kind enough to share with me their adventures; and to my late Uncle Herb, for whom I caddied as a youngster and who opened my eyes to the finer points of the game. And finally, thanks to Saddia, for her love and understanding during all those weekends that were anything but.

BRIAN McCALLEN
NEW YORK CITY
JANUARY, 1993

# HAW

The Hawaiian Islands are actually the tops of volcanic mountains that bubbled up from lava vents in the floor of the Pacific Ocean not so long ago. In that sense, their existence is pure serendipity, a geological miracle. Which probably accounts for the sunny dispositions of the Hawaiians, who, despite the bonds of statehood and the ongoing transformation of their precious islands from places of myth and beauty to the vacation crossroads of the Pacific, still welcome visitors—including those often dour individuals fixated on what locals call "da game"—with a warm aloha spirit.

Resort layouts on Hawaii's three best islands for golf—the Big Island of Hawaii, Maui, and Kauai—are surprisingly diverse. From the Big Island's

# *AII*

desolate lava flows, to west Maui's pineapple field mosaics, to Kauai's rugged green headlands, the islands' beauty quotient is very high. Even serious golfers—the ones who keep track of their putts and discuss ways to save strokes over dinner—have been known to observe their surroundings in Hawaii and comment favorably. And if the dreamy sound of ukuleles and the sight of humpback whales breaching in the blue Pacific don't move you, the weather will: It's perfect. Lots of sun, low humidity, and always a breeze to keep things interesting.

This sybaritic experience does not come cheaply. The $100 green fee is commonplace in Hawaii. So is the $350 hotel room. But it's hard to put a price on the rewards of playing golf in America's closest approximation to paradise.

*Inset: Torchlight ceremony at Kauai Lagoons. Photo courtesy Kauai Lagoons Golf & Racquet Club. Large picture: Mauna Lani, South Course, fifteenth hole*

Golfers bound for the Big Island of Hawaii have William Quinn, the state's first governor, to thank for its best-known resort. It was he who invited Laurance Rockefeller to tour the islands in 1960, hoping the conservationist-developer would be inspired to build a resort hotel along the lines of the environmentally harmonious properties he had opened to acclaim in the Caribbean. Though he had previously expressed no interest in developing a Hawaiian resort, Rockefeller changed his mind when he caught sight of the perfect crescent of white sand at remote Kaunaoa Bay along the Kohala Coast. This would be the place to build his dream property, a resort to fulfill his desire for "understated perfection in unspoiled, beautiful places." Eventually, the building of the Mauna Kea Beach Hotel would be accompanied by a careful search for fine Asian and Pacific arti-

facts that would blend with the open-air architecture and gardens to create an organic whole. When it opened in 1965, Mauna Kea was proclaimed the most beautiful resort hotel in the world.

For starters, the 1,600-piece collection of folk and tribal *objets d'art* is displayed casually, without descriptive placards. Visitors are made to feel like guests in the spacious home of a wealthy collector with exquisite East-West sensibilities. In fact, Rockefeller started a trend that has been imitated by every other high-end Hawaiian resort—the incorporation of art in the hotel. But no one before or since has done it better than Rockefeller.

Hotel guests are free to view the extensive collection on their own with the aid of a tour booklet provided in the guest room, or join twice-weekly tours of the hotel conducted by Don Aanavi, professor of art history at the

*Above: Ninth hole*

*Left: Third hole*

University of Hawaii–Hilo who describes in precise and lively detail the individual pieces, starting with the hotel itself. Sand-colored concrete columns, smooth fieldstone flooring, rough lava rock walls, and teak ceiling panels create a variety of textures. They also provide a frame for the collection. Flanking the hotel entrance are a pair of gilded temple guardian figures, each a model of strength and serenity, while in the open-air breezeways are displayed Thai dragons, Japanese lion dogs, Indian temple toys, Solomon Islands dance wands, framed Hawaiian quilts, and fearsome, plaited rattan head masks from New Guinea on tree-fern pedestals. Temple bells and wind chimes tinkle when a sea breeze enters the hotel's atrium.

Mauna Kea's most prized possession is a large pink granite Buddha from seventh-century India seated atop a long wooden stairway in the north garden court. Positioned in accordance with Buddhist tradition—his heart above the level of the viewer's eye—the statue's sinuous eyes and knowing, blissful smile signal enlightenment. Sharp-eyed guests will notice a slight discoloration above the Buddha's navel. Aanavi smiles when asked about it. "Golfers are known to rub the Buddha's belly for good luck before teeing off," he explains. "They also place lotus blossoms in his open palms." Sure enough, there are flowers in his cradled hands. After tackling Mauna Kea's infamous golf course, newcomers will divine why repeat guests offer supplications to the Buddha.

Robert Trent Jones inscribed the Mauna Kea Beach Golf Course on a prehistoric lava flow the color of distressed leather. On this arid, hilly plain—only scrub and cactus peek through the desiccated remains of the flow—Jones fitted earth-moving equipment with specially ribbed rollers to pulverize the lava, creating a powdery soil in which grass seedlings could sprout. He then built an elaborate irrigation system that still pumps more than a million gallons of water per day onto fairways and greens that receive eight inches of rain annually.

But Mauna Kea is more than a marvel of engineering. Jones, following Rockefeller's dictate that nature reign supreme, did not rearrange the site's natural contours in fashioning a well-balanced layout. Unlike many new resort courses, only the soil, not the landscape, was manufactured.

In typical Jones fashion, Mauna Kea is bold and assertive in its presentation of golf challenges. This is golf course as extrovert, with assets fully exploited: an ocean view *at every hole*; elevated tees with dramatic 100-foot drop-offs to the fairway; and a panorama of the broad, gentle slope of 13,796-foot Mauna Kea ("white mountain"), named for its wintertime cap of snow. Nearly thirty years after they were planted alongside the fairways, the coconut palm, Chinese banyan, monkeypod, wili-wili, plumeria, and rainbow shower trees are now mature. They soften the corners of the course beautifully.

Like the full-size sedans of the mid-1960s, Mauna Kea is plush and roomy. But while its fairways are spacious—there is plenty of room to drive the ball—its undulating greens can be maddeningly difficult. Several were toned down by Robert Trent Jones, Jr. in 1975. Rest assured that plenty of challenge remains. Greens with radical slopes and quick pace may be a source of high entertainment to the casual player, but they usually give serious golfers fits. More than a few head directly to the nineteenth hole for a double mai tai after the repeated embarrassment of a three-putt green.

In 1983, twenty-two new tees were established to provide a wider range of options to golfers. Not only had a younger, limber-backed clientele appeared on the scene thirsting for a big-time challenge, but older guests were finding it increasingly difficult to get around the course. Mauna Kea now sports four sets of tees. Golfers simply pick the color tee best suited to their games. Seniors and women are happiest at the whites (5,277 yards), average golfers do fine from the orange markers (6,365 yards), low-handicappers and most pros choose the blues (6,737 yards), and frequent guest

Isao Aoki, the Japanese star, and a handful of other world-class players tackle the black tees (7,114 yards).

The third hole, one of the world's most exhilarating seaside par threes, has *five* sets of tees—four that are played and one that is not. Golfers play from a lava promontory—this after adequate time for photographs and exclamations—and must carry their shots across an inlet of the Pacific to a large, kidney-shaped green bisected by a sharp ridge and guarded by seven traps. The view is of crashing waves, distant Kohala peaks, and, set back from the beach, an ancient Hawaiian temple. Well behind the pro tee is a modest platform furnished with a koa wood bench for whale-watchers. It was on this platform, 250 yards from the front of the green, that the "Big Three"—Arnold Palmer, Jack Nicklaus, and Gary Player—teed off when the course opened in 1964. (Player, incidentally, could not carry his ball over the water.)

Tougher by far than the third and nearly as scenic is the long par-three eleventh hole, which plays from an elevated tee to a crowned green that falls away to deep bunkers and the exposed roots of giant banyan trees. Miss the green here and you're in for an easy five. The eleventh kicks off a stretch of testing holes that make scoring difficult on the back nine. "Try to make time on the outgoing holes," advises J.D. Ebersberger, Mauna Kea's director of golf, "because the incoming nine is about three strokes harder." Jones's dictate that every hole be a "demanding par and a comfortable bogey" is simply not reliable on the home holes—especially when the trade winds blow.

While the golf course can be trying, Mauna Kea's accommodations are decidedly comfortable. The rooms, simple by modern standards, have large lanais, teak and willow furnishings, woven Thai cotton bedspreads, and floral serigraphs that create a peaceable mood. Following Rockefeller's original instructions, rooms have no radio or television. The idea is to leave behind reminders of civilization and relax.

Mornings at Mauna Kea usually start in the Pavilion, where macadamia waffles or banana pancakes go perfectly with the rich Kona coffee. The luncheon buffet on the Terrace is one of Hawaii's finest (the Hawaiian fern shoot salad is healthful, the macadamia nut cream pie irresistible), while traditional favorites are served in the Batik Room, an elegant salon set off by tangerine and pink Sri Lankan tapestries and a howdah, the thronelike canopied litter used for riding in style on the backs of elephants.

Though the hotel is much less formal than in earlier days, gentlemen are still asked to wear a jacket to the Garden, where cutting edge regional cuisine features guava and coffee-bean-smoked lamb, bamboo-steamed kalua pork dumplings with macadamia nuts, and Hawaiian baby abalone sauteed in kakui nuts with rice noodles, and lime-tobiko caviar sauce. In addition, the Island Clambake at the Hau Tree on the beach (Saturdays) and Sunset Luau at North Pointe (Tuesdays) are two of the best outdoor dining experiences in the islands.

*Left: Breakfast on the terrace*

*Below: Tennis courts overlook the sea*

*Right: Seventh-century Buddha in pink granite*

*All photos courtesy Mauna Kea Beach Hotel*

First impressions can deceive at the Mauna Lani Resort, Mauna Kea's Kohala Coast neighbor. After turning off Queen Kaahumanu Highway and driving seaward, all one sees for miles on either side of the road is a spiky blanket of licorice-black lava that looks as if it might have cooled and hardened last week. It's not every world-class resort that sports a giant pan of overbaked brownies for a front lawn. But eventually the road leads from this scene of withering desolation to the impressive porte-cochere and blue tile driveway of the Mauna Lani Bay Hotel, where arriving guests are greeted by a beautiful Hawaiian girl bearing fragrant leis of carnations, orchids, and crown flowers. After stepping past reflecting pools aswim with torpedo-shaped koi, the multicolored carp prized by the Japanese as symbols of prosperity and good luck (they're raised like Thoroughbreds and are nearly as valuable), visitors are brought to a rosewood desk and offered a glass of fresh orange juice. Check-in was never easier.

Mauna Lani ("mountain reaching heaven") occupies the site of an ancient Hawaiian fishing village where Hawaii's early royalty perfected the art of relaxation. Resort founders have worked with *malama* (enlightened stewardship) to preserve the petroglyph fields, lava tube dwellings, and fifteen acres of spring-fed ponds where seafood delicacies were once raised for the king. It is impossible to stay at Mauna Lani and not sense its mana—spirit of place. The presence of Pele, the volcano goddess, also can be felt, especially when "vog"—volcanic fog from still-alive Kilauea—forms on the mountain ridges that backdrop the resort.

The sleek, chevron-shaped hotel, one of the world's most beautiful properties, features an ocean view from nearly every one of its 351 rooms. Each opens on a dazzling open-air atrium marked by tall palms, silent waterfalls, and a garden café. Most afternoons, grass-skirted dancers perform the hula as musicians strum ukuleles and sing about old Hawaii. At night, a jazz trio sets up in the atrium bar behind one of the Plexiglas waterfalls. When the song is right, lovers dance under the twinkling stars. Small wonder that Mauna Lani is so popular with honeymooners.

The Francis H. I'i Brown Golf Course at Mauna Lani, recently expanded to thirty-six holes, is named for the dashing sportsman and bon vivant, half Hawaiian and half English-Scottish, whose estate at Kalahuipua'a spawned the 3,200-acre resort. Known for his opulent lifestyle, Brown owned fourteen cars, entertained extravagantly, and counted Babe Ruth, Bob Hope, Howard Hughes, John Wayne, and Bing Crosby among his friends. (Crosby was once quoted as saying, "The man I most admired and wanted to be like was Francis I'i Brown.") A champion golfer, Brown was

a nine-time winner of the Hawaiian Amateur Championship and shot a 67 on the Old Course at St. Andrews, Scotland, while tuning up for the 1924 British Amateur Championship. He loved golf as much as the people of Hawaii loved him.

The golf course built in his honor is a work of art in volcanic media. The contrasts among the beautifully manicured fairways, the pitch-black *a'a* lava, the white sand traps, the reddish-brown *pahoehoe* lava, and the turquoise-blue sea are very appealing. So are the challenges: Holes with wide fairways, little rough, and flattish greens not only yield birdies to skillful players, they reward the modest efforts of higher handicappers. It also is a course that flatters a woman's game. Comments hotel manager Charles Park, one of Hawaii's top amateur players, "I don't know of a course where women have a better chance of beating their husbands. I can have a good match with my wife, and she's a 30 handicap."

The original front nine, sculpted from lava deposited by the prehistoric Kaniku flow, was successfully grafted to a new nine (holes two through ten) to form the South Course in 1990. Overall, the composite South retains the characteristics of the original course. Gentle contouring not only emulates the broad slope of distant Mauna Loa ("long mountain"), it tends to contain offline shots.

Mauna Lani's signature ocean hole, formerly the par-three sixth, is now the fif-

*Above: Bedroom and terrace. Photo courtesy Mauna Lani Bay Hotel, © David Franzen.*
*Opposite: North course, seventeenth hole.*

teenth and perhaps is more memorable in the current sequence. Its geography is exquisite: From a series of tee boxes chiseled into a lava rock pedestal (the back tee at 199 yards is particularly daunting), golfers must brave tricky crosswinds and play their shots across a surging inlet of the Pacific to an enormous green staked out by coconut palms and cloverleaf bunkers. The hole is more forgiving than it appears, though the salt-and-pepper beach of rounded white coral and black lava rocks between tee and green is no place to be.

Among the better new holes, the par-three seventh runs along the sea to a sizable green backdropped by stark rock formations that rise from Honokaope Bay, while the par-four ninth features a split-level fairway bisected by a swath of basaltic rubble. (The tempting upper route is shorter but more dangerous than the safer lower road.) Incidentally, there's nothing to gain by trying to retrieve your ball if it skips wide of the fairway: The sharp *a'a* lava rips apart balls (and shoes) on contact.

The North Course overlays fields of 5,000-year-old *pahoehoe* lava, its greens and gently rolling fairways bordered by groves of twisted *kiawe* (mesquite) trees. The landscape resembles the savannahs of East Africa, minus the herds of zebra and wildebeest, though feral goats roam freely.

Designer-builder Homer Flint, in conjunction with Raymond F. Cain of Belt, Collins & Associates, seamlessly joined nine new holes (four through twelve) to the original back nine to create a tournament-tough layout with extended tees, one of which is located in the center of a tidal pond. (No, you don't have to swim it.)

The North's feature holes remain the original layout's short par-five eleventh, where petroglyphs (mostly stick figures with arms and legs akimbo) are carved into the rocks near the tee; the 126-yard seventeenth, its green contained within a banked amphitheater of toasted rock; and the 386-yard eighteenth, where the giant cone of 10,023-foot Mt. Haleakala on Maui is the directional marker from the tee. Pay your respects to the lava gargoyle that glares across the links as you leave the course for Knick-

ers, a clubby mahogany-paneled grill and bar with framed golfiana and antique books lining the walls; and the Golf Shop, which could give a designer outpost on Rodeo Drive in Beverly Hills a run for its money. Not only is its selection of intarsia cashmere sweaters definitive, but what other resort pro shop showcases Italian leather golf bags ($1,500 and up), crocodile loafers by Polo (don't ask), and golf-theme keepsakes wrought in sterling silver?

Two other lodging options have debuted at the resort since the Mauna Lani Bay Hotel opened in 1983. The 542-room Ritz-Carlton at Pauoa Bay, opened in late 1990, is a luxurious hotel geared mainly to incentive travelers and business groups, while the Bungalows at Mauna Lani Bay are quite simply the summit of luxury. Each of the five 4,000-square-foot private

*Swimming pool*

18

seaside residences features a full-time chef and butler to cater to every whim. The bungalows are promoted as the finest accommodations imaginable, and at $2,500 per night, they should be.

Mauna Lani's restaurants are among the best in Hawaii. Go formal at Le Soleil, enjoy any meal of the day alfresco at the Bay Terrace (the breakfast *malasadas*—deep-fried Portuguese crullers—are superb), or stop by the more casual Gallery, located near the exhibition tennis court. The Gallery's feature dish, wok-charred *ahi*, is a must-try: seared chunks of yellowfin tuna served in a fanned arrangement on a bed of radish sprouts with papaya relish on the side. Very tasty.

The resort's newest dining spot, the Canoe House, features Pacific Rim cuisine (defined as Asian-influenced foods presented in a contemporary California manner) in an open-air seaside room that celebrates the site's heritage as a fishing village. A *koa* fishing canoe hangs suspended from the high ceiling. On the wall is a pair of crab-claw-shaped sails woven from *lauhala* trees that propelled early vessels. As for edibles, the pupus, or appetizers, are excellent, particularly the sesame shrimp on crispy noodles with *lilikoi* (passion fruit) glaze, while the main course of bamboo-steamed *mahi mahi* (dolphin fish) and Chinese cabbage with ginger and scallions is nonpareil. But so too is the feeling of tiptoeing round the royal fishponds on a moonlit night when the only sounds heard are those of the juvenile *awa* (milkfish) splashing in the shallows. That is when Mauna Lani's mana is unmistakably felt.

*The Atrium*

# WAIKOLOA BEACH RESORT

*View from a room*

It's currently fashionable to bash mega-resorts as too capricious to satisfy the tastes of sophisticated travelers. Certainly the 1,241-room Hyatt Regency Waikoloa, the $360-million centerpiece of the Waikoloa Beach Resort on the south Kohala Coast, is flamboyant in the extreme. The advertising copy describes the resort as a place where "fantasies come to life, the senses are indulged, passions are requited, and the pursuit of happiness is limited only by the scope of your imagination." Heady stuff. But the sprawling hotel, the largest in Hawaii and one of the biggest resort properties in the world (it was described by writer James Michener at its 1988 opening as "the kind of place God would have built if He had sufficient cash flow"), is nothing if not entertaining. Motorized canal boats and a Swiss tram transport guests to their rooms, while art viewing and exercise can be combined by strolling the mile-long "museum walkway," its corridors decorated with a hodgepodge of Asian artifacts.

Part tropical movie set and part amusement park, the hotel's list of superlative attractions is long. It includes:

• The main lobby, where towering colonnades (the kind Samson toppled) rise from a pink flagstone stairway that descends into a saltwater lagoon stocked with tropical fish;

• A four-acre, beach-rimmed lagoon with a free-form swimming pool marked by waterfalls, a hidden grotto bar, and a giant waterslide;

• A protected saltwater lagoon where the resort's popular dolphin encounter program is conducted (guests must enter and win a lottery to participate, though there's a daily children's event);

• Eight restaurants, from Donatoni's (northern Italian cuisine in a classy villa setting) to Imari (authentic Japanese tabletop cooking on teppanyaki grills);

• A state-of-the-art spa, called ANARA (A New Age Restorative Approach), where a staff of sixty specializes in ancient fitness techniques (yoga, tai chi) as well as serious pampering;

• A full-time director of fantasies who can organize once-in-a-lifetime experiences, such as a gourmet picnic on a remote cliff accessible only by helicopter, or a wild boar hunt on the slopes of Mauna Kea;

• A staff astronomer who trains a high-powered telescope on Hawaii's brilliant night sky and describes to guests what's out there in spellbinding detail.

Then there's the golf. The original Waikoloa Beach Golf Course, a Robert Trent Jones, Jr. design, benefited greatly from a $3-million facelift in 1989. Essentially a parkland-style layout set upon lava, the Beach Course skirts the island's second-largest petroglyph field before bringing golfers to the brink of the Pacific at the 497-yard par-five twelfth hole. This is golf hole masquerading as thrilling temptress: A zigzag double-dog-leg, it asks for length and precision of those heroic dreamers who try for the green in two. Prudent golfers can leapfrog their shots from one safe landing area to the next to reach the green in regulation. The modest remains of an ancient fishing shelter are found in the center of the fairway, while a stubbly lava field borders the entire right of the hole. A pushed shot usually ends up in the rumbling surf of Anaeho'omalu Bay. From the lava promontory that holds the well-bunkered green, breaching humpback whales can be spotted offshore in the winter months. This is Hawaii's finest seaside par five.

The Kings Golf Club, a Tom Weiskopf–Jay Morrish design opened in 1990, is a flattish, inland layout patterned after a Scottish links. In direct contrast to the high-profile hotel, the Kings emphasizes balance and restraint. Not only do holes quarter to nearly every point of the compass, enabling the course to be played when the Kona winds or tradewinds stir, but there's an unusual double green (shared by the third and sixth holes), as well as a pair of short, driveable par fours (the fifth and thirteenth). Driveable, that is, if you happen to play them downwind, manage to thread your drive safely past water, sand, and lava—and are a big hitter to begin with. Deep greenside bunkers, a half-dozen lakes, and gigantic lava boulders that sprout like free-form sculptures from a few of the fairway traps can interfere with low scoring at the Kings, though wide fairways and large greens left open in front enhance more than hinder playability. It is the push and pull of fair and difficult that lends the course its appeal. The clubhouse, its upstairs deck topped by a gold weathervane, is a fine place to review your scorecard before heading back to the hotel for a giant dollop of fantasy.

Beach Course, twelfth hole

Motorized canal boat in hotel waterway. Photo
courtesy Hyatt Regency Waikoloa Beach Resort

# KAPALUA BAY HOTEL & VILLAS

Wedged between West Maui's scalloped lava coastline and a sprawling 23,000-acre pineapple plantation, Kapalua generates the excitement of a world-class resort while retaining an essentially rural character.

To the ancient Hawaiians who lived and fished on Maui, this land was *Kapalua* ("arms embracing the sea"), so named for the lava rock fingers that reach into the ocean and cradle the shoreline's bays. The handsome 194-room hotel terraced down to the sea is a prime example of "disappearing architecture," for the structure is camouflaged by the natural surroundings. The sweeping open-air lobby, its potted trees alive with tropical birds, frames a fantastic view of the Pacific. Garden paths weave through fruit-bearing trees, flowering shrubs, and ti leaf plants to a clifftop pool shaped like a butterfly, where iced pineapple spears are served from a roving cart. Many golfers never get around to unpacking their clubs at Kapalua.

*Above: Bay Course, fifth hole*

*Right: Beachfront*

*Opposite, below: Kayaking*
*Photo courtesy Kapalua Bay Hotel & Villas*

But that would be a shame. The opening of the Plantation Course, added to the Bay and Village courses, gives Kapalua three distinctive layouts. Each is a captivating test of golf. But the soundness of the designs is only a small part of their appeal, because nowhere else are golf courses eclipsed so completely by their natural settings as here.

The Bay Course, an Arnold Palmer–Frank Duane layout opened in 1975, features broad, rolling fairways with little rough and plenty of room to hit the ball. This room is welcome, because wind is usually a factor, particularly at the fourth hole, a short par four that doglegs to Oneola Bay, its green fitted snugly atop a lava promontory. The fifth hole, a thrilling par three of 154 yards, plays across a gaping chasm in the black lava cliffs to a well-bunkered green. To realize what sort of challenge confronted the pros

during the 1988 World Cup, size up the hole from the championship markers at 205 yards, preferably with a twenty-five-mile-per-hour cross-wind racing across the links. If you do manage to reach the green, remember that most putts on the Bay Course break toward the Auau Channel, which separates Maui and the island of Lanai.

Kapalua's Village Course, a Palmer–Ed Seay design circa 1981, sets gravity on its ear at the start—the first four holes play straight uphill—but rewards skybound golfers with over-the-ledge views of great rifts in the fecund earth. Holes five and six, both shortish par fours that enclose a lake, occupy a plateau 800 feet above sea level.

In an age when smaller rather than larger parcels of real estate are made available for new golf course construction, the Plantation Course, opened

in 1991, is a throwback. This is a big course that takes full advantage of its dramatic, large-scale setting. On a 240-acre site, Texans Bill Coore and Ben Crenshaw laid out a par-73 layout that features wide, promenading fairways and enormous greens, à la Augusta National, that snowbirds with rusty swings can find.

Crenshaw, a staunch traditionalist when it comes to golf course design, harked back to several early American classics in seeking inspiration for the design of the Plantation. At least two of the holes, the fourth and twelfth, are taken from the National Golf Links of America in Southampton, New York, the nation's first great course.

"Here we have the rarest combination you can find in golf," Crenshaw said shortly before the Plantation Course opened, "a strikingly beautiful

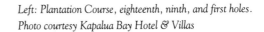

*Left: Plantation Course, eighteenth, ninth, and first holes.*
*Photo courtesy Kapalua Bay Hotel & Villas*

*Below: Plantation Course, seventeenth hole*

location that is also a natural for play. Our design didn't really have to create new holes as much as take the existing land and natural characteristics and adapt them to create the most exciting, challenging play possible. Nature gave us a tremendous head start."

Did it ever! Sloping terrain, low vegetation, and deep ravines mark the course, which lacks a single water hole. Bunkering is pronounced and dramatic throughout, as are tee-to-green distances: the Plantation stretches to a man-eating 7,263 yards from the tips. (It's a more manageable 6,547 yards from the regular men's tees.) Native grasses from Molokai inhabit the rough, but they stand well back from the fairways. Prevailing wind patterns were calculated in the design, which is more strategic than penal. The current site of the Lincoln-Mercury Kapalua International tournament, the Plantation Course is more than Maui's best layout; it's also one of the best new classic courses of the 1990s.

Kapalua's creature comforts are very fine. The open-air Grill & Bar at the Bay Course, with its upcountry and ocean views, is one of the most popular nineteenth holes in the islands. Not only are the mai tais flawless, but the pupu platter (Cajun chicken wings, homemade egg rolls with Maui onion and hot mustard sauce, and sashimi) is superb. More substantial victuals are available at the Bay Club, a candlelit room done in koa-trimmed pine walls and batik-upholstered rattan furniture that was originally intended as a private dining room for resort investors. Built on a lava promontory angled to the west, the room fills with oohs and aahs during one of those orange sherbet sunsets for which Hawaii is known. *Ahi* (yellow-fin tuna), *mahi mahi* (dolphin), *opakapaka* (pink snapper), and other local fish are prepared six different ways, including sautéed with oysters and shrimp in a dill-flavored white wine sauce. The Bay Club's list of California wines is definitive, not surprising for a resort with one of the best wine cellars in the Pacific. (Kapalua's sommelier hosts weekly wine-tasting sessions for guests.)

The spacious accommodations, in muted shades of taupe, rose, and terra cotta, feature his-and-hers marble vanities, gold-tone fixtures, and private lanais. Room bars are stocked with Russian caviar, Swiss chocolates, and Maui potato chips. Chip connoisseurs say they are the best. Golf connoisseurs say the same of Kapalua. In the words of three-time U.S. Open Championship winner Hale Irwin, the resort's touring professional: "There is something distinctly different about playing at Kapalua. Some days, I think it is the setting. Other days, I know it is the way I play. No matter what, it is an experience I always remember as only happening here."

*Kiele Course, sixteenth hole*

Any native of Kauai knows that to build something great, a call must go out to the *menehune*, that mysterious race of diminutive people who sailed north from Tahiti to Kauai long ago. Short and squat and very industrious, they are said to work on projects only at night, using their great strength and vast numbers to accomplish mighty feats.

Perhaps that's who think-big developer Chris Hemmeter recruited to build Kauai Lagoons Golf & Racquet Club and the extravagant Westin Kauai along a half-mile stretch of Kalapaki Beach near Lihue Airport. "We're creating monuments to mankind, to the joy of life, to the majesty of the senses," Hemmeter rhapsodized to the island's citizenry before transforming the former Kauai Surf hotel, a dowdy high-rise, into a five-story complex of 847 guest rooms complemented by some of the grandest public spaces this side of Versailles.

"It all relates to size," Hemmeter explained during construction. "The human race has always put a premium on scale. The pyramids are just

thrilling structures! Washington, D.C., is monumental. Each has a grandness, a scale, a noble feeling."

Ancient Egypt and the nation's capital haven't been eclipsed by Kauai Lagoons, but this is the resort future generations will point to when they want to know what $360 million could buy in the 1980s.

Arriving guests, after being picked up by a complimentary limousine at Lihue Airport and driven along a private road to the resort, are greeted by an enormous white marble Buddha near the hotel entrance. (Hemmeter leased a marble quarry in China and hired a village of carvers to produce the resort's large-scale statuary.) An escalator descends from the open-air lobby to the Palace Court, where the 2.1-acre reflecting pool and its seven larger-than-life white marble horses galloping through a sixty-foot-high geyser of water tend to widen the eyes of even the most jaded travelers. Gargantuan koi (carp) carved from black marble spout water twenty feet into the pool, while matched pairs of black and white swans glide regally across the water's surface. Lacquer paintings the size of movie screens hang in alcoves around the perimeter of the court. Burmese winged lions, teak relief carvings from Thailand, ten-foot-high cloisonné vases, and faux marble columns comparable in size to those that supported the palaces of Imperial Rome compete for attention. And that's just the Palace Court. Other one-of-a-kind features at Kauai Lagoons include:

• A 26,000-square-foot, rosette-shaped "aquatic fantasy" patterned after the turquoise-tiled pool at San Simeon, Hearst's castle.

• Narrated outrigger canoe rides through a forty-acre system of man-made lagoons that pass near islands stocked with wallabies, monkeys, kangaroos, gazelles, llamas, zebras, and exotic birds.

• Custom-made, convertible landaus drawn over eight miles of crushed coral paths by champion draft horses.

• One-hour thrill sails aboard a forty-two-foot racing catamaran that tops off at twenty-five knots, about the speed of the flying fish that usually race the boat.

• An early evening torchlighting ceremony on the beach, featuring traditional Hawaiian singing and dancing to the beat of sharkskin-covered drums.

Yet with all this competition, golf may still be the resort's best amenity. There are two Jack Nicklaus–designed layouts: the big-time Kiele Course (named for the sweet fragrance of the gardenia flower), an outstanding test that sketches the dimensions of an epic journey; and the sportier Lagoons Course, a links-style layout built on former sugarcane fields. The Kiele is the most playable and aesthetically pleasing resort course Nicklaus has designed to date.

At the time the resort was taking shape, Hemmeter claims to have given Nicklaus an unlimited budget (Jack claims to have exceeded it) to build one of the great golf courses of the world. Nicklaus's task was made immeasurably easier by the 262-acre parcel of land set aside for the Kiele Course, encompassing as it does a lush inland jungle and volcanic headlands set high above Nawiliwili Bay. "The site is one of the most magnificent pieces of property I have ever seen," Nicklaus said before breaking ground. After touring the finished links in 1988, Nicklaus, no shrinking violet as a player or a designer, said: "On a scale of one to ten, I'd rate the Kiele a thirteen."

Certainly Nicklaus allowed the inherent drama of the landscape to define the essential shape and routing of the holes. Unlike many previous Nicklaus efforts, which have tended to be suitable only to a player with Nicklaus's ability to drive the ball powerfully from the tee and hit towering, accurate approaches that land softly—like "a butterfly with sore feet," as Lee Trevino once said—the Kiele can be enjoyed by all types of golfers if the right tees are chosen. (There are four sets, ranging from 7,070 to 5,417 yards.)

The Kiele's front nine, longer but less exposed to the wind than the back, opens innocently on gently rolling land west of the sea. The fifth hole, a long par-three called the Eagle (each hole is named for an animal or a deity, and each tee is graced by a large white marble statue of that animal or deity placed on a 6,000-pound granite base), plays over a canopy of the rain forest to a tabletop green backdropped by a pleated volcanic ridge. The forecaddie stationed on the tee—he's there to clean your clubs and discuss strategy—will advise the use of extra club, because the green is far larger than it appears, and because there's nothing but trouble short of the green. Take his counsel.

The ride from tee to green at the fifth is memorable: Golf carts descend a switchback path to the deeply shaded floor of the forest, where wild chickens and guinea fowl scurry through the undergrowth. To emerge in the sunshine and look back over the tops of the mango, guava plum, and broad-leafed schefflera trees and realize that this lush valley doubles as a golf hole is truly exciting.

The back nine of the Kiele is a revelation. Not only are golfers brought to the brink of the Pacific, they are treated to one of the best and most thrilling stretches of resort golf in existence.

The fun starts at the 409-yard twelfth hole, the Alligator, which tumbles down a funnel-shaped, bunker-lined fairway to a two-tiered green set on a ledge overlooking the ocean. The breeze picks up here. So does a golfer's adrenaline. At the 162-yard thirteenth hole, called the Frog, golfers play their tee shots from an elevated seaside perch across a roiling ocean inlet to a green that beckons from a jungly pedestal far below tee level. To experience the true scariness of the hole, walk back to the gold tees at 207 yards, where the prospect of clearing the black sand beach and foaming surf is really daunting, even if the prevailing tradewinds are at your back. As at the fifth, arm yourself with extra club—underhit shots imbed themselves in thick vegetation that cannot be parted to find a golf ball. The green itself is framed by tall palms. Above their fronds loom the broken peaks of volcanic mountains. You are free to jump into the shark tank at Sharkey's Fish Market overlooking the green if you dunk more than three shots.

After a breather hole that turns inland, the par-five fifteenth hole returns to the sea, its fairway canted from right to left and its rippled green set on bluffs above a water spout: From a craterlike hole in the charred rock shoreline, the surf spumes high in the air with each incoming wave.

Often it is the eccentric holes that endear a course to golfers. In his quest to build Great Tests of Golf, with all hazards and landing zones plainly visible, Nicklaus's courses, stripped of mystery, were fair to a fault. The 279-yard sixteenth hole, the Turtle, is a welcome departure from his previous course designs. Again, a forecaddie is on hand to offer encouragement and dispense advice on how to play the hole. The drive is essayed to the crest of a hill—the landing area is blind—while the approach is played with a short iron (but from a downhill lie) to a tricorn green that occupies a lava peninsula. Imagine a turtle on a rock about to slide into the water. It's unwise to attack the pin; the green is as slick as one of the hotel's marble floors. A shot that hits the green on the fly scoots over the putting surface like a scared mouse into a gathering trap fully twelve feet below the level of the green. This is jail. Far better to aim the approach to the bottom of the hill on the right and allow the ball to pitch off the slope, pinball-style.

The 130-yard seventeenth hole turns away from the sea but keeps water in play. Tee shots are played over a lagoon to a green backdropped by seventeen palms and nearly encircled by a deep U-shaped bunker. To the right of the tee is a white gazebo built on pilings—the resort's Chapel by the Sea, a popular wedding spot.

Depending upon the direction of the wind, the Kiele's par-four eighteenth can be a cream puff or a bear. Played into the breeze, it is a punishing hole, despite the generous tee-shot area: Water not only borders the entire right of the hole, it cuts in front of the semi-island green. Screw up your courage for a big second shot—or recognize that discretion is the better part of valor if your drive gets hung up in the wind and lay up short of the lagoon.

Nicklaus, who is listed as Kauai Lagoons's director of golf, was miffed to find that none of the holes was named for his sobriquet when the course was formally opened. Consequently, the Happy Buddha was moved from the eighteenth to the first tee, and a Golden Bear—in white marble it resembles a polar bear—was installed at the home hole, its nose pointed in the direction of the fairway. Call it author's pride, chalk it up to ego, but Jack got the personal totem he wanted.

On agricultural land not far from Lihue Airport's runways, Nicklaus built the Lagoons Course, intended as a sporty companion to the majestic Kiele. A links-style layout marked by gently rolling fairways, sandy waste areas, and well-contoured greens, the Lagoons can play tough when tradewinds sweep the nearly treeless site. According to Nicklaus, "Our goal was to create a course where players would have plenty of room to hit the ball, and still find some exciting and fun-filled golf." The Lagoons poses a gentler challenge than the Kiele—bunkers and water hazards are less severe—but it is no weak sister, especially when stretched to its full length of 6,942 yards.

In addition to the two courses, there's another plus to the resort's golf experience: Hotel guests are made temporary members of the Kauai

*Kiele Course, fifteenth hole*

nese tapestries and a mural depicting Captain Cook's arrival in the Sandwich Islands. The menu is centered on eight to ten types of fresh local seafood prepared by an all-Hawaiian kitchen staff whose preparations of Hawaiian spiny lobster and *lehi* (long-tailed snapper served stuffed with a scallop mousse and accompanied by a delicate puff pastry) are superb. There's an excellent selection of California wines to accompany these dishes, too. After dinner, dancing under the stars is popular on the Inn's torchlit terrace. So is relaxing with an after-dinner drink in a cozy upstairs lounge where a jazz trio performs.

*Horse-drawn carriage*

Lagoons Golf & Racquet Club and receive all the privileges of membership, including unlimited practice balls, a roomy oak locker, admission to the spa and wellness center (where fitness assessment and lifestyle appraisal programs are available), and shoe and club cleaning.

Is there a better place in the golf resort universe to work up an appetite than Kauai Lagoons? Probably not. The resort's roster of restaurants comprises the best and most varied collection of dining places imaginable.

For starters, there's the Inn on the Cliffs, a "destination" dining room reached by mahogany launch boat or horse-drawn carriage. Perched on cliffs above Ninini Point with a 200-degree ocean view available through its picture windows, the high-ceilinged room is set off by large framed Chi-

*Kiele Course, fifth hole*

Prince Bill's, located atop the Surf Tower, is the place for grilled steaks and a grand view of the backcloth for the *King Kong* remake. Is it sizzle you're after? Hot Rocks Dining—patrons prepare meals on heated granite stones—is available at the poolside Cook's at the Beach. So is the Tropical Itch, a pleasantly lethal concoction designed to wipe out negative swing thoughts. It is mixed with a foot-long backscratcher, which can be used as a walking stick when you're finished. Duke's Canoe Club, named for Duke Kahanamoku, the father of Hawaiian surfing, and Sharkey's Fish Market are good choices for informal meals.

But it's the golf at Kauai Lagoons, not the sumptuous dining, that lingers longest in the memory. And if the humps alongside the Kiele's fairways look suspiciously like spectator mounds, Nicklaus did expect that the course might one day attract a tournament. Perhaps the pros will discover what amateurs have known since Day One about the Kiele: Regardless of score, it's the kind of course you simply can't wait to play again.

*Opposite: Kiele Course, sixteenth hole.  Above: Swimming pool*

# PRINCEVILLE RESORT

SILVER MEDALIST

lights in the raised roof. On the dining side, the essence of a southern Italian villa has been re-created at La Cascata by way of terra-cotta floors, a double-vaulted ceiling, and trompe l'oeil paintings. Café Hanalei, overlooking the bay and its endless succession of breaking waves, spreads Kauai's finest seafood buffet on Friday evenings. The hotel's favorite repast is afternoon tea served in the lobby's adjoining living room, its built-in library filled with hardcover classics and comfortable chairs. Cocktails are served on an outdoor terrace off the lobby where the dramatic crushed orange sunsets could find a place in any novel in the library. As for accom-

In a previous life, it was a faceless Sheraton hotel with a cavelike lobby that took no advantage of its spectacular location on Kauai's north shore. But a $120-million surgical demolition in the early 1990s transformed this introverted concrete bunker into a European-style palace terraced down a cliff overlooking Hanalei Bay and the fabled peak of Bali Hai. And while Hurricane Iniki wreaked its own form of demolition when it struck Kauai in September, 1992, the 252-room Princeville Hotel survived the storm and reopened, as grand as before, a year later.

Italian marble flooring, antique tapestries, an ormolu gilded fireplace, an authentic Louis XVI revolving clock, and a hand-painted piano from the 1730s (among other tasteful antiques) grace the hotel lobby, its gurgling fountains and well-appointed sitting areas brightened by giant sky-

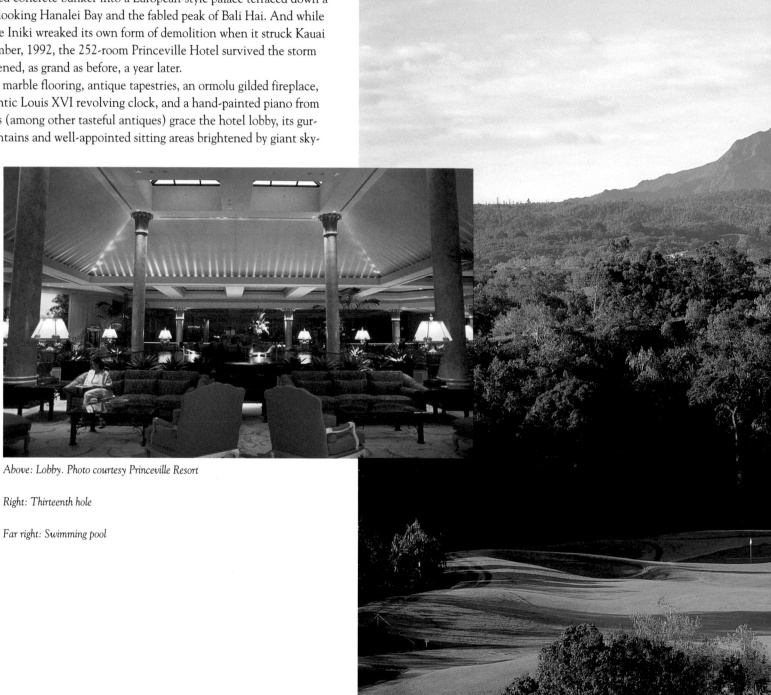

*Above: Lobby. Photo courtesy Princeville Resort*

*Right: Thirteenth hole*

*Far right: Swimming pool*

modations, many of the well-appointed rooms feature fantastic ocean views as well as liquid crystal windows that change from clear to frosted at the flick of a switch. Service? A staff of twenty butlers on twenty-four-hour call assures that guests are well cared for.

Princeville showcases the early and recent designs of Robert Trent Jones, Jr., a part-time Kauai resident who maintains a home in nearby Hanalei. The resort's twenty-seven-hole Makai Course, consisting of three distinct nines that can be played in any combination, provides a near-perfect resort golf experience. Each is fun, challenging, and scenic. The

Ocean and Lakes nines were renovated in 1991 (resurfaced greens, new irrigation system, repaved golf cart paths), while the Woods nine was treated to a facelift in 1993.

On the strength of its outstanding par threes, the Ocean is the most memorable and sought-after nine of the three. The 142-yard third hole calls for a short iron shot from a skybound tee to a green guarded by a lake and backdropped by the verdant Na Pali cliffs. Its beauty to challenge ratio is perfect. The seventh is risky business, especially from the tips at 204 yards. Tee shots here must carry a 160-foot-deep ravine where ocean rollers crash into a pile of blackened rocks, the distant green perched above albatross nests on a cliff garnished with tropical vegetation. When the Pacific trade winds blow, this hole can subdue the best of players.

But even in a gale, the Ocean seventh is a pushover compared to the rigors of the Prince Course. Vital statistics tell the story of Hawaii's most challenging layout: 7,309 yards from the tips, a course rating of 75.6 (par is 72), and a slope of 144, highest in the state. Five sets of tees, minimal bunkering, and relatively gentle greens give everyone a chance, but this is a course for the serious player. On 390 acres of rolling pastureland sandwiched between the blue Pacific and serrated volcanic palisades laced with streaming waterfalls, Jones sculpted a majestic layout that traces the natural heave and toss of the terrain. "Because the site was so dramatic, I tried to extract a golf course from the landscape, not impose one on it," Jones said when the course opened in 1989. Most of the holes are edged or bisected by cliffs, streams, jungles, and gorges—triple-bogey country. Avoiding the edge-of-the-world abysses is the key to success on the Prince.

There are feature holes aplenty, including two that borrow heavily from Pine Valley and Cypress Point, but the best holes are originals. These include the fishhook-shaped tenth, a par five that yields birdies, double bogeys—and very little else. The twelfth, known as the Eagle's Nest, calls for a bombs-away tee shot from a tee perched 100 feet above the fairway. The approach shot is aimed to a green cut into a mossy amphitheater of ferns.

At the 382-yard thirteenth, a stream purls across a slim fairway carved from a rain forest of mango and guava trees, requiring a lay-up shot from those who can't carry the ball 240 yards in the air. A waterfall built a century ago by coolie labor cascades behind the small oval green.

If there's one drawback to Princeville, it's the weather. The north shore of Kauai is cool and rainy in the winter. Bring a rain suit and woolens from December through February, or visit at a more clement time of year. If and when it does rain, the hotel's sixty-seat theater screens new releases as well as *South Pacific, Blue Hawaii,* and other classics filmed in Hawaii. But pray for fair skies—it's the Prince Course that keeps purists on the edge of their seats.

# HAWAII

### TIPS AND SIDE TRIPS

*A helicopter flies over a lava flow. Photo courtesy Papillon Hawaiian Helicopters*

Hawaii has more fun things to do off the golf course than any other state in the nation. Where else can you go surfing, windsurfing, sailing, snorkeling, scuba diving, hiking, camping, hunting, deep-sea fishing (for blue marlin), or horseback riding? Or just plain relax on some of the best beaches in the Pacific? Or join a whale-watching cruise (book one out of Lahaina, Maui, in the winter months when the whales are visiting), or reserve a seat on the forty-six-passenger submarine in Kailua, Hawaii? Looking for bragging rights back home? Arrange to go downhill skiing on the slopes of Mauna Kea on the Big Island from December through May.

Is a thrilling but passive activity more your speed? Then consider flight-seeing, or touring the islands' inaccessible beauty spots by helicopter. Not inexpensive at $150 to $300 per ride, but utterly memorable.

Jokingly referred to by locals as Hawaii's new state bird (they are ubiquitous in wilderness regions), helicopters are the ultimate trailblazers. They are capable of flying into craters and hovering over waterfalls, lava flows, and sea cliffs not accessible any other way. Headsets supply the pilot's narration or music appropriate to the natural wonder being viewed.

*A helicopter follows the Big Island's dramatic coastline. Photo courtesy © Brian McCallen*

Papillon Hawaiian Helicopters, the state's largest helicopter sightseeing company, offers excellent forty-five-minute to two-hour tours of the Big Island of Hawaii, Maui, and Kauai.

On the Big Island, tours depart a landing site at the Mauna Lani Resort for some of the world's most spectacular volcanic scenery. After passing between 13,680-foot Mauna Loa (goats and sheep can be spotted on its slopes) and 13,796-foot Mauna Kea (seven observatories are grouped near its summit), the helicopter passes over still-active Kilauea. If Madame Pele, the volcano goddess, is feeling hot-tempered, orange-red rivers of molten lava can be viewed in their seaward progress. Tremendous clouds of steam are produced when the lava hits the water.

After refueling, the pilot heads to the Big Island's east coast, where the sheer cliffs of the Hamakua Coast are the gateway to the Waipo Valley, a broad cleft in the Kohala Mountains. There, 1,000-foot bridal veil waterfalls, fantastic chasms, and spectacular greenery leave most passengers speechless.

On Maui, flights depart from the Kapalua Hills Heliport for 10,023-foot Mt. Haleakala ("house of the sun"), an enormous cone that dominates all sightlines on the island. After reaching the rim, the helicopter descends nearly 3,000 feet into the volcano's nineteen-square-mile crater (it's nearly large enough to contain Manhattan) to explore its barren moonscape. A stop for lunch can be arranged in the gorgeous Hana district. The excursion also features the state's tallest waterfall and the world's highest sea cliffs.

Seen from the air, Kauai emerges as the lushest and most beautifully eroded island in the chain. Tours departing from Lihue Airport fly to Waimea Canyon, described by Mark Twain as the Grand Canyon of the Pacific; the Na Pali Coast, where verdant cliffs rise 3,000 feet from the sea; and Waialeale Crater, one of the wettest spots on earth and a veritable rainbow factory.

---

DON'T LEAVE HOME WITHOUT...PROPER ALIGNMENT

*A*fter concluding a round of golf in a driving rainstorm on the Monterey Peninsula, Johnny Miller told me, "There is nothing in the Rules of Golf which says that golf will only be played in ideal weather conditions."

*Fortunately for visitors to Hawaii, the weather for golf in these beautiful islands is near-perfect year round. Sunny days, temperatures in the low eighties, and balmy breezes prevail. The only adverse weather conditions are fairly strong tradewinds. Though infrequent, these winds can blow twenty to thirty miles per hour. These conditions make it absolutely imperative to reduce the amount of right-to-left or left-to-right spin applied to the golf ball. The best way to do this is to align yourself properly to your target.*

*Proper alignment is best pictured through the image of a railroad track. If you are right-handed, your ball would sit on the right rail, and you would stand on the left rail. If you were to picture these*

*rails extending all the way to your target, the right rail (your target line) would hit the target, and the left rail (your body line) would miss the target to the left. Violations of these parallel tracks—aiming right or left of your target—mean forcing yourself to work the clubhead across what should be the parallel target line. The end result is side spin.*

*Get on track and eliminate side spin. You'll be better able to cope with Hawaii's tradewinds!*

DENNIS ROSE, DIRECTOR OF GOLF,
WAIKOLOA BEACH RESORT

It's simply not possible to sum up quickly California's attributes as a golf destination. With more geographic diversity among its top resorts than any other state, California proposes a getaway for any season, a course to suit any taste, and the widest array of post-round diversions and amusements imaginable.

"The face of the earth as the Creator intended it to look" is how Henry Miller described Big Sur, but he could just as easily have been referring to the Monterey Peninsula. This rugged fist of land thrust into the Pacific Ocean 120 miles south of San Francisco not only presents the most eloquent coastal scenery in the nation, it is anchored by one of the truly great golf courses of the world, Pebble Beach Golf Links. Next to St. Andrews in Scotland, it is the most recognized course name in all golfdom. Plan to visit in the spring or fall when the weather is at its best.

North of San Francisco, Napa's rolling hills shelter dozens of fine wineries, their vineyards stretched for miles along the Old Silverado Trail. Avid golfers and serious oenophiles rolled into one can do no better than Napa Valley.

# ORNIA

In southern California, Ojai is a sleeper community of artists and potters a ninety-minute drive north from Los Angeles. However, the town and its refurbished resort, walled in by the ridges and spurs of the Topa Topa Mountains, is light years away from the freeways and smog of Tinseltown.

La Costa Resort and Spa in Carlsbad, north of San Diego, is a beacon for golfers seeking play on a television tournament golf course, as well as a sybaritic retreat for look-good, feel-good spa-goers. Both contingents mingle happily.

In the California desert east of Los Angeles is Palm Springs, one of the wealthiest communities in the nation and a place where the palm-treelined thoroughfares are named for such well-known residents as Bob Hope, Frank Sinatra, and Gerald Ford. If you own a flashy convertible, this is the place to drive it. Private clubs inaccessible to transient players greatly outnumber resorts in this winter golf capital, though La Quinta Hotel, opened in 1926, alone retains the charm of its storied Hollywood past.

Meals at California's golf resorts are among the best available, for two reasons: The state's excellent quality of life attracts talented chefs; and the Golden State produces about half of the nation's fruits and vegetables. Also, California's wines now rival the best France has to offer. Cheers, *bon appétit*, and fore!

*Inset: Entrance, The Lodge at Pebble Beach. Large picture: Indian Wells Golf Resort, West Course, sixteenth hole*

Even if you've heard the story, it bears repeating. A well-to-do lawyer fulfilled a life-long dream by taking a year off from his practice to play 100 of the best and most exotic golf courses in the world. He teed up at Los Leones beneath the towering spires of the Chilean Andes, played in the shadows of the Giza pyramids at Cairo's Mena House Golf Club, strolled the crumpled links of Royal Dornoch in the far north of Scotland, and wandered through the sulphurous steam that drifts across the fairways from geysers at Wairakei in New Zealand. Cypress Point, Shinnecock Hills, Pine Valley, Augusta National—all were on his itinerary. After returning home from his golfing odyssey, he was asked if there was one course in the world that surpassed all others. "Yes," he said without hesitation. "Pebble Beach."

The origin of the Pebble Beach Golf Links on the Monterey Peninsula is familiar to most followers of the game. It, too, bears repeating. The links was laid out in 1919 by a pair of local amateur champions who were pressed into service by visionary developer Samuel F.B. Morse, a grand-nephew of the telegraph inventor. After purchasing 7,000 acres of real estate on the peninsula, much of it along the ocean, Morse insisted that the golf course be laid out on land that had been earmarked by previous owners for oceanfront homes. In addition, he reconstructed the Del Monte Lodge (long since expanded and renamed The Lodge at Pebble Beach) to attract visitors to an area he believed was unrivaled for natural beauty. Golfers everywhere owe Morse a great debt of gratitude.

If your appreciation of Pebble Beach is derived solely from viewing the links on television, a big surprise awaits. Pebble Beach doesn't come off that well on the tube. The sweep and scale of holes stretching along the craggy bluffs of Carmel Bay cannot be fully grasped until they are seen in person. Once they are played, a golfer cannot help but sing their praises, for Pebble Beach is by turns the most thrilling, beguiling, and stupendous golf course on the face of the earth.

The first three holes open innocently—but not *that* innocently—on gently rolling land cut from a forest of Monterey pines. Players don't catch sight of the sea until they reach the short, uphill par-four fourth, the left side of its fairway pitted with bunkers and the right side bordered by a cliff that tumbles down to a sandy beach. Miss the putting surface by a fraction, and you're faced with an explosion from sand (or a delicate chip from the vegetal equivalent of steel wool) to a lightning-fast green tilted from back to front. Once you do get a putter in your hands, you'll be confronted with quirky slopes and subtle breaks that even locals claim are virtually unreadable. Welcome to double-bogeyville.

*Above: Dining al fresco. Photo courtesy The Lodge at Pebble Beach*
*Opposite: Ninth and tenth holes*

After detouring uphill through a narrow corridor of trees at the 156-yard fifth hole, serious intentions are signaled at the par-five sixth, where golfers play up a fairway that resembles the deck of an aircraft carrier listing to starboard—and oblivion. The green is sited at the brink of a high escarpment where the breeze, even on a mild day, is usually fresh enough to ripple the flag. It is followed by the 103-yard seventh, its small, firm green embraced by bunkers and set dangerously near the sea. Overshoot the green, and the closest drop area would be Hawaii. The wind dictates strategy: It's a smooth wedge or 9-iron under normal circumstances, but if the wind is whipping the bay into whitecaps, you may have to resort to Sam Snead's strategy: One foul-weathered day in a long-ago Bing Crosby Pro-Am, he putted the ball along the ground to keep it out of the jaws of a squall. Its stunning location and potential for calamity make Pebble's seventh the finest short par three in the world.

There is a moment of truth on every great course, a juncture at which a golfer is tested to the limit of his skills. At Pebble, the curtain usually rises or falls at the 405-yard eighth hole, where the approach—this after a blind drive to the crest of a hill—is played across a gaping chasm in the 100-foot-high bluffs. The shot not only must be of heroic proportions to carry the gorge, it must also find and hold a tilted green the consistency of polished marble. Jack Nicklaus has called it the most dramatic second shot in golf.

The ninth and tenth holes are both long par fours that tightrope the headlands, their vast fairways sloped gently to the Pacific. The views from these two holes of the hulking coastal mountains and the wave-tossed sea, the mist rising like gunsmoke from the rocky shore beyond Carmel Beach, are the best in the sport. Because both greens are situated hard by the edge of the cliffs, they play difficult on the calmest day. When a stiff wind blusters the links, a top-flight pro would be happy to settle for bogey at either hole.

The links leads away from this magnificent stretch at the eleventh hole, its fairway tracing the outward curve of the layout's elongated figure-eight routing. Among the better holes on the incoming nine is the 553-yard fourteenth, which plays much longer than its measured length and deserves well its number-one handicap ranking. The drive is played to a broad fairway that bends gently to the right at about the 250-yard mark. Those who attempt the short route up the right side run the risk of going out of bounds. A gaping mouth of sand protects a two-level green that is extraordinarily slick.

Like an epic poem that gathers steam in its final stanzas, Pebble returns to the sea at the par-three seventeenth, where a narrow promontory holds

a skewed, hourglass-shaped green girdled by sand. Capricious winds have a way of directing all but the truest shots to the wrong side of the midriff bulge that divides the green into two distinct putting areas. Worse, the wind deposits indifferent shots in sand or deep grass, an all-too-familiar scenario for most golfers at this point in the round. The seventeenth was imprinted on the national golfing consciousness when Tom Watson chipped in from off the left edge of the green to secure victory in the 1982 U.S. Open Championship.

Of the many great finishing holes in golf, the par-five eighteenth at Pebble Beach is the best and most memorable. An imposing dogleg that follows the rounded sweep of Carmel Bay, the hole is played from a tee that occupies a broad shelf of weathered rock. Behind it, floating canopies of the bay's dense kelp forests sway in rhythm with the ebb and flow of the ocean. Playful sea otters occasionally peek their whiskers from among the thick strands of kelp, while harbor seals—they look like swollen cigars six feet long—bask on the rocks in the bay. The hole itself, familiar to most golfers from years of televised viewing of the AT&T Pebble Beach National Pro-Am (Jack Lemmon's misadventures are usually the highlight of the broadcast), has a string of out-of-bounds stakes up its right side to discourage golfers from steering too clear of the seawall and pebbly beach up the left side. Played judiciously, it can be reached in three carefully planned shots that cheat the wind. The green is another story. Most first-

time players depart the eighteenth in a state of semishock, either because they exceeded their handicap by a dozen strokes or more, or because the links went way beyond their notion of how great a course can be.

The majesty and grandeur of Pebble Beach tend to obscure its merits as a strategic test of golf. Only precise, intelligent golf carries the day at Pebble. When the elements act up, equal amounts of patience and skill must be summoned. Even on a fair day, the minuscule greens—the smallest of any of the world's great courses—are hard to hit. They're also slippery. Bring your delicate flip shot, your even more delicate flop shot, your square grooves, brake fluid, chewing gum. Think sticky. No wonder Bob Hope, a fine golfer in his day, called the links "Alcatraz with grass." Then again, Jack Nicklaus, who captured the 1961 U.S. Amateur and 1972 U.S. Open championships at Pebble, once said, "If I had only one more round of golf to play, I would choose to play at Pebble Beach."

One last word: Arrange for a caddie or carry your bag. The curbed golf cart paths swing well left and right of the fairways. It's impossible to formulate strategy, much less see the course, from their perspective.

The Lodge at Pebble Beach is often overshadowed by its illustrious links. It needn't be. With 155 rooms and six one-bedroom suites located in thirteen rambling low-rise buildings spread throughout the grounds, the Lodge offers splendid accommodations. Nearly all rooms have working fireplaces, and many skirt the right flank of Pebble's eighteenth fairway,

*Seventh hole*

*Eighteenth hole*

The Lodge's dining choices are as various in mood and character as the links itself. The glass-walled Cypress Room, located on the entrance level of the main building, has incomparable views of the eighteenth green, Carmel Bay, and, looking toward Big Sur, rounded peaks in the Santa Lucia Range. The room itself, set off by wicker chairs, potted palms, tall white pillars, and lanternlike chandeliers, is romantic and elegant. There's soft piano music to dine by, and an excellent selection of wines to accompany regional cuisine. Club XIX has a dual personality: By day, fortifying sandwiches and salads are served on an umbrella-shaded patio located an invitingly short distance from the eighteenth green. At night, Club XIX is transformed into a formal, intimate candlelit room where updated continental cuisine is rendered expertly.

The Tap Room, patterned after an English pub and located across a greensward from an arcade of shops spaced along a breezeway, is the heartbeat of the Lodge. Black-and-white photographs of great golfers and celebrities (including a young, crew-cut Clint Eastwood), as well as memorabilia from the many tournaments held at the great links, warm the walls of this informal gathering spot. Choose from among thirty brands of bottled beer or sample the resort's specialty drink, a Del Monte Fizz (fresh orange and lemon juice, gin, cream, egg white, vanilla extract, and sugar,

placing guests within earshot of barking sea lions and the Pacific's low, muffled roar. Rooms are large (nearly 650 square feet on average), comfortable, and California traditional in motif. Brick hearths are stacked daily with seasoned oak and pine logs. Many of the rooms feature ceilings painted in dreamy swirls of cream and blue, hand-carved chairs, antique bureaus, large vanities, and a private balcony or garden patio. Is there a better view from a fairway villa than Pebble's eighteenth fairway? Not in this life.

Service at the resort—the staff is comprised mainly of bright, young, cheerful Californians—is impeccable. So are the gratuity arrangements: Tipping is discouraged, as a daily service charge is applied to the guest's hotel account.

As much a country club as a golf resort, the Lodge has at its guests' disposal the Beach and Tennis Club (including a sun deck and heated freshwater pool with a distant view of the fourth and sixth holes); horseback riding along upland trails cut from the Monterey pines; and sailing from the resort's private pier on Stillwater Cove.

*Lounge. Photo courtesy The Lodge at Pebble Beach*

all blenderized with ice and served in a twelve-ounce stem wine glass garnished with fresh mint and an orange slice).

The Tap Room's pub fare is terrific. The artichoke soup with lemon is delectable (the artichokes are grown in nearby Castroville, where an unknown actress later named Marilyn Monroe was crowned the town's first California Artichoke Queen in 1947); the Tap Room burger with pepper bacon and cheddar cheese is simply one of the best meals-on-a-bun in America. Rollicking Dixieland jazz and rhythm-and-blues music are featured on weekends in the Tap Room, which attracts a strong local following.

Despite the fine and varied dining choices, a golfer's most memorable meal is likely to be a quick breakfast or lunch before tee-off in the Gallery, a casual second-floor restaurant set above the practice putting green. From a windowside table can be observed the first tee and the nervous practice swings of golfers about to set off on their journey. On a clear, temperate day—or even on a day when the Pacific wind is blowing strong and carrying rain—there can't be a golfer worth his straight left arm who believes by round's end that there's a better place for golf than Pebble Beach.

*Sixteenth hole*

# The Inn and Links at Spanish Bay

Five miles up the road from its sister resort at Pebble Beach, the Inn and Links at Spanish Bay is a tribute to what patient money and environmental constraints can produce. Built on the site of an abandoned sand quarry in the northwest corner of the Del Monte Forest, this new-age, old-style layout is the only authentically designed and maintained links available for resort play in America. Technically speaking, Pebble Beach is a headlands course. Spanish Bay is a links.

After the California Coastal Commission delayed construction of the proposed course at Spanish Bay for twenty years, it fell to a trio of the game's figureheads to come up with a design in the mid-1980s that did everything except save whales and germinate redwoods. The architects of record are Robert Trent Jones, Jr., Tom Watson, and former USGA president Frank ("Sandy") Tatum. Their collaborative effort, a brilliant evocation of a naturally evolved Scottish links, was born of much head-butting.

After 100 acres of sand was sculpted into high, rolling dunes—sand was brought to the site on a two-mile-long conveyor belt—sedge grasses and wildflowers were sown to anchor and beautify the dunes. Stiff, bristly fescue grasses—the kind that grow naturally on British seaside courses and can survive with minimal rainfall—were planted on tees, fairways, and greens. So natural-looking is the appearance of this links, even an educated eye would have trouble guessing its origin. Fairways are cropped close to encourage crisp pitch-and-run shots, and the ball runs smartly along

*Eighth hole*

them, but incoming shots grind to a halt on the greens. Given their liberal contours, perhaps it's just as well they are no speedier.

Spanish Bay opens auspiciously with an impressive par five that parades golfers directly to the ocean. Thereafter, holes play to and from the sea on a treeless sweep of tossed, heaving land pockmarked with bunkers. The canted fairways not only create sidehill lies, forcing golfers to assume awkward stances, they also direct slightly errant shots into cleverly positioned traps. Bunkers, most of the pot variety but a few of them diagonal trenches known as cross bunkers, challenge players to plan their shots carefully. Creativity must be exercised and optional routes searched for, as there's little chance of making a long recovery from these hell holes. Simply take your medicine and explode safely to the fairway with a lofted club. The unthinking golfer who can't cope with swirling winds and the occasional bad bounce—or who is easily unnerved by adversity—will get eaten alive by Spanish Bay.

After skirting a restored coastal marsh and its honking waterfowl at the seventh and eighth holes, the fairways disappear into a forest of tall Monterey pines at the tenth, eleventh, and twelfth holes paralleling 17-Mile Drive. The links marches back to the sea at the 535-yard fourteenth, a truly colossal hole with a freeway-wide fairway full of hillocks

*Lobby Lounge. Photo courtesy © The Lodge at Pebble Beach*

that tumbles to the brink of the Pacific. The course flexes its muscles from here on in, for the remaining holes play along a shore exposed to brisk winds off Spanish Bay.

The best hole on the course? The ninety-nine-yard thirteenth is a sparkling version of the Postage Stamp hole at Royal Troon in Scotland, but the vote must go to the 369-yard seventeenth. Here a broken line of dunes stares golfers in the face from the tee. The approach must carry a band of scrub prefacing a small, slippery green that falls away on all sides to bunkers and beach grass. It's a toughie.

A few words of advice to the uninitiated: Unless you're an exceptionally strong player, bypass the blue tees (6,820 yards) and tee your ball at the white markers (6,078 yards). The everpresent breeze adds 300 yards to the card. Also, as at Pebble Beach, arrange for a caddie. The course was designed to be walked; your appreciation of its tall dunes and sea views will be greatly enhanced by strolling the links. On foot, you'll have a better chance of seeing the herds of red deer that feed at the fringes of the incoming holes.

The low-rise 270-room Inn at Spanish Bay, its ivory-white stucco buildings sheltered by pines, could pass for the vacation compound of a wealthy Milanese. The taupe-colored lobby, a tasteful amalgam of marble,

slate, and burnished walnut, draws guests to its large bay windows angled to the sea. The Lobby Lounge serves refreshments by an outsize fireplace (there's a jazz band to entertain nightly), while the Terrace Grill features barbecued seafood and other local specialties a stone's throw from the second green. Just before sunset, a kilted bagpiper paces this terrace as he skirls his notes in the gloaming.

Each of the 270 rooms (half with ocean views and nearly all with private balconies) has a gas-lit fireplace. Custom furnishings include oversize sofas and chairs, quilted down comforters on the beds, and large bathrooms with separate dressing areas finished in Italian marble. The hooded terry cloth robes in the rooms are especially comfortable.

The Inn's main dining room, the Dunes, is a gorgeous, pink-and-beige salon with floor-to-ceiling windows that features patio dining in the afternoon and excellent regional cuisine at all times of day. The resort's dressiest restaurant, the Bay Club, could pass for a fine supper club in Rome—except for the fantastic views of the Pacific from its banquettes.

# QUAIL LODGE
# RESORT &
# GOLF CLUB

SILVER MEDALIST

A few miles south of Pebble Beach but light years away in terms of climate is Quail Lodge, a tranquil 850-acre retreat nestled among the green and amber hills of Carmel Valley. While fog and inclement weather often cling to the Pacific coast, the weather a few miles inland is invariably sunny and considerably warmer.

Built on a former dairy farm that once belonged to a brother-in-law of Charles Lindbergh (the famous aviator summered here), Quail Lodge is the epitome of rustic charm. Guests enter the cedar-sided lodge with its heavy shake roof through a three-story skylit atrium where oak floors, Spanish tiles, large ficus trees, and a tiny fountain gurgling from a block of wood create a peaceable mood. The resort, first opened as a modest inn in 1967, is the creation of Ed Haber, a man who lacked formal hotel-development experience but who knew what he liked from his years of travel. The 100-room lodge is a personal reflection of his simple, elegant, and countrified tastes. The rooms are comfortable, the food is excellent, and the golf course is way better than average, but it is the personal attention of the staff that sets the resort apart. Not only is each guest's car windshield swept of dew every morning, but a "Good Morning" note is attached. A bottle of chilled champagne is placed in the room of arriving guests, while room service breakfast arrives with a toaster and flowers. Afternoon tea is served in the lobby. Turndown service is rendered at the convenience of guests, not of the staff. And guest comment cards are followed up by a call from a staff member.

Nearly every one of the light, airy rooms in the lodge looks to the golf course, one of the many lakes on the grounds, or the foothills of the Santa Lucia Range. Some rooms have fireplaces and canopied, four-poster, king-size beds; all have balconies.

The lodge's Covey restaurant, built out over a lake crossed by a bowed wooden bridge, is again rustic in mood: Antique farm tools are grouped on the walls of the lounge; fresh flowers in pewter vases are placed on the dining room tables. Not only does chef Bob Williamson season dishes with chives, mint, sage, thyme, oregano, curry, fennel, and sorrel fetched from his private herb garden, but he forages for wild mushrooms in Carmel Valley. The veal, duck, and lamb dishes are the equal of any multistarred gourmet dining establishment; the tableside preparations of the Caesar salad and Covey spinach salad are flawless. In addition, the dining room's selection of California wines is definitive. So is the kitchen's vacherin au chocolat (ice cream, meringue, and roasted almonds topped with chocolate sauce and whipped cream).

The Golf Club at Quail Lodge, previously known as Carmel Valley Golf & Country Club, is a well-manicured Robert Muir Graves design routed around ten lakes frequented by geese, swans, and ducks. Even ardent golfers have been known to trade their clubs for a fishing rod when steelhead trout run in the mile-and-a-half long section of Carmel River that cuts through the course.

Though it stretches to 6,515 yards from the back tees, the course is best enjoyed by the average player from the regular tees at 6,141 yards. A flattish layout that follows the natural contours of the valley floor, the course changes personality throughout the round. Several holes are routed below limestone bluffs overgrown with shrubs and live oaks. Other holes have a classic woodland appearance, with tall aspens, cottonwoods, pines, and river willows lining the fairways. Still others wander across open land dotted with lakes. Site of the USGA Senior Amateur Championship in 1975 and the California Golf Association's 75th Amateur Championship in 1986, the Golf Club at Quail Lodge is very quietly one of the best tests of golf in a region dominated by heavyweights. Not only are accuracy and shrewd shot placement called for, but caution must be exercised on the slick, subtly sloped greens. Also, nicely contoured bunkers and cloverleaf-shaped ponds pinch the fairways in places. The course offers the prospect of relaxed golf in a scenic meadow, but it is not nearly as easy to score as it looks.

After golf, guests are free to explore Quail Meadows, a bowl-shaped area hidden by large oaks a short drive from the golf club. This 600-acre nature preserve has miles of walking trails, nearly 100 varieties of wildflowers, and lots of wildlife (including coveys of quail that scurry along the ground). There's also a lake stocked with very smart trout and several small boats for guest use. Haber maintains a home here, the farm portion of which contains horses, burros, sheep, Andalusian goats, and unusual long-haired Scottish Highland cattle. If a post-round picnic is desired, box lunches can be ordered at the Lodge and spread out on picnic tables beside the lake. On a clear day, the property's highest ridge offers a fantastic view of Carmel and the Pacific Ocean. The cloud bank that often forms above the sea rarely intrudes upon this gorgeous coastal valley.

*The Covey restaurant.*
*Photo courtesy Quail Lodge,*
*© Russell Abraham*

*Sixth hole. Photo courtesy © Brian McCallen*

# NAPA
# SILVERADO
# COUNTRY CLUB
# & RESORT

SILVER MEDALIST

(now the North Course) and author a second course. Both venues are far more typical of classic East Coast parkland layouts than anything Californian. Each is bordered by mature oaks, each is crisscrossed by small creeks.

The North, the longer but perhaps more forgiving of the two layouts, is marked by expansive fairways and well-bunkered greens. It is a championship test with pro tournament pedigree: it hosted the Kaiser International Open Invitational and Anheuser-Busch Golf Classic, both PGA Tour events, from 1968 to 1980. Among the standout holes is the first, a 404-yard firebreather ranked the number-one handicap hole on the course (have an extra cup of coffee before you tee off to make sure you're

*North Course, sixteenth hole*

A ninety-minute drive north of San Francisco's Golden Gate Bridge is Napa Valley, the epicenter of California's wine-producing region. Warm, dry days and cool nights not only produce excellent grapes, they also draw golfers to the Silverado Country Club & Resort.

A 1,200-acre spread set among rolling hills that shelter a maze of neighboring vineyards, Silverado was originally a Spanish land grant. The property was purchased in 1869 by General John F. Miller, the youngest Union general of the Civil War. President Theodore Roosevelt and General John J. Pershing were some of the many distinguished guests in Miller's Colonial mansion, which today serves as the resort's clubhouse. The name Silverado was inspired by Robert Louis Stevenson's story, *The Silverado Squatters*, a narrative placed in a deserted mining town on the edge of the valley. Stevenson, who liked the area, described Napa's wines as "bottled poetry." Perhaps that is why the wine lists in Silverado's dining rooms feature Napa Valley bottlings exclusively.

The resort, first developed in 1953, came into its own in the mid-1960s, when Robert Trent Jones, Jr., was called in to revamp an existing layout

*South Course, first hole. Photo courtesy © Brian McCallen*

alert); the 122-yard eleventh, a shaded glen of a hole where a duck pond gobbles shots that fall short of the green; and the 500-yard sixteenth, its grove of thick-waisted oaks tracing the curve of a creek that guards the entire left side of the hole.

The South Course, while shorter, confronts golfers with hillier terrain than the North. Not only are there a dozen water crossings to negotiate, but putting surfaces have more pronounced undulations than the North's. Opened in 1965, Silverado's South Course was the first layout Jones, Jr. designed on his own after serving an apprenticeship under his father. Subtle and tricky, it calls for shotmaking skills that make it a favorite of the graybeard pros who tackle it every fall in the Senior PGA Tour's Transamerica Senior Golf Championship.

Johnny Miller, who makes his home at Silverado, said of the South: "It's a well-balanced golf course. The par fives are very exciting—every one of them. You have one of the hardest par fives in northern California in the eleventh hole, a definite three-shotter with water in play down the entire left side."

Accommodations at Silverado range from spacious studios to one-, two-, and three-bedroom cottages equipped with wood-burning fireplaces, wet bar, and patio or balcony. Clusters of these units are sited near the mansion and along the first fairway of the North Course. By modern standards they are modest but comfortable.

Silverado's restaurants rank among the best in a region known for its culinary outposts. The Royal Oak, overlooking gardens and the eighteenth green of the South Course, features mesquite-broiled dishes in a countrified room set off by high-backed chairs, hand-carved tables, copper trimmings, exposed beams, and brickwork. It's a fine place for a grilled steak and a rich Cabernet Sauvignon.

Vintner's Court is an elegant, chandeliered salon with a wall of windows that face the resort's fairways. It is lit by candles and, on enchanted evenings, by the moon. Wine lockers from area vineyards panel the interior walls. After dinner, live entertainment and dancing are featured in the Patio Terrace, a glass-enclosed portico near the mansion's main entrance.

Breakfast is a big deal for most golfers who have arranged morning tee times— few good rounds are played on an empty stomach. Appetites are satisfied at the Silverado Bar & Grill, which adjoins the pro shop. There can't be better fresh-made waffles in America than the Bar & Grill's large, crisp cakes made from a special malt batter and served with Vermont maple syrup.

While the resort can arrange a wine tour for guests, it's more fun to tour the vineyards on your own. Not far from the resort entrance is the Old Silverado Trail, a winding road traveled by the *vaqueros* of old California that today cuts a swath through a mosaic of the nation's best vineyards. There is perhaps no better way to cap off a round of golf at Silverado than in the cool tasting room of a quality winery. By the second glass of a crisp Chardonnay, the bad shots don't seem quite so bad, and the good ones emerge as glorious.

# Ojai Valley Inn & Country Club

"Relaxed elegance" is the sort of brochurese used by many resorts to describe themselves to the traveling public. In an increasingly commercial world, the hard reality is that precious few properties are able to do more than pay lip service to a mood and style that hark back to an earlier, more carefree time. A resort with the requisite breeding and savoir-faire to advertise "relaxed elegance" honestly is the refurbished Ojai Valley Inn & Country Club, located seventy-five miles north of Los Angeles. Though readily accessible to L.A., the sequestered enclave of Ojai nevertheless is light years away from Lah-Lah land.

As a rule, southern California doesn't conjure fertile valleys hemmed by rugged peaks rising to 7,000 feet, but that is the surprise Ojai (pronounced OH-high, and translated as "the nest" from the Chumash Indian language) holds in store for first-time visitors.

In the 1920s, Midwest glass tycoon Edward Drummond Libbey built a beautiful town (now the center of a lively arts scene) patterned after the rural architecture of Andalusia. Later, he built a resort, hiring George C. Thomas, Jr., designer of Riviera Country Club and other courses of distinction in the Los Angeles area, to create on a 200-acre spread a golf course to rival the best layouts back East. Money was no object. Libbey gave Thomas and his associate, William P. Bell, a blank check. They spent $200,000 to build the course, quite a sum in those days. Ojai opened in 1925 to immediate acclaim. In the years that followed, Hollywood celebrities—Clark Gable, Lana Turner, Walt Disney—flocked there.

Thomas wrote of Ojai at the time, "Two ideals were followed in its design and construction. First, a course was to be built on which an average golfer could enjoy his round without too great a penalty, and second, a test must be afforded requiring the low handicap man to play fine golf in order to secure pars." His original conception remained intact until the 1970s, when the resort fell on hard times. But a $35-million makeover in the late 1980s, some $3 million of it spent to recondition the golf course, has restored Ojai, a resort once owned by Loretta Young and Hoagy Carmichael, to its previous prominence.

Jay Morrish, an architect with great respect for classic designs, was brought in to update Ojai's golf course. He completed the job without leaving a single trademark of his own. Working from Thomas's original sketches, Morrish dished out and redefined driving zones, reshaped Thomas's distinctive multifingered bunkers, and recontoured several greens to make them fairer. In places where specimen trees had encroached on a green's air space, putting surfaces were enlarged or relocated. Then as now, the front nine is a pleasant parkland test, its fairways open in some places but lined in others by burly California oaks, big sycamores, and eucalyptus trees.

Ojai's back nine is a complete change of pace from the front: the tenth hole is a roller-coaster par four of 406 yards, the 330-yard eleventh hopscotches a nasty barranca not once but twice, while the twelfth is a 105-yard shortie that may be responsible for more high scores than any other hole on the course. Suffice it to say that if you miss the green, you may not be heard from again. By the time players cross the trestled bridge that leads from tee to fairway at the short par-four thirteenth, golfers disgruntled by the proceedings may be ready to leap. Then again, stellar views of distant mountain ridges and the tangy scent of citrus and eucalyptus in the air usually stave off drastic action.

It's a mistake to judge Ojai's relative difficulty by consulting the scorecard: The par-70 layout measures a scant 6,252 yards from the blue tees, a paltry 5,909 yards from the whites. Not only do many of the holes play uphill, but the greens invariably are elevated above the level of the fairways, requiring the use of extra club. Finally, a swirling breeze off the sea fifteen miles to the west usually arrives by midafternoon. In the words of the senior pros who participate in the GTE West Classic held at the resort, "Ojai is the longest short course we play all year." Fun from start to finish and never discouraging to the novice, Ojai is where the canny, accurate player can bankroll the long-ball artist. It's a shotmaker's course all the way.

The hotel, like the golf course, has retained its original character since its refurbishment. Expanded from 110 to 218 rooms, accommodations are contained in a low, rambling hacienda with a red tile roof. Many have terraces that overlook the two-tiered sixth green and its sentinel oaks. The public rooms in the resort's original adobe structures, wonderfully human in scale, are worth exploring. Of particular interest is the Neff Lounge, named for the hotel's original architect, Wallace Neff. Its exposed beams, tile-trimmed fireplace, eloquent caged birds (K.B., a cockatoo, grew up with a baby elephant and can reproduce its call), and tables set for chess and checkers create an ideal atmosphere for relaxation. The room's beautiful vases and bowls were fashioned by Ojai Valley potters.

Hungry? The flagstone Terrace is the place to lunch (or brunch) al fresco under the spreading oaks, while the Club Bar, with its wood paneling, plank floors, captain's chairs, and prints of famous British links, is an ideal place to rehash the round.

Ojai's Vista dining room serves up an extraordinary view of a long valley framed by successive rows of misty peaks. If you happen to see them snow-capped in winter, you might recognize them as the Shangri-La view featured in Frank Capra's 1937 film, Lost Horizon. Local produce, including oranges, avocados, almonds, and a variety of hybrid vegetables, are used whenever possible. Dishes are garnished and seasoned with fresh herbs grown in the Inn's garden. There aren't many resort dining rooms that attempt a wild mushroom strudel, or a salmon and halibut terrine, or would dream of sprinkling edible pansies on its salads. The Vista does and does it well.

And then there is the "pink moment." At the valley's east end, looking toward the tops of the Topa Topa peaks, the sun, barely dipped below the horizon in the west, turns the highest bluffs a vivid pinkish-orange hue. It is an ephemeral moment of exquisite beauty, an incredible signoff to the day, and much more reliable than the green flash variously reported in the Caribbean.

*Courtyard*

*Fourth hole*

# L A  C O S T A
# R E S O R T  &  S P A

Feeling stressed out? La Costa Resort & Spa in Carlsbad, thirty miles north of San Diego, has been soothing the nerves and tightening the tummies of harried executives, overvexed celebrities, and ageless matrons since 1965. The ingredients for relaxation at this sumptuous decompression chamber are as appealing as one of its spa cuisine entrées: two fine golf courses, a composite of which is played in the annual Tournament of Champions; superb weather year round; and a world-class spa where fitness and diet programs (as well as the treatments themselves) alleviate stress, revitalize the body, and uplift the spirit.

Bordered on three sides by haystack-shaped hills studded with expensive homes, La Costa's 400-acre spread is centered on its North and South courses. The most significant sections of each were designed by Dick Wilson, with later additions and modifications by Joe Lee. There is little to choose between them. Each is an excellent, beautifully conditioned layout with enough water and sand in play to keep the most skillful players alert. The North is the slightly longer, more rolling and more open of the two. In fact, its middle realm nearly departs civilization, playing to sagebrush-covered hills that appear lifted from an early Hollywood western. Its feature hole is the 141-yard sixteenth, where the rounded corner of a lake must be carried to reach a large but well-protected green. However, six other equally dangerous holes on the back nine cross or skirt water.

The South Course, a more compact layout, is routed closer to the peachy-pink buildings of the main resort complex. Like the North, it is distinguished by slick, medium-small, elevated bent grass greens undercut by deep bunkers, their faces flashed above the level of the putting surfaces. These greens are hardly the inviting, featherbedded targets one often sees at resorts. In fact, there's a phalanx of traps staring you in the face on nearly every single approach shot. In the words of a former staff pro, "You must have a good understanding of the sand game to play well at La Costa."

You must also stroke the ball a fair distance if you are to survive holes fifteen to eighteen on the South Course. Known as "Golf's Longest Mile," the final four holes measure slightly more than a statute mile of 1,780 yards from the championship markers. When a breeze sweeps in off the Pacific, located a mere three miles from the resort, these round-crunchers can play to a mile and a half. Even the yardage book isn't very cheerful about a golfer's prospects on them. The notations in the book, starting at the 320-yard fifteenth, read: "Position of drive is critical." At the par-four sixteenth: "Plays long. Into the wind." The par-five seventeenth: "Plays long. Position second shot carefully. You may need three woods." (And a ball retriever, it might have added; there's water up the entire right side of the fairway.) At the 377-yard eighteenth, the news is dire: "Plays long and into the wind. May require a lay-up short of creek."

More encouraging advice may be proffered by the resort's corps of forty caddies, each of whom reports to work in a white jump suit and logo visor. Perhaps your bag will be assigned to a grinning, mirror-shaded gentleman by the name of James Brown, who will mark your ball with a silver dollar and sagely inform you that all putts break toward Las Vegas. It's hard to argue with this opinion, as La Costa was conceived by a Las Vegas syndicate of casino heavyweights.

*North course, eighteenth hole*

If you think spa treatments are the sole province of the fairer sex, think again: Not only does La Costa maintain separate spa facilities for men and women, but the afternoon queue for facials in the men's spa is longer than in the women's area. Facials are given in a darkened, church-quiet room by technicians who huddle over their charges with fine camel-hair brushes and steam cleaners, and who fit each gentleman's hands and feet with mittens and booties filled with vitamin E-based creams while impurities are removed from facial pores.

Above: Lunch at the Aquatic
Center Pool. Photo courtesy
La Costa Hotel & Spa

Right: Massage al fresco.
Photo courtesy La Costa
Hotel & Spa, © Bachmann

Is it time to remove the top layer of dead cells from your skin? Sign up for a loofah scrub, ideal for those seeking the literal pink of health. The body is smeared with a gel, sprinkled with coarse salt, and then scrubbed vigorously with a natural sponge. The rinse, which can induce yowling, takes place in a needle-nosed Swiss shower regulated from very hot to icy cold. There's also a eucalyptus inhalation room, individual whirlpool baths, an outdoor massage area (*the* place to hear of the latest advances in cosmetic surgery), competitive games of water volleyball, a walking/running track with a crushed brick base, and a team of clinicians to perform manicures and pedicures.

Even if you are more of a live-it-up golfer than a committed spa-goer, a meal should be taken in the resort's Spa Dining Room to experience how good a low-calorie, low-sodium, low-fat meal can taste. For example, a four-course dinner of asparagus soup, sliced tomatoes with fine herb dressing, roast leg of lamb with mint sauce, carrots l'orange, and a dessert of butterscotch mousse looks and tastes like 3,000 calories, but actually totals fewer than 300. Dealcoholized wines can be ordered to accompany these healthful dishes.

La Costa's top nonspa dining spots include Pisces, one of the finest seafood restaurants in the San Diego area (a consignment of fresh Dover sole is flown in each Thursday); and the Brasserie La Costa, an indoor café and garden terrace with an old-fashioned soda fountain and New York deli specialties on the menu.

La Costa runs an excellent program for children. On weekends and during winter holidays, Camp La Costa Nightclub invites kids to dress up for an elegant theme dinner (tables are set with fresh flowers, candelabra, crystal, fine bone china, and silver). Afterwards, kids can "cut some rug" to a live band just like the grownups do in the Tournament of Champions lounge. Aside from the golf courses and spa, La Costa's best amenity may be its 180-seat movie theater, where first-run feature films are screened nightly. The free all-you-can-eat popcorn, unbuttered, isn't fattening.

Rooms at La Costa (there are 478 accommodations in all) were recently redone in contemporary colors with pink Brazilian marble in the bathrooms. The resort's own line of cosmetics and skin care products is featured throughout. If ever you dreamed of wearing rhinestone-studded socks (on or off the course), or of wearing a pony tail for that special evening (the resort's salon specializes in hair extensions), this most Hollywoodish of getaways is the place to let your hair down. Even if it's not your own.

# LA QUINTA
# HOTEL GOLF &
# TENNIS RESORT

Greater Palm Springs—a collection of more than twenty communities in the Coachella Valley 100 miles east of Los Angeles—has more than eighty golf courses to its name. Unfortunately, most are private clubs immediately recognizable by high walls, stay-away gates, and bubbling fountains set in elaborate gardens. These clubs require that guests be invited (and often accompanied) by a member. Rarely are the rules bent to accommodate visitors.

But these havens of privilege haven't put a lock on tradition. La Quinta Hotel Golf & Tennis Resort is the most venerable of the valley's getaways, and its guest list reads like a Who's Who of American filmmaking. Opened in 1926, La Quinta ("the country retreat" in Spanish) began as a modest collection of cottages, named alphabetically for saints, that soon became the preferred retreat for the stars of Hollywood's "Golden Era." Clark Gable and Carole Lombard honeymooned there. Greta Garbo was one of the resort's early investors. Bette Davis, William Powell, Joan Crawford, Errol Flynn, and many others traveled the extra twenty miles past Palm Springs to this stylish outpost backed into the Santa Rosa Mountains. "It was the kind of place everyone was looking for," said movie director Frank Capra, who passed away at the resort in 1991. "It was a wonderful green oasis in the middle of the desert, and it was absolutely private." Capra first visited the desert in 1934 to turn the short story "Night Bus," which he had read in a Palm Springs barber shop, into the script for *It Happened One Night*. When the film swept the Academy Awards that year, Capra became superstitious about the desert and returned annually to the same cottage at La Quinta to write several film classics, including *You Can't Take It with You* and *Mr. Smith Goes to Washington*.

La Quinta Hotel has undergone several ownership changes and has expanded greatly since its inception, but still the resort maintains an air of quiet sophistication and charm. The 640 accommodations, including sixty-eight suites, are housed in Spanish-style adobe casitas spread out on forty-five acres of manicured lawns. Date palms, climbing rose bushes, and gardens of cascading bougainvillea beautify the grounds. The decentralized setting adds to the resort's air of relaxation. Most casitas are situated near one of twenty-five pools on site, and many have wood-burning fireplaces to warm the rooms on cool nights. The decor is vintage California with contemporary Southwestern accents.

Among the dining choices within the resort's flower-decked plaza of specialty shops is Morgans, named for the hotel's founding family and patterned after a traditional 1920s café, with black-and-white tile floors and blue plate specials. Upstairs from Morgans is the Adobe Grill, which not only mixes a superb margarita, but serves up Cal–Mex, Tex–Mex, and regional Mexican dishes that go way beyond the standard salsa-and-tacos fare.

Every afternoon from 2 to 5 P.M., tea is served in the Santa Rosa lobby lounge. The room's wood-beamed ceiling, adobe walls, wood-burning fireplaces, and plump, roomy sofas make it a perfect place for this civilized ritual.

While the hotel's original layout, La Quinta Country Club, was long ago sold to its club members, Pete Dye was hired in the late 1970s to build a pair of courses at the resort. The Mountain Course remains a private club for members only (limited play is accepted in the summer months, not an enjoyable time to be in the desert), while the Dunes Course, a classic Dye design opened in 1980, is the venue set aside for hotel guests.

Built six years before Dye's infamous torture chamber, the Stadium Course at PGA West, opened on PGA Boulevard in the town of La Quinta, the Dunes Course is a sane, subtle layout that does not require superhuman skills to play or survive it. As a target golf course, however, it constantly confronts a player with a risk-reward factor. Assessing the correct angle of attack and overcoming the depth perception dilemma common to all Palm Springs courses (targets are not as close as they appear in relation to their mountain backdrops) are the keys to success.

The challenge of the Dunes is fully realized from the tips at 6,861 yards, though even from the champion tees (6,300 yards) and to a lesser extent from the regular tees (5,798 yards), golfers must think their way round this brilliant composite of water, sand dunes, desert vegetation, and undulating greens buttressed by railroad ties.

Despite a succession of fairways woven through a residential community, the look of the Dunes is for the most part naturalistic. For example, bunkers and mounds are in harmony with and in fact mimic the valley's natural land forms and mountain foothills.

Among the feature holes is the 171-yard sixth (measurements are from the misnamed champion tees, which are readily managed by the average player), a deceivingly difficult par three with a green set well below tee level and surrounded by pot bunkers; and the 416-yard seventeenth, which must rank as one of the very best par fours in southern California. A testing dogleg that veers to the left, with water in play off the tee and again on the approach, the seventeenth calls for two first-class shots at a point in the round when most golfers are reeling from Dye's sleight-of-hand tricks on the previous holes.

In addition to the Dunes Course, La Quinta Hotel guests also can arrange to play the Citrus Course, a newer Pete Dye design routed through orange groves that is a favorite of sometime La Quinta resident Lee Trevino. (Tee times at the Citrus are reserved for club members until 11 A.M. from December through May.) Also available to hotel guests on a space-available basis is the nearby PGA West Jack Nicklaus Resort Course, a solid test opened in 1987 that is known by its stark mounding and sharp-edged waste bunkers.

It's heresy to talk about tennis in a book devoted to golf resorts, but La Quinta's tennis facilities cannot go unmentioned. There's a choice of three playing surfaces (grass, clay, and hard) among the thirty courts, all of them placed in groves of olive and date palm trees, and several of them lighted for night play.

*Above: Dunes Course, seventeenth hole*

*Opposite, above: Watercourse in the plaza*

*Opposite, below: An adobe casita*

Shortly before the sun sinks behind the mountains, the desert floor cools, the air becomes scented with evening jasmine, and the convivial banter of cocktail hour gatherings emanates from the private patios of the casitas. By the time the snow on the valley's 8,000-foot peaks turns a deep shade of indigo, La Quinta's appeal to the great stars of Hollywood becomes plain to see.

# INDIAN WELLS GOLF RESORT

SILVER MEDALIST

La Quinta's next-door neighbor, Indian Wells, has a ton of golf to its name, most of it private. But the Hyatt Grand Champions adjacent to the Indian Wells Golf Resort has something else going for it: superior creature comforts. The low-rise hotel, a 336-room, all-suite property, is a dramatic amalgam of Moorish-style columns and arches tinted sand and sage to blend with the desert. This is one of the best-appointed and most glamorous hotels in the California desert.

Inside, the oversize rooms, done up in pale shades of peach and apricot, are decorated with European furnishings, silk fabrics, and original artwork. Private terraces allow secluded sunbathing. The resort also maintains ten one-bedroom and ten two-bedroom villas, each with living room, wet bar, stereo, fireplace, and private courtyard with Jacuzzi. Each villa is staffed by a butler, many of them trained by Ivor Spencer, toastmaster to the Queen of England. The two-bedroom villas are more than $1,000 per night in

season, but there are no more sumptuous dwellings in the Coachella Valley.

The Ted Robinson–designed courses at the Indian Wells Golf Resort, built on land once owned by Bob Hope's sons, are lush, forgiving, and, rare in these parts, without condominiums lining the fairways. They are two of the best maintained public-access layouts in Palm Springs. Both share fantastic views of the stark Santa Rosa Mountains, their bristly, treeless flanks rising abruptly from the desert floor at the southernedge of the property.

While the layouts were designed to flatter a player's game, not expose or exploit shortcomings, they are not creampuffs. Curiously, better players gravitate to the shorter but more rolling West Course (6,115 yards from the regular tees, 6,478 yards from the tips). In fact, the West lays to rest the theory that low-handicappers automatically tee it up on the course with the longer yardage. Placement, not power, is the key to scoring well

*Left: Overhead view of the swimming pool. Above: West Course, thirteenth hole*

here. The idea is to direct the ball, not necessarily with a driver, to a flattened area of the fairway to set up the approach. Overly long drives at more than a few holes leave a player with an awkward downhill lie. The ability to feather a wedge from a difficult stance is not given to everyone; it is more practical to aim for level ground with a long iron or fairway wood than to blast away with the driver.

Rather surprisingly, there are elevation changes of up to sixty feet on the West Course. Earth was moved to enhance what nature provided by way of massive sand dunes to create elevated tees, pedestal greens, and a lot of rolling ground in between. Of course, elevated greens take away the opportunity to pitch or roll the ball onto the putting surfaces. A high carry shot is needed here.

An easy equation applies at Indian Wells: the longer the hole, the more undulations in the greens. The par fives are triple-tiered, for example, while the par fours and threes have two tiers. A player must be able to gauge the break and speed of multiple-slope putts to have any chance on the greens.

The West's signature holes include the first and second, each of which wraps around ancient burial grounds of the Agua Caliente Indians (flower beds cover the site); the watery thirteenth, short but deadly at 126 yards, with water front and back of the green; and the will-o'-the-wisp par-five sixteenth, which tempts big hitters to carry a walled lake to reach the roller-coaster green in two strokes.

The slightly longer but flatter, more wide-open East Course is the perfect venue for players who aren't interested in executing delicate cut wedge shots from hanging lies to small, elevated greens. With plenty of margin for error, there's room to swing away, though the course does present seven water holes and cannot be negotiated without a rational game plan. As on the West, a pair of holes skirt Indian burial grounds, though the most daunting sight on the East is the "island fairway" at the tricky 352-yard thirteenth hole.

When the game is done, the Grandview Grill & Lounge, with its beamed ceilings, wraparound bar, plump sofas, and working fireplace (winter afternoons can be chilly), is a fine place to review the round.

A good variety of cuisine styles are available in the resort's three restaurants. Trattoria California, a sunny terrace, is known for designer pizzas baked in a wood-burning oven; Charlie's, named for original resort investor and tennis star Charlie Pasarell, features Southwestern dishes in a room not far from the resort's 10,500-seat stadium tennis court; and Austin's, a steakhouse adjoining the hotel lobby, serves wood-roasted prime rib, vegetable breads, and microbrewery beers to purists who manage to tackle the East and West courses in one day.

# CALIFORNIA

## TIPS AND SIDE TRIPS

*In a Napa Valley wine cellar.*
*Photo courtesy Beringer*
*Vineyards, © Gary Quiring*

A multitude of natural and man-made wonders—and sometimes a combination of the two—make California one of the best states in the nation for post-round excursions.

No visit to the Monterey Peninsula is complete without a tour of 17-Mile Drive, which traces a loop along the shoreline and through the Del Monte Forest between Pacific Grove and Carmel. (The nominal per car entrance fee to 17-Mile Drive is waived for guests of the Lodge at Pebble Beach and the Inn at Spanish Bay.) Stop at the Cypress Point Lookout for a view of the stunning oceanside holes at the ultra-exclusive Cypress Point Club. The most famous landmark along the drive is the Lone Cypress, a gnarled tree that clings tenaciously to bare rocks high above the surf.

For a memorable half-day trip, head south thirty miles from Carmel along Highway 1 to Big Sur. The road traces a serpentine path along steep cliffs, the surf crashing into the rocks far below against a backdrop of coastal mountains. It is one of the most dramatic seaside drives in the world.

Three miles south of Big Sur State Park is Nepenthe, a redwood bar-restaurant with an outdoor deck perched 800 feet above the sea that is popular with locals and visitors alike. Regardless of what happened earlier in the day on the links, a cocktail at sunset here will bring "surcease from sorrow"— a loose translation of Nepenthe.

Closer to Pebble Beach is Point Lobos State Reserve, a mosaic of granite headlands, irregular coves, and rolling meadows sprinkled with wild-flowers. There's a network of hiking trails within the park, as well as picnic areas and steep wooden staircases built down to secluded beaches. Between December and May, migrating gray whales spout and dive off

*Aerial tram. Photo courtesy Palm*
*Springs Aerial Tramway*

Point Lobos. Bring binoculars. Half the reserve is an undersea marine park open to qualified scuba divers.

On the site of a former sardine cannery in Monterey is the Monterey Bay Aquarium. One of the best of its kind anywhere, the aquarium features a three-story kelp forest exhibit, a bat-ray petting pool (the velvetlike creatures can be touched as they swim by), a simulated tidal surge habitat, a 55,000-gallon sea otter tank, and other one-of-a-kind maritime

*Glider over the Napa Valley. Photo courtesy © Joseph Woods*

creations. Avoid summer weekends, when the aquarium draws a big crowd.

Fisherman's Wharf and Cannery Row in Monterey, both of which figured prominently in several of John Steinbeck's novels, today contain dozens of factory outlets, souvenir shops, and inexpensive seafood restaurants.

Carmel, a classy seaside village just south of Pebble Beach, where the buildings have no street numbers and first-time visitors usually can't resist ducking their heads into Hog's Breath Inn to see if the proprietor, Clint Eastwood, happens to be around, is known for its smart cafés and more than forty art galleries.

The Napa Valley, synonymous with fine wine, is ideal for a tastings tour. Among the better choices: Domaine Chandon, a French-owned winery that serves its excellent sparkling wines in an attractive outdoor café; Robert Mondavi Winery, which offers instructive tours along with a superb Cabernet Sauvignon; and Beringer, its impressive Rhine House dating to 1876 and its wine storage caves cut deep into limestone hills.

Good food, local wine, and sightseeing can be combined by riding the Wine Train, a three-hour, thirty-six-mile roundtrip excursion from Napa to St. Helena. Lunch, dinner, and weekend brunch trips are offered in refurbished vintage Pullman cars.

*Touring the San Diego Zoo. Photo courtesy and © Zoological Society of San Diego, by Ron Garrison*

There is perhaps no better way to see Napa's vineyards than from the air, either by hot-air balloon or by glider. Those seeking serious relaxation should sign up for a two-hour treatment called "The Works" at Dr. Wilkinson's Hot Springs in Calistoga. A mud bath in a mixture of local volcanic ash, imported peat, and naturally boiling mineral spring water is followed by a mineral water shower and whirlpool, a visit to a mineral steam room, a blanket wrap, and a half-hour massage.

Not far from La Costa is the community of La Jolla, which bears favorable comparison to the Italian Riviera with its serrated cliffs, sea caves,

and stylish bistros. The San Diego Zoo and Wild Animal Park, located in Balboa Park, the city's cultural center, showcases more than 4,000 animals in open-air habitats within a 125-acre botanical garden. Ride the Skyfari Aerial Tramway for a bird's-eye view of the zoo.

For a spectacular seventy-five-mile overview of the Coachella Valley, board the Palm Springs Aerial Tramway, which ascends from the desert floor to the 8,516-foot mountain station in Mt. San Jacinto Wilderness State Park in fourteen minutes. The preserve offers fifty-four miles of hiking trails as well as camping and picnic sites. Cross-country skiing—and snowman-building—are available in the winter months.

---

DON'T LEAVE HOME WITHOUT...GETTING IN SHAPE

*There is a prevailing, mistaken notion that golf is a nonathletic game and, therefore, does not require a toned and conditioned body to play it well. Many golfers erroneously believe the only way to improve their games is to bang balls on the practice range. For years, no matter what the swing flaw, golf instructors could only advocate practice, practice, practice.*

*New technology has enabled us to evaluate, in minute detail, the muscles golfers use to play golf. At La Costa, we believe that players of all ages and levels of expertise who combine body conditioning with qualified instruction can vastly improve performance—and prevent nagging injuries.*

*Golfers don't get weaker as they get older, they lose elasticity and flexibility due to lack of exercise. The human body*

*is the most forgiving machine ever designed: Specific muscle training and stretching exercises can do wonders for the power game as well as sharpen touch with the short irons and putter.*

*Here's a tip from our Muscular Conditioning Program to stretch and strengthen key muscles.*

*If you're missing to the right or not getting the clubhead through the ball, weak flexor and/or extensor muscles in the wrists and/or forearms may be the reason. To correct the problem, fold a twenty-four-inch by eighteen-inch towel in half until it measures twelve by nine inches long and roll it up. Grasp with both palms facing upward about four inches apart. Squeeze the towel; roll and rotate the right wrist under the left in a wringing motion. Reverse with the left wrist under the right and continue for five minutes. Follow the regimen, and you'll start hitting crisper, straighter shots.*

FROM MIKE SULLIVAN, DIRECTOR OF GOLF, LA COSTA RESORT & SPA AND JUDIE NIXON, DIRECTOR, LA COSTA SPA

# THE NOR

If you're a V.S.G. (Very Serious Golfer), the Northwest is probably not for you. Not only would recreational opportunities in the great outdoors (hiking, fishing, river rafting) be lost on those bent solely on a singular passion, but there's a chance the region's matchless natural splendor would go unnoticed. That would be a great shame, for Washington, Oregon, and Idaho provide three of the greatest—and least heralded—forums for golf in the nation. Where most destinations provide stages on which to play the game, these states have veritable *arenas* in which the drama unfolds. Tall firs and pines tower over fairways, while massive snow-frosted peaks often backdrop greens.

The best resorts in this neck of the woods are among the most casual, low-key, and unpretentious in the nation. Which in no way detracts from the quality: Taken together, Semiahmoo, Port Ludlow, Sunriver, Black Butte Ranch, and Coeur d'Alene are among the finest, especially if you're traveling with children. (Central Oregon in particular is without parallel for vacationing families.) There's no appliqué of trendy sophistication at these resorts. Rustic charm will do just fine, thank you.

# THWEST

All it takes to fully enjoy the Northwest is a genuine ability to relax. Not every golfer can manage it. The tone is set by a health-conscious citizenry who more often than not choose to walk instead of ride, who revel in the larger-than-life scenery, and who can identify by name the wildflowers and native critters. These folks take superb locally produced wines and fresher-than-fresh salmon found on every menu for granted. Golf is treated as just another pleasant amenity.

The weather is good, too. The maritime influence of the Puget Sound makes year-round play a possibility at Semiahmoo and Port Ludlow, while central Oregon's high desert region has an enviably sunny climate.

The increasing stature of Seattle as a model city (Portland is purported to be the region's up-and-coming city of the 1990s) has certainly put the Northwest on the map. Still, there's no pretense in these parts. Golf at the top resorts exists as you once knew it. Do like the locals: Tee up and have some fun.

*Inset: River otter near Sunriver. Photo courtesy High Desert Museum, Oregon*
*Large picture: Black Butte Ranch, Oregon, Big Meadow Course, eleventh hole*

# THE RESORT SEMIAHMOO

Not many resorts would choose to delay the opening of their golf course by more than a year so as not to interfere with a pair of nesting bald eagles holed up in a tall fir alongside one of its fairways. But then Semiahmoo, located at Blaine in the far northwest corner of Washington a two-hour drive from Seattle, is a place unto itself. Actually, two places. The Arnold Palmer–Ed Seay golf course was carved from a second-growth forest of hemlocks, firs, and lichen-splotched alders on high ground a mile or so from the resort complex. The Inn at Semiahmoo occupies a former salmon cannery on the tip of a mile-long sand spit near the United States–Canadian border. It is not true, as some golfers have jested, that you must go through customs to retrieve a ball that's been knocked out of bounds.

Palmer, who usually relegates himself to ribbon-cutting formalities and an inaugural round on the opening day of one of his golf courses, was more involved than usual in the design of the Semiahmoo project. Perhaps the setting made the difference. "I knew we had the design opportunity of a lifetime the first time I saw the natural flow of the terrain," he said.

Semiahmoo is a stately, well-balanced layout that presents appealing, not overbearing, challenges. This is especially true from tee to green. For example, the gently rolling fairways are quite spacious, the hardwoods and old cedar stumps lining the course only brought into play by seriously wayward shots. Also, much of the fairway and greenside bunkering is more decorative than penal, though in truth there are hidden bunkers to contend with in places. The greens, however, are very large, and liberally contoured. At least one, the green at the 314-yard sixteenth hole, resembles a lolling tongue, while more than a few are humped down the middle by a hog's back. They, not the woods or the water on the course, pose the chief obstacle to low scoring, particularly when a Stimpmeter rating of 9.5 (very speedy) is achieved in the summer months. When Semiahmoo opened in 1986, Palmer was quoted as saying that the greens were designed to give the resort player a feel for what touring pros face every week—just in case you wanted to know what it is like to make a living waving a putter at a few thousand square feet of bent-grass treachery.

The key to enjoying Semiahmoo is to choose the markers that suit your game. The member tees are a modest 6,003 yards, the blues stretch to 6,435 yards, and the Palmer tees are a daunting 7,005 yards. Indeed, each hole offers the challenge of a risky route for the advanced golfer, as well as a less dangerous line of play for the more conservative (or less capable) player. Because of the lush, beautifully conditioned fairways and often moist air, the course can play long.

Semiahmoo is a remarkably well-balanced golf course. While the par threes are varied in length and direction, and the par fives evenly split between reachable and untouchable, the prime interest lies in the par fours, several of which dogleg out of view from the tee.

One of the best and most intriguing is the second, a 362-yard hole that bends gently to the right. A sentinel fir dominates the left side of the hole about two-thirds of the way down the fairway. In its topmost branches 120 feet above the ground is the tangled aerie of a family of bald eagles. Even stalwart golfers have been known to lose their concentration for a moment when one of the adults takes flight.

The course emerges from its corridors of trees at the ornery 316-yard eleventh, which wraps around a lake and culminates in a well-protected green rife with swales. The twelfth is simply the best par three on the course: A do-or-die shot of 138 yards is played over water to a rock-walled green staked out by three large cloverleaf bunkers.

As is true throughout the fitness-conscious Northwest, walking is not only permitted but encouraged at Semiahmoo. Also, to avoid congestion and enhance enjoyment of the beautiful surroundings, tee times are staggered at 10-minute intervals. Another plus: It stays light in these northern latitudes until 10 P.M. in the summer, offering that most tantalizing of possibilities: a quick nine after dinner. Because the Puget Sound basin enjoys mild winters, the course is open year round. Winters

*Twelfth and thirteenth holes*

can be rainy, but an excellent drainage system makes Semiahmoo "perhaps the driest course in western Washington," according to Ed Seay.

The 200-room Inn at Semiahmoo, constructed from the skeletal remains of turn-of-the-century salmon cannery buildings, is perched on a substantial sand spit that divides Semiahmoo Bay and Drayton Harbor. The four-story property, built to the original roofline, resembles the saltbox structures constructed by prosperous sea captains on Martha's Vineyard and Cape Cod during the heyday of the whaling era. Its steeply gabled roof, modest dormers, and driftwood-gray shingles are attractive in an understated way. Inside, public rooms glow with a striking variety of polished woods. The dark hemlock walls contrast nicely with floors, pillars, and wainscoting of burnished yellow pine. Burgundy-and-teal sofas and wingback chairs are ideal for lounging near a double-faced brick fireplace (the bricks were found in the cannery's old boiler room), while the library is a study in good taste: leather loungers, lighted globes, brass planters, and a good selection of leather-bound classics. What a place to curl up with *Moby Dick!*

Guest rooms are large, simply constructed, and furnished with clear pine armoires, desks, and chairs. Top-floor rooms have bedroom skylights with louvered closures. Rooms with even numbers have sea views. Request one, as the odd-numbered rooms look to the marina or parking lot. Thirty-six of the Inn's accommodations are equipped with fireplaces, but only three offer a fireplace *and* a good view: 4104, 4114, and 4122.

A health club attached to the Inn is equipped with an indoor-outdoor heated pool, an indoor track, and squash, racquetball, and tennis courts. Bicycle rentals are available, while trails leading along the spit and through wooded uplands can be traveled on horseback.

Semiahmoo's fine dining is at Stars, named for the mighty Star Fleet that once sailed from the cannery docks. The shutters of this formal bilevel room, where a pianist entertains nightly, open to a patio graced by flowers and backdropped by the sea.

The resort's most popular gathering spot for post-round refreshments and informal meals is Packers Oyster Bar & Lounge. In a terrariumlike room that enjoys as fine a view of the sea as you'll find between Seattle and Vancouver, British Columbia, patrons can belly up to the gray marble bar to sample beers from the region's top microbreweries. The fish and chips (white cod in beer batter with a side of curlicue French fries) are nonpareil, but so too are the plump steamer-clams dug from local tidal

*Packers Oyster Bar & Lounge. Photo courtesy The Resort Semiahmoo*

*Main Lobby. Photo courtesy The Resort Semiahmoo*

flats. If you are serious about shellfish, order up a dozen raw oysters on the half-shell, including golden mantles and quilcenes, both highly prized by connoisseurs. (Semiahmoo, by the way, is named for the region's native Americans, and translates as "people who eat shellfish.")

By day, beachcombing directly in front of the resort for driftwood, sand dollars, and chitons is popular. So are visits to the 300-slip marina, its fashionable shops, and the small museum at the base of the sand spit. Actually, most guests who have spotted a bald eagle soaring overhead never seem to take their eyes from the sky. And that includes normally implacable golfers.

# PORT LUDLOW
# GOLF &
# MEETING
# RETREAT

SILVER MEDALIST

How can something so forlorn as a tree stump be the key feature of the Northwest's finest resort course? A quick review of Port Ludlow's history and geography reveals the answer. Located on an inlet of the Puget Sound ninety minutes by car and ferry from Seattle, Port Ludlow was once a prominent logging site where hundreds of old-growth cedar trees were felled for ships' timbers. The sawmill operation ceased during the Depression, but the cedar stumps, many of them up to twenty-five feet in circumference, remain. Small firs, hardy mosses, creeping vines, maidenhair ferns, and wild berry bushes have since colonized them. Most of the granddaddy stumps and their upended root systems (surrealistic friezes of twisted wood and dirt) were integrated by Robert Muir Graves in the design of a golf course that is by turns the most exasperating and beautiful in all of Cascadia.

*Seventeenth hole*

*The marina*

A holdover from another age, Port Ludlow is one of the last of the hand-built golf courses. A team of sixty lumberjacks armed with chainsaws and machetes spent months clearing the heavily wooded site. Half the course was hewn from a mantle of rock; the other half was routed over a soggy peat bog stabilized with tons of sand and rock. The finished product, opened in 1976, is a splendid, well-balanced layout, each of the holes isolated and distinct from the others, the water views vying for attention with occasional glimpses of snow-capped Mt. Baker. It is not unusual during a round at Port Ludlow to hear a deer bleating for her fawns, or see bald eagles soaring overhead. Belying the region's drizzly reputation, Port Ludlow, situated in the lee of the Olympic Mountains, receives one-third the rain (and therefore two-thirds more sun) than Seattle.

With a course rating of 74.2 and a slope rating of 142 from the tips at 6,787 yards (par is 72), Port Ludlow shapes up as a man-eater. The layout is somewhat more forgiving from the white tees at 6,262 yards, but this is a course that demands judicious shotmaking and unfailing accuracy from any set of tees one might choose to play. Drive with the club you hit straightest—there is little hope for recovery off the fairways. Not that the unmown acreage is unpleasant: Volleyball-sized blossoms of wild rhododendrons brighten the forest. Throughout the course, well-tended flowerbeds of pansies, foxgloves, and marigolds bloom from spring to fall. The logging days have not been forgotten: Rusty old boom chains once used to bundle logs in the harbor rope the tee boxes.

Steering clear of trouble and finding the greens is only half the battle at Port Ludlow. Once there, golfers must cope with enormous, undulating putting surfaces, a few of them up to fifty yards deep. The green at the par-four seventh is about the size of a ballroom dance floor, though hardly flat enough for a waltz. Built atop a peat bog, it returns a hollow sound when tapped with a putter.

Among Port Ludlow's signature holes is a beast-and-beauty combo found on the back nine. The 396-yard thirteenth is an uphill, right-to-left dogleg that funnels through a tight landing area and calls for a nerveless second shot to a giant, sloping green guarded by gaping sand pits, an overgrown stump, and tall Douglas firs. It's one of the toughest par fours in the Northwest. The beauty is the 148-yard seventeenth, where golfers play from an elevated tee across a pond to a sprawling green. On an island in the center of the pond (and reflected in its waters) is yet another gargantuan cedar stump festooned with greenery.

After gentle persuasion by resort management, Graves returned to the site of his masterpiece to build a third nine. Opened in May 1993, the layout is hillier and even more compelling than the original eighteen, with numerous forced carries over wetlands and ravines. The compensation for lost balls? Exquisite views of Puget Sound, a clamorous symphony of foghorns and bell buoys, and the sight of frisky raccoons splashing in the lakes.

More rustic than sophisticated, Port Ludlow nevertheless offers comfortable accommodations (loft bedrooms, full kitchens, bayside balconies) in renovated condominiums spread throughout the grounds. Hardwood floors have been refinished and an outdoor circular sun deck added to the Wreckroom Lounge, but the most noticeable (and welcome) change at the resort is found in the Harbormaster Restaurant, where an updated color scheme, private booth seating, and a brilliant new chef have transformed a previously drab room into one of the region's best eateries. Favorite dishes include boneless quail stuffed with homemade apple sausage, Hood Canal crab and shrimp cakes, poached king salmon, oyster stew, and an exceptional Dungeness crab-stuffed halibut.

A family-oriented resort, Port Ludlow encourages guests to guide a small sailboat around its protected cove, angle for salmon, or arrange a skippered cruise to the San Juan Islands from its 300-slip marina. Golfers, of course, will have none of these diversions. Not with a golf course that artfully blends behemoth stumps, a primeval forest, and the call of the sea.

# SUNRIVER LODGE & RESORT

## SILVER MEDALIST

Located in the striking high desert region of central Oregon near Bend, Sunriver is not only sunny (an average of 265 blue sky days per year), it is bisected by an eight-mile stretch of the Deschutes River. Which is why resort founders had no problem finding a name for this 3,300-acre residential community-resort development in the late 1960s. Curiously,

this family-oriented complex within the Deschutes National Forest was a former infantry camp for the Army Corps of Engineers during World War II. The soldiers left behind the cavernous Great Hall, a masterfully constructed lodge built entirely of logs that hosts the annual Sunriver Music Festival. Its acoustics for classical music are surprisingly good.

But culture is not the magnet that draws visitors to the sparsely populated east flank of the Cascade Range. Sunriver's main appeal is the great outdoors. For a few weeks each spring, hyperactive sportsmen can seek out more high-quality recreational opportunities here than at any other resort in the land. Rise early on a fine May day, and you can ski nearby Mt. Bachelor, tackle Class IV white-water rapids in the Deschutes River, windsurf in nearby Elk Lake, angle for trout and landlocked salmon in back-country lakes, ride a bike (or a horse) along scenic riverside paths and, if your muscles haven't turned to jelly by day's end, tee up for a predinner round on one of the resort's two courses.

For the accomplished player, Sunriver's venue of distinction is the North Course, a scenic Robert Trent Jones, Jr., design opened in 1981. The annual site of the Oregon Open, the 6,208-yard layout (6,823 yards

*South Course, sixteenth hole*

*A guest room. Photo courtesy Sunriver Lodge & Resort*

from the championship markers) is laid out on a semiarid plain marked by vignette outcroppings of lava rock. The rough is inhabited by several varieties of sagebrush, its silvery-gray, bitter-aromatic foliage rising to six feet in places. Should your ball lodge in its branches, you'll find it as formidable to play from as the gorse in Scotland.

Rising above the layout's rolling fairways are fragrant juniper trees, stands of lodgepole pines encrusted with cones, and giant ponderosa pines, the cinnamon-colored plates of their bark fitted together like the pieces of a jigsaw puzzle. The great volcanic cone of 9,065-foot Mt. Bachelor, its slopes frosted with snow all summer long (the U.S. Ski Team trains there), dominates all sightlines.

Though it appears wide open from the tees, the North Course creates a false sense of spaciousness at several holes. Accuracy, golf's Holy Grail, is generally more valuable here than distance. Sunriver, it must be said, is a slicer's nightmare: Water comes into play seven times, the lakes encroaching more often than not on the right side of the greens and fairways.

Then again, slicers and hookers alike can be victimized by the 371-yard eighteenth, a near ninety-degree dogleg left with a lake in its bend and a green pinched on both sides by water. A misaimed approach—assuming the drive finds terra firma—has drowned many a chance for a decent round. In fact, the nineteenth hole at the North Course is a halfway house for broken hearts. Of course, golfers with exaggerated fades and draws have been known to come unhinged much earlier in the round, usually at the eighth, a 138-yard par three with a horseshoe-shaped moat fitted like a collar around two-thirds of its green.

The thinner air at higher elevation—Sunriver is 4,158 feet above sea level—enables golfers to pick up an additional ten to twenty yards on their drives and perhaps a half-club with irons. This extra distance can be crucial, as most of the water alongside the fairways is designed to snare the average player's slightly errant drive. A slightly longer tee shot can spell the difference between disaster and excellence.

The greens on the North Course require careful scrutiny. Not only are they smooth and fast, but many have interesting contours ranging from

subtle to barely survivable. To keep them that way, putting surfaces are roped off in the winter months to prevent herds of migrating elk from trampling them.

Actually, Sunriver's nature show has a way of taking your mind off the rigors of the game. A pair of inquisitive horned owls nest beside the second hole. Occasionally, a golden eagle passes high overhead. Coyotes roam the course at night. Cougars have been known to bed down on the greens. And until quite recently, mountain lions were occasionally spotted in the area.

Apart from its slick plateau greens, the resort's South Course lacks distinction in its design. A long, flat, bland course routed through meadows, its prime challenge consists in manufacturing pitch-and-run shots to the firm, elevated greens. Because many of the fairways are lined by earth-toned homes and condominiums, the South lacks the rugged beauty, much less the inventiveness and variety, of the North. Surprisingly, the South is not unpopular with Sunriver residents and resort guests. Which probably means that it's far too easy to get hung up on a layout's architectural shortcomings. Golfers speak with their green fees, and at Sunriver, the South Course receives a substantial amount of play, though less than the North. Management is confident that the two Bob Cupp–designed courses (Cupp was formerly one of Jack Nicklaus's chief designers) planned for Sunriver on a 600-acre parcel of land south of the existing complex will put the South Course in the shade.

Incidentally, bring your most comfortable golf shoes to Sunriver—the gently rolling North and the flattish South are both ideal for walking. And wear your most casual golf togs—dress codes in rural Oregon are very relaxed.

Despite its dress-down attitude, Sunriver's rusticity is not without its comforts. Rooms and suites, remodeled in 1988 to coincide with the resort's twentieth anniversary, feature cathedral ceilings, decks with mountain views, and large stone fireplaces stocked daily with seasoned wood. One-, two-, and three-bedroom homes with full-kitchen facilities and optional maid service are also available. Do you fly your own plane? Sunriver has a 5,500-foot lighted runway that is rated one of the best in the state.

At the resort's elegant Meadows Dining Room, the "High Desert" cuisine features black bear consommé (chunks of flavorsome bear meat in a clear broth), venison in a black currant glaze, and wild game ravioli. Many of the dishes go perfectly with the superb red wines produced by Portland-area vineyards. (More than forty Oregon Pinot Noirs are found on the Meadows' wine list. Many vintages compare favorably with the better French red Burgundies.)

After hours, the renovated Owl's Nest Lounge features live entertainment and dancing. No need to dress up: flannel shirts and jeans are fine. Same thing goes for The Provision Co., Sunriver's informal restaurant, which has exposed cupboards on its walls reminiscent of an old general store.

Kids may have the best of it at Sunriver. Resident naturalists at the resort's Nature Center schedule nature walks, bike rides, canoe floats on the Deschutes River, campfire programs, slide shows, guest lectures, and field trips. The accent is on the interaction of plants and animals (including humans) in the high desert region. The center also houses one of the largest bird rehabilitation centers in Oregon (kids get to see hawks and other raptors up close) and has on display obsidian tools and projectiles used by prehistoric Indian tribes. Youngsters are also free to enjoy a play area filled with swings, slides, and a small fort. Small wonder that Sunriver is so popular with kids—and with golfers able to steer clear of the water and sagebrush on the North Course.

# BLACK BUTTE RANCH

SILVER MEDALIST

An hour's drive from Sunriver and eight miles from the re-created Old West town of Sisters and its thriving llama ranches is Black Butte Ranch, an 1,830-acre complex set in a crown of seven mountains. The resort functions not only as a four-season, family-oriented community for the likes of the Guggenheim family and the retired editors of big-city newspapers (like the *Washington Post*), it welcomes golfers to an utterly low-key, noncommercial atmosphere. Community members and resort guests have the right of way: No outside tournaments or convention groups are scheduled at Black Butte. What it lacks by way of self-promotion and hoopla, it more than compensates in beauty. The .encircling peaks in the eastern Cascades, many of them snow-covered dormant volcanoes in the 10,000-foot range, make Black Butte the most glorious mountain resort in the nation.

The resort's two golf courses are routed through highland meadows hemmed in by aspen-lined streams and tall ponderosa pines. The better of the two tracks is the 6,456-yard Big Meadow Golf Course, a Robert Muir Graves design opened in 1969. The front nine is a plain-Jane spread on gently rolling land sculpted a few eons ago by a retreating glacier. These holes comprise a pleasant parkland test, with greens nestled in the pines and beautifully scalloped bunkers (the architect's specialty) defining the play. The back nine, however, departs the cattailed marshes and beaver ponds stocked with rainbow trout for higher ground. The 356-yard

twelfth, for example, calls for a second shot to a green that resides atop a hill. Carry your approach too far, and a delicate chip from earthen mounds awaits to a very slippery green. The hulking stack of tree-covered rock known as Black Butte backdrops the green at the par-five sixteenth (wispy clouds often conceal the summit of this massive cinder cone), while the 373-yard eighteenth returns golfers to flatter terrain and the familiar sight of ponds and meadows. It is not unusual to see great blue herons tiptoeing in the shallows of the ponds as they hunt minnows.

The newer Glaze Meadow Course, designed by Black Butte's former director of golf, Gene ("Bunny") Mason, is a tricky, treelined layout that reflects the local pro's prejudices about the type of challenges a golfer should face. Mason, who believes that David Graham's final-round 67 at Merion in the 1981 U.S. Open was one of the best competitive rounds ever played, points out that Graham drove with an iron at nearly every hole. Perhaps to emphasize pinpoint shotmaking, Mason effectively takes the driver out of the hands of the better player at Glaze Meadow: The

*Left: Big Meadow Course, eleventh hole. Above: Glaze Meadow Course, tenth hole*

lion's share of the layout's par fours and par fives dogleg sharply to the left or right about 200 yards from the tee. If free swingers are to have any chance of landing their tee ball on the fairway, shots must be judiciously positioned with a long iron or fairway wood. The sight of a long, straight tee shot ricocheting off trees or splashing into water on the far side of a fairway is proof enough that Glaze Meadow was laid out with the short knocker in mind.

Black Butte's Western-theme lodge facilities and accommodations appeal mainly to activity-oriented family vacationers seeking good value. For example, the lead price for a room is under $150 per night in high season. Accommodations range from bedrooms in the main lodge to one-, two-, and three-bedroom condominiums. Private homes designed to accommodate four to eight persons are also available.

The Lodge restaurant, the main (and only) dining room at the resort, has large windows set in a high-ceilinged room that faces a lake and beyond it the clumped trio of peaks known as the Three Sisters. Waitresses wear floral smocks, while the dress code for diners is relaxed. (The tone of the resort is best expressed by a sign in the pro shop at the Big Meadow course, which states: "Shirts Required on Course.") The informal setting belies the quality of the meals, particularly the grilled beef and seafood presentations. The chocolate sourdough cake is also a winner.

Upstairs from the restaurant is the Lounge, a loftlike area set with antique chairs and warmed by a fireplace. No heavy-metal acts or Vegas revues here: Guitar-accompanied balladeers perform the kind of folk-rock music that never went out of style in this part of the country.

In addition to superb trout fishing on and off the resort (only fish over

six pounds are considered keepers), Black Butte has its own stable of horses. Pony rides for kids as well as hourly, half-day, all-day, and meal rides are available, many of them traveling far into wilderness areas. There are also sixteen miles of bike and jogging paths at the resort. The truly fit can hike to the top of the 6,415-foot Black Butte for an unparalleled view of the Cascades.

*Birches*

# THE COEUR D'ALENE RESORT

On a course brimming with gorgeous holes, the 155-yard sixth is a knockout that stairsteps downhill to a green framed by tall pines and backdropped by the lake. However, Coeur d'Alene's *pièce de résistance* is the par-three fourteenth, the hole with the world's first and only floating island green. Resting on foam-filled concrete honeycombs and linked to cables and winches, the 15,000-square-foot, 7,500-ton green is moved daily and anchored anywhere from 100 to 175 yards offshore. (A computerized digital display on the tee flashes the precise yardage). The

In the upper reaches of the Idaho panhandle some thirty miles from Spokane, Washington, is Coeur d'Alene, one of the most refreshing new resorts opened in the 1980s. Built on the shores of Lake Coeur d'Alene, rated "one of the five most beautiful lakes in the world" by *National Geographic*, and home to the largest population of osprey in the western United States, the resort is anchored by a gleaming white eighteen-story tower, its roof crowned by sloping copper turrets and belfries. Inside, the oversize rooms, each with a lake or mountain view, are thoughtfully conceived, with separate living, sleeping, and dining areas, balconies, fireplaces, an entry hall, bar, even a doorbell and light outside the door. (Prototypes were tested at the resort's headquarters for months before the most useful and attractive layouts and color schemes were chosen.)

Other amenities include three lounges (one with nightly live entertainment); an indoor recreation center complete with a pool, bowling alley, and racquetball courts; and the world's longest floating boardwalk (it's three-quarters of a mile long) skirting a 300-slip marina. Thirty shops and restaurants within a climate-controlled plaza are accessible from the resort hotel's lobby via a glass skybridge.

Beverly's, Coeur d'Alene's premier restaurant, serves Northwest cuisine with a continental flair, if dishes like sautéed breasts of quail with macadamia nut crust and rosemary chili sauce fit that description. Located on the seventh floor overlooking the lake and marina, this elegant but informal room changes its menu daily to incorporate fresh, seasonal ingredients in its preparations. Beverly's wine list is exceptional. Service in the dining establishments and throughout the resort is first class.

In all the world, Coeur d'Alene's golf routine is unique. Players are whisked to the course in one of two custom-designed mahogany launches (Eagle and Double Eagle), introduced to their forecaddies, and shown to the lakeside practice tee, where floating balls are hit to a series of floating targets in the water. Golf bags are lashed to custom-designed golf carts, each with built-in ball washer, tee dispenser, refuse bin, and cooler. Then it's off to the first tee of one of the most enjoyable resort courses in America. Also one of the best conditioned: Perfectly manicured bent grass covers not only tees and greens but fairways, too. The rough is a smooth blanket of bluegrass. Course maintenance is performed at night by a greens crew that wears helmets fitted with lamps, so as not to intrude on the golf experience. With no trash receptacles, drinking fountains, or ball washers on the grounds (even the rest rooms are located underground), the golf course calls to mind a beautiful, uncluttered park. Ironically, the holes were routed on the site of an abandoned sawmill stockpiled with industrial and wood wastes following an extensive cleanup.

A par-71 layout conceived by Scott Miller, a former Jack Nicklaus design associate, Coeur d'Alene's golf course measures a scant 6,309 yards from the tips. However, it plays longer and includes three distinct experiences: sculptured linkslike holes bordered by Austrian pines; mountainside holes carved from forest and rock; and water holes played over or around Fernan Creek and Lake Coeur d'Alene. Forecaddies, their services included in the price of the green fee, are adept at pathfinding.

target is not only attractive—small conifers, red geraniums, and a pair of bunkers frame the putting surface—it is actually much less intimidating than island greens at newfangled stadium courses. After their tee shots, players board a ferry to the green, where the boat's skipper tends the pin, rakes the bunkers, and records the scores. A true novelty, Coeur d'Alene's island green may soon replace the potato as Idaho's most recognizable symbol.

*Left: Sixth hole*

*Below: The resort and marina*

*Bottom: Fourteenth hole*

through heavily wooded, lightly populated areas where oysters and clams can be gathered at state parks along the way. Wine lovers can stop by the Hoodsport Winery, known for its excellent white wines.

A few miles from Sunriver is the High Desert Museum, where interpretive trails cut through a pine forest lead to a pond where frolicsome river otters can be viewed from below water level. Other exhibits feature porcupines, birds of prey, and re-creations of the region's Indian and Gold Rush settlements.

Also near Sunriver is the Lava Lands Visitor Center, located at the base of Lava Butte, an ancient cinder cone. Automated tremors and dramatic visual displays jog the imagination to experience the area's turbulent volcanic past. A paved road leads to the top of Lava Butte, where an interpretive trail winds around the crater's rim and serves up spectacular views of the Cascades.

The curious may obtain a lantern and explore the mile-long Lava River Cave, the longest uncollapsed lava tube in Oregon; or follow the 0.9-mile,

*Nature talk at the High Desert Museum. Photo courtesy High Desert Museum*

Departing from the marina at Semiahmoo, early evening cruises on the *Star of Semiahmoo*, an eighty-foot motor yacht, are a great way to view Mt. Baker, the North Cascades, and the San Juan Islands, which resemble bluish-green pincushions set against the horizon. A six-hour San Juan Islands cruise passes by Peace Arch Park at the United States–Canada border before reaching Clements Reef National Wildlife Refuge and the rugged coastlines of Orcas, San Juan, Waldron, and Speiden Islands. Porpoises, seals, sea lions, and orca whales are often sighted. The cruise includes a two-hour shore excursion to the beautiful island town of Friday Harbor.

In addition to fly-fishing for sea-run cutthroat trout from the beach at Semiahmoo Park (a county preserve within the resort), fishermen can arrange charters to the San Juan Islands aboard the *Star Fisher* to angle for salmon, ling cod, rockfish, and red snapper. Skippers guarantee a catch or welcome fishermen back for a complimentary trip. (All cruises and fishing charters are operated by Gray Line Water Sightseeing.)

At Port Ludlow, sailing or fishing excursions in Puget Sound can be arranged at the resort's full-service marina. Majestic Olympic National Park, where primeval rain forests vie with glacier-capped mountains for a visitor's attention, is a half-hour's drive from the resort. (The Port Ludlow staff will pack box lunches for nature jaunts.) Also nearby is Port Townsend, a historic seaport town noted for its Victorian homes and many fine antique shops. Ferries depart Port Townsend for pristine Whidbey Island and Deception Pass, a scenic lookout. For those willing to venture further afield, ferries depart Port Angeles (a ninety-minute drive from the resort) for the city of Victoria on Vancouver Island, British Columbia. Known for its grand 19th-century buildings, well-kept parks, and lovely gardens, Victoria, still very British, is one of Canada's most charming cities. A pleasant drive can be made from Port Ludlow to Seattle via Olympia by following the west side of the Hood Canal

*Rafting on the Deschutes River. Photo courtesy Sunriver Lodge & Resort and Sun Country Tours, Inc.*

self-guided trail through the Lava Cast Forest, a stark wonderland of volcanic sculpture that was formed when molten lava flowed through an ancient forest, later cooling to a hard coating that remains today as a tree cast.

Near Black Butte, the Sisters–Metolius River Recreation Area is home to majestic old-growth ponderosa pines, hundreds of miles of hiking trails, fifteen full-service campgrounds, and the Metolius River, known as one of the finest wild trout streams in the nation (fly-fishing only).

Wine lovers transiting through Portland can visit some of the Northwest's top wineries in the Willamette Valley, an hour's drive southwest of the city. Among the top vineyards are Eyrie, Knudsen Erath, Sokol Blosser, Rex Hill, Adams, Adelsheim, Cameron, Ponzi, Elk Cove, Tualatin, and Veritas. The Pinot Noir, white Riesling, Chardonnay, and Gewürztraminer grapes produce exceptionally fine wines in this microclimate. Check with the Oregon Winegrowers Association for a map and details on suggested wine-tasting tours.

Coeur d'Alene makes the most of its beautiful twenty-six-mile-long lake. The resort organizes a weekly dinner cruise during the summer as well as visits to remote Huckleberry Beach, a six-acre hideaway ideal for wilderness barbecues. Aqua cycles, paddle boats, canoes, kayaks, and jet skis are available at the city dock, while Hobie Cats and windsurfers can be rented through North Idaho College. Parasailing above the lake is also popular. So is fishing for kokanee salmon. Brooks Seaplane, adjacent to the resort, offers aerial tours of north Idaho's lakes. Ready to go to the dogs? The Coeur d'Alene Greyhound Park features parimutuel racing Tuesdays through Saturdays on an enclosed track. The world's longest single-stage gondola runs to the top of nearby Silver Mountain, where hiking, mountain biking, and outdoor entertainment are available. The resort's boardwalk and adjacent Tubbs Hill nature trail are ideal for hiking and jogging. Twenty minutes north of Coeur d'Alene is Silverwood Theme Park and Country Carnival, a family-oriented park with rides, entertainment, and a steam-chugging locomotive.

---

### DON'T LEAVE HOME WITHOUT . . . A GAME PLAN

*Playing a great golf course for the first time can be truly memorable and exciting. However, a lack of local course knowledge can wreak havoc with your score, as well as your enjoyment of the game. The solution is to do some homework before departure and arrive at the resort with a clear game plan.*

*First, know the distance you hit each club. Through practice sessions, determine which iron you consistently hit 150 yards. There is generally a ten-yard difference between clubs, assuming a 7-iron shot travels 150 yards.*

*After calculating your personal yardages, request a scorecard and yardage book (usually available for a small fee) from the resort you plan to visit. Study the layout of the course,*

*including landing areas, water hazards, and bunker placements. Devise a realistic strategy of how to play the course based on the strengths (and weaknesses) of your game.*

*At the resort, check with the pro shop to find out how the course is marked for yardage. At Semiahmoo, for example, the yardages stamped on the sprinkler heads were measured by laser to the center of the greens. In addition, 150-yard markers are found on either side of the fairways.*

*Doing a little research in advance of your trip—and asking the pro shop staff for yardage information—will greatly enhance the enjoyment of your golf vacation.*

BRIAN SOUTHWICK, DIRECTOR OF GOLF,
THE RESORT SEMIAHMOO

On the surface, Arizona's high Sonoran Desert would seem the last place on earth an enterprising resort developer or golf course architect would choose to build. The ground is hard and stony. Most of the plant life bristles with thorns. The sunsets are beautiful, but Bermuda grass won't grow on a sunset. Because water (and permissible fairway acreage) is at a premium in the desert, golfers at newer resort courses play their tee shots not to broad welcoming lawns, but to slim landing pods hemmed in by cactus and arroyos. Should your ball stray from the short grass, you will require the wiles of a prospector to find it, the skills of a pro to extract it, and a pair of rip-stop pants to avoid finishing the round in shreds.

But not all of Arizona's challenges are so closely defined by the environment. Older establishments, such as the Arizona Biltmore and the Wigwam in the Phoenix area, present mile-wide fairways built at a time when winter escapees liked to be reminded of their hometown parkland courses. They are a good choice for golfers who tend to spray the ball.

Newer properties—the Boulders in Carefree and the Ventana Canyon resorts in Tucson, for example— give golfers a chance to play *in* the desert—tees, fairways, and greens are embraced by a devil's garden of scorched earth and prickly cactus. Bring extra balls.

The Grand Canyon State offers dry, clear air and more than 300 days of sunshine annually. Except when temperatures soar above 100 degrees in the summer months, Arizona is *the* place to be when winter arrives early or lingers late in the northern states. Traditionally

# THWEST

favored by Midwestern snowbirds, the Arizona desert has taken on international appeal of late. Everyone, it seems, wants the chance to tee it up among the giant saguaro cacti that thrive here.

Texas is a great place to play golf. Just ask the Texans, the least bashful of Americans. The Four Seasons Resort and Club adjoining the TPC at Las Colinas is probably the most unusual resort setup in the nation: The complex is contained within a corporate greenbelt a short drive from Dallas–Fort Worth Airport. The golf course, one of the more enjoyable (and playable) stadium courses in existence, gives traveling players a chance to test their skills on a television tournament track.

The Texas hill country, marked by waterfalls, limestone outcroppings, and dramatic elevation changes, belies the popular image of a dusty, pancake-flat Texas. Barton Creek's three courses outside Austin and, farther afield, the three Robert Trent Jones–designed layouts at Horseshoe Bay trace the natural contours of a hilly corner of Texas still associated with native son Lyndon B. Johnson.

While Colorado's major ski resorts are hurrying to jump aboard the golf train by building new courses to expand their appeal, one resort, the Broadmoor, has been attracting golfers since 1918. It is not only the finest resort in the Rockies, it features a composite thirty-six hole spread that showcases the design talents of both Donald Ross and Robert Trent Jones, two of the unlikeliest bedfellows in golf. The hotel, built by a copper tycoon with bottomless pockets, is unrivaled in this neck of the woods for Old World luxury.

*Inset: Tennis Center, Horseshoe Bay, Texas*
*Large picture: The Boulders, Carefree, Arizona*

*Latilla dining room. Photo courtesy The Boulders*

They have no geological business being there, these enormous tawny granite rocks extruded from the earth eons ago and left piled on the floor of the high Sonoran Desert twenty miles north of Phoenix. Rounded and creased over the years by wind and rain, they provide a fantastic backdrop for the Boulders, a 1,300-acre resort with 136 adobe casitas that blend so seamlessly into the granitic setting, they look as if they too might have issued forth from a split in the earth's crust. The desert floor was not "scraped" during construction of the Boulders: Vegetation at the building site was placed in a nursery and later replanted. Resort structures were designed to play off the shapes of the boulders and be as unobtrusive as possible. Ditto for the golf courses.

Until recently, architect Jay Morrish's make-over of a preexisting course in 1981, and his creation of a third nine four years later, gave the resort twenty-seven holes of superlative mix 'n match golf, permitting three different eighteen-hole combinations. However, the game's growing popularity spurred management to rehire Morrish to construct a fourth nine, opened in 1991. Guests choose between the Boulders South Course, comprised of holes from the original Boulders nine grafted to Morrish's new holes; or the Boulders North Course, formerly the Saguaro and Lakes nines. Taken together, they are two of the most visually striking resort golf courses in the world. The shot values are a match for the scenery.

According to Director of Golf Bob Irving, "All of the holes are tough but entertaining. To score well, a golfer needs a little imagination, and there's not much room for error. The Boulders rewards those who play sensibly," especially those sensible enough to follow one of the local rules printed on the scorecard: "Ball

hit into the desert may be played as a hazard with the following option: Drop the ball in the grass at the point last crossing the margin of the grass; penalty, one stroke." Depart the fairway, and you enter the desert at your own peril. The rough is *really* rough, not the usual long grass or hardpan. Playing the desert as a lateral hazard avoids wear and tear on your shoes, slacks, golf clubs—and ego. Poisonous creatures such as rattlesnakes, scorpions, and Gila monsters are rare, to be sure, but cactus is ever-present. More than one golfer has presented himself to the Boulders staff with the barbs of the notorious chainfruit or "jumping" cholla (many claim the plant actually lurches forward to snare unsuspecting passersby) imbedded in an arm or leg. Bid your ball adios and reload if you happen to hit a wild shot.

With only ninety acres of turf and lake surface permitted per eighteen holes due to current water restrictions, no sprawling lawns of green were planted at the Boulders. Target areas are tight. Accuracy and shrewd club selection are all-important, as golfers play to landing pods fitted snugly into the raw desert. Similarly, greens are backdropped by piles of sorrel-colored rock or chiseled into an inhospitable landscape of spiny plants. Most are well bunkered, too, but sometimes catching a bunker can prevent a golfer from ending up in no man's land. Lastly, there are no adjacent holes at the Boulders: Each serves up its own slice of desert reality.

Even if you haven't the game to tackle the pro tees, it makes good sense to visit a few of them for their scenic values. Shading the elevated back tee at the par-three seventh on the South Course, for example, is a huge balancing rock. (It's the favorite perch of a large turkey vulture.) The tee shot is played to a green framed by a spreading ironwood tree to the left and a large, shallow trap on the right. In the center of the trap is a 300-year-old saguaro cactus, its great candelabra arms bleached by the sun and its perforated trunk inhabited by singing cactus wrens.

*A terrace. Photo courtesy The Boulders*

*Main Lodge pool*

Next is the long par-four eighth hole, fully 460 yards from the tips. The pro tee is found only by looking up. A spiral staircase carved in rock leads around the side of a massive boulder to a tee that fits the shaved top of the rock like a green crewcut. (Morrish snaked a pipe through a crack in the rock to provide irrigation.) Spread forty feet below the tee is a broader-than-usual fairway that leads to a sprawling green protected at the rear by bunkers. Not that many players are victimized by overshooting this green in two strokes.

Adventure strikes again at the 313-yard eleventh hole, where the fairway is divided by a median strip of cactus and scrub, leaving golfers to choose between the narrow high road, with its better angle of attack to the green, or the much wider low road, where the approach must swing in over trouble. The preternaturally deep bunker that prefaces the right side of the green can cause serious problems, even to those who believe they have mastered the explosion shot.

Perhaps the toughest hole on the course is the short par-four twelfth, a lay-up hole where the drive is aimed to a directional flag at the crest of a hill, and where the approach shot is carried to a long, narrow, kidney-shaped green that sits well below fairway level. The grass bunkers to the right of the green are no place to be.

The North Course opens with a short par five that crosses a pair of dry washes, one on the tee shot and one on the second shot, and is quickly reprised by the longer par-five third, a spectacular right-to-left dogleg with

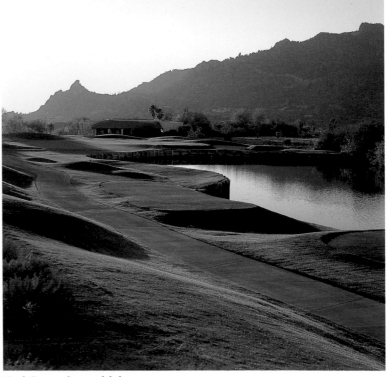

*North Course, fourteenth hole*

*South Course, seventh hole*

Meals at the Boulders Club, recently expanded to include an exhibition kitchen, can be taken indoors or outside on a shaded terrace. Both seating areas have good views of the golf courses and surrounding desert. Menu items range from deli-style sandwiches to seafood, steaks, and chicken grilled over Kentucky white charcoal. The Boulders margarita, a mixture of three types of aged tequila and fresh lime juice, is peerless.

The resort's Palo Verde restaurant, named for the leafless desert tree that conducts photosynthesis in its chartreuse bark, serves lunch and dinner in an airy room with an open, Mexican-tiled kitchen where white-toqued cooks preside. The Latilla, the Main Lodge's dining room, is dominated by the trunk of an enormous ponderosa pine that supports a vaulted ceiling, its supporting beams radiating out like the spokes of a wheel. The unusual banquettes were hand-molded in muted tan

sand traps on one side and grassy pots on the other designed to gather wayward tee shots. A conservative second shot sets up an approach to an elevated green guarded in front by a troublesome brook. It may well be the finest par five at the resort.

Although the seventh hole is a mere 323 yards, no fewer than eight pot bunkers pit the left side of the fairway to snare hooked tee shots. Take aim at the lone saguaro at the far end of the fairway and select an extra club on the approach to carry the pot bunker that guards one of the smallest and slickest greens on the course. A marvel of strategic design, this hole must be finessed, not bullied.

If the seventh isn't the best short par four at the Boulders, the 309-yard eighth is. The surprisingly wide driving zone leads past a clump of boulders and an appendage of desert laid into the fairway to a two-tiered green protected on all sides by deep bunkers. Here again, accuracy and careful judgment of distance are called for.

The back nine of the North Course favors long hitters but penalizes golfers who go for broke and fail. Without boulders and tall saguaros to frame them, these holes are less stirring than the other twenty-seven, though they do not lack for challenge.

Not only is the pro shop at the Boulders one of the most stylish in the nation—lots of beautifully displayed designer golf togs—but the level of service and courtesy provided by the staff is usually found only at the best private clubs. Players are handed a course guide by the starter, while staff members indicate to golfers engrossed in practice on the range how much time they have until tee off.

plaster to emulate the shape and color of the boulders. The view from the room's picture windows is of a slender waterfall creasing a formation of boulders above the free-form swimming pool. After hours, the Discovery Lounge, adjacent to the dining room, features a trio that knows every Cole Porter and George Gershwin tune you can name.

In all three of the resort's restaurants, selections low in fat, cholesterol, and salt are available. In addition, healthful breakfasts feature whole-grain cereals, homemade fruit muffins, and fresh fruits and juices. Breakfast served on the furnished balcony or patio of the casita, the desert sun just beginning to evaporate the dew on the grass, is inarguably the best way to start a day at the Boulders.

Much thought was given to the design of the resort's accommodations. The spacious one-bedroom casitas, each with a private entrance, have wood-beamed ceilings with fans, a fireplace set with fragrant boughs of juniper wood, a wet bar, a large dressing area with two six-drawer dressers and plenty of closet space, and a bathroom with double sink and vanity done up in glazed Mexican tiles. One wall of the stall shower (there's also a large oval tub) is made from glass blocks, so that a rainbow effect is created when the sun filters through in the morning. For total peace, guests may request that the phone, clock radio, and television be removed from the casita during their stay.

Before or after golf, consider touring the grounds with a staff horticulturist who can identify the three distinct palettes of desert vegetation assigned to each area of the property. No palm trees or showy ornamental flowers are found at the Boulders—desert exotics from Australia and South Africa enhance the indigenous plants and flowers.

The more adventurous can hike the one-third mile Boulders trail, a narrow path that leads through a natural tunnel of boulders and over a ravine inhabited by bobcats to a rock shelf 400 feet above the resort. The panorama of stark hills in the Tonto National Forest, as well as the view to Phoenix over the high chaparral, is inspiring, especially when the sky streaks with orange at sunset.

Within the main lodge, Navajo blankets, woven baskets, twelfth-century Native American pottery and other handicrafts grace the walls and niches of the public rooms. A stained-glass skylight floods the lobby with color, while the massive entry doors, pieced together from four different hand-rubbed woods, take their design from the boulder formations. There's also an artist-in-residence who makes models of Indian cliff dwellings designed to be lit from within by a candle. These "illuminaire sculptures," built with miniature adobe bricks, are available for purchase in the resort's gift shop.

The resort's concierge can arrange Jeep tours of the desert, hot-air balloon rides, as well as rounds of golf at neighboring private clubs. Most of these clubs feature very strong golf courses staked out by pricey real estate, but precious few guests race off to play them. There's a reason: The sumptuous envelopment of the boulders, and the Boulders, is unduplicated elsewhere.

*South Course, fifth hole*

# ARIZONA BILTMORE

Golf isn't necessarily the best reason to visit the Arizona Biltmore. The Phoenix area has many resorts with better layouts than the Biltmore's Adobe and Links courses. What they don't have is the self-proclaimed "Jewel of the Desert," a legendary hotel inspired by visionary architect Frank Lloyd Wright that opened in 1929, when Phoenix was nothing more than a laid-back town of 70,000 residents. Entering its doors is like entering an Art Deco time warp.

"Craftsmen actuated merely by mercenary motives could never have created such a structure," claimed one of the front-page stories in the *Arizona Republican* when the hotel made its smashing debut. The Biltmore cost $2.5 million to build, a small fortune in those days, but it's anyone's guess what a 32,500-pound copper roof, lavish gold-leaf ceilings (justified with the explanation that they would "never need painting"), or more than 250,000 hand-cast filigreed blocks used to face the building would cost today. One-time owner William Wrigley, Jr., the chewing gum magnate and owner of the Chicago Cubs, whose family controlled the hotel for forty-four years, knew from day one that the Biltmore would be a money-losing proposition. The hotel never could cover the interest on its debts, much less pay them off. Perhaps Wrigley realized that any place that gave him goosebumps every time he stepped inside could afford to run in the red.

*Links Course, third hole*

*Swimming pool*

Many changes of ownership and several facelifts later, most recently a $20-million makeover in 1991, the Arizona Biltmore remains one of the classiest acts in the American resort business. Located in the foothills of Squaw Peak and now embraced by a tasteful residential development, the 506-room property (including seventy-seven suites) doesn't look like any other hotel in the world. A stylized fortress of ornamental sandy-gray textile blocks that were fired on site and inspired by the trimmed trunks of

palm trees or ancient Aztec designs (depending upon your point of view), the hotel is lighted by semiopaque glass blocks inset to match the walls and supporting pillars of the lobby.

Guest rooms are spacious and comfortable. The housekeeping staff uses three sheets per bed, with the third sheet placed over the blanket so the guests don't pull rough fabric against their chins when they tuck in for the night. The pillows are 100 percent goose down.

The Biltmore's main dining hall is the Gold Room Grille, famous for its vaulted gold-leaf ceiling (reputedly the world's largest), its stained-glass windows along two walls, and its pair of enormous tapestry murals that depict scenes from Native American mythology. Dancing to live Big Band music on a parquet wood floor in a room that literally glows with the metallic richness of its ceiling is more than enjoyable. It's inspiring. The Gold Room was mildly scandalized by Harpo Marx and his bride during their honeymoon at the Biltmore: The couple would hold hands and skip through the room after a meal.

In the Orangerie, an intimate, gardenlike room lit by sparkling clusters of drop-tier chandeliers and enlivened by the sounds of a harpist, the gourmet continental cuisine leans to the eclectic: wild boar-bacon-wrapped loin of rabbit, skillet-seared medallions of south Texas venison, three-lentil relish on watercress and arugula. Celebrating a special occasion? The hotel's trio of wine cellars, containing more than 20,000 bottles, comprise one of the best sources for great vintages (particularly red Bordeaux) of any American resort. Jackets are required of gentlemen in both Biltmore restaurants after 6 P.M., though only first-timers would

considerably longer than they appear. Take an extra club for the approach at the home hole, for a devilish little creek purls in front of the green.

It should be remembered that the Adobe was not designed to cause paroxysms among guests who desire a relaxing round of golf. Except for the Aleppo pines that serve as 150-yard markers and a few palms at the outer perimeter of the fairways, the layout is wide open. There's room galore to spray the ball from the tee, but approach shots must be delivered with a fair amount of finesse. Comparable to a mature country club layout in a temperate region of the country, the Adobe has been described by guests and members alike as a great place to air out your swing.

The newer Links Course, designed by former Biltmore director of golf Bill Johnston in 1978, is a horse of a different color. Created as a greenbelt for a residential community, the Links is a short (5,726 yards from the whites), frivolous layout rife with eccentric holes. This is especially true of the back nine, which traces a wide loop behind the hotel on surprisingly hilly terrain. (The front nine is flat, watery, and thick with out-of-bounds stakes.)

The Links's feature hole is the 162-yard fifteenth, which drops precipitously from a forbidding expanse of desert scrub to a well-trapped green. The views of Squaw Peak and the Phoenix skyline from the tee are outstanding, though the aesthetics are marred by the sound of passing cars on busy Lincoln Drive, which borders the hole to the left. Stick with the Adobe and play it in the morning when the desert air is fresh.

At some point during the stay, sign up for a tour detailing the hotel's history and architecture, available three days a week following a cold luncheon buffet in the Gold Room Grille. The guided tour is a trip back in time to the days when only those with Social Register standing were permitted to reserve a room at the Biltmore, a time when the resort functioned as an upper-crust dude ranch and exclusive retreat for a clientele that shrugged aside the Great Depression as if it didn't exist.

dream of appearing without a tie as well. In years gone by, formal dress—tuxedos for men, gowns for women—was mandatory in the lobby and dining rooms. Dress codes have been relaxed over time, but this is no place to wander down to the lobby in a bathing suit.

Another of the Biltmore's features is its concierge desk. Of the three concierges in Phoenix who are members of Les Clefs d'Or ("the gold keys"), an international association of elite concierges, two work at the Biltmore. Whether it's the Grand Canyon or an Arabian horse show you wish to see, these concierges make swift arrangements.

The hotel, set in thirty-nine exquisitely landscaped acres, has an annual budget of more than $100,000 for petunias alone. The pool, built with turquoise-blue tiles from Catalina Island in California, is a delightful place to relax in the sunshine. Cabanas are available, including the one favored by Irving Berlin during his frequent stays. In addition to a pair of putting greens on the hotel grounds, lawn chess is also available. Square tiles form a checkerboard with alternating patches of grass. The playing pieces are knee-high.

The Biltmore's golf is almost an aside to the hotel and its grounds. The Adobe Course, a William P. Bell design circa 1929, is an old-fashioned parkland test still remembered as the place where Clark Gable lost his wedding ring (an employee recovered it). There's plenty of room to drive the ball on this spacious 6,455-yard layout, but the small, subtly contoured greens are well protected by bunkers. Holes are routed longitudinally on a gently sloped mountain foothill. The downhill holes generally play into a breeze, nullifying the seeming advantage, while the uphill holes, particularly the sixteenth and eighteenth, both testing par fives, play

*Lavish landscaping*

# THE WIGWAM RESORT

SILVER MEDALIST

Located seventeen miles west of Phoenix in sleepy Litchfield Park, the Wigwam was originally built in 1919 as a guest house for visiting representatives of the Goodyear Tire & Rubber Company. Their business, surprisingly, was agricultural: the fibers of long-staple cotton cultivated in the arid valley were used to strengthen the rubber carcasses of the company's pneumatic tires.

Converted to a modest thirteen-room resort in 1929 (in that era, guests were assigned a horse with their rooms), the Wigwam eventually blossomed into an exclusive vacation colony favored by well-to-do Midwesterners. After falling on hard times in the early 1980s, new ownership and a recent $28-million overhaul have recaptured the resort's luster and charm. Not only have the 241 single-story adobe casitas been refurbished (ninety new accommodations were added in 1991), the Territorial-style pueblo architecture of the main lodge and its public rooms has been carefully restored. Antler chandeliers, adobe hearths, exposed ceiling beams, and a painted elkhide wall hanging greet arriving guests in the lobby.

Authentically Southwestern, the Wigwam makes no attempt to compete with the opulent, high-profile resorts in nearby Scottsdale. Relaxation is the order of the day. Jasmine-scented paths lead through beautifully manicured grounds shaded by palms to a free-form heated swimming pool. Bicycle use is free of charge. Shuffleboard is popular. So is badminton. There's also croquet on the greensward, a sure cure for the yips. If blasting clay pigeons out of the sky appeals, a visit to the Phoenix Trap and Skeet Club can be arranged. But best of all, for a resort of its size, the Wigwam's golf amenity is a surfeit of riches: three courses, each distinctive, all beautifully kept, and none heavily trafficked.

The trio's Great Humbler is the Gold Course, a Robert Trent Jones design built at the height of the architect's powers in the mid-1960s. The Gold was laid out in the days when the idea was to imprint an oasis of water, palms, and wall-to-wall greenery on the desert floor and then fashion a lush parkland course upon it.

Which is not to suggest that the Gold is easy. Stretching to a lusty 7,074 yards from the tips (6,504 yards from the white tees), this stern examination of power and skill owns one of the highest course ratings in the Phoenix area. Not only are the Gold's challenges big, but so too are its pedestal greens (they average more than 10,000 square feet each); its tees (the tee at the 391-yard thirteenth hole, for example, is 150 yards in length); and its sand traps (there are 100 of them, most large cloverleafs that guard the corners of the doglegs and pinch the fairways in the driving zones).

Among the Gold's feature holes is the 360-yard second, its fairway narrowed by salt cedars and its crowned green guarded by a pair of ponds; the 409-yard eighth, where a culvert must be crossed twice to reach an elevated green angled diagonally to the fairway and guarded by two deep sand pits that look as if they might have been gouged by a giant ice cream scoop; and the grand 555-yard tenth, a double-dogleg with a complete checklist of potential trouble: out of bounds, water, sprawling bunkers, big trees, and a wickedly undulating green. Without a single weak hole to its name, the Gold was intended to weed out the pretenders from the champions.

*Blue Course, thirteenth hole*

*Swimming pool*

Mercifully, Wigwam guests have a better chance of playing to their handicaps at the 5,960-yard Blue Course, a second Jones layout adapted from a links dating to 1930. All the trappings of the Gold are present on the Blue in smaller form. The better player can make time on the short par fives of this par-70 layout, while the average player can reach all the par fours in regulation.

The West Course, located a half-mile from the main resort complex on the site of a former airplane landing strip and blimp mooring circle, is a Robert ("Red") Lawrence design that is roomy, pleasant, and fair—for fourteen holes. The layout's final four, long and tough from the white tees, are well-nigh impossible from the blues. Even with the latest graphite technology at their disposal, few golfers can hope for more than an up-and-down par at the par-three seventeenth, which measures an ungodly 254 yards from the tips.

The Wigwam's formal restaurant, the Terrace, offers both prix fixe and à la carte continental dining in an understated room set off by stained-glass windows and wrought-iron chandeliers suspended from peeled aspen rafters. However, the resort's signature dining room is the Arizona Kitchen, where unusual regional specialties such as smoked corn chowder, rattlesnake fritters with salsa, pheasant tamales, and veal medallions with

*Bedroom in a villa. Photo courtesy The Wigwam Resort*

cinnamon-tequila-lime sauce are served in a hive-shaped room of whitewashed adobe walls.

One evening during a stay at the Wigwam, guests are encouraged to travel by hay wagon, horseback, stagecoach, or air-conditioned van (for spoilsports) to Sunset Point for an old-fashioned steak fry. Gathered round the campfire, the hired hands strumming guitars and calling to the coyotes, the cookout is a chance to catch a glimpse of the West as it was experienced by Goodyear executives who journeyed to the region more than sixty years ago to watch their cotton (and fortunes) grow.

# THE PHOENICIAN

SILVER MEDALIST

The resort's golf course, a compact design laid out on 130 acres by Homer Flint (his credits include Mauna Lani in Hawaii), starts out on flat terrain landscaped with tropical greenery before scaling the flanks of Camelback Mountain. Measuring 6,487 yards from the championship tees (the resort tees are 6,033 yards), with an unbalanced par of 34 on the front and 37 on the back nine, the course gets off to a rigorous start, its 177-yard third and 377-yard fourth holes both calling for savvy play over sand and water. And while there is room to hit the ball, seven pronounced doglegs,

*Mary Elaine's Restaurant. Photo courtesy The Phoenician*

Fanned out at the base of Camelback Mountain in Scottsdale, The Phoenician, a sumptuous palace patterned after the Crescent Hotel in Bath, England, is a glittering testament to the opulence of the 1980s. A curving drive lined with stately palms brings visitors to an impressive porte-cochere beside an enormous fountain made all the more spectacular by the arid surroundings. Inside, the $290-million hotel must rank among the most lavishly appointed in America. Four types of Italian marble were used to create a stunning geometric pattern in the entry area. Crystal chandeliers cast soft light on the twenty-three-carat gold leaf coffered ceilings. The Phoenician's eclectic art collection ranges from photorealist waterscapes and Indian-theme bronze sculptures to eighteenth-century Italian landscapes and striking ammonites (large snail fossils from central Mexico).

The resort's 580 rooms, suites, and casitas all offer at least 600 square feet of space, their art and decor carefully chosen to coordinate with the muted color schemes, wool Berber carpeting, and authentic McGuire furniture with Philippine leather strapping. Oversize bathrooms are sheathed in marble and feature twin vanities. For those who like to communicate, The Phoenician does not disappoint: Rooms have three telephones, each with two lines plus a dedicated line for a personal computer. Many of the spacious decks look to Camelback Mountain, a distinctively shaped rock pile described by GOLF Magazine correspondent Robert Sommers as looking "exactly like a supine dromedary resting from a long and thirsty trek across the Sonoran wastes."

Few resort hotels can match the diversity of cuisine found at The Phoenician. The top dining room is Mary Elaine's, serving Mediterranean country cuisine in a rooftop setting enlivened by a jazz combo. Diners can enjoy superb Italian food inside or out at The Terrace, while golfers seeking a casual dinner usually gravitate to Windows on the Green, where cilantro, jicama, Nopales cactus, and other local ingredients are used in authentic Southwestern dishes. After hours, Charlie Charlie's features dancing and socializing in a weathered wood and stone room. In its center stands the reproduction of a 2,000-year-old African baobab tree.

including a 90-degree bend in the fairway at the 371-yard seventh, quickly separate players from tourists.

The golf course gains altitude at the eleventh, an uphill par five, before attaining a height of 1,400 feet at the fifteenth tee, which looks to the city of Scottsdale, the snow-capped Superstition Mountains, and the resort's two-acre Cactus Garden, where 350 varieties of rare and unusual cacti and succulents are cultivated. The finishing holes draw near the five-story hotel, its exterior earth-tone colors hand-tinted to blend with the desert terrain. The greens, resurfaced with bent grass in 1991, are among the speediest and best kept in the area. Varied and testing, The Phoenician's golf course provides a satisfying stage for the game. Any shortcomings in the course design—the semiblind shots at the thirteenth and fourteenth holes are slightly suspect—are more than compensated for by one of the most luxurious (and best-run) resort hotels in the nation.

*Fifteenth hole. Photo courtesy The Phoenician*

# LOEWS VENTANA CANYON RESORT

SILVER MEDALIST

Probably the best way to introduce Loews Ventana Canyon in Tucson is to note that the resort location was shifted from its original site to ensure the safety of a 300-year-old saguaro cactus. Opened in 1984, the 398-room, low-rise hotel was a prime forerunner of the environmentally sensitive resort. A U-shaped structure backed into the foothills of the Santa Catalina Mountains, the hotel was designed to agree with the desert the way a painting relates to its frame. The exterior block, an indeterminate shade of grayish-brown, was selected to duplicate the tone of the surrounding mountains, while the vertical ribbing in the texture of

*Refreshments on a guest room terrace. Photo courtesy Loews Ventana Canyon Resort*

*Canyon Course, sixteenth hole*

the block imitates the pleated trunk of a saguaro. Viewed from afar, the hotel is suggestive of the cliff dwellings built by Arizona's earliest inhabitants.

Within, the Loews property has a slab of limestone imbedded with sea fossils for a front desk counter, an unusual copper woven sculpture behind it, and mammoth geodes of Brazilian amethyst on display in the lobby.

Guest rooms, each with a private balcony, serve up views of the Tucson skyline or the Coronado National Forest (the king of the forest is the saguaro cactus, a thorny colossus that reaches a height of fifty feet). Spacious and comfortable, each room features a minibar, stocked refrigerator, and three telephones. A split of the resort's champagne bubble bath is placed beside the oversize tub.

As for the golf, Tom Fazio created an appealing resort layout in the 6,282-yard Canyon Course (6,818 yards from the tips). Fazio, who considers his work as more of an artistic effort than a civil engineering project, was the perfect choice for a resort that sought to blend in with the desert, not impose itself upon it. And while Fazio's Mountain Course at the nearby Ventana Canyon Golf & Racquet Club places a premium on accuracy, the designer cleared out considerable amounts of desert scrub to widen fairways and enhance playability at the Canyon Course. The front nine leads golfers through Esperero Canyon, the holes shoehorned into a tight parcel of land. The shot values on these holes are sound, but the encroachment of housing and the tightly cornered cart paths detract somewhat from their appeal.

Notwithstanding the long drive from the ninth green to the tenth tee, the back nine of the Canyon Course redeems the shortcomings of the front. The tenth hole, a short par four, ends at a kidney-shaped pedestal green tucked up against a free-flowing volcanic rock that creates a natural amphitheater for putting. After rolling downhill through the desert at the 423-yard eleventh hole, the layout raises the ante at the 535-yard twelfth, a tremendous uphill par five that leads golfers by the nose up a

canyon of grassy swales to a narrow, deep green. The hole is backdropped by a V-shaped opening in an outcropping of rock high in the Catalinas. Describing the effect of this natural crack, the Spaniards named this valley Canyon de la Ventana, or "Canyon of the Window."

The short par-five eighteenth proves that Fazio, a classicist, has a little Hollywood in him. Intended as a grand finale, this hole entices gamblers, long hitters, and those who stopped keeping score after the twelfth hole to go for the green in two shots. Not only must a dry wash in front of the green be carried, but the shot must not drift right (into a pond) or carry long (into a waterfall).

Not far from the eighteenth green and opposite the pro shop is the Flying V Bar & Grill, named for the dude ranch that predated the resort. Inside, the ambiance is contemporary cowboy saloon with a Hollywood theme. Outside, a spacious patio set with wood-stump cocktail tables and tall director's chairs looks to the eighteenth green and its complex of watery graves. It's a great place to watch approaching golfers lay up or go for the gusto with their second shots. Margaritas, mixed by one of the best corps of bartenders in Arizona, are a house specialty. At night, the Flying V is transformed into Tucson's hottest nightclub, with University of Arizona students, wealthy Mexicans, and party-minded golfers all hitting the multilevel dance floor with abandon.

For fine dining, excellent new American cuisine is featured at Ventana, located on the second floor of the hotel facing the twinkling lights of Tucson on one side and the upper level of the canyon waterfall on the other. Superb preparations of seafood, venison, and quail (the chef burns different woods in the grill to flavor the meats) are served in one of the most romantic settings in the American West. Seeking romance and intimacy? The full-course dinner for two served in the guest room or terrace overlooking the desert (candlelight and flowers included) is nonpareil.

# VENTANA CANYON GOLF & RACQUET CLUB

SILVER MEDALIST

The nondescript brick exterior of the Ventana Canyon Golf & Racquet Club pales by comparison with its more glamorous neighbor up the street, the Loews Ventana Canyon Resort. In fact, the forty-eight-suite property was originally conceived as a timeshare development. When the "alternative ownership" concept failed to blossom, an all-suite hotel was created. Why stay here rather than the Loews property, one of the most elegant, environmentally correct resort hotels ever designed?

One very simple reason: Guests of the Golf & Racquet Club enjoy playing privileges at the Mountain Course (Loews's guests are restricted to the newer Canyon Course). Both are Tom Fazio layouts, but the Mountain, its greens slightly smaller and its landing zones narrower than the Canyon, is the superior course.

Fazio, who rarely works west of the Mississippi River, created one of his best-balanced designs at Ventana Canyon. From the gold rock tees at 6,356 yards, two of the par fives are reachable by long hitters, two are out of reach except to serious crushers. Two of the par threes are short, two are long. Similarly, the par fours range from short and tricky to long and dangerous. In fact, there isn't a single weak or indifferent hole on the course. Throughout, Fazio was content to showcase the natural beauty of the desert, not call attention to his skillful handiwork. Holes nestle into dead-end canyons, crisscross dry washes, trace the edge of *bajadas* (long slopes of sediment) and bring golfers abreast of the desert, particularly at the tee boxes, many of which are seamlessly integrated into the cactus and rock. As for wildlife, golfers are likely to encounter an appealing cast of characters during a round: Cottontail rabbits and coveys of Gambel's quail scurry in the underbrush, roadrunners streak across the fairways, and javelinas (wild pigs) forage noisily in the brittlebush. At night, bobcats snooze on the sixteenth green. Coyotes call to each other from one end of the course to the other, their calls more sustained and insistent when a mountain lion descends from its lair.

In typical Fazio fashion, the holes rely more on clever shaping and visual deception than on forced carries or artificial hazards to provide challenge. For example, fairways bottleneck just beyond the distance of a normal drive, while subtle elevation changes play havoc with distance assessment. A firm but fair test from the regular tees, the Mountain can be murderous from the black rock tees at 6,948 yards. (The slope rating from the tips is a hefty 144.) Bob Boyd, who won the 1990 Wilson Club Professional Classic played at Ventana Canyon, described it this way:

"This course is very punishing if you don't hit the ball straight. You can't get away with a bad shot. You hit it out in those weeds, and you're going to be constantly reteeing it." Local members maintain the only way to enjoy the course is to select a club that will keep the ball in play. There isn't much hope from the understory of thornscrub found beneath the giant saguaros that line the fairways.

The overall excellence of the design tends to be overshadowed by the eye-catching, infamous 104-yard third hole, a tiny transcanyon par three described by Fazio as the "shortest and most expensive hole I've ever built." (The price tag for the hole is listed at $1 million.) As a stage set, this hole is unparalleled: A tortuous, hairpin-turn cart path climbs seventy feet to a series of tees set atop outcroppings of rock. On the far side of a canyon, chiseled into the foothills of the Santa Catalinas below tee level, beckons an extra-firm, bilevel green the size of a child's wading pool. It's strictly a hit-or-miss proposition. You can't afford to be short or left: The weak or pulled tee shot cannot be retrieved. Produce the smoothest three-quarter wedge shot you've ever hit in your life, putt with delicate restraint on the slippery green (imagine putting down the windshield of your car and stopping the ball at the hood ornament), and success may be yours. Regardless of the tee shot's final destination, make an about-face on the tee to take in a southern panorama of the high Sonoran Desert, the city of Tucson, and the Mexican border 100 miles distant.

The feature hole on the back nine is the 413-yard fifteenth, a rugged, uphill par four with a friendly catch-all bunker guarding the left side of the fairway. (It's designed to prevent stray shots from leaving the premises.) Behind the generously sloped green is a large basaltic mound that looks for all the world like the topmost portion of a breaching whale. The whaleback rock partitions this hole from the tenth green on the Canyon Course. Appearances to the contrary, putts at Ventana Canyon break away from the mountains and toward Tucson. The greens, of bent grass, are uniformly fast and true.

The Mountain Course finishes in grand style at the 564-yard eighteenth hole, a hole that in shot value and appearance sums up everything that has gone before. Ironically, the hole plays no longer from the sky-high black tee at 589 yards than from the gold tee at 564 yards, the exalted height of the rear tee nullifying the extra distance. Certainly the view of the bristling cacti lining both sides of the rolling fairway, the faraway green guarded by a long skinny bunker, is superb from the topmost tee.

The golf cart return at the Mountain Course is most unusual. Golfers drive carts to an underground garage, where resort personnel clean and store players' clubs. An elevator returns golfers to the clubhouse level.

The Golf & Racquet Club is nearly as unfussy and spare inside as out. The one- and two-bedroom suites, ranging in size from 800 to 1,500 square feet, feature full kitchens and dining areas, king-size beds, large baths with oversize tubs, and good views of the golf course or surrounding mountains from the private balcony or patio. All the amenities afforded local club members—fireside lounge, card rooms, exercise and aerobic facilities, heated swimming pool, and salons—are available to guests. A popular meeting site for small business groups, Ventana Canyon attracts country clubbers who don't require the bells and whistles of a more bustling operation, but who do insist on access to the best course in town.

*Mountain Course, third hole*

# WESTIN LA PALOMA

SILVER MEDALIST

In the stark foothills of the Santa Catalina Mountains on the outskirts of Tucson, golf is played not as a tight-lipped test of character, but as if golfers were extras in a freewheeling, shoot-'em-up cowboy movie. Perhaps that is as designer Jack Nicklaus intended, for his twenty-seven-hole La Paloma Country Club layout is without question the most formidable and arresting resort course on his résumé.

Designed in the mid 1980s, a time when Jack built courses to satisfy his own formidable standards of "challenging" play, La Paloma is a target-style

layout stretched across the High Sonoran desert with half the grass and twice the trouble of an ordinary course. Stray from the manicured turf, and you'll find yourself among the spiny shrubs of the high chaparral. Presiding over the small artillery are the big guns, the giant saguaro cacti, thousands of which were tagged, mapped, and relocated during course construction. Several of these thorny colossi are 200 years old, stand fifty feet tall, and have upraised arms that sprout crowns of white flowers in the spring. Rattlesnakes, tarantulas, and horned toads live beneath the saguaros, providing added motivation for staying on the fairway.

Actually, driving zones on the Hill, Ridge, and Canyon nines are wider than they appear, a point La Paloma's forecaddies try to impress upon first-timers. (The club's forecaddies, many of them enthusiastic college students well-versed in the nuances of the game, act as scouts and nature guides for each group, offering advice on how to attack—or survive—the often intimidating holes.) Nearly every hole at La Paloma requires a forced carry over a dry wash or desert habitat. Ground balls and pop-ups disappear in no man's land. Finding the fairway is no guarantee of success: Craterlike hollows, bear-shouldered mounds, and deep pits of sand guard the slick, multilevel greens. It is not for nothing that the Ridge-Canyon combination, measuring 7,088 yards from the gold tees against a par of 72, carries one of the highest slope and course ratings (147, 75.8) in Arizona. And while sharp ledges were softened and several desert transition zones cleared in 1991, La Paloma remains a test for the fearless player. Staggered tees (there are as many as five sets at selected holes) give everyone a chance, but the casual player can expect to lose an average of a dozen balls per eighteen holes. Why bother? The scenery. It is compelling. The flanks of the stony Santa Catalinas, bristling with rocks and scrub, soar to 9,000 feet at the perimeter of the layout. The setting sun colors these peaks a brilliant shade of roseate pink. There's wildlife, too. Jackrabbits scamper and roadrunners scurry beneath the saguaros. For sheer beauty, La Paloma (the dove) may be the fairest bird in the desert.

The Hill nine, which opens with a pair of modest par fours, is the easiest of the three nines, though its 409-yard fifth hole, routed through a long valley, puts the screws to the unwary. The Ridge nine, marked by edge-of-the-world drop-offs from several of its fairways, claims a spectacular par three, the fourth, its green backdropped by mountains and embraced by grassy swales. The Canyon nine is the backbone of La Paloma, its risk-reward holes subjecting golfers to a giddy roller-coaster ride through the desert.

After the round, guests can unwind at the Westin La Paloma, its 487 rooms contained in low-rise complexes arranged in a villagelike setting. The Mission Revival buildings, painted a distinctive hue of dusty rose, glow at sunset. Corbeled beams, wrought-iron balustrades, and shady recesses create a Spanish mood. The accommodations, each with private exterior entrance and spacious patio or balcony, feature copper tables and lamps with a verde iron finish, nubby cotton on the furniture, and woven raffia headboards on the beds. Drought-resistant brittlebush, desert marigolds, Arizona poppies, and Cochise lovegrass were used to landscape the property.

The resort's dining spots are varied and good. Also scenic. The multilevel Desert Garden (inspired by Frank Lloyd Wright's description, "The desert with its rim of arid mountains spotted like the leopard's skin or tattooed with the amazing patterns of nature is a desert garden . . . ") has 30-foot-high arched windows in its rear wall that bring the Santa Catalinas into view. La Villa, a Southwestern hacienda overlooking the city of Tucson, offers seafood specialties (a surprise in the desert), while La Paloma Dining Room, available to resort guests from Tuesday through Saturday (jackets required), features classic country club dining. It should be noted that gold-plated "Members Only" signs appear near the grill beside the pro shop, though hotel guests are no longer made to feel they have stumbled into out-of-bounds territory at the club, as they were in years past. Perhaps the toughest rough east of Tombstone on the Southwest's burliest resort course has softened up the membership.

*Left: Resort and pool. Photo courtesy Westin La Paloma, © Derriak Anderson. Above: Canyon Course, eighth hole. Photo courtesy Westin La Paloma*

# THE BROADMOOR

Shortly after the Indian Wars in the Colorado Territory subsided, Spencer Penrose, a Philadelphia blueblood who journeyed west to make his fortune in copper and gold mining, decided to build a grand luxe hotel in Colorado Springs. His lofty plans for the property, conceived from the start to be both "permanent and perfect," were every bit as auspicious as its location. The eighteen-acre hotel site, purchased from a Prussian count, would accommodate a hotel to be built on the rim of a man-made lake in full view of the stately Front Range

*Left: Skeet shooting. Photo courtesy The Broadmoor*

*Above: Living room of the MacNeill Suite. Photo courtesy The Broadmoor*

*Right: East Course, fifteenth hole*

of the Rocky Mountains. For good measure, the outskirts of Colorado Springs happen to mark the exact topographic break between the Continental Divide to the west and the plains of Kansas to the east.

Only the best claimed the interest of Penrose and his partner, Charles L. Tutt, a childhood friend whose descendants are still actively involved in the operation of the resort. Warren and Wetmore, the architectural firm responsible for the design of Grand Central Terminal in New York, was hired to design a hotel that resembled nothing less than an Italian palace. Another famous firm—Olmsted Brothers of Brookline, Massachusetts, the landscape architects who had laid out Central Park in New York—was contracted to plan and order the grounds. Next to arrive was golf course architect Donald Ross, who sculpted and molded a splendid layout from 135 acres of scrub oak and underbrush on the lower slopes of Cheyenne Mountain. Thousands of pine seedlings were planted to define the fairways and enhance the beauty of the course. Today these pines stand thirty feet tall.

Penrose and his wife Julie traveled widely during the time the hotel was under construction, shipping back paintings, sculptures, rugs, fine pieces of furniture, and other adornments for the public rooms from art centers in Europe and the Far East. Italian artisans were brought in to create the plaster latticework on the vaulted ceilings. Gorgeous frescoes and bas-reliefs were created on ceilings, staircases, and arches. Marble stairways lead to ornate loggias of the kind found in opulent Florentine villas. To greet guests arriving at the pale pink facade of the nine-story hotel, a large, antique fountain of mythical horses imported from Italy was placed on a lawn opposite the porte-cochere.

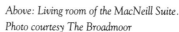

Small wonder The Broadmoor earned immediate acclaim as the "Riviera of the Rockies" when it opened in 1918. Quickly embraced by high society, it was to The Broadmoor that the Palm Beach crowd gravitated for a change of pace, and it was here that sportsmen quartered their polo ponies for the winter season. Certainly the climate was favorable: Though 14,110-foot Pikes Peak is barely seven miles distant, the average daily temperature in the winter months is fifty degrees. Sunny days and clear nights are the norm in spring, summer, and fall. Golf soon became one of The Broadmoor's feature attractions.

The resort's golf history was colorful from the start. Long Jim Barnes, The Broadmoor's first professional, was the highest-paid pro at the time (he received $15,000 for the summer, handsome pay in those days). In 1918, Barnes teamed with Charles ("Chick") Evans, the reigning U.S. Open and Amateur champion, against Jock Hutchison and Warren Wood, two top pros of the day. Barnes and Evans later toured the country as The Broadmoor Golf Club Team, playing exhibition matches and raising more than $1 million for the Red Cross. More recently, The Broadmoor was the site of Jack Nicklaus's first major title, the 1959 U.S. Amateur. Nicklaus, then nineteen, holed an eight-foot birdie putt on the thirty-sixth hole to defeat defending champion Charlie Coe, 1-up. Jack never looked back.

In 1950, Robert Trent Jones was brought in to update the original eighteen-hole layout and add a new nine on terrain far hillier than the land Ross used. Fifteen years later, Jones returned to author another nine, rebuilding four holes to shape the complex into two eighteen-hole layouts.

The composite East and West courses at The Broadmoor showcase Ross and Jones at their best. Commodious, gently inclined fairways that lead to large, undulating greens—the Ross influence—are contrasted by fairways that narrow in the landing zone and pivot around cloverleaf bunkers before leading to pedestal greens guarded by sand or water—a Jones trademark.

In addition to the pines planted in Ross's time, holes on the thirty-six-hole spread are punctuated by stands of blue spruce, Douglas fir, and scatterings of aspens. The thinner air at the resort's 6,500-foot altitude (it has two-thirds the oxygen found at sea level) accounts for noticeably longer tee shots and iron shots. This is the land of the endless drive and the 150-yard 8-iron.

The 6,555-yard East Course is a very well-balanced design, with much of Ross's influence embodied in the holes. Longer but more forgiving

green. The stately white clubhouse, a former casino, and the majestic hotel preside over the greens at these two testing holes.

The heart of the 6,109-yard West Course is found in its middle stretch. Holes seven through twelve are routed through heavily wooded terrain close to the looming granite ridge of Cheyenne Mountain. Presiding over these holes is the Will Rogers Shrine of the Sun, a tall gray-pink granite tower built by Penrose in 1937 as a memorial to the popular American humorist. The ringing chimes in its bell tower can be heard throughout the day by golfers on the East and West courses.

A third course, the South, was designed by Ed Seay for the Arnold Palmer organization in 1976. Located a mile away from the main resort complex, the 6,108-yard South is a scenic joy, perhaps the prettiest of The Broadmoor's three layouts, though strategically less sound. Carved from a low forest of scrub oaks, the South can prove to be an exercise in exasperation for the first-time player. On the front nine, players are permitted a view of the green from the tee on only one hole! In addition, brush-filled ravines crease eight of the first nine holes. The back nine eases up a bit, though tees throughout feel like tiny islands in the scrub oak. Small wonder the pro shop distributes a tip sheet to players noting

than the West, the East presents extremely wide fairways and very large greens. There's plenty of room to maneuver the ball, but coaxing it into the hole is another matter entirely. The putting surfaces are exceptionally fast and deceptively undulating. Putts that look as if they'll come to a stop well within tap-in range keep rolling . . . and rolling . . . and rolling to six, ten, often twelve feet past the hole. Visual appearances to the contrary, all putts break *away* from Cheyenne Mountain. No putting success is possible at The Broadmoor without this dynamic foremost in mind.

Two of the best holes on the East Course, the 385-yard fifteenth and 554-yard eighteenth, are both slight left-to-right, downhill doglegs that ask for big drives to generous but rolling fairways. Punctuated by evergreens, each hole requires a forced carry over water to a large, slick

the placement of white directional flags on eleven fairways.

Having recently concluded a five-year, $15-million facelift, The Broadmoor has gracefully ushered itself from a storied past to the present tense. The hotel's 544 rooms, including sixty suites, are contained in the original Broadmoor Main and a pair of newer annexes, Broadmoor South and Broadmoor West. Not only have traces of dowdiness been removed, but guest rooms have been brightened with new color schemes. The hotel feels lighter, fresher, more buoyant than it had in previous years. Fine French reproductions and antiques rest on knotted wool rugs inspired by motifs in The Broadmoor's elaborate ceilings. Original scored walls have been re-created in the lounges, while the furniture layouts in the public rooms are nearly identical to the hotel's early days. Imposing portraits of European royalty, Qing Dynasty ornaments, and Maxfield Parrish's

*Left: South Course, thirteenth hole. Above: West Course, ninth hole*

dreamy painting of the hotel (it hangs in the mezzanine sun lounge) preserve the requisite grandeur.

In the Main Dining Room, draperies have been swagged, festooned, and artfully trimmed to admit more light, which makes the room's soft peach color scheme all the more pleasing.

The Penrose Room, located atop Broadmoor South, features haute cuisine in an opulent Edwardian-style setting dominated by a massive crystal chandelier. Windowside tables command fine views of the plains, mountains, and city. In addition to perennial favorites that have appeared on the menu since the hotel's inception, including Wiener schnitzel, beef Wellington, and pepper steak, the Penrose Room also features more contemporary offerings. Dancing to old favorites played by the Stanley Colon Orchestra, a house institution, remains the Penrose Room's favorite after-dinner pastime.

Charles Court, located in the Broadmoor West lobby, overlooks the lake and calls to mind the cozy interior of an English country manor house. The dining room's all-time favorite appetizer is the lobster melon cocktail, served with fresh ginger sauce. Save room for the fresh raspberry soufflé—it is incomparable, as are all the fresh berry desserts. The Broadmoor's wine cellar is not only very deep in French red Bordeaux and Burgundy selections, it holds the largest collection of German wines in Colorado.

The Tavern, specializing in robust luncheons, is best known for the original Toulouse-Lautrec lithographs that decorate its walls. Lining the corridors outside the Tavern are glass cases displaying Penrose's extensive bottle collection. (Penrose, a connoisseur of fine wine, surely would approve of the wine lists in the dining rooms.) Incidentally, the hotel's dress code suggests sport coats for gentlemen in the Tavern after 6:30 P.M. Coat and tie are appropriate for dinner in the Penrose Room and Charles Court.

The resort's best casual restaurant is the Golden Bee, a re-creation of an early nineteenth-century English pub (elaborately carved mahogany back bar, Victorian-framed mirrors) that serves steak-and-kidney pie and yards of ale. Sing-alongs to ragtime piano music are popular after 8 P.M. On weekends, the Golden Bee is heavily patronized by cadets from the U.S. Air Force Academy, located in Colorado Springs.

Lavish and elegant from top to bottom, there is one drawback to The Broadmoor: The resort attracts many large business groups. In fact, corporate meeting and convention business comprises more than 75 percent of the hotel's bookings. Request a room in the original Broadmoor Main (most groups are lodged in the two annexes), book an early tee time on the East Course, and find out which dining room is taking the fewest reservations. Follow these recommendations, and Spencer Penrose's legacy to the good life shines brightly.

# BARTON CREEK

In the heart of the Texas hill country on the outskirts of Austin is Barton Creek, a 4,000-acre country club and resort community that until the early 1990s operated almost exclusively as a business conference center. But the excellence and variety of its fifty-four-hole golf complex, signaled by the opening in 1991 of a new course by native son Ben Crenshaw and the acquisition of an existing club, has broadened Barton Creek's appeal to vacationing golfers.

The resort's centerpiece is the Fazio Course, a brilliant test dynamited from limestone in 1986. Its sharp elevation changes, rock outcroppings, huge live oaks and cedars, and greenside creeks and waterfalls create enough challenge to raise even a Texan's eyebrows. Site of the Liberty Mutual Legends of Golf, the Fazio Course is perennially ranked among the most scenic and popular in the state. Playability, the chief virtue of Tom Fazio's designs, is the byword here: each hole has a multiple set of tees,

fairways are generously wide, and water, especially falling water, is to be admired rather than avoided. Also, several of the longer holes play downhill, thereby shortening their effective distance.

On a layout with one fascinating hole after another, there are several standouts. The ninth, a mere 125 yards from the white tees, calls for a wee pitch (preferably bounced off a slope to the right) to a green framed by a rock wall and a waterfall. At the 376-yard tenth, players launch their drives from a tee perched more than 100 feet above fairway level. Locals measure their drives at the tenth not by distance but by hang time. The 374-yard sixteenth is as treacherous as it is picturesque, with the approach played over a series of low stepped waterfalls to one of the smallest greens on the course.

The Fazio Course finishes in high style at the par-five eighteenth. After a drive has split a fairway narrowed by water and trees, players are faced with three options: lay up short of a limestone cave cut into the side of a hill; carry the ball above the cave but short of the clifftop green; or go for the green, which is guarded by a waterfall and a creek. Few finishing holes can match its drama.

Barton Creek's second layout was designed by its touring professional, Ben Crenshaw, and his partner Bill Coore. During construction, Crenshaw, a true-blue traditionalist, said: "Ours is an old-style philosophy. We believe that nature is the best architect and that the best 'players'

courses' make good use of, rather than ignore, existing natural terrain." By necessity, Crenshaw and Coore followed this credo exactly. On a bedrock of limestone, 250,000 cubic yards of sandy loam from the Colorado River were spread as a base for the fairways. The site, its undulations less radical than those of the Fazio Course, nevertheless has nice uplifts and plateaus—"the kind of contours that are very adaptive to good golf," according to Crenshaw. Green sites were chosen first. They range from tiny to enormous (the putting surface at the par-five sixteenth is the size of a skating rink). Several of these greens are tipped back from their midpoint, making putting (Crenshaw's specialty) a true adventure. Prairie buffalo grass, a newly developed strain that requires no fertilizer and very little water, was planted in buffer zones and transition areas. It has a feathery look and waves in the wind.

Though only 6,066 yards from the blue tees (6,678 yards from the tips), the Crenshaw and Coore Course is a strategic delight. Among the feature holes is the 505-yard twelfth, where a huge live oak commands the center of the fairway; the 110-yard seventeenth, calling for a short iron shot to a wide, shallow green; and the dramatic 362-yard eighteenth, where the approach is played over a rock-strewn creek to a well-bunkered green etched into a hillside.

Barton Creek's Lakeside Course, a former private club in nearby Lake Travis, is an Arnold Palmer design with excellent bent-grass greens—and panoramic lake views from its hilltop fairways. A twenty-minute drive from the resort, it is worth a visit.

Plan to visit Barton Creek in the spring, when the bluebonnets, Indian paintbrush, and other native wildflowers burst into bloom; or in early fall, when the leaves on the oaks and cedars turn scarlet and orange.

The resort's Golf Advantage School, patterned after a successful program of the same name at Pinehurst, features a 5:1 student/instructor ratio, computerized video equipment, and a new short-game practice area. The European-style spa (indoor pool, jogging track, and a wide range of personal services) is exemplary, as are spacious guest rooms in the chateau-style buildings. Lastly, the Terrace Room, overlooking the Fazio Course, offers a fine buffet. But the fifty-four holes of golf, which have muffled the resort's commercial buzz to a quiet whisper, are the best reason to visit Barton Creek.

*Opposite: Fazio Course, eighteenth hole*

*Below: Crenshaw and Coore Course, eighteenth hole*

# HORSESHOE BAY COUNTRY CLUB RESORT

But the *pièce de résistance* at Horseshoe Bay is found in the formal dining room, the Captain's Table ("Acclaimed by many . . . Created for the few . . ."), with its black-and-gold-trimmed china, black stem crystal, black candles, black ashtrays, black napkins, and furnishings with the black-and-russet color scheme. Yellow roses are presented to ladies on weekends, while matches (flocked black cover, gold matchsticks) can be personalized on request. Tuxedoed captains and waiters, many of them Europeans well schooled in the art of fine dining, prepare tableside flambé dishes from Steak Diane and Châteaubriand Garni to desserts such as Bananas Foster and Cherries Jubilee. All are set aflame with great ceremony.

If Hurd's dream resort is a hill country version of Las Vegas set on the shores of Lake Lyndon B. Johnson, the golf is vintage Jones. His first layout for Hurd was Slick Rock, a pleasant 6,358-yard member's course opened in 1973. The front nine is routed through colorful outcroppings of granite and stands of varnish, corkscrew, and persimmon trees; the back nine is more open and rolling. The bent grass greens, syringed (sprayed with water) in the hot summer months to keep them alive, are very smooth and medium-fast. Hurd, while not a golfer, has supplied some nice touches: Hollywood juniper clustered with purple sage serves as a yardage marker, while extensive plantings of bamboo and pampas grass have added color and texture to the course.

The waterfall at the fourteenth hole is the scenic highlight of the round, though Slick Rock's succession of tough finishing holes captures everyone's attention. The 405-yard

With three big-time Robert Trent Jones layouts, the best little golf resort in Texas isn't so little. Located in the hill country fifty miles northwest of Austin, Horseshoe Bay is the singular creation of Norman C. Hurd, a real-estate developer who is constantly fiddling with his pet project. Not content with the look of the par-four fourteenth hole at Slick Rock, the resort's original layout, Hurd "harvested" massive granite boulders from an upcountry site and scoured the banks of a silted-up creek to create a two-level, 100-foot-long waterfall that gushes 8,000 gallons of water per minute. He also created a new ladies' tee at the fourteenth backdropped by fifteen-foot-high Stonehenge-like pillars of rock and surrounded by water. The price tag for the beautification project: nearly $1 million.

The waterfall is typical of Hurd's tinkering and tastemaking at Horseshoe Bay. Everything at the resort, from the landscaping of the grounds to the distinctive black-and-russet theme colors, is a direct reflection of his personal tastes. Hurd loves birds, so several varieties of exotic finches are kept in glass aviaries in the darkened, rock-walled lobby. Beside the black marble pool is a tall vertical cage filled with large, colorful macaws capable of snapping a broom handle in half with their beaks. (These birds are known to maintain a running commentary on the daily proceedings.) On a center island of the Yacht Club pool, a huge bronze eagle wheels on a wingtip. Decorative elements within the property range from slick Erté silk constructions in the bathrooms to rustic wall hangings of feather, yarn, and macramé. Mirrors are held in gold-veined frames. An enormous 100-year-old clock from London graces the wall of the Anchor Lounge.

*Above left: Twenty-five-person hot tub. Photo courtesy Horseshoe Bay Country Club Resort*

*Above: Ram Rock Course, twelfth hole*

*Opposite: Waterfall on Slick Rock Course, fourteenth hole*

sixteenth is a sharp left-to-right dogleg that leads to a slippery green, the 180-yard seventeenth calls for a brave carry over Slick Rock Creek, and the 380-yard eighteenth confronts players with water along both sides of its fairway, its well-trapped green sited atop a hill.

Slick Rock's finish may be testing, but Ram Rock, opened in 1981, is devastating from start to finish. When the wind swirls up from Mexico, which is often, this Jones firebreather is easily the toughest course in Texas. Local pros who've played in competitions at Horseshoe Bay claim that when the breeze flaps the flags at Ram Rock, "You wish you weren't playing golf."

A sandy brute crisscrossed by dry creeks, its out-of-bounds areas marked in places by barbed wire, Ram Rock stretches to 6,946 yards. Only those willing to inflict serious damage to their golfing egos play from the back tees. (The par-71 layout is somewhat more manageable for the better player from the regular tees at 6,408 yards.) Not only is the terrain at Ram Rock undulating, but its narrow fairways are pinched by cavernous bunkers. Drives must be long *and* well placed, for the simple reason that rattlesnakes live in the rough. Natural springs flow through the layout, feeding several greenside ponds (water is in play at ten holes). Step carefully round the perimeter of these ponds—water moccasins live in them. The greens are medium in size, hogbacked in places, and very slick.

While the island green at the 138-yard fourth hole attracts a lot of attention, the best hole on the course is the 509-yard ninth, a treacherous dogleg that bends inexorably to the left. A deadly funnel-effect is created by channels of water routed up both sides of the hole from the 100-yard

mark to the green. A turtle mound fronting the green tends to ricochet unlucky approach shots into the water on either side of the putting surface. Electric fans mounted on trees framing the greens circulate the air to cool the delicate bent grass. They do a poor job of cooling off disgruntled golfers.

Regardless of what score you've made on the front nine of Ram Rock, you must carry on, as the ninth hole does not return to the clubhouse. The incoming nine is hillier, more scenic, and every bit as challenging as the front. Blind drives, forced carries over dry washes, a rigorous uphill eighteenth hole—Jones held nothing back at Ram Rock. More than any other of his courses, this rough-and-tumble layout was designed to maintain the sanctity of par.

At Applerock, the resort's newest layout, Jones was given the choicest land available to route a course that deviates markedly from his previous designs. Very little earth was moved—fairways and greens flow with the natural heave and toss of the terrain—while bunkering was kept to a minimum. Scenically, Applerock is the best of the lot: The higher points of the course serve up sixty-mile views of Lake L.B.J. and the hill country's limestone-studded hills. In terms of challenge, Applerock splits the difference between Slick Rock and Ram Rock. For example, the layout's water hazards (except at par threes) are less in evidence than at the other two courses. Also, fairways are considerably wider on the 6,536-yard track. The pampas grass in the rough lends the courses a savanna look, though the black-eyed daisies that sprout near the bunkers are pure Texas.

# FOUR SEASONS RESORT AND CLUB/TPC AT LAS COLINAS

SILVER MEDALIST

barely noticeable until the final four holes. Best of all, Las Colinas is one of the very few courses designed to host a professional tournament (the Byron Nelson Classic) that is not intimidating to the recreational golfer.

A par-70 course with only two par fives, the TPC at Las Colinas looks like easy pickings on the score card. It isn't. While sporty from the member tees at 5,937 yards, the layout can prove testing from the blue tees at 6,397 yards and downright hellacious from the tips at 6,767 yards. A collection of strong par fours is the reason.

The 445-yard third hole (that's the yardage from the member tees) is a case in point. Ranked the third toughest hole on the PGA Tour in 1990, with an average score during the Nelson tournament of 4.587, this long, narrow hole with a channel of water along its right side was designed to be played downwind. It is said the prevailing wind in Texas blows from the

*Fifth hole*

You would hardly expect to find a first-rate golf resort within an office park located seven miles from a major airport, but the Four Seasons Hotel and the adjoining TPC at Las Colinas outside Dallas are the exception: The TPC course, laid out by Jay Morrish (with input from Ben Crenshaw and Byron Nelson) at the edge of the Trinity River's flood plain, is one of the most playable of all stadium courses. In fact, it was accorded the ultimate accolade by tour professional Mark Calcavecchia, who said of Las Colinas: "I don't even consider it a TPC course. It's more like a real course."

Certainly it's a TPC without a lot of fabrication and tricks. Massive waste bunkers do not line the holes. Railroad ties are nonexistent. Greens are receptive to well-played shots. Mounding is unobtrusive, and in fact is

south, but in truth it gusts and swirls from all directions. Reaching the green in two shots borders on the impossible when the breeze is against, even for the pros. Play for bogey if conditions are less than favorable.

The 126-yard fifth hole is a clever par three that crosses water to a huge double green (the flag of the ninth is found on the left portion of the putting surface), while the back nine contains a Morrish specialty: a driveable par four. This is the 278-yard eleventh (331 yards for the big guns), a right-to-left dogleg where players who take the "tiger line" (the dangerous line of attack) must flirt with water that flows up the entire left side of the hole. The green itself, the smallest on the course, is tucked behind a bend in the river and is guarded on the right by deep pot bunkers.

It is followed by the par-four twelfth, a wicked uphill dogleg that has cracked the top fifty of the toughest holes on the PGA Tour. Somewhat incredibly, the number-two handicap hole at Las Colinas is the fourteenth, a mere 333 yards from tee to green. Ah, but what lies in between! The tee shot must be delicately placed—a lay-up shot is advisable—because the fairway bends sharply to the right before stopping short of a stream. The green sits on the far side of the water. Beware the tree that stands sentinel beside the green: Tangle with its branches, and your ball has a greater chance of splashing into the water than of falling safely to the grass.

Holes fifteen through eighteen give players a feel for stadium golf. Mounds are more prominent here than on previous holes, but the strategic features of the course—alternate routes for tee and approach shots, ample

The 315-room Four Seasons Hotel, its undulating brick facade set on a hill overlooking the golf course, maintains a low-key, English Regency ambiance. There's a reason Four Seasons has attracted a loyal following, especially among discerning business travelers: Phone for a wake-up call, for example, and the staff will record the time requested and ask if you'd like your clothes pressed. Shoes are shined overnight. Alternative cuisine (low-fat, low-cholesterol) is available in the hotel's cafés and dining rooms, while the guest room itself—especially the marble bathroom with its twin vanities, glass-walled stall shower, and oversize tub—is a delightful place to call home for a few days.

For those who wish to leave the resort in better shape than when they arrived, the hotel is joined by a tunnel to Las Colinas Sports Club, one of the best of its kind in the nation. It features an indoor lap pool, two

*Eighteenth hole*

opportunity to bump-and-run the ball to the green—remain. What Las Colinas lacks in aesthetics—tall glass towers belonging to GTE, Exxon, and other major corporations loom at the perimeter of the course—it more than makes up for in shot values.

After the round, repair to the resort's Game Bar, located near the practice putting green. Inside, the high-ceilinged room is set off by zebra-print wallpaper, two dozen stylized paintings of animals, and the mounted heads of exotic game, including greater kudu and wildebeest. Two full-size pool tables, a shuffleboard table, and a pair of video games help settle deadlocked matches. The Game Bar is jammed by Tour pros during the Nelson tournament. (Many of the pros shoot pool the way they putt—very well.)

outdoor pools, four indoor tennis courts, six racquetball courts, and two squash courts. There's also a small, cushioned indoor track, a quarter-mile outdoor track, and a half-court basketball gym. (High-top sneakers are available.) The latest stationary exercise bicycles, treadmills, and Nautilus equipment are also found at the club. The men's and women's locker rooms have sauna and steam rooms, whirlpools, cold plunges, and an outdoor sun deck, while the spa offers Swedish, shiatsu, and aroma-therapy massages.

Small wonder that major entertainment figures, including Madonna, Smokey Robinson, Eric Clapton, and the Rolling Stones, book into the Four Seasons when they perform in Dallas. Or why the pros look forward to competing in the Nelson tournament at this one-of-a-kind resort.

# THE SOUTHWEST

## TIPS AND SIDE TRIPS

*Pikes Peak Cog Railway. Photo courtesy Pikes Peak and Garden of the Gods,*
*© Finley Holiday Films*

Interested in seeing Phoenix and the Valley of the Sun from the perspective of a slow-moving bird? Consider hot-air ballooning, arguably the best way to experience the beauty of the desert. Passengers stand in an oversize wicker basket suspended below a propane-filled balloon that floats serenely over the desert floor. This aerial nature walk is staged twice daily by Unicorn Balloon Company, based at Scottsdale Airport. Duration of flight averages ninety minutes, though the exact course and destination cannot be predicted (the balloon goes where the wind takes it). The tour concludes with a champagne toast to the Montgolfier brothers, the Frenchmen who pioneered the concept of hot-air ballooning in 1783.

Want a grander view from fixed-wing transportation? Concierges at the Phoenix-area resorts can supply information on charter flights that circle the Grand Canyon, one of the great natural wonders of the world. The vistas from the plane of multicolored canyon walls sculpted over the millenniums by the Colorado River are unparalleled.

Sedona, poised to become the "next Santa Fe," is a two-hour drive north of Phoenix. A mecca for art lovers and collectors, the community is backdropped by the stunning red rock spires, mesas, and buttes of Oak Creek Canyon. Area galleries sell Native American and Southwestern arts and crafts. Stop by Tlaquepaque (pronounced T-lockey-POCkey), a shopping village named for a Mexican town, and Jerome, a ghost town revitalized by a community of artists who operate curio shops that specialize in mining paraphernalia.

More traditional (if pricier) shopping opportunities are found at Borgata, in Scottsdale, a re-created medieval Italian village with dozens of designer shops, galleries, and cafés.

By popular consensus, Tucson's top attraction is the Arizona–Sonoran Desert Museum. Wandering the trails of this "living" museum is like taking an enchanted walk through the desert: no fear of poisonous snakes, and a lot of closeup views of bobcats, coyotes, Mexican wolves, prairie dogs, roadrunners, reptiles, birds, and local desert vegetation. The walk-in hummingbird habitat and the tortoise enclosure are unique. The museum is adjacent to Saguaro National Monument, one of the densest cactus forests in the Southwest.

A five-minute drive from the Desert Museum is Old Tucson, a Western film location with staged gunfights and other amusements scheduled daily. More than 150 movies and television shows have been shot outside the low wooden buildings that line the town's dusty streets. (Sets for old television shows like "High Chaparral" are on display.)

A five-minute ride via complimentary shuttle from the Ventana Canyon resorts is Sabino Canyon, which features the most camera-

*Gunfight reenactment at Old Tucson Studios. Photo courtesy Old Tucson Studios, © Faces Photography*

worthy scenery in the Tucson area. Narrated tours aboard open-sided trams travel a winding road to the head of the canyon. Moonlight rides are available three nights a month from April through December. Reservations are suggested.

In Dallas, the sixth floor of the former Texas School Book Depository, the place from which Lee Harvey Oswald allegedly shot President John F. Kennedy, has been made into a Kennedy museum, with an emphasis on the events surrounding the assassination.

*Emmy Lou Harris performing at Austin City Limits. Photo - Scott Newton/Austin City Limits.*

Some other Dallas attractions include Old City Park, an oasis of greenery that preserves the flavor of the city's pioneers and Victorian heritage; the downtown Arts District, anchored by the Dallas Museum of Art and its fine sculpture garden; and in Arlington, west of Dallas, Six Flags Over Texas, the state's most popular theme park.

A forty-five-minute drive from Horseshoe Bay is Fall Creek Vineyards, a winery located on the shores of Lake Buchanan that produces an excellent Cabernet Sauvignon and Chardonnay. A tour of the premises and wine tastings are available.

Austin, a half hour's drive from Barton Creek, has one of the liveliest music scenes in the nation. The top club in town is Austin City Limits, though dozens more feature well-known country, blues, and rock bands. Check local papers for details.

The Broadmoor is convenient to a number of fine attractions. Pikes Peak Cog Railway, highest of its kind in the world, travels via Swiss-made train well above the timberline to the mountain's 14,110-foot summit. From here, the Great Plains stretch as far as the eye can see. Roundtrip by train is three hours and ten minutes. The railway operates May through October, weather permitting.

*Hot air ballooning near Scottsdale. Photo courtesy Unicorn Balloon Company*

Garden of the Gods, a 500-acre, city-owned park located a short drive from the resort, contains enormous red sandstone formations eroded over the years by wind and rain into dramatic fins, spires, and other unusual shapes.

The Cheyenne Mountain Zoo, adjacent to the hotel, is home to more than 600 specimens of animals, birds, and reptiles. The entrance building to the zoo, the Thundergod House, is a striking example of Southwest Indian architecture. At an elevation of 6,800 feet, it is the only mountain zoo in America.

Tours are available to the U.S. Air Force Academy in Colorado Springs, an 18,000-acre facility with a truly inspiring Cadet's Chapel and a superb planetarium. It is Colorado's most visited man-made attraction.

### DON'T LEAVE HOME WITHOUT . . . GETTING READY FOR THE FIRST TEE

*I*f you are like most golfers, getting off to a good start early in the round is sometimes difficult. Not only can a slow start put a dent in your score, it often sets the mood for a long, unenjoyable day.

*If you're bedeviled by indifferent golf at the start of the round, try my approach. Spend the first few minutes of your warmup on the driving range stretching your muscles. Next, concentrate on hitting the ball solidly. Work on connecting the clubface squarely to the back of the ball. After establishing solid contact, imagine that you are playing the first and second holes of the course you are about to tackle. Hit your tee shot with a picture of the landing area in your mind's eye. Then play your second shot to the green. On the practice putting green, try stroking a putt to the cup from the approximate spots your approach shots landed on the make-believe first and second holes you played on the range.*

*By playing the first and second holes on the range, you effectively create a feeling of having been on the course*

*before you get started. This mental rehearsal will facilitate your ability to get off to a good start. By the time you arrive at the first tee, you will have already "played" the hole. Playing the opening holes beforehand in your mind coupled with the simple goal of striking the ball solidly on the range are the best and easiest ways to eliminate faulty starts.*

KEITH KALNY, DIRECTOR OF GOLF, THE WIGWAM RESORT

# THE MID

The Midwest gets a bum rap from most golfers who don't live there. Michigan, Wisconsin—these are not states one thinks of running off to on a golf holiday. But the heartland is full of surprises. It does not, as coast dwellers believe, experience "nine months of cold weather and three months of winter." Warm, sunny days and cool nights are the norm from mid-May through early October. Further, retreating glaciers not only left behind the Great Lakes and many smaller ponds, they smeared a thick layer of till over the bedrock. From this rich soil sprang vegetation: Norway pines, silver birches, white oaks, sugar maples, and, eventually, fairway grass.

Robert Trent Jones, Jack Nicklaus, and Pete Dye (Nicklaus and Dye are Midwesterners by birth) have all had a hand in the design of the region's best resort courses. The Heather Course at Boyne Highlands, a landmark Jones layout, opened the door to golf course development in northern Michigan around the time Arnold Palmer

# WEST

was making every putt he looked at. More recently, the Pete Dye–designed River Course at Blackwolf Run in Wisconsin has come to rival the Bear, the Nicklaus brute at Grand Traverse Resort, as the toughest resort layout east or west of the Mississippi River.

There are other advantages to playing golf in the Midwest that often go unheralded. Because of the northern latitude, the sun doesn't set till very late in the summer. As in Scotland, it is possible to play golf in Michigan and Wisconsin until 10 P.M. in July. More than one late-to-finish golfer has looked up from the eighteenth green to see the throbbing lights of the aurora borealis on the horizon. It is a phenomenon that renders most players speechless.

Then there's the warmth and hospitality of the people. Perhaps it's true what they say: landlocked people are more secure than coast dwellers. Certainly the heartlanders have kept quiet about a collection of resorts that deserve wider notice. But then it's not their style to crow about their assets. They rely upon visiting coast dwellers for that.

*Inset: Sand dunes at Sleeping Bear Dunes National Lakeshore on Lake Michigan. Photo courtesy © National Park Service Photo*

*Large picture: Grand Traverse Resort, Michigan, the Bear, fifth hole*

# BOYNE HIGHLANDS

SILVER MEDALIST

What began in 1948 as a modest ski area with a single chairlift and a glorified goosebump of a ski hill has since evolved into one of the Midwest's premier four-season resorts. Not only was Boyne Mountain in northern Michigan the brainchild of Everett Kircher, a former Studebaker salesman from Detroit who patented the first commercial snowmaking gun, but so too was Boyne Highlands, a sister ski property he developed sixteen years later in neighboring Harbor Springs.

Seeking a way to keep his winter-season employees and lodges occupied in the summer, Kircher gambled that golf would take hold in this lovely corner of the state. He called in Robert Trent Jones to fashion a layout on a rolling, heavily wooded site spread below the ski mountain. Opened in 1965 and named the Heather Course, this stellar Jones design quickly gained a national reputation as that rare breed of course capable of foiling the expert without discouraging the novice. The Heather Course was not only a trailblazer that paved the way for future golf course development in

*Above: Moor Course, eighteenth hole. Below: The Main Lodge*

northern Michigan (there are today more than thirty courses in the area), it remains one of the best resort layouts in the state.

Designing at the summit of his creative powers, Jones deployed his full arsenal at the Heather without sacrificing the essential fairness of the course. Fairways are very wide, but they need to be: Many of them skirt blueberry bogs, cedar swamps, and cattail-rimmed ponds. Greens are enormous, subtly contoured, and brilliantly defended by Jones's trademark cloverleaf bunkers. Mature and well conditioned, the Heather has few parallel holes. Each serves up its own verdant playing field framed by tall hardwoods. The strength of the course is its great collection of sweeping dogleg par fours and par fives, many of which cartwheel around trees, water, or sand (and sometimes all three). Medium- to high-handicappers who follow the advice on the scorecard ("We suggest that you use our white tees") can have a fun day on the Heather from 6,090 yards. Better golfers will have their hands full from the gold tees at 6,533 yards, while scratch players encounter the true severity of the course from the blue tees at 7,210 yards.

The Heather was followed in 1974 by the Moor Course, a William Newcomb design built in tribute to Jones's handiwork. Here again, holes disappear into a dense forest of birch, maple, cedar, and beech trees, with plenty of water in the clearings. As on the Heather, landing zones are generous, but water is in play from start to finish, often more than once on the same hole. Bring your ball retriever. And don't neglect to carry a sand iron: Deep bunkers frame the large, gently sloped greens.

The Moor's par fives are unusually distinctive. At the boomerang-shaped 489-yard eighth hole, the fairway makes a hairpin turn around a tree in the center of the fairway, while the 503-yard eighteenth is probably the toughest finishing hole at Boyne: a zigzag double-dogleg, with water in play to the left off the tee and again to the right of the green.

The opening of Boyne Highlands's third layout in 1989, the Donald Ross Memorial Course, caused a favorable stir in the golf world, especially among those with a fondness for classic designs. Kircher, his son Stephen, Newcomb, and noted swing doctor Jim Flick traveled extensively to Donald Ross–designed courses to select holes for a layout that would pay tribute to the great Scottish-born designer. (Ross is credited with formalizing golf course architecture in the United States during the early 1900s.) Known for his ability to meld golf holes into existing terrain without disturbing the natural features of the land, Ross believed "golf should be a pleasure, not a penance." Always strategic and never unduly penal in his designs, Ross built courses readily enjoyed by all golfers.

In the course of their research, Kircher and his team charted distances, mapped bunker and hazard placements, and in particular took note of the subtle putting surface contours that were a hallmark of Ross's designs. The holes, chosen from among the Scotsman's finest creations (including Seminole, Pinehurst No. 2, Oakland Hills, Scioto, Inverness, and Oak Hill), are not carbon copies but rather close facsimiles. It would be impossible, for example, to re-create the look of Ross's southern courses in Michigan: Northern hardwoods will never resemble Seminole's palm trees, or Pinehurst's conifers. But the essential shape, spirit, and playing value of the selected holes have been artfully mimicked. The yardage is identical to the originals. So are elevations between tees and greens. Landing zones, bunkers, and ponds have been carefully sized to match their models. Even the mowing patterns at individual clubs have been taken into account in the maintenance of the design. Best of all, the Ross Memorial enables resort guests a chance to play replicas of famous holes not otherwise available to them.

Set on a gently rolling, wooded site of 300 acres, the Ross Memorial is somewhat more difficult than it at first appears. (Deception is a prime characteristic of all Ross courses.) Driving zones are forgivingly wide, a key component of Ross's design philosophy, but most of the greens are crowned and slippery. The worthiness of short pitch and recovery shots is fully examined, though no aspect of the game is "called for in a proportion that will not permit excellence in any department to largely offset deficiencies in any other," as Ross mandated long ago. Though the layout has met with the enthusiastic approval of the Donald Ross Society, Stephen Kircher expects to tinker with the layout for the rest of his life, "until every knoll and bunker lip is as Ross might have intended." The course, as it stands, is a faithful representation of some of Ross's best work.

The new $2-million Country Club of Boyne clubhouse behind the eighteenth green of the Ross course is every bit as classy as the golf holes. Contemporary Victorian in design—the exterior resembles the turn-of-the century lakeside homes in nearby Harbor Springs—the clubhouse, with its marble floors, mahogany paneling, granite bar, Lenox china, and crystal drinking glasses, is the type of establishment you would expect to find at a distinguished private club. The Dornoch Room features superb multicourse meals, while the more casual Seminole Room, with its grill menu, is the perfect place for a club sandwich and post-round refreshments.

A new circular driving range near the Ross Memorial course, patterned after the state-of-the-art practice facility at Muirfield Village in Ohio, comprises fifteen acres and features several target greens to shoot for. A Jim Flick–Jack Nicklaus golf school is open in the summer to those who wish to retool their swings.

Boyne Highlands has greatly improved its accommodations of late. All 165 rooms in the Main Lodge, a Bavarian-style inn of timbered stone studded with lacy balconies and topped with turrets and gables, have been recently renovated. The bathrooms in particular have benefited from the makeover.

The resort's seventy-two-unit Heather Highlands Inn, a condominium hotel ideal for families, has a number of two-bedroom lofts that sleep up to seven people. The rooms, originally designed with skiers in mind, feature full kitchens, fireplaces, and balconies. The additional fifty-six units opened at Heather Highlands in 1992 reflect Boyne's metamorphosis from a regional ski area with modest overnight facilities to an elegant resort with national appeal. The new wing measures up to the design standards of the clubhouse.

But Boyne hasn't totally mortgaged its wooden ski and rope tow past: Casual cookouts are often held on Heather Highlands's lakeside patio, while the Young Americans, a troupe of youthful performers, stage a spirited variety show of singing and dancing at the Highlands Dinner Theatre in July and August. And while the shows do not quite rival the best Broadway musicals, they are entertaining. So are the golf courses at Boyne Highlands.

# GRAND TRAVERSE RESORT

## SILVER MEDALIST

Six miles east of Traverse City, Michigan, a modest town of bait-and-tackle shops, woolen outlets, fudge stores, and turn-of-the-century lumbermen's taverns, is Grand Traverse Resort. Built around an inlet of Lake Michigan, Grand Traverse received instant notoriety in the mid-1980s when the Bear, a Jack Nicklaus creation, was unshackled.

The story goes that real-estate developer Paul Nine, a local attorney known for his ability to raise money, was touring the proposed site of the resort's second course with Nicklaus when the following conversation took place:

"I think I can build a good resort golf course for you here," Nicklaus told Nine.

"I don't want a resort course, Jack. I've already got one of those," Nine replied. "What I want is a *championship* golf course."

This exchange was repeated a number of times, eventually accompanied, according to witnesses, by name-calling and sod-throwing.

"O.K., you S.O.B., I'll build you your championship course," Nicklaus fumed. Nine, a former Chrysler lobbyist well schooled in the arts of persuasion, had prevailed.

"Nobody writes about the excellent, pretty courses," Nine said in defense of his heated insistence that the game's all-time great player build a course that plays like a wounded grizzly. "They write about the beasts. Everybody wants to say they played the toughest course in the world." When the wind sweeps in from the lake, the Bear is very nearly that.

Given free rein, Nicklaus and then-design associate Bob Cupp converted a flat field into a hillocky meadow by mounding up the earth in an endless sea of swales. In most places, the Bear resembles a fleet of Volkswagen Beetles that have been grassed over. Tilt the course at a forty-five-degree angle, and you'd have the equal of any mogul field in Vail or Aspen.

Better golfers who aren't easily intimidated can survive an outing from the white markers at 6,176 yards, but from the blue tees at 7,065 yards, the course would size up nicely as the home venue in Dante's *Inferno*. Ponds, streams, and water-filled ravines come into play on ten of the holes. Slick putting surfaces are not only multitiered and severely sloped, they are surrounded by cavernous bunkers and shaggy mounds. There is room to drive the ball, but the penalty for a misplayed approach shot is severe. After a string of double- or triple-bogeys, even accomplished players soon find themselves steering the ball away from the wrong side of a bilevel fairway, away from the bottomless traps guarding the greens, away from the cherry orchards that hem in many of the holes. The caveat printed on the scorecard often goes unread. "Attention Golfers," it reads. "Beware of deep bunkers and terraced fairways." At least you can't say you weren't warned.

Among the Bear's more memorable holes is the 143-yard fourth, the hole with no fairway. The tee shot must carry a wetland bog of cattails and pickerelweed to a narrow, slightly angled green cut into a hillside. Simply reload if you miss the green—there's no way to retrieve your ball in the rugged mat of heathlike plants that blanket the swamp.

While the fourth hole has no fairway, the 142-yard ninth has a fairway *behind* the green, in the event you carry the ball beyond a slender green protected on three sides by water.

The Bear finishes with a growl. The eighteenth is a par four of 386 yards (467 yards from the tips) that sets up as a left-to-right dogleg with a double fairway divided by a ridge of moguls. From either side, the second shot must be played over a lake to a very large, very undulating green. If you've managed to survive the other seventeen holes, this is the one that will chew up your scorecard. Promise.

The Bear has been softened somewhat since its opening to enhance its playability, but it has not been declawed. From the tips, the course rating is 75.8 (par is 72), with a slope rating of 145, highest in the state. The layout's difficulty was put in perspective by the designer himself, who said: "I wouldn't want to play all eighteen holes from the back tees. It would be too much golf course for me." And that's Jack Nicklaus talking.

Most first-timers slink off the course in a despondent funk, their egos whittled to the quick. But more than a few sign up for a rematch with the Bear despite the extravagant fee to play it (at press time, $110 for resort guests, including golf cart). Maybe course conditioning brings them back:

With an annual maintenance budget of more than $500,000, the Bear is beautifully groomed. It needs to be, given its take-no-prisoners philosophy of design. It looks and plays like what it is: a behemoth born of a conflict.

A name change at the resort's second course (now called Spruce Run) coincided with the planting of 15,000 conifers, many of them thirty-five feet high. The course, a William Newcomb design, serves up good views of Grand Traverse Bay, an arm of Lake Michigan, and features forgivingly wide fairways routed around the property's imposing seventeen-story glass Tower. (It's the tallest building north of Grand Rapids.)

Assuming you still have an appetite after tackling the Bear, sample the hearty buffalo sausage pizza at the aptly named Sandtrap in the clubhouse that serves both layouts. For more elegant dining, there's Trillium, Michigan's answer to Windows on the World in New York City. Located on the top two floors of the Tower, the view from Trillium's tables is of rolling hills and cherry orchards bordering the bay. It's an ideal place to take in a Technicolor sunset. Trillium specializes in seafood, mainly walleye, trout, and whitefish taken locally. Dishes are complemented perfectly by Chateau Grand Traverse, L. Mawby, and other locally produced wines. (The microclimate of Old Mission Peninsula on Grand

*Above: The Bear, fifth hole*

*Left: The Bear, tenth hole*

Traverse Bay is ideal for the growing of grapes, especially those pressed for white wines.) Live entertainment by Detroit soul revues is scheduled most evenings in the Trillium Nightclub one floor above the restaurant, with dancing encouraged on the strobe-lit floor.

The best accommodations at Grand Traverse are found in the 186-room Tower. Standard features in the spacious rooms include a whirlpool bath (for two) as well as great views of the surrounding countryside. Tower guest rooms are convenient to a gallery of fine retail outlets in the lobby. The 920-acre resort also maintains a number of well-appointed suites and condominiums angled to Grand Traverse Bay and the fairways of the golf courses.

In addition to an indoor sports complex, Grand Traverse has a private white sand beach. Not only can sailboats and catamarans be rented, but sailing lessons can be arranged. They're just the ticket for those interested in learning another sport after posting a bowling score on the Bear.

# THE AMERICAN CLUB

KOHLER, WISCONSIN • GOLD MEDALIST

*Meadow Valleys Course, fourteenth hole*

Built in 1918 to house immigrant employees of the Kohler Company (a leading manufacturer then and now of bathroom fixtures), the American Club has been transformed from a dormitory for "single men of modest means" into a hotel and resort of true distinction. Placed on the National Register of Historic Places and guided by a master plan drafted by the Frank Lloyd Wright Foundation, the club, located an hour's drive north of Milwaukee, Wisconsin, was converted in the early 1980s to a sterling hotel embracing formal gardens. The original structure, a stately neo-Tudor red-brick building with a gabled blue-slate roof, was retained. So was the 100-foot flagpole that flies a huge American flag on the front lawn. Inside, oak-paneled hallways lead to salons decorated with stained-glass windows, crystal chandeliers, Oriental rugs, and antique furnishings.

All 110 of the original club's rooms have been completely redone and individually decorated. Each room is dedicated to a prominent American, from John James Audubon to Wild Bill Hickok, with portraits and memorabilia of that personage decorating the room and a brass plate engraved with the namesake's signature on the door. True to the spirit of company founder Walter J. Kohler, who hoped the high standard of living and emphasis on patriotism would instill a love for America among the boarders, the images of hardworking immigrants who lived and worked here are remembered throughout the building in photographs. But not at the expense of luxury: The four-poster brass beds in the rooms are covered with European goose down duvets. Guest rooms also feature the finest bathrooms imaginable. Fixtures range from mirror-walled, marble-lined

106

whirlpool baths to the Kohler Habitat Masterbath, an environmental enclosure which "indulges the senses" with cycles of sun, steam, soft rain, and gentle breezes. It's the Rolls-Royce of showers.

Additional accommodations are located in the fifty-two-room Carriage House, a period building known for its fine collection of Currier & Ives prints depicting horse-and-buggy themes. (To celebrate its seventy-fifth anniversary in 1993, the resort added seventy-five accommodations in a new wing, many of them parlor suites and two-story rooms.) Throughout the property, the bookmark placed in the guest rooms alongside the deluxe mints each evening lists not only local television stations but also the following day's weather forecast written in by hand!

The American Club's former laundry room is today the resort's—and very possibly Wisconsin's—top restaurant. Known as the Immigrant, it consists of six connected rooms, each designed to salute a different ethnic group of early settlers. Delft and terra-cotta tiles decorate the cozy Dutch Room, while antique walnut furnishings are found in the French Room. Open for dinner, the Immigrant showcases fine continental and regional American cuisine, from smoked and pan-grilled breast of pheasant served with black-eyed peas and winter greens, to pecan-crusted lake trout with citrus segments and brandy butter sauce. The Winery, built to resemble a European wine cellar and located adjacent to the Immigrant, is ideal for a leisurely after-dinner drink, particularly on weekends, when live entertainment is featured.

Other dining spots, each distinctive, include the Wisconsin Room, with its tapestries, drawings of distinguished Wisconsinites, and leaded windows containing the company medallion (and cherished quotations, like this one

*The Dutch Room in the Immigrant Restaurant. Photo courtesy Kohler Co.*

from John Ruskin: "Life without labor is guilt, labor without art is brutality").

The club's former bowling alley was converted to the Horse & Plow, a casual tavern decorated with antique farm tools and hundreds of sepia-toned photographs. The Greenhouse, once part of an English solarium, serves homemade ice cream, European pastries, and cappuccino at marble-topped parlor tables. Health-minded guests gravitate to the Lean Bean and its floating outdoor terrace, the Marine Bean. Both are located in the Sports Core, a health and racquet complex.

Pete Dye, who takes on only three or four projects each year so that he can shepherd his designs through each phase of construction, was enticed to visit the region by the current generation of Kohlers. Viewing the site for the first time, Dye said: "There could not be a better natural setting for golf."

His creation, Blackwolf Run (named for Black Wolf, a courageous Winnebago Indian chief of the early 1800s), consists of two eighteen-hole layouts. Both are very difficult target-style courses occupying land shaped by glacial runoff and deposits, though each is playable by the duffer if the appropriate tees are chosen. Encompassed by a 600-acre nature preserve, Blackwolf Run is operated as a public facility. However, guests of the American Club are offered reduced green fees as well as advance tee time reservations not available to the general public.

The River Course follows the meandering path of the Sheboygan River, one of the finest trout streams in the state, with water in play at twelve holes. The beautiful setting—woods frame nearly every hole on the rolling layout—disguises some of Dye's most intriguing hole designs. For example, the ninth, called Cathedral Spires for its ninety-foot-high cottonwood trees, offers a perplexing choice of three fairways. Golfers must decipher the architect's intentions before deciding to follow the high, middle, or low road to the streamside green. Not only is the best choice the least obvious, but once a route has been taken, there's no turning back. Dye's modus operandi for Blackwolf Run applies to this hole. "I put a gambling element into the course, where players will be greatly rewarded for taking a chance, but penalized if they fail." Attempts to bludgeon the course with a power game fail utterly. Thoughtful course management and finesse are the keys to success here.

Arguably the most difficult hole on the River Course is the 372-yard twelfth (465 yards from the tips, 433 yards from the blue tees), a demanding par four that calls for a solid, well-placed drive that must carry a small lagoon and its nearby bunker. Then again, there aren't many pushovers on a layout that stretches to 6,991 yards, carries a course rating of 74.9 (par is 72), and flaunts a slope rating of 151. But the River Course is not just a beast. It's a beauty, too. Locals rate the 376-yard fifth the prettiest of the bunch. The Sheboygan River runs the entire length of the hole, cutting below a tee that commands a bluff nearly fifty feet above the river. The name of the hole? Made in Heaven.

The Meadow Valleys Course at Blackwolf Run is rife with multiple personalities. Rolling hills and open plains set against wooded glades and numerous lakes greet players on the opening holes. Halfway through, the course displays its Ice Age origin, the holes interspersed among ridges, bluffs, and valleys sculpted by a retreating glacier. There's also evidence of the Locomotive Age: Two flatbed railroad cars, one with wheels intact, serve as bridges over Weeden's Creek on two of the back nine holes.

*River Course, ninth hole*

Longer than the River Course, Meadow Valleys is nevertheless a stroke or two easier than its brawnier cousin. Recent course improvements include the lowering of the green at the 330-yard tenth hole, for improved visibility, and a dramatic new set of tees at the 379-yard fourteenth, yet another alluring but very demanding hole with the river coiled like a snake around most of the green.

All the usual Dye trademarks are sprinkled throughout the River and Meadow Valleys layouts: elephantine mounds, split-level fairways, deep pot bunkers, greens bulkheaded by railroad ties (or telephone poles), and hybrid grasses that delineate safe landing areas from hazardous zones. And while the man-made features are striking, Dye took care to meld them to the natural surroundings.

For golfers scathed, unscathed, or merely jittery from the mental outlay required to play the two courses, the Blackwolf Run clubhouse is a comforting place to repair after the round. Built of lodgepole pine logs and wooden shingles, with a large fieldstone fireplace in the dining hall, this handsome building is set into a hill overlooking the Sheboygan River. Indoors or out, golfers enjoy a panoramic view of the huge double green that accommodates the eighteenth holes of both courses. Arrowheads unearthed during course construction, as well as photographs of Indian tribes native to Wisconsin, are on display throughout the clubhouse. Much of the hearty, traditional fare—salmon steaks, mustard lamb chops—is charcoal grilled.

Sportsmen can arrange to rent canoes or drift boats to fish the Sheboygan River, hike along the thirty miles of trails within River Wildlife, or hunt for pheasant from September to early spring assisted by guides and well-trained pointers and retrievers. Homeowners can visit the Kohler Design Center, a three-level exhibition hall that showcases the company's fantasy bathrooms and high-technology products. Golfers may experience déjà vu upon entering the center, for rare is the player who hasn't taken a bath on either the River or Meadow Valleys layouts.

# THE MIDWEST

## TIPS AND SIDE TRIPS

*Charter-boat fishing near Grand Traverse Resort. Photo courtesy Grand Traverse Resort*

Do you like to tackle more than one sport on vacation? Consider timing your visit to Boyne Highlands in mid-April, when the rare opportunity to ski and play golf at the same resort exists.

In any season, the best day trip from Boyne is a visit to nearby Sleeping Bear Dunes National Lakeshore. This 71,000-acre park contains the world's largest moving freshwater dunes (they migrate a few inches each year), as well as more than thirty miles of beaches along Lake Michigan. Comb the beaches for Petoskey stones (petrified coral in hexagonal shapes), hike marked trails, visit the Coast Guard's Historic Maritime Museum, or take the seven-mile Pierce Stocking Scenic Drive, which winds through vast dunes overlooking Lake Michigan and the Manitou Islands. Information and maps are available at the Visitor's Center in Empire.

*The Rowe Inn. Photo courtesy The Rowe Inn*

*Interior of the log cabin headquarters of River Wildlife, near the Sheboygan River, Wisconsin. Photo courtesy Kohler Co.*

At Grand Traverse Resort, full- and half-day fishing charters can be arranged through the resort's recreation department to Grand Traverse Bay or Lake Michigan. Trophy-size lake trout, brown trout, coho and chinook salmon, and whitefish swim in these waters. The resort can arrange purchase of fishing licenses, transportation, and box lunches for these expeditions.

An hour's drive from Grand Traverse is the hamlet of Ellsworth, where two of the Midwest's finest restaurants draw patrons from as far away as Detroit (a five-hour drive). Tapawingo ("restful place" in the Chippewa Indian language) is an elegant, white-shuttered house with an outdoor deck set on the shore of St. Clair Lake. You'll see the occasional golfer practicing the Vardon grip on a table knife at Tapawingo, but you'll see many more couples holding hands across the table.

At the Rowe Inn a mile up the road, it's easy to be lulled into a café state of mind by the blackboard menu, pine paneling, and casually dressed patrons. The woodsy appearance is a cover for first-class regional cuisine prepared by Wes Westhoven, a former schoolteacher who was an early proponent (the Rowe opened in 1972) of fresh, local ingredients. Menu selections range from chilled wild blackberry soup to char-grilled buffalo sausage. The wine list, for a seventeen-table restaurant, is amazingly complete. Reservations are a must at both establishments.

River Wildlife, the 600-acre nature preserve at the American Club, offers resort guests a chance to commune with nature along a seven-mile stretch of water and on more than thirty miles of hiking and horseback trails. A secluded log cabin situated at a bend in the Sheboygan River is headquarters for the preserve. After fishing, hiking, or hunting, this comfortable retreat (wood floors, lofty beamed ceiling, fieldstone fireplace) is a fine place to unwind. Hearty entrées on the lodge's "countrified gourmet" menu—pheasant in applejack cream, barbecued rabbit, broiled stuffed brook trout—hit the spot after a day in the woods.

## DON'T LEAVE HOME WITHOUT . . . A FAIRWAY BUNKER SHOT

*B*lackwolf Run has nine acres of sand traps, so there's a good chance you'll find one of Pete Dye's bunkers while touring the River and Meadow Valleys courses. Playing fairway bunker shots can be greatly simplified with a few swing adjustments. When using an iron, the ball should be positioned in the center of your stance. To establish a firm base, widen your stance and dig the insides of your feet into the sand. Because your feet will be lower than the golf ball, you'll have to choke down on the club. Keep the lower half of your body still and swing mostly with the top half. Assuming the ball has come to rest in a good lie, the club should first contact the ball, then the sand, just as if you were taking a divot in the fairway.

Because the wider, lower stance will restrict your arc and, therefore, the power of your swing, club selection should be one or two clubs more than normal. Be sure to take into consideration the height of the bunker lip. Many modern course designs, like those at

*Blackwolf Run, feature very steep-faced bunkers. If the ball must climb quickly to escape the bunker, your only choice may be a sand wedge.*

PAUL BECKER, HEAD GOLF
PROFESSIONAL, BLACKWOLF RUN
AT THE AMERICAN CLUB

Pennsylvania, New Jersey, New York, New Hampshire, Vermont—these are not states one typically associates with fashionable golf resorts. Perhaps it's the abbreviated golf season, or the quirkiness of the courses: The region was heavily glaciated during the last Ice Age, which means flat lies are rare on the rough-and-tumble landscapes.

By and large, resort properties in the Northeast do not trumpet their assets or attempt to compete with the Sun Belt's golf factories. Northeastern resorts tend to be patronized by loyal followers from nearby population centers who enjoy the region's pleasant, sunny days and cool nights from May through October.

Milton S. Hershey, the chocolate titan, only dabbled at golf. However, he arranged for his friend Maurice McCarthy to plan a number of courses in a central Pennsylvania town built by foil-wrapped Kisses and a famous chocolate bar (with or without almonds). The crowning achievement of McCarthy's design career was the West Course at Hershey Country Club, a Jazz Age classic that starts flat and ends flat, but is anything but level in between.

A century ago, Atlantic City and the Jersey shore was *THE* area to see and be seen in the summertime. Its popularity as a summer resort reached a pinnacle in the Roaring Twenties, a time when Clarence Geist, a real-life Monopoly kingpin, was at the helm of Seaview Country Club (now a Marriott resort). Among his many farsighted moves, Geist hired Donald Ross to design a course that today sits in quiet repose across the water from Atlantic City and its cluster of flashy casino hotels crowding the famous Boardwalk.

Ross is credited with designing more than 500 courses in the United States, though in truth he often did little more than lend his name to his associates' work. (He had 3,000 men in his employ in the mid-1920s.) But where he agreed to spend time at a site, sketch a routing for the holes, and supervise construction of the course, his mark is unmistakable.

# THE AST

The Sagamore is a two-part experience: The resort's white clapboard hotel occupies a seventy-acre island in Bolton Landing, New York; its golf course is located 1,700 feet above Lake George. Ross made the most of the hilltop site: Some of the holes are carved from a forest, others are as open as a seaside links. His signature crowned greens, their subtle contours molded from the existing terrain, provide the main challenge. After years of neglect, the layout was revived in the mid-1980s. So was the grand hotel, an Adirondacks landmark.

Up in New Hampshire, a place where retreating glaciers sculpted the land and creased the mountains, The Balsams has functioned as a summer home-away-from-home for generations of New Englanders. Since its purchase in the mid-1960s by four former employees who believed in the hotel's potential, the resort has operated like clockwork. The room rate includes three squares daily and as much golf as you can manage at the Panorama Golf Club, where Ross's original drawings for the holes are displayed in the pro shop. The golf course, one of the most scenic on the Scotsman's extensive résumé, remains a side-of-the-mountain puzzle where first-timers ponder how a putt can race uphill!

To properly introduce The Equinox in Manchester, Vermont, a little village history is in order. Ethan Allen's Green Mountain Boys met at the Marsh Tavern (now a cozy dining room) in 1769 to secretly organize themselves against the British Tories. By the mid-1800s, the distinctive white-columned hotel had become a favorite summer retreat of well-to-do families who arrived by coach from Boston, New York City, Saratoga, and the Berkshires. Four sitting presidents stayed at the Equinox. So did Abe Lincoln's widow and children. In 1867, advertisements for the resort cited the region's "pure air, fine drives, and good troute [sic] fishing." In 1926, good golf was added. Following years of neglect, the hotel and golf course at The Equinox reopened to acclaim in 1992. The pulse of patriots tends to quicken within this once-again remarkable and historic property.

*Inset and large picture: The Balsams, New Hampshire. Inset photo courtesy The Balsams*

# THE BALSAMS

*Swimming pool and lake*

No man-made entrance can match the natural gate to The Balsams, located in the northern reaches of New Hampshire thirteen miles from the Canadian border. The portal to the resort is a titanic rock defile known as Dixville Notch, its foliage-tufted granite walls rising 1,000 feet from the roadway. The notch was created, locals claim, by one swing of Paul Bunyan's axe.

Opened in 1873 as a modest farm hotel with accommodations for fifty guests, The Balsams today is a grand 232-room resort property on a 15,000-acre estate. The sprawling, beautifully landscaped complex, reminiscent of a vintage Swiss resort snuggled in the Alps, could have served as the backdrop for the filming of *The Sound of Music*.

The Balsams is one of the few remaining resorts to offer a full American Plan. Aside from golf cart rentals and a bar tab, all amenities (including green fees and three meals daily) are included in the room tariff—a splendid bargain.

Two-and-a-half miles up a lovely shaded road from the hotel is the Panorama Golf Club, a Donald Ross design circa 1912 that stretches up, down, and across the face of Keysar Mountain.

The beautifully restored par-72, 6,097-yard layout is a match for the vistas. (Panorama is a match for *anyone* from the blue tees at 6,804 yards: From the tips, its course rating of 74.5 and slope of 142 are the highest in New Hampshire.)

*The hotel and putting green*

There are some classic golf holes. Broad, rippled fairways lead past oval hills of glacial drift and small irrigation ponds rimmed by purple lilacs and cattails. Most of the fairways pitch and roll directly to medium-size greens that accept bump-and-run shots. The greens, in typical Ross fashion, are crowned in the center, their edges tapering off to grassy hollows and swales. Panorama's distinctive flat-floored, grass-faced bunkers stand well back from the greens and exist mainly as signposts for the holes.

Among the outstanding holes on the course—and there are very few that aren't in one way or another exceptional—are the short par fours

from the eighth through the twelfth. The 316-yard ninth is a case in point. After a drive has been coaxed up a steep hill, the approach is played to a humpbacked green set on the crest of a knoll below an impressive stone clubhouse that doubtless has fended off many an overclubbed shot.

The only touch of cruelty on the course is found at the eighteenth hole, a 480-yard par five (560 yards from the tips) that climbs 145 feet straight uphill. (Think of a fourteen-story building sodded with grass and tilted at a forty-five degree angle.) Even Panorama's yardage book is a bit defeatist in its clipped description of the eighteenth: "The hardest hole in the state. Good luck."

The 1,917-yard, par-32 Coashaukee executive course, a flat, open links laid out on a former polo field near the hotel, is an ideal training ground for novices. The course can be walked with ease. Only billy goats or golfers who work out on a Stairmaster for months before arrival attempt to walk the Panorama.

As for the rest of The Balsams experience, the hotel can be compared to the fabulous country estate of a rich uncle who wishes everyone to be happy and comfortable. There's a billiard parlor with four antique slate-bottom pool tables, a well-stocked library set with comfortable chairs, a 250-seat movie theater, a nightclub with cabaret entertainment and dancing nightly, a small lounge with a rock 'n roll duo, a late night piano bar, and chamber music recitals on Sunday evenings.

Guest rooms, comparable to those found in a fine New England country inn, are rated in four categories according to size, convenience of location, and view. Mountain spring water flows from the taps, and guests receive a pint bottle of pure maple syrup in the room. Old-fashioned rituals prevail. Guests are assigned a table in the dining room for the duration of their stay (no dinner reservations are necessary). The multicourse dinner, a blend of American and continental dishes, is excellent, from the chilled fruit soups to the wide range of meat, fish, and vegetarian entrées. For those who wish to tackle the Panorama Golf Course fully fortified, Scottish kippers, smoked salmon, and herring in wine sauce are available at breakfast.

The list of summertime activities is extensive. There is fly-fishing for stocked rainbow trout in Lake Gloriette. Rowboats, canoes, and paddleboats can be used to explore the lake and its islands. Lawn sports

*Panorama Course, eighteenth hole*

include badminton, croquet, horseshoes, and volleyball. The Olympic-size heated swimming pool is popular with those who wish to avoid a "refreshing" dip in the alpine waters of the lake. A bocce court is available poolside. Hayrides depart the hotel entrance regularly. The natural history program features guided tours along an extensive system of marked hiking trails. A supervised children's program is available seven days a week for youngsters five to twelve years of age during the summer. Teenagers usually gravitate to the hotel's arcade of electronic amusements or to the Bedrock Club in La Cave, a soft drink bar (refreshments are half-price to those under twenty-one years old).

The "social season" at The Balsams, from the Fourth of July through Labor Day, is reserved for individuals and families. The hotel is booked near total capacity during the summer. Reservations must be made at least six months in advance for this time period. Convention and business groups predominate during the spring and fall seasons, though programs for individual travelers (minus the busy social calendar of events) are available in May, June, and September. The golf course is open from late May through mid-October. Spring can be a chancy time to visit this far north; autumn, when the tamaracks, birches, and sugar maples turn gold, is more reliable weatherwise.

*Panorama Course, ninth hole and Clubhouse*

# THE EQUINOX

Snuggled in the storybook village of Manchester, Vermont, among the rolling Green Mountains, is The Equinox, a rambling edifice that has been "Serving the Republic since before there was a Republic." A meeting place for the fathers of the American Revolution, the hotel was shuttered and dilapidated throughout the 1970s, endured an underfinanced rehabilitation in the mid-1980s, and in 1992 was brilliantly resurrected by the Guinness Corporation (operators of the Gleneagles Hotel in Scotland). Reopened following a $9-million renovation of all 164 guest rooms and public spaces, the national landmark, subjected to seventeen major architectural changes in six distinct styles since 1769, epitomizes "country grand" splendor. Not only has the eclectic Greek Revival and Federalist character of the hotel been reestablished—tall white fluted columns grace the porch and facade of the property—but the airy, oversize guest rooms, offering a choice of garden, village, or mountain views, have been decorated with Vermont antiques and Audubon prints. Guest bathrooms have also been completely reconstructed using eighteenth-century tile patterns, pedestal sinks, and beaded pine-paneled ceilings. The presidential suites (named for Ulysses S. Grant, William Howard Taft, Benjamin Harrison, and Theodore Roosevelt, all of whom were guests at The Equinox) have been redone, while the Mary Todd Lincoln Suite, named in honor of the First Lady, who spent her summers at the resort hotel with her two sons in the years before and after the president was assassinated, reflects her Victorian tastes.

The hotel's previously dowdy public spaces have been reconfigured and brightened. Guests now enter a traditional Federalist lounge with two-story views of 3,816-foot Mt. Equinox. The relocation of the lobby permitted the expansion of the historic Marsh Tavern, a famed gathering spot for Ethan Allen and the Green Mountain Boys. (When owner William Marsh chose to side with the British, his tavern became the first Tory property in America seized to support the independence effort.) Not only have a second fireplace and lounge been added to the hotel's showpiece restaurant, but area rugs, bookcases, and a collection of

*Thirteenth hole*

*Lobby. Photo courtesy The Equinox*

authentic objects detailing the region's storied past are on display. Live entertainment is featured at the Marsh Tavern on weekends. Cocktails are served after hours on the tavern's porch in July and August.

The resort's golf course, a Walter Travis design laid out on reclaimed swampland in 1926, has been treated to a $3.3-million makeover at the direction of Rees Jones, who has proven himself a master in the faithful reconstruction of classic designs. Jones, recognized for his sensitive restoration of four U.S. Open courses (The Country Club, Hazeltine, Congressional, and Baltusrol), retained Travis's original routing while preserving the layout's rustic Yankee character. Greens were recontoured and rebuilt to at least their original size, bunkers were reshaped (and in some cases restored), and a much-needed irrigation and drainage system was installed. Jones also filled in the spidery network of watery ditches that crisscrossed the fairways, rerouting the water parallel to the line of play. Mindful of recent advances in golf equipment, he modernized the course by moving tees back and repositioning fairway bunkers to bring them into play.

Renamed the Gleneagles Golf Course at The Equinox, the par-71 layout stretches to 6,423 yards from the blue tees (6,069 yards from the white markers). But mere yardage doesn't tell the whole story. Many of the holes march uphill. Elevated, knobby greens abound. A heavy morning dew carpets the fairways and keeps the grass lush and green, minimizing roll. And while the rough is mown to a reasonable height, dense woods line several of the fairways. Jones, who softened the penal aspects of the course, nevertheless paid homage to Travis's design principles. Several holes call for deliberate fades and draws; carefully sited hazards force players to think strategically; and greens are always undulating, never flat. Though far more forgiving of errant shots than the

original design, the golf course, in its current incarnation, favors those who hook the ball. Faders will survive, but slicers will eventually come undone.

The front nine, while appealing, is a warm-up for the stellar back nine. The 401-yard thirteenth, named "the best thirteenth hole in America" by none other than Ben Hogan when he played it, is notorious for its fearsome "Snake Pit," a gaping maw of scrub and loose soil cut into the right side of a domed hill that supports the green. Even without the snakes, it is a hazard to be avoided at all costs.

The travails of the thirteenth are softened by the view from behind the fourteenth tee. Rising from Manchester is the soaring white steeple of the First Congregational Church and beyond it a hedgerow of blue-green peaks. It's a vista that quiets the restless and stirs the phlegmatic.

The course reasserts itself at the two finishing holes, both long, right-to-left doglegs that play directly into a prevailing wind that sweeps through the valley. Each places a premium on distance and accuracy, although the 403-yard seventeenth, with a nest of eight bunkers guarding the elbow of its dogleg, is particularly vexing.

The outdoor verandah at the handsome clubhouse, overlooking the ninth green and two large practice putting greens, is a fine place for post-round refreshments. Back at the hotel, which fronts a marble sidewalk shaded by spreading elms and tall sugar maples, the concierge can recommend self-guided tours to natural and historic attractions in one of the loveliest corners of New England.

Like the early Republic itself, The Equinox has had its share of ups and downs. Thanks to the deep pockets of Guinness and a restoration staff dedicated to historical authenticity, one of the nation's earliest and most distinguished summer getaways flourishes again.

# THE SAGAMORE

SILVER MEDALIST

In 1883, four Philadelphia millionaires financed the construction of the first Sagamore Hotel on a private island in Lake George joined to the mainland by a small bridge. For decades, the hotel functioned as one of the liveliest social centers in the Adirondack Mountains of upstate New York, attracting the wealthy summer residents of the lake's west shore mansions, known then and now as Millionaires Row. Twice destroyed by fire—in 1893 and in 1914—the third Sagamore Hotel, a 100-room white clapboard Victorian-style structure with green shutters, opened in 1930.

Two years previous, Donald Ross, the most renowned designer of golf courses in the 1920s (between 1919 and 1926, six of the eight U.S. Opens were played on courses of his design), laid out the Sagamore Golf Club on rolling, wooded land atop Federal Hill two miles from the hotel. Almost overnight, it was acclaimed the best golf course in the Adirondacks and one of the best resort layouts in the Northeast.

Fast forward to 1981. Not only must the hotel be closed as a fire hazard, but the golf course is totally overgrown, with no distinction among its tees, greens, and fairways. In fact, two of the lower-lying holes have reverted to swampland.

Enter Norman Wolgin, a Philadelphia real-estate developer who owned a summer home near The Sagamore and who long ago had been smitten by the Lake George region. Wolgin formed a consortium to buy the hotel and golf course, pouring more than $75 million into their refurbishment. The makeover, completed in 1985, not only preserved the charm of the existing hotel (since entered on the National Register of Historic Places), it created a full-service resort with a new conference center, 240 new lodges, and an executive retreat with ten bilevel suites.

Working from Ross's original drawings, the golf course was skinned to bare earth before new drainage and irrigation systems were installed. The layout's original Scottish character was brilliantly conjured: The undulating, bent grass greens retain their hogbacks, the cross bunkers and greenside traps were shaped along the lines of the originals, and large patches of heather originally imported by Ross from Scotland were revived on the front nine. A pond was added in a boggy area at the fifth and sixth holes to improve drainage, and a few tees were extended, but otherwise the restoration was faithful to Ross's plan. With a staff that tends to the course with the diligence of curators, The Sagamore purrs as smoothly as a reconditioned Packard.

The strength of the par-70 layout, which stretches to 6,794 yards from the tips and 6,410 yards from the middle tees, is its par fours. Each demands precise shotmaking in return for par. The 405-yard seventh hole, for example, calls for a long, straight drive to a crowned fairway that slopes from left to right. At the base of a hill, the hole doglegs abruptly to the left, away from the slope, to a slippery, oblong green that beckons from the crest of a hill.

At the 427-yard thirteenth, golfers play their drives from an elevated tee sheltered by birches over a hill that blocks a view of the fairway. Water guards the right side of the fairway, trees hem in the left side. A pond filled with lily pads and rimmed by cattails indents the left side of the fairway about 150 yards from the green, providing more strategic interest. Wisely, Ross built a large, flat, bunkerless green at thirteen to compensate for the potential trouble that precedes it.

Although The Sagamore's first six holes play on relatively open ground, much of the course occupies a dense forest of pines, hardwoods, and silver-white birches. No condominiums or other signs of civilization intrude on the golf experience. Nor will they ever: The course is located within the Adirondack Forest Preserve. Lastly, the view from the first tee of the hulking Adirondack peaks looming above Lake George, the broad fairway spread between rows of trees far below tee level, is very impressive. It should be savored, for it is the only view of the lake from any hole on the course.

Twilight golf, when the air cools and the shadows lengthen, is a special summer pleasure at The Sagamore. Also noteworthy is the restored stucco and stone Tudor-style clubhouse, which dates to 1928 and resembles a hunting lodge with its timbered ceiling, heads of trophy bucks mounted on the walls, and displays of Native American artifacts. The Club Grill's dinner menu, particularly the grilled steaks and chops, is excellent.

Back at sea level, the resort has a modest sand beach and swimming area. A caveat: The chilly water of Lake George will turn your legs blue early in the summer. The heated indoor pool is a safer bet for those sensitive to cold. Jogging loops of 1, 2.6, and 4.5 miles are popular with runners, while the spa features first-rate massages and the latest beautification treatments. There are also six tennis courts (two indoors) and a racquetball court.

Fishing charters for pike, lake trout, and bass are available through the resort, though the quarry, perhaps due to the boat traffic on the lake, is very wary.

The best way to tour Lake George is aboard the hotel yacht, *The Morgan*, a seventy-two-foot wooden replica of a turn-of-the-century touring vessel. Sightseeing, cocktail, and dinner cruises are available. (Dinner is covered in the resort's meal plan; the boarding fee is $10.)

The main hotel's 100 rooms, including forty-seven suites, have been as meticulously restored as the golf course. Adirondack-stick and American-country furniture was used throughout. Rocking chairs, quilted bedspreads, botanical prints, and small writing desks add warmth to the individually decorated rooms. The newer lodges offer 240 rooms, including 120 suites with fireplaces, private balconies, and wet bars. They are spacious and nicely furnished but lack the charm of the original hotel.

The Sagamore's best dining room is Trillium, where a musician plays classical guitar and lute in a formal, candlelit setting. The cuisine, with entrées ranging from lobster thermidor to roasted squab, is exceptional. So are the desserts. The Sunday brunch at Trillium is arguably the best in upstate New York.

The elegant Sagamore Dining Room, with views of Lake George and the mountains, serves fine meals from its table d'hôte menu, while relaxed dining (with the accent on Cajun specialties) is available in Mr. Brown's, named for one of the original developers of The Sagamore. Van Winkle's, a 1940s-style nightclub featuring live music six nights a week, books Broadway-style musical revues during the summer season.

A favorite room of repeat guests is the Veranda, a nicely appointed lobby lounge with a spectacular view of Lake George. It's a fine place to enjoy morning coffee, afternoon tea, or an evening cocktail, and there's dancing and live entertainment nightly.

The golf season at The Sagamore is somewhat limited—the course is open from mid-April until ice forms on Lake George in early November. But for as long as it's open, The Sagamore gives golfers a chance to tackle a phoenix risen from its ashes thanks to the T.L.C. (and deep pockets) of a man in love with the Adirondacks.

*Right: Sixteenth hole. Inset: Aerial view. Photo courtesy The Sagamore, © Joe Viesti*

Located on the fringes of the Pennsylvania Dutch country, the Hotel Hershey is the legacy of chocolate baron Milton S. Hershey—and a monument to America's sweet tooth. Completed in 1933 on the heels of the Depression, the 250-room hotel, set high on a hill, was styled after the grand nineteenth-century palazzos Hershey had seen in his travels through the Mediterranean. The world traveler Lowell Thomas pronounced it a "palace that out-palaces the palaces of the Maharajahs of India." Thomas may have overstated the case, but he was more right than wrong. The Iberian-inspired lobby, the hotel's feature room, is highlighted by a sculptured fountain lined with colorful mosaics, stucco arches leading to long halls, lustrous tiled floors, and an oak-railed mezzanine set with overhanging balconies. The classical piano recitals and formal afternoon tea service in the fountain lobby are well attended. The Iberian Lounge, an attractive bar and nightclub within earshot of the lobby's gurgling fountain, features live entertainment nightly and a long list of specialty drinks. There are the usual crowd pleasers—Kamikazi, Melon Ball, Sex on the Beach—but the preferred after-dinner libation is Paris Is Burning, a blend of Chambord (raspberry liqueur) and cognac warmed in a brandy snifter. A live band takes the stage most nights of the week to belt out dance tunes.

A few steps below lobby level is the Circle Dining Room, a large, pillarless room built to Hershey's specifications and graced by thirteen stained-glass windows inlaid with vines, flowers, and birds. Dinner is generic banquet fare served in five courses, but the breakfast and luncheon buffets are very good.

On the north lawn of the hotel outside the dining room are formal gardens inset with gazebos and a pair of reflecting pools graced by lighted fountains. New brick walkways trace a path through the gardens. Street lamps, benches, and a sound system have also been added recently. It's a lovely place to read a book on one of the comfortable wooden benches while listening to piped-in Mozart or to stroll the gardens and admire the rolling green mountains in the distance.

The hotel, renovated in 1990, strives for Old World charm. Twin bell towers mark the facade of the massive beige brick structure and its chocolate-brown window frames that, designwise, could only work here, in a palace built by chocolate. To bring the point home, hotel guests are handed a pair of Hershey bars upon check-in, while a foil-wrapped "Good Night Kiss" is placed on the pillow each evening.

At nearby Hershey Country Club, where hotel guests are accorded playing privileges, the venue of distinction is the West Course, a Maurice McCarthy design circa 1930 that is wonderfully evocative of America's Golden Age of golf course architecture. A classic parkland course routed on narrow fairways through a thick forest of hardwoods and evergreens, the West calls for accurate tee shots and unerring approaches. The circular greens, while large and relatively flat, are well defended by bunkers. (There are nearly 120 sand traps in all shapes and sizes.)

A par-73 layout with five par fives, the West Course stretches to 6,860 yards from the blue tees, 6,480 yards from the whites. There are but two structures on the course: the tiny Derry Church School behind the third green, where Milton Hershey attended classes (he never went beyond the fourth grade), and his great stone mansion overlooking the 279-yard fourth hole, a devilish par four where brawn is more a hindrance than a help. The tall gray smokestacks of the chocolate factory dominate sightlines at the 164-yard fifth, where the aroma of cocoa can be quite strong, but the course thereafter departs the sight and fumes of the predominant local industry. The par threes, each aligned to a different point on the compass, are very fine, though the burly par fives, one hillier and more challenging than the last, are the heart and soul of the course.

Hershey's West Course has championship pedigree. The Lady Keystone Open, an LPGA event, has been held there since 1978. Byron Nelson defeated Sam Snead in the 1940 PGA Championship on the West Course in a thrilling thirty-six-hole final decided at match play. (Nelson birdied two of the last three holes to snatch the title from his arch rival.) Ben Hogan was associated with Hershey Country Club from 1941 to 1951, during which time he won three of his four U.S. Open titles.

One footnote: Guest access to the West Course is limited. Local members are accommodated first, especially on weekends, when visitors cannot play until after 2 P.M. Monday, Tuesday, and Friday are the best days to book a game on the West. Caddies are available at the club. If your legs can handle the hills and dales, walking is the best way to experience this stylish, well-bred golf course that remains the resort's best asset.

Hershey's East Course, designed by George Fazio and opened in 1969, is a sterner and less charming test than the West. Its preponderance of uphill holes, bottleneck fairways, sneaky water hazards, sand traps (100 in all), and superfirm pedestal greens that reject all but the truest approach shots tend to overmatch the average hacker. However, the East has its compensations. Like the West Course, its greens and fairways are beautifully conditioned. And while it lacks the woodsy charm of the original course, its front nine, routed on open pastureland framed by corn fields and horse trails, is attractive. But the demands of the 6,363-yard layout (7,061 yards from the tips), particularly its wicked elevated greens, are simply too severe for casual players.

More pleasant by far is the nearby Hershey Parkview Course, a McCarthy-designed layout with a meandering creek in play at thirteen holes that is ranked among the best public courses in the nation. In addition, the resort's pair of nine-hole layouts are perfect for novices as well as those seeking a relaxed two hours of fun. There's 2,318-yard Spring Creek, a nine-holer originally built by Milton Hershey strictly for youngsters but now open to golfers of all ages; and the hotel's own nine-holer, a hilly par-34 layout that skirts a pine forest. Many of the holes on this course are tough for the wrong reasons—a few are built on the sides of hills—but this has the virtue of convenience going for it. The first tee, located near an outdoor pool, is a hop, skip, and jump from the hotel. For a quick warmup, the Hershey Lodge & Convention Center maintains a par-three chip-and-putt course that wraps around a lake on its front lawn.

Despite the varied selection of golf courses, kids have the best of it at Hershey. Hersheypark, a full-fledged amusement park open from mid May to late September, features fifty rides and attractions, including the Carousel, built in 1919 by the Philadelphia Toboggan Company and one of the oldest operating rides of its kind in the nation. Sixty-six hand-carved wooden horses prance beneath blinking lights to the sounds of a wheezing Wurlitzer band organ. For the more adventurous, there is a death-defying roller coaster, and other hair-raising rides. However, a good portion of the park is devoted to kiddie rides designed to entertain small children without frightening them. All rides are free once the main admission fee has been paid.

Among the resort's other attractions is ZooAmerica, a walk-through zoo showcasing seventy-five species of animals native to five North American regions, and the Hershey Museum of American Life, which details early Pennsylvania life styles as well as Milton Hershey's own rags-to-riches story. (The former pushcart vendor had a weak spot for kids, establishing a boys' orphanage and a tuition-free school for children that are still underwritten by the Hershey Trust Company. For those who wish to know more of this benevolent despot's life, each room in the hotel is stocked with a copy of Hershey's biography, *One of a Kind*.)

A five-minute walk from the hotel is Hershey Gardens, a twenty-three-acre botanical garden with a three-acre plot of roses and hundreds of specimen trees and shrubs. At Chocolate World, a twelve-minute simulated factory tour explains the process of chocolate manufacture. Needless to say, visitors are handed Hershey Kisses when they depart Chocolate World and are free to purchase "I'm kissable" T-shirts, boxes of Reese's Peanut Butter Cups, and other Hershey products in the gift shop. For avid golfers and chocoholics traveling with children, Hershey, with one foot in the Old World and the other ankle-deep in cocoa beans, is the promised land.

*The hotel seen across a reflecting pool*

*West Course, fifteenth hole*

# MARRIOTT'S SEAVIEW RESORT

SILVER MEDALIST

Situated on the outskirts of Atlantic City along the New Jersey shore, Marriott's Seaview Resort was born eighty years ago as the result of a millionaire's impatience. Clarence Geist, who earned a reputation as a feisty, shrewd businessman during his rise from railway brakeman to utility magnate, threw a temper tantrum one day at the Atlantic City Country Club when play did not proceed as quickly as he wished. A friend commented, "If I had as much money as you, I'd build my own golf course."

Geist went one better. Not only did he hire top architect Donald Ross to design a course on a bayside farm, he built a 250-room clubhouse (since expanded), an indoor saltwater swimming pool, tennis courts, and a trap shooting range. The swanky club became an instant success, attracting such notables as President Warren G. Harding, Bing Crosby, and Alfred E. Smith, governor of New York. According to the late Leo Fraser, an early pro at the club who knew Geist well, "There was nothing like Seaview in the rest of the country except when Geist later bought Boca Raton in

Florida, which he made even grander. How many other clubs at the time had an indoor swimming pool, a French chef, and liveried chauffeurs who drove Rolls-Royces and Pierce Arrows?"

Marriott, in command since 1984, has gone to great lengths to retain Seaview's country club ambiance while expanding and refurbishing the property. The blending of modern conveniences and traditional furnishings at the four-story, Colonial-style resort has been quite successful. Stately guest rooms feature restored wood paneling and brass door knobs, while corridors connecting the wings are wide, carpeted promenades. The hotel's suites, featuring private balconies, regally appointed bedrooms, and prized antiques, are extra special.

Geist would feel right at home in Seaview's restaurants. Traditional breakfasts, lunches, and dinners are served in the window-walled Main Dining Room, which offers a panoramic view of Reeds Bay and the Atlantic City skyline from its rotunda. The more informal Grill Room, patterned after an English pub, is ideal for post-round fare, while the piano bar in the Lobby Lounge is a fine place to enjoy a cocktail. During the summer months, the Oval Room, off the main lobby, serves exceptional seafood entrées. Gentlemen wear jackets and ties at Seaview in the evening.

After a day of recreation, guests can unwind in Seaview's indoor and outdoor pools, book a session in the state-of-the-art fitness center—or work out the kinks in their swings at a twenty-two-acre Learning Center opened in 1991. A swing tinkerer's Camelot, the center simulates virtually every playing condition encountered in the Northeast, from deep and shallow bunkers to downhill lies and thick grasses. There are four greens for chipping, putting, and bunker play, plus a total hitting area of 60,000 square feet. If you like to practice, this is the place. There is also a reputable golf school attached to the Learning Center.

For swings grooved and ungrooved, Seaview offers two distinct golf experiences. The Pines Course, its original nine built by William S. Flynn and Howard Toomey in 1931, is a long, tight layout carved from a pine forest. Several of the holes, notably the par-three sixth, are framed by sandy wastes and scrub pines. A superior test of driving and course management, the Pines is a no-frills test of golf and a frequent site of regional competitions. Sharp doglegs hinged on imposing bunkers coupled with slick, well-protected greens prevent easy scoring. Plan to visit in the spring, when the layout's understory of dogwoods and azaleas is in bloom.

The kinder, gentler Bay Course, opened in 1915, plays to the cattail-lined shores of Reeds Bay, its elevated greens sculpted by Ross from sand mounds. Though short by modern standards (6,263 yards from the blue tees, 5,981 yards from the whites), everpresent sea winds, clever bunkering, and clumps of vegetation warrant against easy pars. The layout's short holes are especially appealing. The eighth, a straightaway, 280-yard par four, appears hazard-free and nearly drivable—until a deep, ominous bunker is spied in front of the shallow green.

Because Seaview is a neighbor of the Brigantine National Wildlife Refuge, it cannot spray for mosquitoes. These voracious insects can be a problem on windless days. (The pro shop sells repellent and places after-bite unguent in all golf carts.) Mosquitoes tend to disappear in the fall, a time when the exclusive Seaview tartan sweater available in the pro shop can be worn comfortably at the most Gatsby-esque resort in the Northeast.

*Left: Pines Course, sixth hole. Inset: The resort*

# The Northeast

## Tips and Side Trips

The Hershey Hotel has a variety of attractions on its doorstep, from Hersheypark, an eighty-seven-acre park filled with rides and amusements, to ZooAmerica and its displays of North American wildlife. Those who wish to peek inside the bowels of the earth can join a forty-five-minute guided tour through colorful rock formations at nearby Indian Echo Caverns.

The Capitol Building of Pennsylvania in Harrisburg, fifteen miles west of Hershey, is open daily for tours. It is one of the most beautiful state capitol buildings in the nation.

An hour's drive east of Hershey is Reading, one of the largest factory outlet centers in the Northeast. A forty-five-minute drive southeast from the resort is Lancaster, gateway to the Pennsylvania Dutch country. Farmers' markets offer fresh produce, homemade baked goods, and canned condiments and jams. Simulated Amish communities are also found in Lancaster.

Seaview operates a complimentary shuttle on Friday and Saturday nights to Atlantic City, located ten minutes from the resort. The Las Vegas of the East, Atlantic City is home to a dozen glittering casino hotels, including Bally's Park Palace and the Trump Taj Mahal. Visitors can try their luck at the gaming tables—or take in a show. Seaview is also convenient to the Brigantine National Wildlife Refuge and its colonies of shorebirds. Five miles from the resort are the quaint shops and restaurants of Smithville's historic village. Shoppers can hunt for bargains at the nearby Lenox China factory store, while oenophiles can head for the Renault Winery, the oldest vineyard in the nation.

A thirty-minute drive north from The Sagamore is Fort Ticonderoga, which played a key strategic role in American history. The restored fort illustrates the founding of the nation from the Colonial Wars through the American Revolution. A thirty-minute drive south, in Glens Falls, is the Hyde collection. An outstanding museum of European and American art, including works by Leonardo da Vinci, Degas, Rembrandt, Turner, and Winslow Homer, is informally displayed among antique European furnishings. The Adirondack Museum at Blue Mountain Lake features twenty exhibit buildings that detail the development of industry and art in the region.

*Roadside produce stand in Vermont. Photo © Fred M. Dole–f/Stop Pictures*

At the Lake George Opera Festival, classic operas and American premieres are staged by well-known performers in July and August. Opera-on-the-Lake cruises are available on Sunday evenings.

An hour's drive south of The Sagamore is Saratoga Springs, where the Saratoga Performing Arts Center presents concerts and ballet performances from June through August. The peak of the season arrives with the Thoroughbreds in August, when the Saratoga Race Track, the oldest and one of the most beautiful in America, opens.

Outside the front door of The Equinox, four miles of marble sidewalks lead to Manchester's bookstores, cafés, and confectioneries. Also in town is the original Orvis factory (maker of superb split-bamboo fly rods) and a large number of designer outlets, including Polo/Ralph Lauren, Anne Klein, Cole-Haan, Timberland, Brooks Brothers, and many more. For hiking enthusiasts, The Equinox is convenient to the Appalachian and Long trails. In addition, mountain bikes can be rented at the hotel. Nearby Windhill Farms offers guided trail rides through the local countryside. The Battenkill, one of the great trout streams, flows through Manchester. The Equinox Skyline Drive, a 5.2-mile tour to the top of Mt. Equinox, serves up panoramic views of five neighboring states. Hildene, a twenty-four-room Georgian Revival estate built by Robert Todd Lincoln, the president's son, is open for tours. The estate hosts concerts by the Vermont Symphony Orchestra and stages numerous craft and antique shows.

*Racing at Saratoga. Photo courtesy © Ted Spiegel*

The Balsams, 220 miles north of Boston, is remote. As such, it operates as a self-contained world. That said, a picnic can be staged on the east side of 1,871-foot Dixville Notch near the Flume, an impressive waterfall. Box lunches are available through the maître d'hôtel. In addition, the roadside antique shops along Route 26 and Route 3 are well worth exploring.

## DON'T LEAVE HOME WITHOUT . . .
## A SETUP AND SWING FOR HILLY LIES

*Visiting golfers must learn to cope with uphill, downhill, and sidehill lies on the hilly golf courses of the Northeast. The key to solid contact is an adjusted address position and an understanding of how the ball will behave in flight.*

*To play a shot from an uphill or downhill lie, set the line of your hips and shoulders parallel to the slope. Adjust your balance so that most of your weight is on the lower foot. For a right-handed player, that's the right foot for an uphill lie, the left foot for a downhill lie. Take a few practice swings to test your balance and to get a feel for the grade of the slope.*

*Ball position is critical. Play the ball forward in your stance for an uphill lie,*

*toward the back of the stance for a downhill lie. These positions will enable you to contact the ball at the bottom of the downswing.*

*The setup for an uphill lie adds loft to the clubface, resulting in a higher shot with less carry. For example, where normally you would choose an 8-iron, you should hit a 7-iron from an uphill lie. The opposite holds true for a downhill lie: The angle of the slope and shape of the swing delofts the club, promoting a lower shot. Where normally you would hit an 8-iron, select a 9-iron from a downhill lie.*

*For a sidehill lie with the ball below your feet, play the ball slightly forward in your stance. Flex your knees and bend from the waist to get close to the ball.*

*Aim the shot twenty to thirty feet left of the target, as the slope of the hill and a more upright swing plane will cause the ball to fade from left to right.*

*For a sidehill lie with the ball above your feet, stand erect and play the ball more in the center of your stance. Take one more club than normal and choke down an inch or two on the grip. Aim twenty to thirty feet to the right of the target and swing with the contour of the hill on a flatter plane than normal. The ball will draw from right to left*

TOM SMACK, DIRECTOR OF
GOLF, THE SAGAMORE

The South isn't just the South—it's the *Confederacy*. The thirteen states that seceded from the Union were marked for all time by the "Recent Unpleasantness," a sly reference to the Civil War. (Diehard Confederates still refer to the fraternal conflict as the "War of Northern Aggression.") These many years later, memories of the outcome still permeate the region.

In truth, there was friction between North and South long before the first shots were fired at Fort Sumter. Over the years, the North has done a good public relations job of appropriating much of Colonial history for itself. With all due respect to Plymouth Rock and the arrival of the pilgrims, the first permanent English settlement in the New World was begun at Jamestown, Virginia, in 1607. One of the South's grand spa resorts, The Homestead, was accommodating guests ten years before the Declaration of Independence was signed. Across the border in West Virginia, Thomas Jefferson wrote the first published mention of The Greenbrier's sulphuric waters in his *Notes on the State of Virginia* in 1784.

But the South has more than history. Southern hospitality is a reality; visitors are welcomed graciously. And while you'll hear your share of drawls and "y'alls" below the Mason–Dixon line, the inflections of Gullah that creep into the speech of Charlestonians and the faintly English accents of tidewater Virginians have little in common with the exaggerated vowel dragging often associated with Southerners. However it comes out, the hospitality shines through.

The golf courses at the South's finest resorts are extraordinarily varied, ranging from the flattish, windswept courses occupying the barrier reef islands strung along the coast—Sea Island, Hilton Head, Kiawah—to the rugged mountaintop layouts at Linville in North Carolina and Wintergreen in Virginia. And then there's that seventy-five-mile-long band of white quartz sand and pine trees that runs through the interior of North Carolina south of Raleigh. Created eons ago when a deep trench in the ocean floor filled with coastal sediments that later emerged as sand hills when the sea receded, this barren area, passed over by farmers, attracted the interest of a wealthy Northerner who built a charming New England–style village to attract ailing Yankees. He also hired a recent Scottish immigrant, Donald Ross, to plan a few golf

# SOUTH

courses for the amusement of the guests. The settlement was originally called Tuftstown. A resort-naming contest turned up a more suitable sobriquet: Pinehurst.

The South attracts and breeds good golfers, and for good reason: There's more world-class resort golf in Dixie than anywhere else in the nation. Pinehurst No. 2, Ross's masterpiece, is ranked thirteenth in the world by *GOLF Magazine*. Tommy Armour, the legendary "Silver Scot," was quite enamored of the course: "The man who doesn't feel emotionally stirred when he golfs at Pinehurst beneath those clear blue skies and with the pine fragrance in his nostrils is one who should be ruled out of golf for life. It's the kind of course that gets into the blood of an old trooper." From 5,966 yards (par 74), women can enjoy the course, too.

The Cascades Course at The Homestead in Virginia, ranked sixty-second in the world, offers an aesthetic golf experience second to none. The hand of man is generally responsible for most of the truly fine golf courses in America, but nature must be credited with creating the holes at the Cascades. It stands alone as the best mountain golf course in the nation.

From the day it opened, greatness was predicted for the Ocean Course on Kiawah Island, near Charleston, site of the 1991 Ryder Cup Matches. This remarkable Pete Dye layout, with more than half its holes pressed to the edge of the Atlantic, made good on its promise: Barely four months out of diapers, it cracked *GOLF Magazine*'s top 100 world list.

Of the more than 500 golf courses built by Robert Trent Jones, Sr., none is more charming or more skillfully routed than his original layout at the Golden Horseshoe in Williamsburg, Virginia. His son, Rees, built a perfect companion to his father's design in the Green Course, a majestic beauty located within the 3,000-acre greenbelt that serves as a buffer between Colonial Williamsburg and the modern-day world.

Except for the mountainous regions to the west, golf is played year round in Dixie, though spring and fall are the most temperate seasons and generally the best times of year to visit. If you love flowers, April and May are a must. If you like grits and can quote long passages from the writings of Robert E. Lee, any time of year will do just fine.

*Inset: The Williamsburg Inn, Virginia. Photo courtesy © Colonial Williamsburg Foundation*
*Large picture: Kiawah Island Inn and Villas, South Carolina, Osprey Point Course, eighteenth hole*

# THE WILLIAMSBURG INN/
# GOLDEN HORSESHOE GOLF COURSES

*Welcoming flowers. Photo courtesy © Colonial Williamsburg Foundation*

The nation's founding fathers and the Joneses—Robert Trent and his son Rees—have something in common. Both parties left their mark on Williamsburg, Virginia. The capital of England's largest and most populous New World colony from 1699 to 1780, Williamsburg is where George Washington, Thomas Jefferson, and other patriot leaders established the basic principles of American self-government and individual freedom.

Long after the British were booted out of the colonies, the elder Jones arrived in Williamsburg to design the original Golden Horseshoe Golf Course (now known as the Gold Course). He also built a sporty nine-holer, the Spotswood, within a 3,000-acre greenbelt that insulates sporting amenities from Colonial Williamsburg, an eighteenth-century time capsule that occasionally tempts the dedicated golfer to walk its streets and savor life as the colonists lived it. Since its opening in 1963, the "Shoe" has been ranked among Trent Jones's best efforts. A textbook golf course that follows the natural flow of the terrain, it is a fitting complement to the colonial town's vivid outdoor civics lesson.

Built shortly before the bulldozer became the golf course architect's chief shaping tool, the Gold Course plays across draws and ravines, its fairways heaving and tossing from ridge to ridge. There is excellent variety in the holes: doglegs, a few blind shots, fairways routed to and from a lake that reflects the beauty of the trees. Stretched to its full length of 6,700 yards, this compact, par 71-layout calls for long, accurate drives to lush fairways that give little roll. Its small, undulating greens are difficult to hold with a long approach shot. Bunkering is minimal but magnetic. It's the type of course that seduces a golfer to play a risky shot. If well executed, it is rewarded; if not, expect the appropriate penalty.

Others may clamor for the recognition, but the Gold Course has the finest quartet of par threes of any resort course in the United States. Best known is the 141-yard sixteenth, where the tee shot is played from a small clearing in a wooded hillside to a pear-shaped green that sits in the middle of a lake. This island green, the first of its kind, is unusually large—over 25,000 square feet—and is circled by a generous fifteen-foot-wide collar from which to chip if the tee shot misses the mark.

At the twelfth, the view from the championship tee of a long, slim peninsula with a pin in it does not inspire confidence—there's far more water in view than land. Overshoot the green, and you're left with a chip from deep brush to a tabletop green that slopes to the water. It can be taxing. So, too, can the finish. According to golf director Del Snyder, "If you can play holes fourteen through eighteen in even par from the back tees, you can match par anywhere."

Among the feature holes is the gargantuan par-five fifteenth, which stretches to an unconscionable 631 yards from the tips. (The tee itself

*Pro shop. Photo courtesy © Brian McCallen*

measures 135 yards!) Load up with every bit of ceramic or graphite or titanium in the bag—you still won't be getting home in two shots.

The Gold Course finishes in grand style at the par-four eighteenth, a right-to-left dogleg that leads to a deep but narrow green that slopes away to a pond. Match your handicap at the "Shoe," and you've played a solid round of golf.

In September 1991, Rees Jones put the finishing touches on the Green Course, a larger version of his father's handiwork. To his credit, the younger

*Gold Course, twelfth hole*

dogwood, crabapple, Japanese cherry, and plum trees are in bloom, the golf courses at the Golden Horseshoe rival any in America for beauty. The fall foliage show is equally glorious.

The nine-hole Spotswood Golf Course, which can be played from a different set of tees twice to complete an 18-hole round, is a miniature version of the Gold Course. It's no pushover—holes vary in length from ninety to 480 yards, and many of its slippery pedestal greens are situated on the far side of ravines. There's also water in play at four holes. The layout, open to walkers at all times, is named for Alexander Spotswood, an eighteenth-century Virginia governor who led a daring expedition from Williamsburg over the Blue Ridge Mountains. Upon return, Spotswood presented each member of the expedition with a golden horseshoe.

Jones said the site's natural attributes, not the pressure to compete with his dad's highly regarded work, tempered his design efforts. Carved from 250 acres of virgin timberland—huge beech, oak, and pine trees line the fairways—the routing fits the land beautifully. "The quality of the course is in its framing," Rees said. "We had to clear the fairways a little wider because the trees here are so tall. We had to get the sunlight down to the fairways."

From the tips at 7,120 yards, the Green Course could host a pro tournament, yet staggered tees (the whites are 6,244 yards) and wide, dished-out fairways that gather stray drives assist players of lesser attainment. As on the Gold, no fairway housing will be built around the course; it is and will remain a pure golf experience. In the spring, when the

The Gold Course is located beyond the south terrace of the Williamsburg Inn, a noble edifice of white-washed brick built in 1937 and modeled after the region's nineteenth-century spa resorts. Decorated in the English Regency style, the Inn reflects the wish of John D. Rockefeller, Jr. and his wife, Abby Aldrich, the benefactors of Colonial Williamsburg, that the town's lodging facility capture the understated coziness of a Virginia country estate. It has been called the most perfectly appointed hotel in America.

*Gala in the Regency Room. Photo courtesy © Colonial Williamsburg Foundation*

Replicas of Colonial antiques decorate the public areas, which are warmed in three seasons by crackling wood fires at either end of the lobby. The air is scented with bayberry candles. On the floors are faithful reproductions of carpets that wealthy colonists imported. The flower arrangements are exquisite, the staff unfailingly courteous and helpful. In sum, everything is refined and welcoming, without a trace of pretension.

The Inn has a total of 232 guest rooms: 102 in the main structure; 43 in the contemporary Providence Wings opened in 1972, many with private terraces and fireplaces; and 87 in a score of authentic Colonial homes, taverns, and cottages in the historic area. These range from the commodious Brick House Tavern, its pair of buildings providing eighteen guest rooms; to the Lightfoot House, a tiny building tucked away in a garden that housed President François Mitterand of France during the 1983 Summit of Industrialized Nations.

*Lobby. Photo courtesy © Colonial Williamsburg Foundation*

No two of the Inn's rooms are alike. In fact, the nonprofit Colonial Williamsburg Foundation maintains its own design studio, which custom-makes all draperies and wallpaper for the guest rooms. The rooms, modest in size, are comfortable and quiet, the gray marble baths not the kind in which you'd find a Jacuzzi. What you do find in the bathrooms is a bayberry-scented wash ball placed on the sink for "Ladies and Gentlemen who wish to polish the Skin and rid it from wrinkles."

For setting and cuisine, the Inn's Regency Room is one of the finest dining rooms in America. The lower room, its French doors opening to a flagstone patio shaded by tall white oaks and Camperdown elms, is graced by hand-painted, gilt-framed Oriental murals of birds and flowers, fluted columns, and a pair of bronze-and-crystal chandeliers suspended above a teak parquet dance floor. A harpist or orchestra provides a combination of classical and popular music nightly.

Dinner is continental in style, with an abundance of fresh regional ingredients used in the preparations. Among the classic entrées: rack of lamb Provençal, Chateaubriand, Chesapeake crabmeat Randolph, and fillets of Norwegian salmon poached, pan grilled, or sautéed. The Regency's sommeliers are expert at suggesting wines to accompany the dishes. Garden vegetables are crisp, the Caesar salad prepared tableside is definitive, and the desserts—Southern pecan pie, authentic English trifle, Black Forest cake—are irresistible. Warm lemon-rosewater finger bowls are brought to the table at meal's end.

Even stalwart golfers should budget a day or two to explore the historic area of Colonial Williamsburg, a living museum that appears much as it did when Patrick Henry thundered his defiance of King George III in his "Caesar–Brutus" speech. The 173-acre site, utilizing the still-existing street plan drawn up in 1699, encompasses eighty-eight original eighteenth- or early nineteenth-century houses, shops, taverns, public buildings, and dependencies. Another fifty major buildings and hundreds of smaller structures have been rebuilt on original foundations following extensive documentary research. More than ninety acres of gardens and public greens add warmth and authenticity to the restored capital. No other restoration in America compares in scale or quality.

The scene is brought to life by costumed interpreters, guardsmen, gaolers and other "Colonists" who relate the history of Williamsburg. Artisans employ hand methods and eighteenth-century tools to manufacture articles similar to those made by their Colonial predecessors. Blacksmiths, bootmakers, gunsmiths, printers, coopers, wheelwrights, milliners, musical instrument makers—all are highly skilled in extinct trades. It is they who open a window on early American society and culture.

There are also sensory cues: the sound of fifers and drummers parading down the treelined streets, the pungent smell of burnt gunpowder from a military muster, and the taste of Colonial dishes (peanut soup, spoon bread, and game pie) prepared at the town's colorful taverns. George Washington was partial to the seafood served at Christina Campbell's, though golfers congregate at Chowning's Tavern, a typical English-style alehouse known for its savory victuals, including Brunswick stew and Welsh rarebit. It's a wonderful place to recount the round. Gambols, scheduled nightly, feature balladeers, Colonial games, and other "diversions" popular in the eighteenth century. The town's taverns are a welcome respite from the usual post-round watering holes and their large-screen televisions.

Products from the various craft shops are sold along Duke of Gloucester Street. Where else to find a lace-trimmed infant mobcap, a white-powdered wig, or a handsome tricorn hat? Leather ale mugs, bone dice, pewter teapots, wooden spice boxes, old-fashioned alphabet puzzles, hair combs made from cow horns—all are unique to Colonial Williamsburg.

Other special attractions in town include the Abby Aldrich Rockefeller Folk Art Center, containing an impressive American folk art collection; the

DeWitt Wallace Decorative Arts Gallery, its ten galleries containing rare American and English antiques; the Governor's Palace, former residence of Patrick Henry and Thomas Jefferson; and the Capitol, where the idea of a democracy got its start in the United States.

The early stages of a nation detailed in a restored capital city, golf courses from two generations, the classiest inn in America—Colonial Williamsburg offers nothing less than the best vacation in history.

*Left: Gold Course, third hole. Photo courtesy © Brian McCallen. Inset: Gold Course, sixteenth hole*

# KINGSMILL RESORT

SILVER MEDALIST

Traveling golfers have a weakness for television tournament courses. Most of them appear manageable from the vantage point of an easy chair, but the fact is, the majority are too difficult for the average player. A rare exception is found at Kingsmill, a 2,900-acre resort built along the James River in Williamsburg, Virginia. The River Course, an ungimmicky Pete Dye design set on rolling land bisected by deep ravines, hosts the Anheuser–Busch Golf Classic each summer. Unless the sea breeze is unusually strong, the game's top players eat up the par-71 course from the championship markers at 6,776 yards, though the full measure of the layout often unravels even a better player's game. Then again, the white tees at 6,003 yards present a firm but fair challenge to the average player. (Wisely, Kingsmill posts a "Which Tees Are for You?" sign in the pro shop that guides players of different ability levels to the correct tees. For example, the executive gold tees at 5,010 yards are a good bet for the senior golfer.)

Many of the better holes on the River Course are not televised during the tournament. Among them is the first, a short par four where golfers can aim left or right but not straight. A shaggy hill pockmarked with bunkers lies directly ahead. A fairway shaped like a lobster claw surmounts the hill. The high road, to the left, is the better route, if you have it in you to carry your first drive of the day 180 yards over trouble.

The 151-yard fifth is an attractive but deadly par three—a tiny creek snakes its way from tee to green, the putting surface set above the stream—while the 341-yard sixth, at the east end of the course, is within olfactory range of a large Anheuser–Busch brewery. Suffice to say that beer, the finished product, tastes better than it smells during fermentation. For proof, drop by the resort's Thomas Pettus Grille and Peyton Grille rooms—both serve all six Anheuser–Busch beers on draft. They're ice cold and super-fresh.

Dye left the heaving contours of the land intact at the 371-yard eighth, the layout's number-one handicap hole. The drive at this left-to-right dogleg is played from an elevated tee across a deep swale to a narrow shelf of fairway that falls off dramatically to the left. A hooked drive ends up at the bottom of a hill, a sliced drive disappears into trees. The elevated green, shaped like an acorn squash, is ringed by bunkers and tucked in a grove of shade trees. Pars here border on the miraculous.

The back nine of the River Course weaves through a thick forest of walnut,

cypress, and poplar trees before emerging for a view of the James River at the sixteenth, the resort's most controversial hole. The pros don't give the sixteenth a second thought, but the careless amateur can ruin a round on this 413-yard killer. The drive—it must be accurate—is played to a ledged fairway buttressed to the right by a wooden retaining wall overgrown with ivy. From this treelined fairway, elevated eight feet above the level of the golf cart path, the downhill approach shot is played to a shallow green that beckons from a shaded glen. There are traps galore short of the green.

The 138-yard seventeenth is Kingsmill's signature hole. The tee, set atop a hill, adjoins an earthen fortification built by Colonial forces in 1775 to defend themselves against the British. The earthworks were later reconstructed by Confederate troops during the Civil War. The hole itself is not as scary as it looks, but neither is it easy, especially when a breeze sweeps in from the James, which parallels the hole. The long, slender green, forty yards deep, is guarded to the left by trees. Shots pushed to the right roll down a long slope to a broad crescent of sand that prevents balls from tumbling into the river. The old wooden pilings in the James below the green are all that remains of Burwell's Landing, a thriving ship and ferry port in Colonial times. More recently, the seventeenth is where Curtis Strange, Kingsmill's touring pro and best-known resident, was cheered wildly by local supporters from their rocking boats during the 1988 Anheuser–Busch tournament. The previous week, Strange had captured his first U.S. Open title at Brookline.

In 1986, Arnold Palmer–Ed Seay opened the Plantation Course, a sporty, 6,109-yard layout (6,590 yards from the tips) marked by steep hills, marshy lowlands, and historical landmarks. The short par-five second, for example, leapfrogs a weedy stream before doglegging around restored brick homes within the Richard Kingsmill Plantation, one of Virginia's more prosperous tobacco plantations in the 1700s. The layout's par threes—notably the 102-yard ninth, with its forced carry over marshland; and the 161-yard

*River Course, seventeenth hole*

*River Course, sixteenth hole*

seventeenth, its green set in a natural amphitheater protected by a tidal marsh—are excellent. So is the 367-yard eighteenth, a stirring finale where a well-placed tee shot sets up a midiron approach across Moody's Pond to a three-tier green. The Plantation's greens, larger and in some cases more undulating than those found on the River Course, are superbly conditioned. Unfortunately, too many of the Plantation's holes play through the backyards of post-Colonial fortresses. The lines of demarcation between homeowner and golfer are marked by out-of-bounds stakes.

Kingsmill's most pleasant surprise is found at the Bray Links, a short nine-hole, par-three course opened in 1989 and overlooking the James River. Named for a seventeenth-century plantation, the Bray attracts families, novices, and low-handicappers alike. (Use of the Bray Links is complimentary to resort guests.) Built on mounds and swells in view of the James, its minimal landscaping reminiscent of a Scottish links, the layout's holes range from forty-five to 109 yards. Holes three and four share a common putting surface, while the ninth features an island green. The links is mildly challenging when the wind picks up.

Curtis Strange can often be found refining his stroke on the large practice putting green at Bray Links when he's not on Tour. Strange, an avid fisherman, will tell you where the fish are biting if you ask. When in doubt, head for the mothballed ghost fleet of World War II ships—they resemble an island of gray trees from afar—situated at the mouth of the James River. Striped bass, bluefish, croaker, spots, and flounder are the usual quarry. Charter fishing trips can be arranged through the Kingsmill Marina.

The 360 guest accommodations at Kingsmill consist of one-, two-, and three-bedroom villas with spacious living rooms and fireplaces, outdoor terraces, and complete kitchens. The Riverview Villas, opened in 1990, offer the choicest rooms: The spacious, attractively furnished units overlook the James River and Wareham Pond.

Kingsmill's restaurants, emphasizing Chesapeake Bay seafood and regional dishes seasoned with herbs from the resort's garden, are uniformly excellent. Most formal among them is the Riverview Dining Room, a high-ceilinged, candlelit hall set off by red cedar beams and a large brick fireplace

The Bray Dining Room, designed to cater to the needs of business guests (Kingsmill operates a large conference center), features sumptuous buffets, while the Peyton Grille in the Sports Club is the place to sample Michelob Shrimp—jumbo shrimp deep fried in a Michelob beer batter.

Kingsmill's Summer Splash program, available from Memorial Day through Labor Day, organizes a variety of activities for children and adults. Fitness enthusiasts can join a brisk, two-mile Wake Up Walk daily at 7 A.M., while pool parties, with dancing under the stars to beach music, are featured on Fridays. Kids can take advantage of free golf and tennis clinics, freshwater fishing in Wareham's Pond, and twice-weekly movies.

The best entertainment is often found at the Bray Links, where a youngster may outshine a grownup for the first time, or where a senior player may regain his touch on the greens and emerge victorious. Overnight, the links has become Kingsmill's most popular family attraction.

# WINTERGREEN

Wintergreen is that rarest of creatures—a resort that embraces conservation as the guiding light of its growth and development. At many real-estate/resort properties, crabgrass in the fairways and cracks in the walls of the condominiums begin to appear shortly after the initial developer cashes out. At Wintergreen, conservation-minded property owners bought the resort for themselves in 1984, formed a nonprofit organization, and later set aside 6,740 acres of the 11,000-acre complex as a permanent mountain-forest refuge.

Wintergreen, which adjoins the Blue Ridge Parkway, is located 113 miles west of Richmond, Virginia, and about 170 miles southwest of Washington, D.C. It is worth finding for its Jekyll-and-Hyde pair of golf courses, one perched atop a 3,851-foot mountain, the other routed on rich bottomland. These two layouts elevate the resort from a rustic, laid-back East Coast ski area to a prime golf getaway.

You've heard of crowned greens? At Devil's Knob, Wintergreen's original layout, the *entire golf course* crowns a craggy summit that serves up spectacular views of the Blue Ridge Mountains, the rolling Piedmont foothills, and several broad valleys. It is the highest golf course in Virginia and one of the toughest par-70 layouts imaginable. Designed by Ellis Maples and opened in 1977, the 6,003-yard layout (6,576 yards from the blues) challenges players to maneuver the ball from canted lies to firm, fast, and severely undulating greens. These greens more than compensate for the layout's shortness. Accuracy, control, and inspired shotmaking are required to score well at Devil's Knob.

Carved from a forest of hardwoods, the holes are bordered by rock outcroppings, tiny brooks, and small ponds. In the spring, which arrives late at the top of the mountain, rhododendrons, mountain laurel, azaleas, dogwoods, and wildflowers brighten the premises. In the summer, temperatures hover between seventy-five and eighty degrees—perfect golf weather.

There is little rough at Devil's Knob—it isn't necessary. The rapid transition from the short grass to the tall trees is penalty enough. Holes are routed to relatively level mountain ridges, though dropoffs from tee to fairway can be dizzying. For example, skiers generally feel more at home on the tee of the 388-yard sixteenth hole than golfers—there's a 250-foot plunge from the front of the tee to the landing area.

Local knowledge is essential at Devil's Knob. This is especially true of the greens, for it's not enough merely to reach the putting surfaces. Depending on pin placement, the ball must come to rest in the correct section of the green if a golfer is to have any chance of holing a putt. The course seems fairer and less severe the second time around.

There are only two par fives at Devil's Knob. One of them is lethal. This is the 560-yard seventh, an uphill double dogleg where the drive must carry a small pond to reach a slim fairway. The second shot must be straight as an arrow to avoid rock outcroppings and old oaks, while the approach must find and hold a tiny, well-bunkered green positioned on the far side of a stream. The seventh may well be the toughest par five in the Old Dominion.

A few tips: walk fifty yards through the woods behind the fourteenth tee to a lookout point. From here, the blue ridges of the Shenandoah Valley stretch for more than 100 miles to the West Virginia border. It's as good a view as you'll find from an American golf course. Also, if you've emptied your ball pocket (or forsaken your putter) by the twelfth hole, you can always abandon the game and join the hikers on the Appalachian Trail, which passes nearby.

A twenty-minute drive down a winding, switchback road that drops 2,500 feet from the main resort complex is Stoney Creek, Wintergreen's second course. Routed on the floor of Rockfish Valley, Stoney Creek, a Rees Jones design, is a perfect counterpoint to its high-altitude brother. In fact, with a temperature difference of ten to fifteen degrees (and a substantially longer golf season), Stoney Creek is open for play when Devil's Knob is still covered with snow. In December, February, and March, guests can ski and also play golf at Stoney Creek on the same day for the price of one sport.

Stoney Creek's open, spacious front nine occupies former pastures and corn fields, its fairways spread below weathered humps and domes in the Blue Ridge Mountains. Gathering mounds emulate the shape of these peaks, while gurgling brooks meander through the fairways and cut in front of the greens. Lake Monocan, popular with canoeists in the summer, guards the front of the fourth and fifth greens.

The incoming nine at Stoney Creek disappears into a forest of black pines, pin oaks, and huge beech trees, with several of the tees elevated well above tree height. As with all Rees Jones layouts, Stoney Creek preserves the existing character of the land.

For example, the architect claims the 155-yard twelfth hole "was already there, just waiting to be discovered." The green is situated at a bend in Stoney Creek, which was rerouted slightly to accommodate the shape of the hole, but not at the expense of the native brook trout that grow to good size in its pools. A large bunker stands between the stream and the green, while tall beech trees backdrop the putting surface. A camel's hump of forested rock looms in the far distance. For challenge and beauty, this may be the best hole on the course.

Regardless of handicap, make a visit to the upstairs tee at the par-three sixteenth, where the 125-foot elevation change between tee and green shortens the hole considerably. From any of the stepped tees, it takes a good, solid shot to avoid the pair of bunkers that cozy up to either side of the large, undulating green. Especially if you become mesmerized by the postcard view of the distant blue ridges.

"I tried to build a playable course, not a monument to myself," Jones said shortly before the layout opened in 1988. "Life is tough enough—golf is a recreation that should be enjoyed." Amen. High-handicappers encounter substantially wider target areas from the white tees at 6,312 yards than the more accomplished player sees from the blue markers at 6,740 yards. The tips at 7,005 yards create a tunnel effect that can give the best of golfers a severe case of claustrophobia.

Wintergreen offers nearly 400 condominiums and rental homes ranging in size from studios to seven bedrooms. Most of the condominiums, all nicely furnished, are chiseled into the side of the mountain and serve up fine views of the valleys below. Fireplaces and fully equipped kitchens, both staples of ski resorts, are featured in most of the units. Accommodations are also available at the Trillium House, a privately owned twelve-room country inn located in Devil's Knob Village that was built to resemble an old farmhouse. Rates at the Trillium include a golfer's favorite repast, a full breakfast.

Of the resort's six restaurants, the top choices are the Rodes Farm Inn, a restored nineteenth-century farmhouse that offers family-style home-cooking; the Verandah, located at the Stoney Creek clubhouse, its seafood presentations and regional cuisine both superb; and the Garden Terrace at the top of the mountain, a casual restaurant with great views of the

*Devil's Knob Course, sixteenth hole*

*Breakfast on the terrace. Photo courtesy © Wintergreen Resort*

Shenandoah Valley. The resort's private label wine, produced by Barboursville Vineyards near Charlottesville, is worth a try.

Recreational amenities at Wintergreen include twenty-five tennis courts, one indoor and five outdoor pools, a full-service spa, canoeing on Lake Monocan, horseback riding, and lectures and field trips along a twenty-five-mile trail system. The resort's canopy of oaks and hickories shelters more than 450 varieties of northern and southern wildflower species. Some of North America's oldest geologic formations are found along these trails. Tours are led by staff naturalist Doug Coleman, who reviews Wintergreen's development plans before ground is broken on new projects.

Rare is the property that willingly submits its blueprints to a "tree-hugger." Rarer still is a resort that offers players two fine courses completely dissimilar in style and climate.

The Homestead sits on 15,000 rolling acres in a valley cloistered by the Allegheny Mountains of west central Virginia. Its address is a sleepy spa town called Hot Springs, and directions to two of its golf courses are given from Sam Snead's Tavern, a barnlike watering hole where the local-born pro with the still-fluid swing is often on hand.

The Homestead's central edifice, a rambling red brick structure topped by a white clock tower, is the essence of Colonial simplicity. The Great Hall, a 240-foot-long, peach-and-white lobby supported by a forest of Corinthian columns and set off by crystal chandeliers and a pair of marble fireplaces, is truly impressive. From a balcony hangs the Stars and Stripes. Below it is a livery desk that arranges horseback riding or horse-drawn surrey rides for guests. Tea is served in the Great Hall every afternoon, the tuxedoed violinists and piano player serenading guests with "The Blue Danube" and other house favorites. The resort has reached out of late for a newer clientele, but the old guard is the mainstay, and it is they who have complained about the hotel's relaxed dress code. Until fairly recently, no gentleman would be caught dead in the lobby after 4 P.M. without a coat and tie, and formalwear was de rigueur most evenings for dinner. The Homestead now offers a European Plan, a more flexible dining program that enables guests to choose when and what they eat. Previously, the resort operated only a Modified American Plan, with breakfast and dinner included in the room rate.

*The hotel*

While the resort's celebrated hot springs (they're as warm as new milk) have attracted pilgrims eager to "take the cure" since 1766, The Homestead has welcomed golfers since the end of the last century. A rudimentary six-hole course laid out in 1892 was later expanded to nine holes, then fifteen, then eighteen to accommodate the rising number of players. Several nameless architects had a hand in shaping its design, but William S. Flynn revised the course in 1924 to its current configuration as a sporty 5,957-yard, par-71 layout. Now known as The Homestead Course, it is marked by hilly fairways, small

*Sam Snead's Tavern, Hot Springs. Photo courtesy © Brian McCallen*

greens, and great views of the mountains. Not only is it convenient to the hotel, it claims the oldest first tee in continuous use in the United States.

However, better players not easily swayed by history's allure proceed directly to the Cascades Course, located five miles up the road from the hotel in Healing Springs. Designed by Flynn, who is best known for his work at Cherry Hills and Shinnecock Hills, both U.S. Open sites, the Cascades is conceded to be the nation's finest mountain course. It is a throwback to the days when the inclination and technology to move tons of earth to build a golf course did not exist. The challenge and charm and trickiness of the Cascades derives from the natural heave and toss of the terrain. It can truly be said that nature created these holes; Flynn identified them. As such, they are unique and require golfers to produce a special brand of golf to play them successfully.

A quick inspection of the scorecard reveals the Cascades as a maverick. A par-70 layout that stretches to 6,566 yards (6,282 yards from the white tees), the course features five par threes and three par fives. Two of the long holes (the sixteenth and seventeenth) play back to back. While not unreasonably long, a premium is placed on accuracy. An ability to manufacture a variety of shots is vital, for seldom do golfers face two shots that do not require different methods of attack.

Snead, who grew up a mile and a half from the Cascades and caddied there as a youngster, once described the rugged layout as "the most complete golf course I know of. I find it the perfect place to practice . . . because you have to hit every club in the bag. The driver, long irons, fairway woods, delicate pitches over water, sidehill, uphill, downhill lies, long and short trap shots—everything!"

Holes one through thirteen are routed on the tilted insteps of the Allegheny foothills, with several tees perched 100 feet or more above wooded ravines. The remainder of the holes flatten out on a valley floor. Blind, canted fairways have only yellow-and-black directional flags as targets. Greens throughout are small to medium in size, very slick, and difficult to read. Errant shots bound into the woods, occasionally flushing grouse from the underbrush, or splash into Swift Run Stream, which meanders through eight of the holes.

For two-thirds of the way, the Cascades is a lopsided golf course, with many of the holes cut on the bias of the mountain slopes. Players must beware the effects of gravity and aim to the high sides of the fairways when lining up their drives. These are special holes which call for special shots.

The Cascades's most thrilling hole is the 425-yard ninth, which plays from a sky-high tee above a deep, wooded gorge, the rolling fairway beckoning from 175 yards away. The second shot is played blind, with only a bull's-eye target tacked to a huge tree behind the green to aim for. The green itself is large and undulating. "I can't remember when I've had a straight putt on it," said Snead, who's probably played the course 2,000 or 3,000 times.

The 434-yard twelfth is generally ranked among the best par fours in America. This right-to-left dogleg is framed by a creek (usually dry) and by a heavily wooded mountain slope. Cross bunkers crease the fairway some seventy-five yards short of the green. An enormous maple tree backdrops a deep, narrow green embraced on both sides by bunkers. It has everything a good player could want in a golf hole.

The clubhouse at the Cascades, a creamy white brick Victorian mansion with eccentric Moorish touches built by a Wall Street tycoon, serves fortifying breakfasts and lunches on a shaded verandah overlooking the course. Inside, the pine-paneled walls are decorated with photographs and mementos of the many tournaments staged here, including more than fifty Virginia State Amateur championships. The locker room has low wooden stools from another time that make the changing of shoes a pleasure.

The Lower Cascades Course, located eight miles from Hot Springs in the opposite direction of the Cascades Course, is a Robert Trent Jones design circa 1963. It is routed on flatter, more open land than the main track and presents more conventional challenges. All of Jones's trademarks, including long tees, large, well-trapped greens, and a good variety of doglegs are here in full force, though this 6,240-yard, par-72 layout is somewhat gentler than many of his designs from this period. Yes, there are a few blind drives to be aimed at directional flags, and Cedar Creek comes into play at several holes. But like Flynn, Jones was content to shoehorn his golf holes into the existing landscape. As a running mate to the Cascades, it is ideal.

*A bridge on the Cascades Gorge Trail. Photo courtesy © The Homestead*

archery is available at the four skeet and trap fields. The Homestead maintains nineteen tennis courts and eight 10-pin bowling alleys. Badminton, croquet, horseshoes—no recreation has been overlooked. At night, feature films are screened in the theater. Cocoa and cookies follow the show. In addition to the fine clothing and jewelry shops found in the hotel's Palm Beach Corridor, the resort's Cottage Row, a group of turn-of-the-century cottages, now houses interesting shops (fly-tying kits, decorative items) as well as Café Albert, a bright little restaurant. The café serves the perfect summer afternoon repast: a strawberry spritzer to start, followed by watercress and cucumber finger sandwiches with fruit salad.

Then there is The Homestead's spa, an antiquated stone house opened the year the first tee on the original course came into use. The basis of most spa treatments remains the naturally heated mineral water that emerges from the resort's hot springs. The hottest temperature is 106 degrees, the coolest 102.5 degrees. A twenty-minute immersion in a tubful of these waters will do no harm. The spa has a steam room, sauna, whirlpools, exercise tanks, and hot packs. Aerobics classes and modern weight resistance machines are available, but take a peek inside the Zander Room to view the medieval-looking exercise equipment introduced by an early staff physician. Small wonder

*Lawn bowling and the first tee, Homestead Course. Photo courtesy © Brian McCallen*

Golf is only one of many pastimes to be pursued at The Homestead. There's lawn bowling on a perfectly manicured pitch near the Casino. Swimming is available in a spring-fed pool that averages eighty-four degrees. (The ornate ceiling and large bay windows of the 1903 pool house can be admired as you perform the backstroke.) Equestrians can travel 100 miles of scenic trails cut through the mountain foothills, while hikers can follow the beautiful Cascades Gorge Trail. Horse-drawn surreys and buckboards with coachmen can be hired. (There is perhaps no more delightful way to tour the countryside.) The resort's fishing guides can direct guests to pools in the Cascades Stream stocked with plump rainbow trout. Target and field

earlier generations were so sedentary.

Serious spa-goers make the pilgrimage to the Warm Springs Pools, located five miles north of the resort. Here are found two covered pools, one for men and one for women, as well as a sheltered drinking spring. The octagonal Men's Pool, built in 1761, is a rickety antique, but the soft, alkaline waters, which flow at a rate of 1,200 gallons per minute, are unusually clear and sparkling as champagne.

The hotel, sectioned into four wings, has 600 rooms, including seventy-five suites, some with fireplaces. The rooms vary greatly in size and decor, depending on location. Most, however, are large, high-ceilinged, and

*Above: The Cascades Course, twelfth hole. Right: Lower Cascades Course, eighteenth hole*

traditionally furnished, the original polished fixtures in the small bathrooms quite attractive. Nearly all the rooms have views of the surrounding Alleghenies. The top floors in the tower section of the hotel are perhaps the choicest accommodations. There are nice touches throughout: scented drawers in the bureaus, a bookmark by the bedside, and spacious closets. And something else: A conference center opened in 1973 was specifically designed to keep business delegates separate from social guests. With so little in common between these two factions, the separation is welcome.

Guests may also book into the nearby Cascades Inn, a more modest establishment with lower rates, yet with the same privileges extended to guests of The Homestead. Located in Healing Springs, the forty-nine-room Inn and its three cottages are quite convenient to the Cascades Course. For golfers on a budget, this is a logical choice.

Well aware that the mountain air tends to stimulate the appetite, The Homestead has traditionally gone the extra mile in its dining rooms. The tradition dates at least to the arrival in 1962 of its brilliant Swiss-born executive chef, Albert Schnarwyler, whose orchestration of food presentation at the hotel is peerless. In the main dining room, a cavernous hall separated into three sections by Doric columns, most couples dance the fox trot to the strains of a live orchestra between courses of smoked wild boar and Allegheny Mountain trout, to name two perennial favorites from a six-course dinner menu that changes daily. In the more intimate Grille, with its polished wood walls and candlelit tables, the appetizer of baked oysters on the half-shell with crabmeat gratiné Remick is a meal in itself.

On Sundays, a lavish brunch is spread out in the large white Casino, a building that dates from the early 1900s. During the golf season, the Casino's grand luncheon buffet features more than 150 items. Meals are also available at the more casual Sam Snead's Tavern.

Despite its three fine golf courses, storybook hotel, wide variety of activities, and superb dining rooms, The Homestead is not perfect. Parts of the hotel and spa, pending future renovation, are curling up at the edges. But given the excellence of the Cascades Course, the sunny attitude of the staff, and the poetic setting of the resort ("What a spread," exclaimed Lyndon B. Johnson upon seeing The Homestead for the first time), this dowager deserves its acclaim. Opened before the nation was born, The Homestead has managed to perfect its imperfections over time. Repeat guests find its idiosyncrasies endearing. First-timers marvel at the property's charm and character. Besides, is there any other resort in America that would offer a free round of golf in its chamber music weekend package?

# THE GREENBRIER

WHITE SULPHUR SPRINGS, WEST VIRGINIA • GOLD MEDALIST

The Greenbrier's address—White Sulphur Springs, West Virginia—is somewhat misleading. West Virginia sided with the Union in the Civil War, but The Greenbrier was (and always will be) the lap of Confederate luxury.

The resort traces its history to 1778, when a woman helpless with rheumatism was placed in a hollowed tree trunk filled with sulphuric waters from the spring. The woman jumped out of the tree trunk under her own power and claimed to be cured. Soon rustic

*The Spring House. Photo courtesy © Brian McCallen*

shelters and log cabins were constructed around the healing spring. Rows of attached cottages, many still in use today, appeared later. In the early 1800s, the Spring House, a small rotunda built over the spring that serves as The Greenbrier's symbol, was erected. White Sulphur Springs became a convivial center for aristocratic Southern families who followed a time-honored ritual of drinking the waters three times a day.

The current Georgian hotel dates to 1910. From the front, the grand edifice looks like the kind of multicolumned, ivory white wedding cake a millionaire would select for a favorite daughter's wedding. It also resembles a larger version of the White House, only here the columned portico is studded with the flags of the original thirteen Colonies. No small coincidence that twenty-two American presidents have stayed at The Greenbrier.

An air of romance and charm still pervades this magnificent 6,500-acre estate tucked away in an upland Allegheny valley. Taken over as a military hospital during World War II, The Greenbrier was totally redecorated from 1946 to 1948 by Dorothy Draper, the celebrated New York interior designer. Draper once described her vision for the resort as "romance and rhododendrons," referring to the state flower that adorns everything from the hotel's trademark hallway wallpaper to the dinner plates. White is the basic color used throughout, but it is splashed with bold reds, pinks, blues, and greens. Large stripes and outlandish prints match the huge scale of the building itself. Authentic Colonial and Oriental antiques, as well as excellent reproductions, capture the flavor of the spa's early days.

Decor and furnishings were individually selected for each of the hotel's 650 rooms and fifty-one suites, which in design style split the difference between Palm Beach and Florence. No two are alike. The grand salons in the upper lobby are unmatched for grandeur. A few could have served as backdrops for the love scenes in *Gone with the Wind.* One room features a venerable oil painting of George Washington with this sobering quotation below his name: "Beware of Foreign Influence." Another contains the plaster busts of the nation's founding fathers, rumored to have been modeled after Draper's lovers.

The smaller, west-facing salons look to acres of formal gardens. For those inspired to dash off letters to friends back home, the antique writing desks are stocked with Greenbrier stationery. Correspondence describing the

resort tends to wear out the same adjectives that timelessly apply to The Greenbrier: lavish, palatial, majestic, incomparable. The lower lobby contains the registration desk, a movie auditorium, a post office, a "street" of stylish shops, and a mosaic-tiled indoor pool.

Next door to the pool is the resort's Spa, Mineral Baths and Salon, a full-service complex reborn in a $7-million wing opened in 1987. Ultra-stylish, the spa is highlighted by peach-hued walls, a white billowing sailcloth ceiling, white bamboo furniture, and a philosophy based on exhilaration and rejuvenation for body, soul, and spirit.

According to Greenbrier president Ted J. Kleisner, "We've just enhanced what was envisioned when the spa opened in 1912. We went back to our history books. In 1912, guests were bathing in mud from Italy. Today, they are wrapped in French algae. The Swiss needle showers and Scotch spray were borrowed from Germany and Switzerland in 1912, and they're still

*The Rhododendron Suite. Photo courtesy © The Greenbrier*

being used today. We offered hydrotherapy in 1912 and still offer it. Nothing's new in the whole spa realm. It's just better."

The baths reign supreme at The Greenbrier. Several types of hydrotherapy are available. Opt for a soak in the famous White Sulphur Springs water (hold your nose, the water smells of rotten eggs poached in brimstone); or choose a foaming algae bath in local Alvon Springs mineral water. Sixteen different bath packages are available, including one specifically designed to follow a round of golf. The custom-made, oversize tubs are set in private bathing salons, where soft lighting, New Age music, and soothing colors combine to create optimum conditions for relaxation. Swedish, shiatsu, and aromatherapy massage is performed by twenty massage therapists. The spa's fitness equipment uses hydraulic pressure instead of weights, so that the exercise room rings not with clanging metal but the sound of music.

To a golfer, the point of all this feel-good activity is to relax mind and body for the resort's three fine courses. The Lakeside Course, The

Greenbrier's oldest layout, opened in 1910 as a nine-holer and was expanded to eighteen holes by Dick Wilson in 1962. A par-70 course marked at 6,068 yards from the white tees (6,333 yards from the blues), it is a pleasant spread with dozens of flower beds providing color. Wooden bridges span the many lakes and streams that give the course its teeth and muscle. For while rated the easiest of the three courses, Lakeside asks golfers to negotiate water at the first six holes and frequently thereafter. Despite the flattish greens, it's no cakewalk.

The Greenbrier's most cherished and popular layout is the Old White Course, named for the original hotel that stood from 1858 to 1922 near the present structure. Charles Blair Macdonald, a towering figure in the early history of golf in America, incorporated several famous Scottish holes in his design. For example, the par-three eighth hole was patterned after the Redan at North Berwick; the par-four thirteenth on the Alps at Prestwick; and the par-three fifteenth after the Eden at St. Andrews. The original course, opened in 1914, was a par-72 layout totaling 6,205 yards. The current design stretches to 6,640 yards (6,353 yards from the white tees) and plays to a par of 70. It is one of those rare courses that appeals to every class of player.

Most original is the Old White's first tee, which rises forty feet above the fairway and backs into a corner of the clubhouse verandah. Like it or not, golfers often have a discerning gallery on hand to witness their opening salvos, and in fact a big backswing can very nearly knock a drink off a table. The view from the tee is of a broad, treelined fairway backdropped by bear-shouldered peaks in the Alleghenies. The distant green is generously contoured. Each hole is cut from the same cloth. The Old White is a straightforward course that gives players a fair chance to match their handicaps, though water must be avoided on the final four holes to post a good score. The 140-yard eighteenth is perhaps the best-known hole at the resort: sentinel oaks shade a large teeing ground, from where an iron shot is played over a wide creek to an elevated green guarded by a pair of traps. The green is set below the clubhouse and its colorful awnings.

The Greenbrier Course, designed by Macdonald and Seth Raynor in 1924, was retooled by Jack Nicklaus in preparation for the 1979 Ryder Cup Matches. It is today a solid, fair test of golf blessedly free of architectural frills. At 6,709 yards (6,311 yards from the whites), it presents the stiffest challenge of the three courses. Routed on hilly land, the holes afford plenty of room to drive the ball, but beware the wayward approach shot: Most of the greens are elevated and undercut by steep-faced bunkers.

Among the layout's feature holes is the 441-yard sixth, a giant killer that calls for an approach shot to be guided with pinpoint accuracy to a shallow pedestal green cut into the side of a hill. The green is set diagonally from the ideal angle of attack. It's the kind of hole Nicklaus in his prime could count on playing in four strokes.

*The hotel seen from the rear*

The Greenbrier finishes in grand style at the 537-yard eighteenth, a gargantuan uphill par five that culminates in an unusual fishhook-shaped green staked out by five bunkers. Fortunately, the spa and its therapists are not too distant.

All three courses have slick, bent grass greens and thick stands of close-cropped bluegrass in the fairways. Each is impeccably maintained. Excellent caddies are available for hire. They add immeasurably to the golf experience. Very conveniently, the first tees and eighteenth greens of the three courses meet at the refurbished Golf Club, which turns out a superb buffet lunch daily.

But save room for dinner. The main dining room, sectioned into three chandeliered salons where chamber music is played nightly, offers a masterful blend of continental and American cuisine in its six-course presentations. A typical meal might go like this: brandied chicken livers, chilled strawberry soup (a Greenbrier classic), mixed green salad, roast loin of pork stuffed with apples, currants, and pecans, braised red cabbage, additional potatoes and vegetables, a choice of eight cheeses, and an irresistible selection of desserts, including a chilled ripe peach with whipped cream. The dining room is dressy: Coats and ties are required for gentlemen. Many longtime guests wear black tie on Saturday evenings.

Spring through fall, excellent à la carte dinners are available in the Tavern Room. The room's brass lanterns and equestrian prints capture the feeling of a cozy post-hunt lounge. The Golf Club dining room serves dinner, primarily seafood specialties, on a terrace overlooking the eighteenth green of the Old White Course. For a sunset view of the fine old links, this is the room.

For those watching their waistlines, lighter menu items with reduced calories and sodium are offered in most of the restaurants, most especially in Draper's Café. The café's rich aubergine walls and plaster baroque ornaments were designed in 1990 by Carleton Varney, Draper's protégé and The Greenbrier's keeper of the flame.

*Left: Greenbrier Course, eleventh hole*

*Below: Lakeside Course, tenth hole*

*Bottom: Old White Course, fourteenth hole*

Dependable, loyal service is perhaps The Greenbrier's greatest asset. Second- and third-generation employees are common among the staff of 1,500. Turnover is well under 5 percent. "Ladies and Gentlemen Being Served by Ladies and Gentlemen" is the hotel motto.

All the recreational amenities expected of a world-class resort are here: tennis (fifteen outdoor and five indoor courts), indoor and outdoor pools, bowling, trap and skeet shooting, croquet, fishing, and horseback riding. A carriage drawn by a matched team of horses that tools slowly through the estate is undoubtedly the best vehicle from which to view The Greenbrier's finery and perfection.

Of special interest is the Alabama Row Arts Colony, where artisans display their pottery, paintings, and other handicrafts in tiny cottages dating to the early 1800s. Gibson's, one of the more eclectic shops, sells chunks of meteorites, bookends of petrified wood, and jewelry made from mammoth fossils. At the lilliputian Doll House (duck your head to enter), miniature dolls and other tiny handicrafts are for sale.

Of historical interest is the President's Cottage, built in 1834 by a wealthy sugar planter from New Orleans and so named because it accommodated five United States presidents before the Civil War. A simple, two-story colonnaded home shaded by great white oaks and set on a hill overlooking the Spring House, the rooms of the cottage are lined with sepia-tone photographs of long-ago cotillions and great Confederate leaders. The library of Robert E. Lee is kept here, and a cursory review of his letters reveals clearly how he felt about the Union victory in the "War of Northern Aggression." Yet Yankees have always had a soft spot for The Greenbrier. From 1861 to 1865, both the North and the South occupied it at different times. Each side used it as a hospital for their wounded soldiers. When a Union general in 1864 ordered the hotel to be burned, Captain Henry du Pont (of the Delaware family) countermanded the order and thus preserved the fabled hostelry.

It was once said that the film *Casablanca* should be required viewing for American citizenship. For an American golfer, the axiom could apply as well to The Greenbrier.

*Aerial view of the hotel. Photo courtesy © Pinehurst Resort and Country Club*

Not only is Pinehurst synonymous with golf in America, it arose from a geological oddity called the Sandhills, interior North Carolina's answer to authentic linksland. It was here that Boston philanthropist and soda fountain inventor James Walker Tufts purchased more than 5,000 acres of desolate cut-over timberland for $1 per acre in 1895. His idea was to create a healthful resort for consumptive Yankees. Using the Colonial settlements of New England as his model, he hired Frederick Law Olmsted, the nation's first great landscape architect, to plan a tidy little village. Later, when local dairy farmers complained that guests were disturbing their cows by knocking a little white ball around their pastures, Tufts arranged for a New York doctor to lay out a rudimentary nine-hole course. In 1900, he commissioned a young Scotsman, Donald Ross, who had apprenticed under Old Tom Morris at St. Andrews, Scotland, to develop golf more fully at Pinehurst. Ross remained at Pinehurst until his death in 1948. With mules and manual labor at his disposal, he laid out four courses in the pine barrens. One of them, No. 2, he once described as "the fairest test of golf I have ever designed." Completed in 1907, Ross tinkered with No. 2 for more than thirty years seeking architectural perfection. He was known to sit beside a green all day observing the approach shots of golfers. These observations guided his changes.

Pinehurst No. 2 underwhelms. Its subtlety of design puts most first-time players to sleep, its strategic brilliance masked by a certain sameness to the holes. If No. 2 had a wardrobe, it would be white shirts, gray slacks, and black shoes. Unassuming, void of drama—No. 2 embodies the feel of an inland links but is naturalistic almost to a fault.

At first glance, there seems nothing to spark a golfer's attention. Fairways are unusually wide—Ross believed that golf should be a pleasure, not a penance. However, better golfers soon realize that the drive must be played to a specific area of the fairway to set up the ideal approach.

Each hole is separated from the other by tall long-leaf pines. Wire grass, pine needles, and clumps of *Eragrostis carunta*—lovegrass—occupy the sandy rough. Fairway bunkering is minimal. The heart of each hole is a crowned green replete with swales. The beveled edges of these greens fall away on all sides to muffin-shaped mounds and hollows, making the target area effectively smaller than it appears. Miss the green and you're left with a testy little chip to a firm, fast green. (Short-game wizard Ben Crenshaw has called No. 2 the best test of chipping in the world.) Players who can manufacture soft lobs, running pitches, and everything in between tend to do well. Because the targets put such a premium on the accuracy of the approach shot, Pinehurst No. 2 is generally regarded as the finest course in the world from fifty yards in to the green. Yet with no forced carries and only a single water hazard, No. 2 can be enjoyed by the high-handicapper from the middle tees at 6,401 yards. There's a dynamic at work here: The better the player, the harder it is to score. "It is not difficult," Ross wrote, "to make courses impossible, but that is a betrayal of true principles. The real capacity of every great course lies in its enjoyment value; enjoyment for every class of golfer."

That includes the best players in the world. Because they must reach deep into their bag of tricks to produce a variety of greenside finesse shots, No. 2 has always attracted players anxious to demonstrate their skills.

To fully savor No. 2, hire a caddie. In the words of Don Padgett, Pinehurst's director of golf, "Walking straight down the fairway on No. 2 with a caddie is the only way in the world to see its ultimate and utmost beauty." Just don't expect to be wowed the first time. Ross's masterpiece, like the recording of a great symphony, must be played a few times to be fully appreciated. The thirty-dollar surcharge to play No. 2 is readily justified.

The other six courses at Pinehurst are no less endearing. The No. 1 Course, short, tight, and treelined, is a favorite of local members. (Ross redesigned the layout from an earlier design dating to 1899.) The No. 3 Course, sporty at 5,593 yards, begins in hilly, forested terrain, opens to a links-style setting and returns to trees at the conclusion. Aesthetically, it is marred by rows of condominiums built alongside the fairways.

Pinehurst No. 4 has undergone a number of facelifts over the years. For his part, Ross continuously changed, added, and subtracted its holes. In 1973, Robert Trent Jones lengthened and toughened the layout in preparation for a PGA Tour event. Ten years later his son, Rees Jones, softened the course to make it fairer for average players, removing more than half the bunkers and replacing them with mounds. No. 4 today is a solid and seamless test of golf, despite the many changes.

The No. 5 Course, designed by Ellis Maples (his father, Frank Maples, was for years the keeper of the greens at Pinehurst), was revamped by Robert Trent Jones in 1974. It is the most watery of all the courses at Pinehurst, and its expansive, undulating greens pose major putting challenges. Its signature hole is the 150-yard fifteenth, where the shot is played from an elevated tee over a pond to a small green framed by towering pines. In the spring, flowering pink and white dogwoods add color to the cathedral-like backdrop. Unfortunately, previous management saw fit to build condominiums nearly to the edge of many of the fairways on No. 5.

Three miles from the main club is the No. 6 Course, a George and Tom Fazio effort opened in 1979. Hillier than the original Pinehurst layouts, No. 6, with its crowned fairways and tiny greens, was unduly stern to all but the best players. In 1990, the greens were enlarged and recontoured, and several fairways were widened. No. 6 now offers a solid, fair test of golf with an unusually hilly and scenic back nine.

The newest star in Pinehurst's roster and a perfect counterpoint to No. 2 is the No. 7 Course, a thoroughly modern Rees Jones layout opened in 1986. Located two miles from the main complex on a sprawling tract of land near the PGA World Golf Hall of Fame, the multitheme layout has diverse natural features. The high ground is hilly and wooded, while low-lying holes skirt bulkheaded marshes and weedy streams. Pot bunkers and pronounced Scottish-style mounding define the fairways, though elevated tees are more typical of a mountain than a Sandhills course. Jones made good use of vast sandy wastelands and natural berms at a few of the par threes. These one-

*No. 2 Course, fifth hole*

shotters are the strength of the course. Tops among them is the 151-yard sixteenth, where the tee shot must carry a Sahara-like expanse of sand. The subtle green contours throughout are a salute to Ross. From the tips at 7,114 yards, No. 7 is the toughest course at Pinehurst. It is also the most beautiful, unless you play No. 2 often enough to appreciate its subtle rhythms. There's a twenty dollar surcharge to play No. 7. It's an amount basketball great Michael Jordan happily pays whenever he's in town: No. 7 is his favorite resort course in the world.

Despite the fact that nearly 300,000 rounds are played at Pinehurst annually, the golf operation runs smoothly. Hotel guests are permitted (and urged) to arrange golf starting times up to sixty days in advance.

As it approaches its centennial and bids to host major tournaments, Pinehurst is quietly fine-tuning its facilities. Maniac Hill, the practice area named by Ross for the legions of golfers who now, as then, lash away at

practice balls from dawn to dusk in search of improvement, has been widened, leveled, and reshaped to include eight mounded target greens. The pro shop, already as large as a department store, has been expanded; the men's and women's locker rooms have been remodeled; and the ninety-first hole has been enlarged to include outdoor seating. There is perhaps no more perfect backdrop for golf in America than the white-columned clubhouse and the brick terrace of the Donald Ross Grill set near an enormous practice putting green.

The 310-room hotel, the largest wooden frame hotel in North Carolina, exudes Southern charm—and golfiana. Nearly every hallway is lined with framed photographs of golf's greats, all of whom have played at Pinehurst. Here a raven-haired Sam Snead (who called No. 2 "my number-one course"), there a smiling, youthful Ben Hogan; here a dapper Walter Hagen, there a chubby, crewcut kid named Jack Nicklaus, who won the North and

South Amateur in 1959 as a nineteen-year-old. The most popular bar? The recently renovated Ryder Cup Lounge, a gorgeous little hideaway set off by mahogany display cases of golf memorabilia, tartan green wallpaper, and framed photographs of every Ryder Cup team since 1927. A door in the lounge opens to a wide, green-carpeted porch set with white wicker rockers.

The hotel's Carolina Dining Room is at its best in the early morning hours, when sleepy-eyed golfers trundle down to breakfast to fortify themselves for thirty-six holes of golf, the usual amount of sport for a typical Pinehurst guest. All a hungry golfer could ever want is available at the buffet: cereals, fresh fruit, custom omelettes, creamed chipped beef, and biscuits with red-eye gravy; chafing dishes brimming with grits, sausage, potatoes, and corned beef or venison hash; plus made-to-order waffles, French toast, and pancakes, not to mention four kinds of muffins. There's also a pianist on hand whose breakfast melodies invariably catch the mood of the day.

*Above: The hotel*

*Left: No. 7 Course, eighth hole. Photo courtesy Pinehurst Resort and Country Club, © Paul Barton*

The rooms themselves, tastefully refurbished in the early 1990s, have full-length mirrors fastened to the guest room door. They're ideal for swing rehearsals.

Nights at Pinehurst are quiet. Golfers need rest for a daily diet of nonstop golf. One of the staff pros is on hand after dinner to discuss the finer points of the game in the lobby. (Golfers seeking more detailed instruction can enlist in the Golf Advantage School, which features on-course classrooms, individual video analysis, and a 5:1 student-teacher ratio.)

Quieter still is the forty-nine-room Manor Hotel, a lovely inn near the main hotel dating to 1923 and extensively renovated in 1990. Many of the rooms contain a bedroom and parlor-style living area, ideal for families seeking separate space for their children.

A leisurely five-minute walk or a narrated horse-and-buggy ride from the hotel is the quaint village of Pinehurst, its wide, tree-shaded lanes circling out from the village green. Join the chorus in the piano bar at the Pine Crest Inn (once owned by Donald Ross), shop for antiques or golf clothes, or stop by the drugstore for something fizzy at the authentic soda fountain.

Although golf is king at Pinehurst, there are other activities, too. Lake Pinehurst is ideal for sailing and fishing. The twenty-four court tennis complex is one of the best in the nation. The Pinehurst Riding Club offers hayrides, carriage tours, and instruction. Nine trap and skeet fields are available at the resort's Gun Club, where Annie Oakley, sharp-shooter and star of the Buffalo Bill Wild West Show, once instructed guests in the art of marksmanship.

Then there's the weather, Tufts's prime reason for choosing the area. The Sandhills climate is ideal for outdoor activity year round, though spring and fall are best for golf. If it is pure serendipity that Donald Ross chose Pinehurst as the place to unfurl his genius, consider that the sandy soil heats up rapidly under the sun's rays and radiates quickly after sunset, resulting in warm days and cool nights with low humidity. Perfect weather to tackle a different course for every day in the week.

# LINVILLE GOLF CLUB/ ESEEOLA LODGE

Looking for an alternative to the sharp edges of modern golf courses and the zippy pace of newer resorts? Consider stepping back in time to the Blue Ridge Mountains in western North Carolina, to the Linville Golf Club, a rugged, well-preserved course opened in 1929. The layout was designed by Donald Ross, its fairways shaped with mule-drawn drag pans. Nature wasn't displaced by such rudimentary technology: Golfers today follow an elemental routing etched in the foothills of 5,964-foot Grandfather Mountain. True enough, the fairways are no longer mowed by horses shod in huge leather mitts (so as not to mark the ground), but Linville is a genuine holdover from a time when stagecoaches, not automobiles, were the only transportation available to the resort.

So exemplary was Ross's design that Bobby Jones often made the long, overland trip from Atlanta to play Linville. Billy Joe Patton, the colorful amateur who nearly won The Masters in 1954, and Clifford Roberts, the late Augusta National autocrat, were members of Linville. The club's current membership roster reads like a Who's Who of movers and shakers. Wooden markers and plaques posted around the course commemorate former and present club associates. Impressive stone mansions built into the mountain foothills and, on the first two holes, neat little cottages, border the course. Linville today is not only a prebulldozer museum piece, it's one of the finest mountain courses in America. (Guests of Eseeola Lodge enjoy playing privileges at the club.)

Played from the tips at 6,780, the par-72 layout is a rigorous test of golf that has taken the starch out of more than a few scratch golfers. The regular course, at 6,286 yards, is more readily managed by the average player. All of Ross's trademarks are conspicuous at Linville—forgivingly wide fairways, crowned greens, spare bunkering. Sturdy par fours and long

*The brook*

*Eseeola Lodge*

quilts on the beds are not only decorative, they provide welcome warmth on cool nights. Most of the rooms have porches overlooking the flower gardens surrounding the Lodge. Nice touches include terry cloth robes, fresh flowers, a fruit and cheese basket upon arrival, and turndown service each evening. Thanks to the construction of a bypass to Highway 221 in 1991, rooms in the front of the Lodge are no longer subject to the sounds of passing traffic, as they once were. Eseeola Lodge and Linville Golf Club is that rare creature: a historic, superbly run country inn with a championship golf course on its doorstep.

Breakfast and dinner for two are included in the room rate, a fabulous deal considering the quality of the meals served. The breakfast menu offers everything from fresh local berries and homemade waffles to the Angler's Breakfast: sautéed fillet of rainbow trout with scrambled eggs. Dinner is an elegant five-course meal featuring fine French and New American cuisine.

Note that Linville is a dry town. The Lodge will provide setups for drinks, but guests must supply their own libations.

A seasonal resort open from mid-May through mid-October, the Lodge is often booked solid in July and August. Make early reservations or consider visiting before or after the peak season. Late spring and early

par threes, the layout's bone and sinew, require the competent use of a long iron, the club Ross believed separated genuine golfers from casual sportsmen. Still, even the beneficiaries of advanced technology must find a way to keep their balance on the awkward sidehill, downhill, and uphill lies.

Several of the holes are out-and-out classics of design. The 414-yard third is not only Linville's number-one handicap hole, it is one of the best par fours in America. The landing area for the tee shot is unusually generous, though the second shot must carry a meandering brook to an elevated green that rejects all but the truest shots. The brook, which contains trout, reappears often: It is ingeniously routed through more than half the holes.

Beauty vies with challenge at the eleventh hole, a downhill par four of 422 yards where the tee shot must come to rest short of the brook that gurgles across the fairway 260 yards from the tee. The approach is played to an undulating green framed by a pair of bunkers and backdropped by the craggy face of Grandfather Mountain. It is magnificent. So is the lofty elevation: At 3,800 feet above sea level, Linville is one of the highest courses east of the Mississippi River. Plan on a little extra distance in the thinner air.

If the canted lies and slick greens extract a pound or two of golfing ego from your flesh, there is always the sight of the charming, twin-gabled Tudor clubhouse backdropping the eighteenth green to look forward to at round's end. Lunch is served in the clubhouse's Par-Tee Room, while refreshments can be enjoyed on the verandah overlooking the eighteenth green.

Built in 1926, Eseeola Lodge was one of North Carolina's first resorts and is listed in the National Register of Historic Places. (The original inn, destroyed by fire, opened in 1892.) Beautifully restored Appalachian antiques decorate the Lodge's twenty-eight rustic rooms. The handmade

*Fifth hole*

summer bring wildflowers and rhododendrons; the autumn blaze of russets and golds is fantastic. At most times of year, sunny days in the high 70s and cool nights prevail, a big plus for golfers who like comfortable playing conditions and great sleeping weather.

In addition to golf in Linville, other guest facilities include a croquet lawn, heated swimming pool, hiking trails, and excellent trout fishing in nearby streams. Not far from the Lodge, quaint shops retail antiques and native crafts. Nightlife is nonexistent: The room porches and hotel grounds are ideal for stargazing, while card games are popular in the parlor. The atmosphere of the Eseeola is restful and distinctly noncommercial. Kids are not overlooked: a recreation program for children is organized during the summer months.

# KIAWAH ISLAND INN AND VILLAS

Kiawah (pronounced KEE-a-wah), a 10,000-acre barrier island located twenty-one miles south of Charleston, South Carolina, had had its ups and downs as a resort before it was chosen to host the 1991 Ryder Cup Matches. Enter Pete Dye, who was tapped to design a world-class, oceanside course at the far eastern end of the island along a 2½-mile stretch of tumbling duneland. Before ground was broken, the yet-to-be-built course was declared the site of the 1991 Ryder Cup Matches, a tremendous gamble on the part of the PGA of America. But not if you hear Pete Dye's side of the story.

From day one, Dye's enthusiasm for Kiawah's potential was uncontained. "This is the best undeveloped site for a golf course in the United States," said Dye, who took a room at Kiawah so he could join his construction crew at the crack of dawn each morning. (Dye, to his credit, is a hands-on designer who doesn't mind soiling his clothes during a day's work.) After the Ocean Course was opened in May 1991, Dye suggested he might throw in the towel. "I think it's time for me to go back to the insurance business," said the former insurance salesman. "There's nothing more to do. I'll never get another chance like this." He may be right.

Unique among stateside layouts, the Ocean Course features ten holes stretched along the sea, with the balance routed among coastal marshes. Even the slightly inland holes have a view of the Atlantic. Dye, who feels strongly that technological advances in golf equipment are rendering many classic designs obsolete, built the Ocean Course to withstand any conceivable challenge well into the next century. The course can be stretched to nearly 7,600 yards if necessary, though the Ryder Cup contestants played the par-72 layout at 7,240 yards.

With its exceptionally wide fairways and skimpy rough, the Ocean Course is readily managed by the average player from the regular tees at 6,244 yards. However, the championship tees at 6,824 yards can quickly overmatch better players, as slightly mishit approach shots to the greens, many of them crowned, tend to roll off into grassy swales. Greenside bunkering was kept to a minimum. So were forced carries over water: There's only one, at the 152-yard seventeenth.

Though Scottish in motif, this is a Pete Dye creation all the way, minus the railroad ties. The designer moved more than one million cubic yards of muck and sandy soil to build up the tees, fairways, and green sites. The course does not flow through the rolling dunes, but rather is propped up on top of them, exposing shots to the vagaries of the wind. In the words of Tom Weiskopf, "It's an American-style course on linkslike land, a simulation of what naturally occurs overseas by way of wind and erosion." And while the course has the look of an authentic links, even Dye is quick to point out that the Tifdwarf grass planted in front of the greens, while close-shaved, will not permit bump-and-run shots due to its dense, thatchy texture. (Native seaside grasses on British and Irish links are fast-running and conducive to shots played along the ground.

But this is a technical quibble. The Ocean Course is a glorious celebration of golf and perhaps the most invigorating seaside layout east of Pebble Beach. It was not for nothing that the Ocean Course was ranked eighty-ninth in the world by GOLF Magazine four months after its debut, an unprecedented achievement. This is a course that was born to greatness. Best of all, there is no real-estate development to intrude upon the golf experience. The only building a golfer sees from the links is the modest clubhouse, its entire back wall a sheet of glass that serves up a superb panorama of the Atlantic.

If ever there was a course worth the extra money charged to play it—at presstime, the green fee was $100 for resort guests, including golf cart—this is it.

The first course to open at Kiawah, in 1976, was Marsh Point, originally designed as an executive course and later stretched to a par-71 layout by Gary Player. At 6,203 yards from the tips (5,841 yards from the white tees), Marsh Point is rather short by modern standards. The seduction here is that anyone who can drive the ball 200 yards has a legitimate shot at birdie on

*Turtle Point Course, sixteenth hole*

*A villa*

nearly every hole. What the scorecard fails to emphasize is the importance of accuracy.

A good portion of the course is routed through the marshy nesting grounds of herons and egrets. Blackwater lagoons, invisible from the teeing grounds, lie in ambush on no fewer than thirteen holes. There is also enough sand to make one consider playing in sandals. Golfers make few excursions to the rough—the ball is usually lost when it departs the fairway.

Turtle Point, designed by Jack Nicklaus and opened for play in 1981, was named for the Atlantic loggerhead sea turtle that nests near its three ocean holes. While Marsh Point is loaded with deception, Turtle Point reflects Nicklaus's design philosophy that there be no unpleasant surprises during the round. All hazards are plainly visible and all flags, even on the longest holes, can be seen from the tee. Because Nicklaus believes that reaching the green on a par five in two strokes is one of golf's greatest thrills, his long holes present eagle opportunities to the expert.

For the first thirteen holes, Turtle Point is a stately woodland layout long on shot values but short on drama. The course undergoes a personality change at the 143-yard fourteenth, however, where players emerge from the shade of the maritime forest to a hole placed between a corridor of receding dunes and a hillside of windswept scrub. If the fourteenth hole signals a change in mood, the 407-yard fifteenth transports golfers directly to Scotland. Direct your attention to the back tee, where a sizable expanse of seaside vegetation must be carried to reach a slender fairway framed by stunted trees to the right and a series of rolling dunes up the left side. The second shot is played to a small, crowned, diamond-shaped green guarded by three pot bunkers and a thicket of scrub. In design and challenge, this hole closely resembles the infamous Railway Hole at Royal Troon. Both are long, tight, and extremely difficult.

The 153-yard sixteenth hole, like the fifteenth, parallels the Atlantic, its long, shallow green guarded by a lone pot bunker. Turtle Point's final two holes, a mild anticlimax, turn inland. The seventeenth borders a pelican rookery, while the eighteenth bellies up to a lake where outsize alligators cruise around with their eyes above the water. It's the seaside holes at Turtle Point that linger in the memory.

Environmental restrictions at Osprey Point, Kiawah's fourth course, appeared to free rather than confine architect Tom Fazio. With water in play at fifteen holes, Osprey Point offers a firm challenge from the tips at 6,678 yards. However, the white tees at 6,015 yards offer a more forgiving line of attack and take much of the water out of play for high-handicappers. Among the better holes is the 149-yard third, which calls for a full-blooded carry over the breadth of a marsh to a large, skewed green set above the marsh's cattails and dog fennel. Finding the green is only half the battle, for once there, it's easy to be faced with a difficult sixty-foot putt.

Designed with families in mind, the resort offers biking and land-sailing on the ten-mile-long, firm-packed beach; twelve miles of paved bike trails;

windsurfer and sailboat rentals; and jeep tours of wilderness areas. Night Heron Park is a well-equipped twenty-one-acre play area for kids, though aspiring athletes of all ages form pickup games of softball, volleyball, and touch football in the park. On summer evenings, concerts transform the greensward into an open-air concert ground.

Guests of all ages are welcome to matriculate at Kiawah Kollege, which offers a natural and historical perspective of sea island flora, wildlife, and early plantation living. Marine biologists and naturalists schedule activities ranging from ocean seining and biking tours to island walks and bird-watching.

Accommodations are contained in four separate lodges at the 150-room Kiawah Island Inn. The rooms, airy and inviting, feature dramatic ocean or forest views from private balconies. The resort also maintains 260 villas in a variety of locations throughout the island—near the beach, overlooking a lagoon, or tucked beside a fairway. The one- to four-bedroom villas are ideal for extended family stays. Each has a fully equipped kitchen, washer-dryer, and roomy living and dining areas.

*Swimming pools*

The resort's dining experiences are as well varied as the golf courses. Sunday brunch at the Jasmine Porch offers a great selection of regional seafood dishes, as well as twenty different salads, patés, and terrines. The Southern version of eggs Benedict, served with biscuits and pea meal bacon, is a nice turn on a brunch classic.

Theme dinners and cookouts are offered throughout the year. The oyster roast and barbecue at Mingo Point, held on Saturday evenings, features square dancing to live bluegrass music after dinner. For a more formal affair, a five-course meal with wines to match is presented at the Vintner's Dinner. Seating is limited to allow guests to converse with both vintner and chef.

Not only does the Straw Market sell the usual logo T-shirts and suntan lotion, it regularly attracts a few of Charleston's "basket ladies," who weave and display authentic sweetgrass baskets. With sweetgrass becoming scarce, these handmade baskets are well worth the purchase price. Given the scarcity of oceanside courses open to the public, the Ocean Course at Kiawah is well worth a round or two. Just ask the Ryder Cup contestants.

# PORT ROYAL GOLF & RACQUET CLUB

SILVER MEDALIST

large greens, Planter's Row stretches to 6,520 yards from the blue tees. The layout is eminently manageable by average players from the white markers at 6,009 yards. Not only has the new regime resurfaced the greens and removed fairway bunkers at several holes to enhance playability, but extensive landscaping has brightened Planter's Row considerably. Flower beds surrounding a gazebo in the center of the course create a parklike atmosphere. Numerous birdhouses dot the landscape. As a pure golf experience untouched by reminders of civilization, Planter's Row stands alone on an island that has been steadily developed since the 1960s.

Robber's Row, located on the marsh side of Hilton Head and the longest of Port Royal's three courses, favors power over finesse, especially on the tee

*Lobby. Photo courtesy The Westin Resort Hilton Head Island*

Long before it gained a reputation as a premier golf destination, Hilton Head Island was the scene of a major Civil War conflict. In November, 1861, the largest naval assault on the shores of the continental U.S. occurred on land now occupied by Port Royal's Robber's Row and Barony golf courses. Several of the tees at the two courses, designed in the early 1960s by George Cobb, are built atop earthen embankments that once enclosed a Confederate fort. The name Robber's Row was inspired by an infamous street that sprang up around the encampment of the victorious Union troops. Civil War buffs are treated to an eighteen-hole history lesson at Robber's Row: A monument on each tee details the Union's occupation of the largest barrier island between New Jersey and Florida.

A rapid succession of undercapitalized owners in the mid-1980s allowed Port Royal's courses to degenerate into a drab battleground. New management arrived in 1989 to update the two original layouts—and completely refurbish the marquee course, Planter's Row, a Willard Byrd design opened in 1984. Site of a Senior PGA Tour event in 1985, Planter's Row is the only course on Hilton Head unencumbered by real estate development. A tight, tree-lined layout with well-positioned hazards and

*Planter's Row Course, fifteenth hole*

shot. However, the small greens, many of them elevated and well bunkered, demand precise iron play. Large magnolias and moss-draped oak trees border the fairways, while tidal creeks, lagoons, and the marsh itself must be negotiated at several holes. The second and eleventh holes, both listed at 440 yards from the tips, are especially testing.

The Barony course was intended to be a user-friendly member's course, but with several tricky doglegs, clever bunkering, and water in play at fourteen holes, it is no pushover. Colorful azaleas frame the tiny greens of a course generally regarded as the easiest to score of the three. Still, wayward players stand to lose their vacation's supply of ammunition on a former battlefield where shot placement is all-important.

After the round, golfers can repair to Bayley's, a nineteenth-hole bar and grill within Port Royal's clubhouse. The Bloody Marys at Bayley's are exceptional. At the popular Sunday jazz brunch held on the clubhouse verandahs above the croquet lawns, kids dine free. When accompanied by their parents at selected times every afternoon, kids can also tee up for free.

A five-minute drive from Port Royal is the Westin Resort, its U-shaped hotel built on a superb 24-acre beachfront site. Designed to complement the historic port cities of Charleston and Savannah and reminiscent of the grand seaside hotels built at the turn of the century, the Westin has 410 rooms (including twenty-nine suites), all with large pine armoires and spacious balconies. Most rooms have ocean views. Several face the waterfalls, reflecting pools, and gardens that grace the hotel's central courtyard. A wide boardwalk leads from the pool deck across sandy dunes to a six-mile-long, firm-packed beach ideal for strolling and jogging. Within the public spaces, antiques, tapestries, porcelain planters, brass chandeliers, and light oak floors covered with Oriental rugs create a residential feeling characteristic of the homes of the Old South. The Westin's formal Barony Grill, specializing in Low Country specialties, conjures a cozy hunt club atmosphere, while the island's best seafood buffet (fried oysters, blackened redfish, grilled marlin with pine nuts) is served nightly in the Carolina Café. A steel band entertains at the Pelican Poolside snack bar, where casual meals are served at umbrella-shaded tables.

For those with a taste for whimsical art, life-size statues of people cleverly disguised as birds are stationed throughout the property. "Rhett and Scarlett," for example, is a six-foot-tall sculpture of puffins in antebellum dress. It provides a nice contrast to Port Royal's authentic nature show and history-laden fairways.

# PALMETTO DUNES RESORT

SILVER MEDALIST

*Arthur Hills Course, third hole*

Hilton Head Island in South Carolina isn't the exclusive getaway it was in the 1960s and early '70s. The island's main thoroughfare, William Hilton Parkway (Highway 278), is today lined with fast-food establishments and budget motels, not subtropical vegetation. Traffic jams are not uncommon in high season. However, one resort has managed to distinguish itself from others that have experienced financial difficulties or suffered an identity crisis. This is Palmetto Dunes, a 2,000-acre real-estate/resort development with three golf courses, three miles of white sand beach along the ocean, *twenty-seven* swimming pools, a Rod Laver Tennis Center with twenty-five courts, a 200-slip marina, an excellent windsurfing school, and ten miles of navigable lagoons ideal for canoeing, rowing, or fishing. It's also a great place to fly a kite or build a sand castle. Not only are most activities within walking distance, but the needs of resort guests do not clash with those of the community's permanent residents, a neat trick attributable to enlightened planning.

Within this well-organized colony, golf is the acknowledged star. The feature layout is the Arthur Hills Course, a rolling neo–Scottish links with dramatic (for Hilton Head) elevation changes set among tidal marshes and thick stands of oaks, pines, and palmettos. Borrowing liberally from modern design features pioneered by Pete Dye (bulkheaded greens, prominent mounds, use of different grasses to provide contrast), Hills crafted an eclectic test of golf that fits in well with the natural flow of the land. Not only did Hills incorporate secondary dune ridges into his design—level lies

are rare—he also created new dunes, anchoring their slopes and hollows with sea oats and love grass. Visually, the Hills course is a very striking layout, though not quite as difficult to play as it appears. For example, fairway traps are absent, rough is negligible. Finesse and shotmaking are far more valuable than distance, especially when the wind blows, which is often. Putting surfaces are multitiered and very undulating throughout.

Opened in 1986, the Hills course is readily managed by average players from the white tees at 6,122 yards, though it can play tough from the tips at 6,651 yards. While the front nine brings a lagoon into play at more than half the holes, calling for forced carries to the green at the 334-yard second and 135-yard eighth holes, the back nine is clearly the better half. The 142-yard fifteenth plays from a raised tee directly to a restored ninety-one-foot-high lighthouse (it was in service from 1881 to 1930 and is listed on the National Register of Historic Monuments). An enormous live oak frames the rear of the fifteenth green, the white lighthouse visible beyond. Historical and natural touchstones aside, the 320-yard seventeenth is probably the best hole on the course. The drive is played down a rolling fairway pinched by a lagoon to the left and by high grassy mounds to the right. The long, narrow green, nestled in a forest, beckons from the far side of the creek. The carry over water at this point in the round can be deadly to the unwary.

The George Fazio Course at Palmetto Dunes, opened in 1974, is bar none the toughest course on Hilton Head from the championship tees. And that includes the vaunted Harbour Town Golf Links at Sea Pines Plantation. Fazio's cookie-cutter bunkers, many of them intimidating walls of sand that preface tiny greens, dominate the layout. Fairway traps are proportionally larger and every bit as ubiquitous. A par-70 course with only two par fives, the strength of the layout is its unrelenting par fours. For example, three of the final four holes on the Fazio course are two-shotters that play over 400 yards from the white tees. (The par-three seventeenth, by the way, is no breather: It calls for a carry of 187 yards over water.) It is anyone's guess how many South Carolina beaches George Fazio emptied of sand to build this severe test of golf.

Bring your A-game to the Fazio course or make a tee time at the more user-friendly Robert Trent Jones Course. Opened in 1969 and one of Hilton

*Marina*

*Arthur Hills Course, second hole*

Head's first courses, this layout fits perfectly the description "resort course." Landing areas are generous, while greens are large and receptive. However, beware the lagoons in play at eleven of the eighteen holes, particularly on the back nine. And while five of the holes on the front nine are well within the sight and sound of passing traffic on Highway 278, the back nine kicks off with a straightaway par five that leads golfers directly to the sea. The ocean views from the tenth green are as fine as any on Hilton Head, especially when the shrimpers are hauling their nets or when dolphins break the surface. With its large terrace and extended patio for outdoor dining, the clubhouse, opened at the Jones course in 1990, is unusually attractive.

Green fees at Palmetto Dunes's three courses are on a sliding scale. The Arthur Hills Course is the costliest (fee includes a ditty bag with logo balls, tees, ball marker, divot repair tool, and yardage book), followed by the Fazio and Jones layouts. The Fazio course permits walking after 2 P.M.

The resort's parent company has developed an adjacent property, Palmetto Hall Plantation, with a second Arthur Hills course available to resort guests. Opened in 1991, it is longer and tougher than his original design, with more undulating greens but less water in play.

Accommodations at Palmetto Dunes are varied. Nearly 600 tastefully decorated one- to four-bedroom villas are scattered about the premises beside lagoons, fairways, the ocean, or Shelter Cove Harbour. All have private balconies, patios, or decks, as well as full-service kitchens. Building exteriors are colored in subtle earth tones to blend in with the surrounding landscape.

The 324-room Mariner's Inn features spacious rooms in two wings, all with ocean views, while the 505-room Hyatt Regency Hilton Head, renovated to the tune of $32 million in the late 1980s, is reputedly the largest oceanfront resort hotel between Atlantic City, New Jersey, and Palm Beach, Florida. Opt for one of the ocean-view rooms in the south wing.

Among the Hyatt's features is a health club enclosed in a three-story translucent glass pyramid that admits light to the heated pool, whirlpool, and tropical plants. The hotel's oceanfront restaurants and lounges are equally distinctive. Hemingway's serves grilled or blackened seafood in a relaxed "Key West" atmosphere (ceiling fans, lots of plants, good daiquiris). Possum Point, ideal for casual lunches—a dripping wet bathing suit is suitable attire—is transformed into J.J. Pepperonio's at night. It may be the only oceanside pizza parlor in the South. Point Comfort, a poolside bar, does a brisk business in frozen drinks, while Club Indigo is one of the livelier nightclubs on an island that's lost its blush of youth—but can still point to Palmetto Dunes as one of its enduring successes.

# CALLAWAY GARDENS

Callaway Gardens began with a rare flower and a heart problem. The flower was the brilliant coral-red plumleaf azalea. The heart problem belonged to Cason Callaway, an enlightened textile industrialist. Years earlier, while hiking the land around Blue Springs, a gorgeous corner of Georgia seventy miles southwest of Atlanta, Callaway discovered that the summer-flowering *Azalea prunifolia* flourished only within a 100-mile radius of the spring. Not only did he and his wife Virginia purchase the land to preserve the flower, sowing thousands of seeds from the original azaleas; they planted alternatives to cotton on the eroded land, including oats, muscadines, and blueberries. Callaway shared his ideas of soil restoration and experimental farming through the Georgia Better Farms program. Thousands visited Blue Springs to learn more of his methods. But his days as a farmer became as hectic as those in textiles. A heart attack, in 1947, turned the 53-year-old Callaway to one of life's gentler pursuits—gardening.

Originally, the Callaways planned to build a modest retreat with lakeside homes, fishing, and a nine-hole golf course. Realizing the site's potential, they decided to create a public garden for the enjoyment of families and their children. When the gardens were completed in 1952, their corporate and financial operations were turned over to the nonprofit Ida Cason Callaway Foundation, named for Cason's mother. The current-day property's after-tax profits are channeled back to the foundation to maintain its horticultural and educational programs.

Callaway Gardens is to flowers what Pebble Beach is to seaside golf. Unlike most botanical gardens that feature plant varieties native to other regions of the world, Callaway Gardens propagates flora native to the Southeast. In fact, 1,700 of the 2,500 developed acres at Callaway (the resort totals 12,000 acres) are devoted to regional plant and flower species.

Greatly expanded over the years, Callaway Gardens today lacks for nothing as a natural spectacle. One of its feature attractions is the five-mile Scenic Drive, which rims the shore of Mountain Creek Lake and passes by once-depleted farm terraces on which the Callaways replanted more than 200,000 native plants and shrubs under a restored forest canopy of pines. Sweetgum, tulip poplar, and hickory trees later entered the forest naturally.

Visitors are encouraged to explore on foot the miles of woodland trails that branch off this route, including Azalea Trail (more than 700 species of azalea herald the arrival of spring); Rhododendron Trail, its collection of more than seventy species giving forth volleyball-size blooms in early May; Holly Trail, which has the largest public display of holly in the world (nearly 500 varieties); Wildflower Trail, which begins near an old log cabin and passes near wildlife habitats; and Meadowlark Gardens, most formal of the bunch, with a collection of fragrant Oriental saucer and star magnolias arranged near a cupola-turned-gazebo transplanted from the roof of Mrs. Callaway's childhood home. The thirteen man-made lakes in the gardens, several of them fed by natural springs and creeks, act as reflecting pools for the floral displays.

And that's just the Scenic Drive. At Mr. Cason's Vegetable Garden, arguably the most productive 7½ acres in the United States, guests can gather valuable tips and techniques for the backyard cultivation of vegetables and fruits. The John A. Sibley Horticultural Center features six major floral displays yearly as well as workshops on pruning, landscaping, and cooking with wild plants. The Cecil B. Day Butterfly Center, opened in 1988, is the largest free-flight, glass-enclosed, live butterfly conservatory in America, with more than 1,000 butterflies flitting about in a lush tropical setting.

The resort's sixty-three holes of golf are beautifully integrated into these carefully tended grounds. The star layout is Mountain View, a burly Dick Wilson design routed on rolling land, its fairways narrowly spaced through tall Georgia pines. There's plenty of timber to greet the sprayed drive, though the understory of dogwoods that blossom among the towering pines are fair compensation for a wayward golfer's crooked shots. Updated in 1991 in preparation for the Southern Open, a PGA Tour event, Mountain View is extra-tough from the tips at 7,057 yards.

*Lake View Course, fifth hole*

Gardens View, designed by Joe Lee in 1969, trails along orchards and muscadine vineyards, its generously wide fairways and yardage (6,392 yards from the blue tees, 6,108 yards from the whites) intended to flatter, not flatten, the average player's game. However, players must contend with twenty-five green-guarding bunkers.

The sweetheart layout at Callaway Gardens and one of the prettiest resort courses in the South is Lake View, the property's original test of golf. A par-70 course stretching to 6,006 yards (there is no back tee), the front nine was designed in 1952 by J.B. McGovern, a protégé of Donald Ross. The incoming nine was added later by Dick Wilson. The challenge of Lake View lies in its nine water holes and small, well-bunkered greens, though the surrounding floral beauty is often enough to break the concentration of most golfers. The 152-yard fifth hole, where golfers play from an island tee to a green set in front of the Gardens Restaurant, is one of the best par threes at the resort.

Sky View, a well-groomed nine-hole executive course for walkers only, is an ideal choice for a family outing or a casual tune-up. It's no cream puff, however—this Dick Wilson layout calls for sound shotmaking.

Incidentally, there are no 150-yard bushes or numbers painted on the golf cart paths at Callaway Gardens. The 150-yard markers are well disguised as bluebird boxes.

Of the seven restaurants at the resort, three are especially noteworthy. For fine dining, all the key ingredients—candlelight, flowers, soft music, classic continental cuisine—are found at the Georgia Room within the Callaway Gardens Inn. Braised paté-stuffed quail with Merlot sauce and sirloin of lamb with garlic port sauce are two of the best entrées. There's a wide assortment of wines to accompany these dishes. Also at the Inn is the Plantation Room, best known for its excellent seafood buffet on Friday evenings (try the fresh catfish and fried frog legs).

*The John A. Sibley Horticultural Center. Photo courtesy Callaway Gardens, © Lothner Comm*

High atop Pine Mountain, which is not really a mountain but rather a flat-topped ridge that runs from eastern Alabama into Georgia, the rustic Country Kitchen specializes in hearty breakfasts. Speckled heart grits (made from the heart of corn kernels), blueberry pancakes, muscadine bread, and thick slabs of Georgia-cured bacon are among the offerings.

Accommodations at the resort include motel-style rooms at the Callaway Gardens Inn; one- to four-bedroom units at Mountain Creek Villas, each with a fireplace, fully equipped kitchen, and screened porch or patio; and the two-bedroom Country Cottages, which are free-standing or grouped in small clusters amid tall trees near Robin Lake. During the summer, only families participating in the week-long Summer Recreation Program may stay in these accommodations. Easy to see why: the cottages offer an indoor-outdoor heated swimming pool, whirlpool, children's playground, laundry, and a restaurant, the Flower Mill, patterned after a 1950s soda fountain complete with vintage jukebox. The cottages are also convenient to the man-made beach (one of the world's largest) that nearly encircles Robin Lake.

Callaway's appeal to children is boundless. Since 1960, Florida State University's Flying High Circus has performed at Callaway Gardens. With its big top pitched at Robin Lake Beach, the circus is the focal point of the Summer Recreation Program. In addition to daily circus performances, performers also double as counselors, teaching kids simple circus acts and games. Sailing, swimming, water-skiing, roller-skating, horseback riding, biking, and fishing for bream and bass in Mountain Creek Lake are also available, as are golf and tennis instruction. Family events such as barbecues, square dances, and organ concerts in the chapel on Falls Creek Lake are on the summer agenda. So are guided garden walks that tell youngsters about the region's animals, plants, and ecology.

The sign posted outside the entrance gate to the Gardens sums up best Callaway's appeal to children and adults alike: "Take nothing from these gardens except nourishment for the soul, consolation for the heart, and inspiration for the mind." Golfers would be wise to shoot for more than just a score within this horticultural wonderland.

There is perhaps no more dramatic approach to any golf course in America than the Avenue of Oaks, an ancient archway of massive oaks that hover over the dual carriageway leading to the Sea Island Golf Club. The walls of the main clubhouse are the remains of a corn bin and stable that once were part of the Retreat Plantation, renowned since the late 1700s as the producer of the finest long-staple Sea Island cotton in the world.

It was to these former plantation grounds seventy miles south of Savannah, Georgia, that Walter J. Travis was brought in 1927 to lay out the resort's first nine. Travis, the first American to capture the British Amateur (1904), routed broad fairways through a dense forest of oaks, pines, and palmettos, the holes bordering the marsh or skirting a few of the lagoons that dot the property. Working with mule teams and wagons to recontour the old cotton fields, Travis created modest chocolate drop mounds to emulate the grassy hillocks he saw during his competitive days in Britain. He also moved dirt to form pedestal greens, most noticeably at the 339-yard second and 355-yard sixth holes, where approach shots that are not properly played do not find and hold the putting surfaces.

The Plantation nine was marshy during much of the year until Rees Jones installed a new drainage system in 1992. Jones, an exceptional

Clubhouse and practice green

Main dining room. Photo courtesy The Cloister/Sea Island Golf Club

revisionist, also recontoured greens, repositioned bunkers, and lengthened a few holes to bring them up to date.

Sea Island's second nine, Seaside, was designed in 1929 by H.S. Colt and Charles Alison, a British duo ranked among the foremost architects of the era. Not only did they create one of the finest nine holes of golf in the South, they reworked Travis's Plantation nine as its companion.

Constructed over filled marshland, with several holes drawing near St. Simons Sound, the Seaside nine is fraught with difficulties. Tiny "inverted saucer" greens, gaping pits of sand in the driving zones, and a fiendish breeze that constantly changes velocity and direction do a good job of defending par. So does the ever-present marsh. Seaside is the closest

approximation of a British links in Georgia. It also features two of the best par fours in the nation.

At the 373-yard fourth, the drive must be essayed over a tidal creek that cuts through the salt marsh. There is little room for a bail-out: Three large bunkers snare tee shots that exit the right side of the fairway, forcing players to flirt just a little with the creek, which protects the entire left side of the hole. The fairway doglegs to a green guarded by a pair of enormous traps. Locals claim the swirling breeze off the sound, in view behind the green, adds piquancy to the strokes.

The most talked-about hole at Sea Island is the 414-yard seventh, one of the best strategic holes imaginable. On the tee, golfers must determine how much of White Heron Creek can realistically be carried to reach the fairway. The hole's key ingredient is a yawning fairway bunker that beckons ominously about 240 yards from the tee down the right side of the hole. To avoid this trap, better players must hew to a riskier course closer to the marsh and creek up the left side to set up an open shot to the green. A safer shot to the right, short of the fairway bunker, leaves a longer, blind approach to a green defended by a massive bunker artfully positioned to gather less-than-noble efforts. For anyone bidding for par, the seventh asks for sound judgment and courage. A little luck comes in handy, too. Yet a comfortable bogey can be attained by the prudent high-handicapper who staves off the temptation to flirt with the serpentine creek. The push-pull between success and disaster here is very keen.

Bobby Jones, a Georgian who first played the Plantation–Seaside course in 1930, the year of his immortal Grand Slam, was so impressed by the layout he penned a note to Howard Coffin, the Detroit industrialist who founded the Sea Island complex. The letter hangs in the clubhouse to this day. "Have just finished round on Sea Island course. You should be very proud of your work. Second nine one of the very best nine holes I have ever seen." Jones was referring to Seaside. His score of 67 on the original eighteen stood as a club record for twenty-nine years, until Sam Snead eclipsed it with a 63 in 1958.

Sea Island's core eighteen was supplemented in 1960 by Dick Wilson, who built the Retreat nine, often described as a tighter, woodsier version of the Seaside nine. Swept by constantly shifting winds, the layout is marked by enormous bunkers, giant greens, and a pair of lakes that are very much in play at four holes. The 438-yard ninth is the toughest of the Retreat's long, formidable par fours: water to the left and overhanging trees in the Avenue of Oaks to the right pinch the driving zone, while the approach shot must avoid a necklace of traps that nearly encircle the jumbo green. Pointed like an arrow to the ocean, this hole usually plays into the teeth of the wind.

The shortest, tightest nine at Sea Island is Marshside, a Joe Lee design opened in 1973 that tiptoes through a brackish marsh laced by tidal inlets. Seven of the nine holes play over, through, or alongside an environment that is utterly inhospitable to stray golf balls. Often it's best to tee off with a long iron or 3-wood to thread the ball onto the fairway—anything to avoid donating yet another ball to the bog. Lee, perhaps inspired by the work of Colt and Alison, fashioned a number of risk-reward holes that tempt greedy golfers to bite off more than they can chew. This is especially true at the short par-five second and 349-yard sixth holes, both left-to-right doglegs that dare players to select an angle to the fairway they can live with. Dreamers and underachievers end up in the gook.

A veritable museum of design styles, each of the nines played in any combination presents a scintillating test, though Seaside–Retreat is

reckoned to be the toughest eighteen and is the one used for competitions. Sea Island attracts a dependable corps of caddies year round, readily recognizable in their white coveralls and green caps. Walking is the way to go: Each of the nines is relatively flat and easily covered on foot in two hours. In spring and fall, the best and busiest times of year for golf at Sea Island, walkers, both those accompanied by caddies and those carrying their own bags, nearly outnumber those who choose to ride in golf carts. Sea Island attracts traditionalists.

For those seeking more variety, resort guests have playing privileges at nearby St. Simons Island Club, a well-conditioned Joe Lee–designed layout cut through tall pines and pinched by lagoons.

For those who wish to fine-tune their games, the resort's Golf Learning Center, opened in 1991, features two indoor video studios and five covered hitting stalls for practice in inclement weather. The spacious, rebuilt driving range has five target greens. There's also a pair of short-game practice greens and a full-service club-fitting center on site. If you hear what sounds like a rifle shot on the range, you'll know that Davis Love III, Sea Island's touring pro and a fantastic ball striker, is practicing his irons. Among the staff's teaching pros is Louise Suggs, a founding member of the LPGA and one of the dominant players of her time. She knows how to communicate the sensation of a good swing.

Five miles from the Sea Island Golf Club, which is located, somewhat incongruously, on St. Simons Island, is The Cloister, a bastion of Southern charm that caters to a loyal, conservative-minded clientele drawn mainly from Dixie. Built by Coffin, who wished to entertain his

*Seaside Course, seventh hole. Photo courtesy © Henebry Photography*

friends in high style (among them Calvin Coolidge, Herbert Hoover, Charles Lindbergh, and John D. Rockefeller), The Cloister was designed in 1928 by Addison Mizner, the eccentric architect best known for the design of the Cloister in Boca Raton, Florida.

Mizner kept most of his tricks in the bag here, creating an intimate, Spanish-style hostelry of sixty-one high-ceilinged rooms. While the resort today totals 264 rooms, the majority of them contained in newer guest houses situated along the ocean or near the Black Banks River, the original building, with its red tile roof, peach stucco walls, and antebellum oaks sheltering the grounds, remains the central focus of the resort. Its series of connected dining rooms, each wood-beamed and with stained-glass windows overlooking the gardens or courtyard and fountain, are

*Above: The Avenue of Oaks. Photo courtesy The Cloister/Sea Island Golf Club*

*Right: Plantation Course, seventh hole*

exceptionally inviting, as are the pair of lobbies. Most unusual in this day and age, The Cloister offers a full American Plan—all meals are included in the room rate. Dinner is something special: Low Country shrimp creole, oyster pot pie, and hush puppies are among the specialties of the house. The wine list is not only deep in vintage red Bordeaux, it includes a few Georgia white wines worth sampling. The dessert table is phenomenal—the Georgia peach cobbler is scrumptious, the Southern pecan pie definitive.

More than most resorts, The Cloister adheres to a strict dress code. Gentlemen and boys over twelve are expected to wear a jacket and tie to dinner. In fact, gentlemen are expected to wear a jacket or a long-sleeved sweater with a collared shirt to breakfast and lunch in the main dining rooms. On Wednesday and Saturday evenings, formalwear is encouraged but is optional. There is dancing nightly (except Sundays) to the hotel's Sea Island Orchestra, which plays everything from Jimmy Dorsey to the Beatles.

On Friday nights, an outdoor plantation supper is served at the north end of Sea Island in an oak grove by the sea. Torches and bonfires light the grounds. Seafood, chicken, and hamburgers are grilled by the resort's chefs. Strolling singers entertain diners with songs that were sung by their ancestors on the cotton plantations.

The resort remains devoted to its social guests, many of whom are fourth-generation visitors. Business groups are advised in writing that name badges should be removed upon entering general guest areas of the hotel. (The cookies and milk left for guests in the lobby at bedtime wouldn't be the same with the buzz of commerce in the air.)

Sea Island's natural splendor invites discovery. Situated within a 10,000-acre estate free of commercial development, The Cloister is the only hotel complex on Sea Island. There are five miles of private beach available to guests. A $5-million restoration program in 1991 bolstered the shoreline with two million cubic yards of sand that had been carried away by tidal action. A full-service spa, located next to the Beach Club, offers both fitness programs and "aesthetic services." Romantics can enjoy a horseback ride on the beach or, even better, a moonlight supper ride departing from the resort's stable. There's a cycling center with 300 bikes and a gun club with three skeet ranges. Special programs, from wine-

tasting seminars and bridge festivals to cooking schools and financial planning classes, are scheduled throughout the year. There's even an etiquette class called "Manners Can Be Fun!" for boys and girls ages seven through mid-teen during the summer, designed to produce the ladies and gentlemen of tomorrow.

# MARRIOTT'S GRAND HOTEL & RESORT

SILVER MEDALIST

golf experiences. Holes one through five and sixteen through eighteen, designed by Maxwell, are routed through a forest of towering white pines and giant moss-draped oaks. A spring-fed bayou favored by alligators winds through these holes. They are classic in appearance and demand good shotmaking.

Holes six through fifteen were designed by Ron Garl on rolling land with dramatic elevation changes—and fewer trees. Garl's holes are distinctly modern in appearance: A 450-yard-long waste bunker, arguably the largest sand trap in the nation, separates the ninth and tenth holes, while players at the par-five fourteenth are greeted by the sight of a four-tiered, bulkheaded island green that beckons from the center of a lake.

Situated on the tip of Point Clear, a large peninsula that juts from the eastern shore of Mobile Bay in Alabama, the Grand Hotel's history is emblematic of the Old South. First built in 1847 as a compound of low wooden buildings, the resort was a gathering place for antebellum Southern society. There were separate men's and women's bathing wharves, a popular bar called The Texas, and the Gunnison House, scene of high-stakes card games and other festivities.

A steamboat captain built the first hotel on site to be called The Grand, in 1875. In fact, the heart pine flooring and framing of this hotel were used in the main building of the current Grand. The mint condition of the floors is a tribute to the U.S. Marines, who took over the hotel for a training school during World War II and never permitted

*Putting green. Photo courtesy Marriott Corp.*

shoes to be worn in the main building. Marriott, which acquired the 550-acre property in 1981, has lovingly restored and expanded the resort.

After updating the 308 guest rooms, many of them decorated with white cypress paneling and ceiling fans, the hotel chain directed much of its attention to the Lakewood Golf Club, a private club open to hotel guests.

The club's original eighteen was designed in 1946 by Perry Maxwell, who is best known for his work at Prairie Dunes and Southern Hills. This core layout has since been joined to nine holes built by Joe Lee in 1965 and to a second section laid out by Ron Garl in 1985.

The 6,292-yard Azalea Course (6,770 yards from the tips) is a Jekyll-and-Hyde creation that entices players with two distinct

*Alligator on the Dogwood Course*

In addition to the eye-catching architecture, Garl also reshaped tees, resurfaced fairways, and rebuilt Maxwell's greens. A sizable vein of sand discovered at the base of a cliff near the ninth and tenth holes was mined to underlay both new and pre-existing greens. This strategy assured consistent putting surfaces throughout on the Azalea.

On the slightly shorter Dogwood Course, players commence their rounds on the Joe Lee–designed front nine. Routed near Mobile Bay, which funnels cooling westerly winds in spring and summer, the opening holes are characterized by enormous fairway bunkers, occasional patches of water, and large, well-trapped greens. The 385-yard ninth hole is typical of Lee's handiwork. A slight right-to-left dogleg, there's a lake in play up the left side of the hole and a stream crossing in front of a long, narrow green guarded to the right by a giant bunker.

The Dogwood's par-35 back nine, designed by Maxwell, may well be the best stretch of golf at the resort. It is noteworthy for its tremendous collection of long, tough dogleg par fours, particularly the 11th, 15th, and 16th holes. Each calls for a carefully positioned drive that steers clear of the primordial oaks as well as an accurate approach to a well-protected, medium-size green. The par threes on the Dogwood's incoming nine provide good contrast. The 195-yard thirteenth plays uphill to a minuscule green guarded by deep bunkers, while the 134-yard seventeenth

*A brick terrace*

three-foot Hatteras yacht, is available for day sails, as are smaller craft—skiffs, windsurfers, and paddleboats. Badminton, volleyball, lawn bowling, and putting greens are also popular diversions. For guests with children, the Grand Fun Camp, open during the summer and holiday periods, features supervised activities, movies, and puppet shows for five- to twelve-year-olds.

Fishing is very popular at Marriott's Grand Hotel. Anglers congregate on Pavilion Wharf, a structure that dates to the 1870s. Staff members stand ready to bait hooks, clean the day's catch (mainly redfish, speckled trout, flounder), and carry it to the hotel's chefs, who will cook the fish to order.

The resort's collection of dining rooms is superb. The Grand Dining Room is the height of elegance, its commanding view of Mobile Bay spectacular. Request a bayside table—it's ideal for taking in a lingering sunset. The seafood selections, especially the red snapper stuffed with crabmeat, Bon Secour oysters, and spicy seafood gumbo, are recommended. An orchestra performs nightly for dancing during and after dinner. The Grand's breakfast buffet, one of the best in the South, gets golfers off to a solid start in the morning: baked apples, cherry preserves, blintzes, baking powder biscuits, fresh doughnuts, and grits are among the specialties of the house.

The more intimate Magnolia Room specializes in seven-course gourmet meals and stellar views of the bay, while those seeking an informal meal can dine at the Lakewood Golf Club. Julep Point, a screened verandah located at the tip of Point Clear, is *the* place for moonlight dancing.

The staff, totaling 500 (they outnumber guests 2:1), extend an exceptionally warm welcome to guests. They also go the extra mile. The valet parking staff, instructed to wash the windows of departing guests' cars a few years ago, voluntarily washed out the inside as well. The housekeeping staff rose in minor revolt when Marriott attempted to institute a policy of rotating room cleaning in 1981. The housekeepers insisted on cleaning the same rooms they always had, because the guests who frequented these rooms were "their people."

features a triple-tiered green nearly encircled by sand pits. Lakewood members have a nickname for the hole: "Jaws."

Interested in cooling off after the round? Swimming is available in a 750,000-gallon pool constructed from the hull of a ship (it's reputed to be the world's largest resort swimming pool). There's also a private beach on Mobile Bay. Five miles of trails are routed behind the golf courses, with horseback riding offered from the resort's stables. The *Billfisher*, a fifty-

*Azalea Course, ninth hole*

# THE SOUTH

## TIPS AND SIDE TRIPS

Directly across Mobile Bay from Point Clear and Marriott's Grand Hotel is Bellingrath Gardens, the self-proclaimed azalea capital of the world. The time to visit is spring, when some 250,000 plantings of 200 different species of azalea are in bloom, though flowers are cultivated throughout the year at the 905-acre site. The USS *Alabama*, a mighty World War II battleship anchored in Mobile Bay, can be visited on the drive from Point Clear to Bellingrath Gardens.

Civil War buffs can visit the Confederate Naval Museum in Columbus, thirty miles south of Callaway Gardens. The museum showcases the wreckage of two Confederate gunboats that were sunk in the Chattahoochee River in 1865. In nearby Fort Benning the National Infantry Museum, one of the largest of its kind, displays 30,000 items, including firearms and uniforms dating back to the Revolutionary War.

Five miles from The Cloister is Fort Frederica National Monument, on St. Simons Island. The monument includes the ruins of a fort built by British militia in the 1730s to defend against a Spanish invasion. Around the fort are excavations of the village of Frederica. The National Park Service

Colonial Williamsburg. Photo courtesy © Colonial Williamsburg Foundation

Monticello. Photo courtesy Southern Stock Photos/Everett C. Johnson

Visitor's Center contains artifacts and dioramas depicting life from Indian times through the nineteenth century.

Shelter Cove Harbor, convenient to Palmetto Dunes and Port Royal, is Hilton Head Island's largest deepwater marina. Coastal and Gulf Stream fishing charters are available, as are evening cocktail and dinner cruises. Shops, boutiques, and cafés ring the marina.

A forty-five-minute drive from Kiawah is Charleston, one of the most beautifully preserved Colonial cities in America. The Visitor Information Center can suggest the best carriage, walking, boat, and bus tours of the city. Charleston's

restaurants, many located in vintage antebellum homes, are famous for seafood. She-crab soup flavored with sherry is a local favorite. Boat tours are available from City Marina and Patriot's Point to Fort Sumter National Monument, where the first shots of the Civil War were fired. Charleston's main cultural event is the Spoleto Festival USA, a seventeen-day celebration of the arts held in early summer.

There isn't much to do in Pinehurst except play golf and stroll the lovely village. Golfers with a historical bent may wish to spend a (rainy) afternoon in the Tufts Archives at the Given Memorial Library, to find out how the village and its golf courses came into being; or check out the golfiana in the PGA World Golf Hall of Fame. Also recommended is a driving tour of the area's Thoroughbred horse farms and fox hunting country. Upscale shopping is available three miles from Pinehurst at Midland Crafters, which sells pottery, jewelry, graphics, sculpture, and handicrafts.

A pleasant hour's drive along the Blue Ridge Parkway from Linville and the Eseeola Lodge is Asheville, a gorgeous mountain city. A must-see is the Biltmore Estate, a 250-room chateau built by George Vanderbilt. The grand palace, today a museum with seventeen acres of formal gardens on the vast grounds, is filled with priceless antiques and works of art.

Closer to Linville is Blowing Rock, a popular tourist area; and Boone, where the Tweetsie Railroad theme park is a favorite with young children.

Even committed golfers tear themselves away from the Golden

*The Blue Ridge Parkway. Photo courtesy North Carolina Division of Travel and Tourism*

A short drive north from Wintergreen is Charlottesville, where Monticello, the mountaintop home of Thomas Jefferson, can be visited. Designed over a period of forty years, the house reflects Jefferson's inventive and often playful genius. Also in Charlottesville is the University of Virginia, founded and designed by Jefferson in 1819. The campus, an "academical village" marked by classical pavilions and gardens laced with serpentine walls, has been recognized by the Architects Institute of America and others as one of the finest achievements of architecture in the first 200 years of the nation.

The Homestead and The Greenbrier are both self-contained worlds tucked away in the Allegheny Mountains. There is no compelling reason to leave the sumptuous confines of either resort.

Horseshoe Golf Courses to stroll back in time 200 years at Colonial Williamsburg, its 173 acres of preserved or restored buildings populated by costumed interpreters and craftsmen who bring the eighteenth-century Virginia capital to life. Adjacent to the Colonial village is the College of William and Mary, chartered in 1693 and the alma mater of Thomas Jefferson and James Madison.

Avid shoppers meet their match at the Williamsburg Pottery Factory in nearby Lightfoot, where everything from dried flowers and fine china to casual clothing and power tools is for sale in the giant discount outlet's thirty buildings.

Convenient to Williamsburg and Kingsmill is Busch Gardens, a 360-acre family entertainment park with eight European-style villages and many exciting rides, shows, and attractions.

*Dining hall at the Biltmore Estate. Photo courtesy the Biltmore Estate*

## DON'T LEAVE HOME WITHOUT...
## A RELIABLE CHIP SHOT

*Many golfers consider the Donald Ross–designed No. 2 Course at Pinehurst the best test of chipping in the world. Certainly this course puts a premium on the short game, particularly the chip shot. But getting up and down from off the green is important everywhere you play.*

*On a straightforward run-up chip from the fringe, with no long grass or sand between the ball and the green, the trajectory of the shot should be low, with the ball in the air roughly one-third of the distance to the pin. Assume a narrow, open stance and grip down on the club a few inches for better feel and control. Position the ball back of center, the weight slightly on the forward foot and the hands ahead of the ball. The chipping motion, similar to a pendulumlike putting stroke, is generated by the arms, with very little wrist action.*

*This setup and swing will promote a descending blow and produce a low shot that rolls smartly to the hole with maximum accuracy. A firm stroke, with the back of the left hand leading the shot, helps to prevent scooping and chili-dipping. Trust the club's loft to get the ball airborne.*

*Here's a tip from the Tour pros: Pick a spot on the green where you want the ball to land and then concentrate on hitting that spot with the least lofted* *club possible. The idea is to reduce flight time and increase roll time. Use a more lofted club as you move farther from the green's surface.*

*The ability to chip the ball consistently within "gimme" range of the hole is one of the keys to lower scores.*

RICH WAINWRIGHT, HEAD GOLF PROFESSIONAL, PINEHURST RESORT AND COUNTRY CLUB

Golf is not just another game in Florida. It's a major industry. In fact, it is very likely the largest nonpolluting business in the state. In 1990, the Florida golf industry generated more than $5.5 *billion* in total revenues, or roughly one-fifth of the state's tourism pie. That's a lot of golf balls, room nights, and green fees.

With more than 1,000 golf courses routed up, down, and across the peninsula, Florida must look like one big links from outer space. (If Florida's fairways were stitched together from end to end, they would stretch from Key West to Seattle.) Because more than half of these courses are open to traveling golfers, Florida has more volume than any other golf destination in the world. Moreover, the state's top resorts are well represented by all the leading designers of the modern era, including Robert Trent Jones, Dick Wilson, Pete Dye, Tom Fazio, Jack Nicklaus, and Lawrence Packard. Many of their designs belie the image of a pancake-flat state dotted with palm trees. In fact, a flat runway of grass punctuated by sand and water simply does not qualify as a typical Florida golf course. The state's topography is unusually diverse. From a semitropical barrier island with moss-draped oaks and tidal marshes in the northeast, to the surprisingly hilly and wooded layouts in central and southwest Florida, the state has terrain that would look right at home in the Carolinas.

Florida's mild climate is one of its strongest assets. Indeed, there's nothing quite like escaping the polar chill of a northern winter by booking a flight to Florida—and stepping off a jet plane to face warm sunshine, blue skies, and green fairways. There's a reason more than sixty PGA Tour players choose to live in Florida.

# RIDA

By and large, Florida's venerable resorts are the legacy of bullheaded entrepreneurs with exceptional vision and deep pockets who bucked trends to build their dream properties. Each resort reflects the taste and prejudices of its founder.

Railroad titan Henry Morrison Flagler must be considered Florida's father of tourism for his role in extending the rails from Daytona to Miami, thereby enticing wealthy Northerners to visit in their private railway cars at the turn of the century. It was he who inspired The Breakers in Palm Beach, the *ne plus ultra* of grand resorts.

The Roaring Twenties gave rise to two larger-than-life impresarios, both of whom set out to build blockbuster properties. The original Cloister at the Boca Raton Resort and Club was the grandiose creation of Addison Mizner, a giant of a man and a darling of high society. Circus king John Ringling's dream of constructing the resort equivalent of the "Greatest Show on Earth" on Longboat Key in the Gulf of Mexico was ruined by the Depression. But Ringling surely would approve of the resort that stands there today.

In the modern era, Alfred Kaskel bought land west of Miami that was barely fit for habitation by mosquitos on which to build his dream golf resort. It's called Doral. Don Soffer created Turnberry Isle on a tiny island overgrown with mangroves in North Miami. It soon became a haven for celebrities. Walt Disney wished upon a star and created a Magic Kingdom in the middle of nowhere. Charles Fraser saved Amelia Island from potential destruction (it was slated to be strip mined), developing a resort that remains a model of environmental sensitivity. Finally, the one-of-a-kind TPC Stadium Course at Sawgrass, home of The Players Championship, was the brainchild of Deane Beman. Each of these men believed, and rightly so, that no snowbound Northerner could resist the prospect of fine accommodations, first-class golf, balmy weather, and a great array of off-course attractions.

*Inset and large picture: The Breakers, Palm Beach*

# AMELIA ISLAND PLANTATION

S I L V E R   M E D A L I S T

*A suite. Photo courtesy Amelia Island Plantation,*
*© Paul G. Beswick*

The southernmost and possibly the prettiest of the barrier islands strung along the Atlantic seaboard is Amelia. Located thirty miles northeast of Jacksonville, just below the Georgia state line, Amelia's natural features—tidal lagoons, saltwater marshes, moss-draped oaks—have more in common with the Carolina Low Country than with the palm tree flatlands usually associated with Florida. Discovered in 1562 by the French, it is the only location in the United States to be governed under eight different flags.

Amelia was spared an ignominious fate by Charles Fraser, the far-sighted developer of Sea Pines Plantation on Hilton Head Island, South Carolina. In 1970, Fraser purchased substantial acreage at the southern end of Amelia Island from Union Carbide. (The company had intended to strip-mine the property for titanium and other minerals.) Union Carbide's discovery of better-grade ores elsewhere, as well as Fraser's decision to develop a resort in tune with the environment, is every Florida-bound golfer's gain.

Fraser called in Pete Dye, who had designed Harbour Town Golf Links at Sea Pines three years earlier, to route a golf course among the maritime forests and open marshes stretching to the Intracoastal Waterway. Opened in 1972, long before Dye's current penchant for world-beater stadium courses, the three nines at Amelia Links reflected his (and Fraser's) thinking that golf courses should lie naturally and unobtrusively upon the land. Environmental preservation, not architectural precepts, dictated the design of the course. Several of the tees, for example, are tunneled beneath canopies of live oak. In the words of *GOLF Magazine* contributing editor Stephen Goodwin, "The holes are so tight that even your tee shot feels like a recovery shot." Yet the Links provides a palatable version of target golf readily enjoyed by players willing and able to sacrifice unbridled distance for accuracy.

Oakmarsh, the longest of the three nines (2,978 yards from the white tees, 3,308 yards from the tips), is probably the most solid test of the trio. The short par-four eighth hole, where the second shot must carry a tidal creek to reach the green, calls for pinpoint iron play, while the sturdy 494-yard ninth brings the marsh into play along the entire length of its right side.

For challenge and scenery, Oysterbay is one of the most compelling nine holes of resort golf in the South. The 159-yard seventh is a fine conception that, depending on the strength and direction of the wind, requires a full-blooded carry over the marsh. The eighth is a mere 305 yards from the white tees but a world-class test from the tips at 441 yards. The rear tee is isolated on a slender finger of land raised a few feet above the marsh. This is gator country. From here, golfers must carry their drives nearly 200 yards over an oxbow loop in a tidal creek to reach the fairway. The shored-up green, framed by tall cabbage palms, is well protected by a pair of bunkers. Even professional golfers are happy to walk away with a par.

Oceanside is the shortest and most nautical of the Links trio. If ever there was a predinner nine designed to be played for sheer fun, Oceanside is it.

At the southern tip of Amelia Island, a mile and a half down the road from the main resort complex, architect Tom Fazio was enticed to build Long Point Club. Opened in 1987, the layout's fairways are routed on fingers of raised land within a vast marsh that stretches for miles to thickets of wax myrtles, slash pines, red maples, and other trees able to survive on tiny shoals of land within the swamp. Several of the greens teeter on the brink of the marsh. Seriously offline shots disappear in the gook, but the conservative straight-ahead player isn't overly penalized at Long Point.

The layout, while every bit as pristine as Amelia Links, is a modern big-time championship course that presents a major challenge to the better player from 6,775 yards. The average player, however, is not undone by Long Point from the white tees at 6,068 yards. A surcharge ($15 at press time) is levied to play the course. It is well worth it.

Amelia Island probably attracts more nature-oriented families than gung-ho golfers. The Beach Club, with an Olympic-size pool, children's wading pool, and playground, fronts a four-mile-long, firm-packed white sand beach. For what it's worth, the television show "Lifestyles of the Rich and Famous" has ranked Amelia's beach one of the top ten in the world.

Walker's Landing, centered on an Indian burial mound, offers ideal conditions for crabbing. The Willow Pond Conservancy, a low wetland, is a haven for the island's marsh wildlife (raccoons, blue herons, armadillos),

*Pool and villa*

*Long Point Club, sixteenth hole. Inset: Oysterbay nine, seventh hole*

while the cypress boardwalk at Drummond Point Park extends far into the salt marsh. There is cycling on five miles of paths cut through sunken forests, nature walks on coquina (crushed shell) trails, horseback riding on the beach, and fishing in lagoons for largemouth bass, tarpon, and snook. Serious anglers check in with the Amelia Angler, the resort's charter fishing operation. Fifteen miles offshore, blue marlin, king mackerel, dolphin, wahoo, and other major sport fish can be taken, particularly in the fall. In addition, surf fishing for whiting, bluefish, and sea trout is excellent at the south end of the island.

Kids and Amelia get along famously. Three- to five-year-olds meet from 8:30 A.M. to 1 P.M. daily to dabble in arts and crafts, collect shells, and fish for crabs. (A babysitting service is available for younger children.)

Six- to eight-year-olds, conspicuous in their homemade visors, build sand castles, fly kites, and swim in the ocean (or in one of thirteen pools). Preteens (nine- to twelve-year-olds) often combine learning with fun. Field trips to the Jacksonville Zoo, Fort Clinch State Park, and the Jacksonville Museum of Science and History are scheduled, as are instructional workshops in surfing, volleyball, soccer, and golf.

Activities for thirteen- to eighteen-year-olds are available from 8 P.M. to midnight in the Beach Club. They range from deejay parties and video game tournaments to bonfires on the beach.

A special dinner program, Just For Kids, welcomes all three- to twelve-year-olds to supper at the Coop, a casual restaurant. Movies and games are also planned. The supervised meal gives parents a chance to slip away for a quiet dinner in the Dune Side Club, a lovely candlelit room overlooking the ocean where a pianist tinkles away at '40s standards and jazz classics.

Verandah, a more casual restaurant (the children's menu arrives with a box of crayons), is the place to try grilled marinated shark, shrimp fettuccine, and a thick seafood bisque.

There are few standard hotel rooms at the resort (the Amelia Island Inn contains only twenty-four rooms). The more than 500 units available range from one- to four-bedroom villas with complete kitchen facilities. The units are comfortable, not opulent. They were designed to make families feel at home at the end of a long, active day on one of the most thoughtfully developed—and undeveloped—islands anywhere.

# MARRIOTT AT SAWGRASS

PONTE VEDRA BEACH • GOLD MEDALIST

Sawgrass. Stadium golf. The island green at the seventeenth hole. Mere mention of any of these items ten years ago was enough to send chills up a tour pro's spine. Six million dollars worth of refinements later, the original ego buster is not the grueling test the pros once kicked and screamed about. Nowadays, they leave those histrionics to traveling golfers game enough to play it.

Pete Dye, working under the watchful eye of PGA Tour Commissioner Deane Beman, drained a swamp twenty-five miles southeast of Jacksonville, built a moat around the 415-acre site, and started moving dirt. Lots of it. His Frankenstein-like creation, opened in 1980, featured the starkest examination of golf imaginable. Water *at every single hole*. Vast waste bunkers lining the fairways. Tiny convex greens that rejected perfectly acceptable approach shots, bouncing them like gumdrops into the open mouths of waiting gators. Fairways pinched by water oaks, sweet gums, and pines. Penal holes with no room to bail out. Huge mounds built to serve as spectator bleachers (with grass pews) framing the greens, so that viewers could observe the pros' misery first-hand. Beman said the public wanted to see the pros struggle in the face of adversity. Dye said he wanted to test the pros mentally. The reception among the players to this unkind slice of cutthroat architecture was not warm.

"They messed up a perfectly good swamp," said J.C. Snead. "Do you win a free game if you make a putt on the last hole?" asked John Mahaffey.

No one was happy with the monster.

And so Dye and Beman went back to the drawing board. Wicked contours on the greens were toned down. (It was the steep swales in the putting surfaces that had drawn most of the pros' ire.) Angles of approach were improved. The TPC at Sawgrass today stands as a monument to Dye's remedial enterprise. It is, quite simply, the best-manufactured golf course in the world. After years of outrage and hurt feelings, the Stadium Course today is home to The Players Championship, golf's "fifth major."

Amateur golfers being the fearless creatures they are, this fractured landscape of railroad ties and sandy wastelands receives a tremendous amount of play (more than 65,000 rounds per year) by players curious to see how they measure up to the challenge of target golf at its most extreme. For the majority, it is simply too much golf course to handle. Ironically, tee times can be hard to come by.

*Left: TPC Stadium Course, twelfth hole. Above: Drinks on the terrace. Photo courtesy Marriott Corp.*

The most vilified and notorious hole on the course is, of course, the seventeenth. (It measures 132 yards from the TPC gold tees, 121 yards from the blues, and 97 yards from the white tees.) But yardage doesn't tell the story. A Cyclopean eye of green, smaller by far than it appears on television, beckons from the middle of a lake, the green joined to the fairway by a thin umbilical cord of grass and gravel. It is one of the most naked, unsubtle, in-your-face challenges in golfdom. There is something rude about this hole, for Dye has managed not only to raise the white-knuckle quotient to new heights, he has laid bare every golfer's innermost fear of failure. Miss the green, and you're done. Miss the green again, and you adjourn to a drop area near the ladies' tee about eighty yards from the green. When a breeze sweeps the course, this hole is well-nigh unplayable by the average duffer. Unsurprisingly, more than 200,000 balls are dredged from the lake annually. By the way, taking "an extra club" to get to the green can be as dangerous as coming up short—there's water behind the green, too.

The seventeenth is one of many holes that gives not an inch. There's a risk-reward factor at nearly every hole that draws a fine line between the tantalizing and the intimidating. Bogey here feels like par if you are a decent player, par feels like birdie. From start to finish, far more of a golfer's attention is directed to the hazardous areas (bunkers, water, rough) than to the fairways and greens. Dye's retort: "Everything on the course looks more severe than it is." Still, it's a scary proposition to play the Stadium Course for the first time, not knowing which angles to cut, which part of the green to shoot for, or how to separate appearance from reality. The course does yield a few secrets the second time around. Try to play it twice, if your first round does not leave you debilitated.

The seventeenth gets all the publicity, but the 554-yard ninth hole (all yardages are from the blue tees, which stretch to 6,417 yards; the white tees are only 5,761 yards) is a superb three-shotter, the second shot played over a creek and the third guided to a narrow green walled in by steep mounds. Its brother-in-arms is the 509-yard eleventh, its fairway forked in three directions and its tiered green set above a long waste area. Hit a good drive, and the green can be reached in two shots. Maybe.

Sawgrass has other golf courses far gentler to the ego than the dreaded Stadium Course. The TPC Valley Course, designed by Dye and Jerry Pate, is a flatter spread with superlative greens, though there *is* water in play at every hole. (The gators have to live somewhere.) The original twenty-seven-hole Sawgrass Country Club layout, its East–West configuration the original home of The Players Championship before it moved across Highway A1A to the Stadium Course in 1982, is a spacious, links-style course with an abundance of water, sand, and wind.

Oak Bridge Club, a pleasurable par-70 layout, was completely revamped by Ed Seay in 1982, and gives the average enthusiast a chance to make a few pars on an attractive 6,031-yard layout (6,383 yards from the blues). Resort guests also have limited weekday access to Marsh Landing Country Club, one of the prettiest, most user-friendly layouts in north Florida. Arrange to play it. Unless, of course, you have traveled from the ends of the earth to trace the footsteps of the pros on the Stadium Course.

Set on a hill above the practice ranges, putting greens, and fleets of golf carts is the Marriott at Sawgrass, a symmetrical building of coral-tinted concrete sheathed in emerald-toned glass. Nicely landscaped, with fifteen acres of alligator-filled lagoons encircling the hotel, the Marriott has approximately 550 accommodations. In addition to the 324 rooms and 24 suites in the main facility, 82 rooms and 83 suites (they combine to make two-bedroom suites) are available in the Island Green Villas located near the thirteenth fairway of the Stadium Course. A mile away from the hotel near the resort's beach are the Spinnaker's Reach and Surf Villas, while a handful of TPC Player's Club Villas overlook the tenth fairway of the Stadium Course.

*TPC Stadium Course, seventeenth hole*

*TPC Stadium Course, eighth hole*

Boasting the largest meeting and convention facilities between Atlanta and Orlando, the Marriott bustles with business groups, most of whom convene in Cascades, a rock garden lounge and piano bar set near a waterfall. Seated amongst tropical vegetation, one can readily admire the lobby's seventy-foot atrium and impressive skylight.

The Marriott's top restaurant is the Augustine Room, its walls decorated with hand-tinted etchings and lithographs of St. Augustine, America's oldest city. Strawberry shrimp is the appetizer of choice: the shrimp are dipped and fried in a tempura batter and served in a sauce of fresh strawberries. Veal scaloppine Frangelico garnished with walnuts and hazelnuts, and chicken-wrapped lobster served with saffron mustard buerre blanc, are among the more popular entrées. The desserts in the Augustine Room are exceptional.

Café on the Green, overlooking the thirteenth green of the Stadium Course, is a fine place to start the day with a custom omelette, while the 100th Hole is a poolside retreat designed to mend wounds and ready one for the morrow.

On the site of a former orange grove on the outskirts of Disney's Magic Kingdom in Orlando, Jack Nicklaus has conjured a striking re-creation of his favorite place in golf. His paean to the Old Course at St. Andrews in Scotland is an inspired rendition (not a dull clone) of the humble, crumpled links honored throughout the world as the birthplace of the game.

Nicklaus borrowed liberally from the Old Course's distinctive topographical features to create the New Course. So what if the Swilcan Burn here contains alligators, or that the golf cart paths and rock-and-mortar bridges

*South Course, ninth hole*

have been painted to resemble weathered stone? The nearly treeless site is pockmarked with 145 bunkers, ranging from hidden pots the size of hot tubs to gaping twelve-foot-deep craters with wooden ladders leading to their depths. Completing the fakery are seven double greens (shoot for the yellow flags going out, the white ones coming in); subtle mounds covered with whins and fescue grasses gone to seed; a mirror image of the infamous Road Hole (complete with pebbly road and stone wall behind the green); a Valley of Sin indenting the front of the eighteenth green; and a low white picket fence that wraps behind the home hole. Click your spikes three times on a cool winter's day with a breeze chasing the clouds across a gray sky, and you could be standing in the Kingdom of Fife, not central Florida.

Certainly the first tee does not summon the image of the average Florida resort course. There's the tiny starter's shed, and beside it a closely mowed portion of the tee where golfers can stroke a few last-minute putts. The fairway of the first hole, shared with the eighteenth, seems a mile wide. As at St. Andrews, golfers are tested immediately: The approach shot to the first green must carry a sneaky ribbon of water.

At the short par-five second hole, a nest of bunkers called the Seven Sisters is modeled on the traps at the fifth hole of the Old Course. At the 368-yard fifth, the bunkering on the right side of the fairway is similar to the Principal's Nose and Deacon Sime bunkers found on the sixteenth at St. Andrews. There's a twenty-one bunker salute to players at the 322-yard ninth hole, while the 544-yard fifteenth, much like the great fourteenth at St. Andrews, was designed to undo all the good that has gone before. Here golfers must decide whether to tangle with the Beardies on the drive or to flirt on their approach shots with Hell Bunker, a vast pit every bit as large (but somehow not quite as fearsome and forbidding) as the original. Still, it's no garden spot. Like the original, the green at the fifteenth is guarded by a knoll and slopes, maddeningly, from front to back. The firm, fast-running fairways on the New Course were designed for bump-and-run shots. Golfers have the option to fly their approaches

high, but a low, running shot is often preferable, depending upon wind conditions and pin placement. As at St. Andrews, canted lies in the undulating fairways force players to assume awkward stances, making solid contact more difficult. Yes, the sight of Disney's EPCOT Center buildings on the horizon breaks the heathery spell on the back nine, but overall, Nicklaus has succeeded brilliantly in bringing a bit of the Old Sod to the world's entertainment capital.

A suggestion: Arrange for a caddie. They are available on call through the pro shop. The experience of playing the New Course is enhanced immeasurably by walking it with a caddie. Failing a caddie, arrange for a pull cart or a light carry bag. Walk the course at all costs.

The New Course at Grand Cypress stands in marked contrast to the original twenty-seven-hole layout at the resort, also designed by Nicklaus. The North–South eighteen, opened in 1984, is a stark bit of manufacture—sharply ledged fairways, rows of volcano-shaped mounds shaggy with love grass, and tiny platform greens guarded by sand and water characterize the design. Originally billed as a Scottish prototype links (it is anything but), the North–South tandem is at least three shots harder than the New Course. It is also about half the fun for anyone carrying more than a single-digit handicap. There is plenty of room to drive the ball— Jack allows you that much—but approach shots must be directed with pinpoint accuracy. Otherwise, there's hell to pay around the greens. Bring your 60-degree wedge and a full repertoire of finesse shots to this, Nicklaus's gumdrop manifesto. And read the local rules, which recommend, "in the interest of speed of play," that grassy mounds be played as a lateral hazard. Just drop another if your ball burrows into the thick Bahia grass atop one of the mounds.

Two of the most interesting (and difficult) holes on the layout are the ninth holes of the North and South nines. The fairways of each are separated by a slender lagoon, with a shallow figure-eight-shaped double green accommodating both flags. These two long par fours demand what amounts to a North–South litany: lengthy, accurate drives; well-placed approach shots; and a sure touch on the greens.

The East nine, opened a year later than the original eighteen, is a bit different from the North–South combo. Carved from a forest of pines and oaks, the holes are softer around the edges and strongly reminiscent of an inland course in Georgia or the Carolinas. The East nine's feature hole is the 134-yard fifth, where players must shoot to an island green.

All forty-five holes of golf are served by a stucco-and-glass Mediterranean-style clubhouse with a terra-cotta tile roof. The pro shop has the look and feel of a toney Fifth Avenue boutique. The Grand Cypress staff is exceptionally courteous and helpful. It is they, as much as the distinctive golf courses, that set the resort apart.

Grand Cypress Academy of Golf can make a case as the best practice facility and golf school in the nation. There is a Nicklaus-designed three-hole course (a par three, four, and five) with four tee boxes at each hole and three flag positions on each green. Greenside bunkers, fairway traps, high grass, low grass, mounds for uneven lies—all playing conditions likely to be encountered at Grand Cypress (or anywhere else for that matter) have been reproduced. The enormous practice putting green is contoured at one end for developing touch, level at the other for refining technique. Small wonder that Orlando-based PGA Tour pros, including Payne Stewart, Ian Baker-Finch, and Nick Price, fine-tune their games here.

As for formal instruction, the academy combines biomechanics, computer graphics, and hands-on guidance to teach golf the way the best players in the world play the sport.

Ralph Mann, an Olympic silver medalist hurdler in 1972 and a biomechanics authority, has analyzed the swing patterns of more than fifty top players, including those of Jack Nicklaus, Greg Norman, and Arnold Palmer. From this research, Mann has developed a sophisticated modeling program that portrays the ideal swing. After a computer model is created for individual students based on size, weight, and body type, this ideal swing is then superimposed over the student's actual swing. The learning curve tends to flatten at the moment students grasp how their swing should look, and how it actually looks.

According to Senior PGA Tour player and short-game wizard Phil Rodgers, who conducts a series of three-day clinics at the academy, "You can explain, talk, and demonstrate, but there is nothing quite as effective as showing students on the screen those areas in need of improvement."

The resort's 750-room Hyatt Regency Grand Cypress, a four-sided Maya templelike structure with an eighteen-story atrium, is a sophisticated razzle-dazzle of Asian, European, and American design styles. The ground floor area is particularly attractive. By day, colorful parrots chatter to passersby from their brass rings. At night, a jazz combo performs on a footlit marble island, in a pool of water, landscaped by gardens and tall palms.

A $10-million remodeling program, completed in 1990, gussied up the guest rooms and seventy-two suites in a green color scheme designed to create a residential feeling. Marble baths, improved lighting, and two phones for each room were also added.

For those seeking a virtual home away from home, the resort's forty-eight villas, ranging from club suites to expansive multibedroom villas, are a good choice. The 600-square-foot club suites, comparable in price to a room at the main hotel, include a spacious bedroom with a sunken seating area, luxury bath, and a patio or verandah. The larger villas, spacious and sunny, feature private entryways, fully equipped kitchens, paddle fans in the living room, large picture windows, French doors, and vaulted ceilings. Some units have marble fireplaces and whirlpool baths. All villas are clustered in groups near the fairways and waterways of the North nine. Room service is available in the villas, though the resort's dining spots are worth a visit.

The Hyatt Regency's fanciest restaurant is La Coquina, a formal, candlelit room with shell-themed carpets and chandeliers. The two-story glass-walled dining room overlooks a lake with an attractive white sand beach and an inlet that harbors pink flamingos. The Sunday champagne brunch at La Coquina—guests are led by their waiter into the kitchen, which is decorated to resemble a well-provisioned French market—is tops in Orlando.

Hemingway's is a casual eatery with a Key West motif that specializes in charbroiled steaks, blackened seafood, and potent rum drinks, while the chicken 'n ribs crowd gravitates to the White Horse Saloon, where a bluegrass trio entertains. In Cascade, an informal room serving Italian

*Villa. Photo courtesy Grand Cypress Resort*

specialties, diners are seated near the Mermaid Fountain, a thirty-five-foot-high water sculpture that tinkles soothingly.

Fulfilling its promise as a world-class resort, Grand Cypress has a full complement of amenities. There's a half-acre, free-form swimming pool with a dozen waterfalls cascading into the swimming area and a forty-five-foot waterslide for kids of all ages. An ice cream bar called On the Rocks is located within a cool, dark grotto and can be reached by swimming through a series of caverns. High above the center of the pool, streams course through rock gardens planted with bougainvillea, allamanda, and hibiscus. Tall palms and hot tubs are spaced around the perimeter of the pool. As a place to cool off after a round, this pool is matchless.

*Above: New Course, eighth and tenth holes. Below: South Course, sixth hole*

The resort's equestrian center offers advanced (English saddle) trail rides on the perimeter of the New Course, as well as leisurely trail rides (Western saddle). Pony rides are available to children under twelve. Private, semiprivate, and group lessons are available to riders at all ability levels. For guests arriving with their own mounts, the center maintains a forty-two-stall stable, a covered ring, outdoor jumping ring, regulation dressage ring, exercise track, and a paddock shaded by a canopy of oaks.

For more serious fitness buffs, Grand Cypress has a well-outfitted health club, bicycles for rent, a 1.3-mile exercise trail, and jogging trails of varying lengths. Climbing jasmine vines screen the racquet club's twelve tennis courts, six of them lighted for night play.

Cars are not necessary at Grand Cypress. Four turn-of-the-century, restored Belgian trolleys (leather hand straps, cane seats, oak paneling) circulate the grounds. One of the more popular stops along the way is the forty-five-acre nature preserve and its mile-long elevated boardwalk built into a cypress swamp. An informational brochure and educational signs along the pristine route (the Florida Audubon Society lent a helping hand) familiarize visitors with the ecology of the swamp. Lush and cool on the hottest day, with herons, egrets, and the occasional gator making an appearance, the preserve is as evocative of Florida as the New Course is of Scotland.

Walt Disney World, the forty-three-square-mile entertainment kingdom on the outskirts of Orlando, is the golden pot at the end of every child's rainbow. A glorious and inspired celebration of imagination and technology, Walt Disney World is the best-known and most popular tourist attraction in the world. The whole of this not-so-small world is greater than the sum of its parts, though each of the parts is a major freestanding attraction. The Magic Kingdom, Epcot Center, and Disney-MGM Studios form the core of the theme parks, with Typhoon Lagoon, Pleasure Island, River Country, Discovery Island, Disney Village Marketplace, and the rest joining the party. Stir healthy doses of Americana, phantasmagoria, and cartoon fantasy with a magic wand, sprinkle a little pixie dust on a central Florida swampland, and presto! The ultimate family vacation destination dominates the map. A pair of mouse ears marks the spot.

*Lighthouse and Turtle Crawl pool. Photo courtesy © The Walt Disney Company*

Despite the existence of the well-groomed Magnolia, Palm, and Lake Buena Vista courses, a solid trio that hosts the annual Walt Disney World/Oldsmobile Golf Classic, the resort did not hold the same electric appeal for serious golfers as it did for wide-eyed children until recently. Quick to recognize that golf had established itself as the sport of the 1990s, Disney contacted the two leading architects of the day, Pete Dye and Tom Fazio, both of whom jumped at the chance to design courses near the glow of the Magic Kingdom. According to Dye, the Casey

*The Living Seas–Coral Reef Restaurant. Photo courtesy © The Walt Disney Company*

Stengel of his profession, "When you build at Disney, you know somebody's gonna play golf, and this will be in the limelight." Presented with a large parcel of pristine land, the two designers were asked to choose their sites. Fazio took the high road, opting for the locale with more contour and elevation. Dye, returning to his roots as a minimalist, took the low road. In time, two totally opposite golf courses emerged. The opening in 1992 of Dye's Eagle Pines and Fazio's Osprey Ridge courses launched Walt Disney World into the Tomorrowland of megaresorts.

Located in the northeastern corner of the property a duck hook away from the Fort Wilderness campground, the two layouts share the futuristic Bonnet Creek Golf Club clubhouse, its front lawn spiked with giant spun aluminum golf tees. Inside, the pro shop, located on the top floor, could pass for the cockpit of a space station. From its curved windows can be seen a practice putting green that subtly resembles Mickey Mouse in profile. It's the only hint of frivolity at a place that aims to please the serious campaigner.

Ever the innovator, Pete Dye claims he "emptied the state of Georgia of its pine needles" to spread a thick blanket of pine straw beside several of the dished-out fairways of the Eagle Pines course. The pine needles, suggested by Dye's wife, Alice, are a tip of the hat to Pinehurst, the famous golf complex in North Carolina, though with water in play at sixteen holes, this is very much a Florida golf experience. Dye, who delights in foiling golfers, here tried to help them: It's simply not possible to lose a ball in the rough's brown blanket of pine needles. Also, a golf ball perches nicely on pine straw, assisting recoveries. St. Augustine grass, the vegetal equivalent of steel wool, was planted around the green collars and near the water hazards to slow the progress of wild shots. (A lip on the edge of the lakeside fairways also prevents balls from dribbling into the drink.) Rest assured that plenty of challenge remains on this 6,772-yard layout (6,309 yards from the Crest tees, 5,520 from the Wings tees), much of it found on the liberally contoured greens. To ensure that an imprint of this stark, morning-after-the-forest-fire layout burns in a golfer's memory, Dye designed a pair of round busters at the finish. Both the seventeenth and eighteenth holes are long, tough par fours with water in the crook of their right-to-left doglegs. Pulled or hooked shots meet a watery grave at each.

Where Dye cut and dug, Tom Fazio filled and shaped. Built in a wetlands wilderness, this spectacular course is marked by high, sinuous ridges and thick stands of palmettos, oaks, and slash pines. Fazio, who excels at coaxing golf holes from a landscape and covering his footprints, treats golfers to a nature tour early on. A long, wooden bridge laid through a maritime forest brings players from the second green to the elevated third tee, which commands a fine view of the entire links. Ahead lies one of the prettiest par threes in Florida: A shot of 175 yards is played downhill over a sandy waste area to a large, rolling green guarded to the left by several bunkers. It's not a tee golfers rush to leave.

As if to compete with the resort's overwhelming array of attractions, Fazio crammed as much variety into Osprey Ridge as he could. There are open, linkslike holes framed by waste bunkers, fairways tunneled into thickets of vegetation, and greens carved from the flanks of a meandering ridge. The high mounding and natural framing of the Fazio course is in marked contrast to the low-profile Dye design, where the fairways are built on the same level as (or lower than) the surrounding land. Osprey Ridge is a "looks hard, plays easy" course, with all hazards placed parallel to the line of play (Fazio believes that forced carries over hazards are too daunting for the average resort golfer).

A circulating design with no return to the clubhouse after the ninth hole, Osprey Ridge comes into its own on the back nine. The 501-yard twelfth, completely lined with dense greenery, occupies the best natural site on the course, though the final three holes are the show-stoppers. The par-five sixteenth, a sweeping right-to-left dogleg with a pulpit green sited beyond a lake, is a gambler's delight, though the penalty for missing the green, its pedestal undercut by deep bunkers, is sure perfidy. At the do-or-die, 196-yard seventeenth (yardages are from the Wings tees at 6,103 yards—the two back tees are too much golf for the average duffer), a lake skirts the left side of the hole, the rolling green shored up by rocks and the bailout area staked out by pot bunkers. The 403-yard eighteenth, narrowed by water to the right and mounds to the left, is pinched by large traps in the driving zone. The long, slim green is tucked into a spectator ridge within sight of the UFO-style clubhouse.

Since their debut, Eagle Pines and Osprey Ridge have tended to overshadow Disney's original Palm and Magnolia layouts, though each of these Joe Lee–designed tracks, opened in 1971, presents a strong, satisfying test of golf. The Magnolia, Disney's longest course (7,190 yards from the tips), is a wide-open, free-swingers' delight, its generous fairways lined by moss-draped oak and cypress trees. However, the broad landing areas and giant greens are counterbalanced by ten water holes and a preponderance of sand. (There are fourteen bunkers on the par-five fourth hole, though the most distinctive trap, in the shape of Mickey's ears, is found beside the green at the sixth hole.)

*Aerial view, Grand Floridian Beach Resort. Photo courtesy © The Walt Disney Company*

*Osprey Ridge Course, third hole. Used by permission from The Walt Disney Company*

The Palm is Disney's sleeper layout. It's also a good course for a safari—deer, bobcat, fox, otter, alligator, armadillo, and wild turkey have all been spotted on occasion. But this is no place for distractions—precise shotmaking is required to find the Palm's narrow fairways and avoid its nine water hazards. The toughest hole on the course? The 439-yard eighteenth, which calls for a long, straight drive to reduce the threat of a canal that crosses the fairway in front of the green. The soundest strategy after a less-than-perfect drive is to lay up short of the water on the second shot and play the hole as a par five.

At the Lake Buena Vista course, the nines were reversed and six of the layout's holes were realigned in 1991 to accommodate the Disney Vacation Club, a Key West–themed timeshare housing project. The changes, made by original designer Joe Lee, have resulted in a tight, sporty layout that is testing but not overbearing. For example, multilevel tee boxes and a new island green at the par-three sixteenth (formerly the seventh) have strengthened the hole considerably, though the target here is no lonely speck of green in the middle of a lake, like the seventeenth at the TPC at Sawgrass. Not only is the green king-size, its wide band of light rough collars stray shots.

Mindful that not every visitor wants to go up against a full-fledged course, Disney converted its one-time Wee Links into Oak Trail, an enjoyable nine-hole layout tucked on a forty-acre parcel within the Magnolia course. Positioned as a family-play course, Oak Trail, stretching to 2,913 yards, serves up genuine challenges, particularly on its small, undulating greens. The 517-yard fifth, a double dogleg, and the 489-yard seventh, the right side of its fairway indented by a lake, are two of the best holes on the course. Oak Trail welcomes walkers.

Golf at Walt Disney World is available at three price points. Eagle Pines and Osprey Ridge are at the top; the Magnolia, Palm, and Lake Buena Vista courses occupy the second tier; and Oak Trail is the least expensive. A same-day second round is half-price.

With over twelve lodging options and more than 11,000 rooms, Walt Disney World offers a mind-boggling array of accommodations. At the high end is the Grand Floridian Beach Resort, a large, white neo-Victorian hotel with red gabled roofs and three giant stained-glass domes in its cathedral-like lobby ceiling. Patterned after the fabled Florida beach resorts of yesteryear, the Grand Floridian exhibits signature Victorian trademarks (towers, turrets, dormers, cupolas) in a contemporary vein. Dining choices range from Victoria & Albert's, an intimate, candlelit gourmet dining room where all the waiters and waitresses are named Albert and Victoria; to Narcoossee's, an octagon-shaped room with a show kitchen where fresh seafood, yards of beer, and the "Seven Seas Seven Scoop ice cream spectacular" are featured.

Another example of Disney's "entertainment architecture" is found at the Yacht and Beach Club Resorts, where noted architect Robert A.M. Stern used the grand summer homes and clubs of Martha's Vineyard and Nantucket as his inspiration. The 635-room Yacht Club, done in oyster-gray clapboard and nautical furnishings, features oak floors, antique chandeliers, and a staff decked out in navy blue blazers. The 580-room, pale blue-and-white Beach Club is more casual—lots of white wicker furniture, French limestone floors, and a mermaid-theme restaurant, Ariel's, that serves excellent mesquite-grilled seafood a stone's throw from Stormalong Bay.

Port Orleans, its ornate row houses decorated with wrought-iron railings, is an attractive, sanitized version of New Orleans' French Quarter. The sounds of Dixieland jazz reverberate in its cobblestone courtyards around the clock. Rooms at Port Orleans are moderately priced (under $100 per night). Dixie Landings, a 2,048-room sister property opened in 1992, features stately plantation-style mansions and rustic bayou dwellings designed to conjure the romance of the Old South. The focal point of the complex is 'Ol Man Island, a 3.5-acre recreation site with playgrounds, pools, and a fishing hole.

Even the most fanatical of golfers would be hard-pressed to resist Walt Disney World's incredible attractions. Parents traveling with children have no choice—the Magic Kingdom, anchored by the soaring towers of Cinderella Castle, is a must. Fly with Peter Pan, set sail with the wild and crazy Pirates of the Caribbean, ride a runaway train through an avalanche and under a waterfall, and blast out of this world at Space

Mountain. Extra-special is SpectroMagic, an electric parade of whirling floats piloted by Disney characters down Main Street, U.S.A. each evening.

Epcot (Experimental Prototype Community of Tomorrow) like the Magic Kingdom, overflows with diversions and amusements, some educational, others culinary, all entertaining. Epcot is divided into Future World and World Showcase. At Future World's Journey into Imagination pavilion is "Honey, I Shrunk the Audience," a dazzling 3-D movie. At Wonders of Life, its entrance marked by a giant steel DNA molecule, "The Making of Me" explores the wonderful and mysterious process of pregnancy and birth, with awesome footage of a developing fetus.

World Showcase at Epcot, a celebration of the cultures and people of the world community, highlights the cuisine, entertainment, and merchandise of eleven countries. Each "nation" is a pastiche of recognizable architecture populated by citizens in native dress. Among the charming lanes of France is Bistro de Paris, a bustling, upstairs eatery with a menu fashioned by France's top culinary superstars. The food presentation, service, wine list—all are authentically French. At night, IllumiNations, a spectacular display of fireworks, lasers, and twinkling lights set to a symphony of classical favorites, roars to life in the center of the World Showcase Lagoon.

Exceeding all expectations as a major draw has been the Disney–MGM Studios, a re-creation of a Hollywood movie lot circa 1930. A must-see attraction is Jim Henson's Muppet*Vision 3D, a thirteen-minute film shown in a replica of an old-time opera house complete with plush red velvet drapes and gilded columns topped with Muppet statuary. Though Kermit the Frog initially remarks that "at no time will we be stooping to cheap 3-D tricks," that promise is soon broken. Before the theater is shattered in a grand finale, guests experience squirting boutonnieres, bubble showers, high winds, musket fire, and cannon blasts.

More entertainment? There's Pleasure Island, a complex of nightclubs, live outdoor shows, restaurants, and shops for the eighteen-and-over adult set. Admission to the street party and all nightclubs is included in one admission price. Visitors should dress festively—every night is New Year's Eve on Pleasure Island!

There is more to see and do at Walt Disney World than any visitor, no matter how energetic, could possibly hope to experience in a week. Impressive? Very. Is a visit required of every parent with kids? Absolutely. Should you pack your golf clubs? Most certainly. Even Goofy, avid golfer that he is, has to juggle his schedule to play all ninety-nine holes at Walt Disney World in a week.

*Eagle Pines Course, third hole. Used by permission from The Walt Disney Company*

# BAY HILL
# CLUB &
# LODGE

SILVER MEDALIST

Legend has it that Bay Hill in Orlando coughed up a 66 to Arnold Palmer the first time he played it in an exhibition match with Jack Nicklaus in 1965. Smitten, the King spent the next few years vigorously pursuing the club's lease before finally making Bay Hill his own in 1976. It remains one of Arnie's homes away from home in the winter season.

A Dick Wilson layout dating to 1961, Bay Hill was designed for the Arnold Palmers of the world. Narrow, undulating fairways ask for long, straight drives; sickle-shaped doglegs pivot around evergreens, orange trees, bunkers, and water hazards on surprisingly hilly terrain; and the well-defended putting surfaces are probably the slickest Bermuda grass greens in the state. If you can't break 85 from the back tees of your home course, skip Bay Hill. This is a rugged, demanding test of golf without a single chink in its armor. It is fair, without a hint of caprice in the design, but very intolerant of lackluster play. This is a place for Golf, not just

*Seventeenth hole*

golf. Consider, too, that caddies, that dying breed, are available for hire. *Real* caddies from prestigious northern clubs who winter in Florida, not just bag toters.

Dick Tiddy, Bay Hill's director of golf and Palmer's former college roommate, ranks the layout's par threes among the best quartets of one-shotters to be found anywhere. Each is a formidable challenge requiring a long iron or fairway wood. (The average player would need a driver to get home at the resort's par threes from the 7,114-yard Palmer tees.) These holes exhibit good balance: The 189-yard second hole plays downhill to a well-bunkered green, while the seventh and fourteenth holes play slightly

uphill, with only the topmost portion of the flagstick visible. Take an extra club at these two.

Bay Hill's most feared par three is the 182-yard seventeenth (219 yards from the championship markers), which calls for a nerveless carry over water to a two-tiered green. It has ruined many a fine round in the making. With the wind against and the pin cut close to the pond, it may be the most difficult one-shotter in Florida.

The eighteenth hole at Bay Hill was an unassuming par five before Palmer got his hands on it. The hole today, a 414-yard par four (441 yards

*Fourteenth hole*

from the tips), is a true heartbreaker. Just ask the pros—when a cold wind blows down from the north during the annual invitational tournament held at Bay Hill each spring, the eighteenth is next to impossible for even the best players in the world. (It averaged 4.559 strokes per round in the windswept 1989 tournament, placing it atop the list of the hardest holes on the PGA Tour that year.)

The approach shot at the home hole (assuming you have bombed a long drive) must carry a lake, a.k.a. "The Devil's Bathtub," that indents the bilevel green. Incoming shots must also avoid a trio of large, cavernous bunkers cut into a hill on the left side of the green. It is an amateur's nightmare. However, its difficulty might be lost on tour pro Robert Gamez, who holed a 176-yard 7-iron for an eagle 2 at the eighteenth to win the 1990 Nestlé Invitational by one stroke from Greg Norman. Television tournament courses tend to draw golfers like moths to a flame, though Bay Hill remains a no-baloney layout intended to test low-handicappers to the fullest. It is they who can appreciate a course that raised Palmer's eyebrows (and won his affection) the first time he played it.

In addition to the original eighteen, a third, more relaxing nine, called the Charger, is available. Superbly conditioned, as is the main course, this nine features wider fairways, larger greens, and less severe bunkering than the big track. Only 3,090 yards from the tips, the Charger nine can play tricky when the wind blows. But the skills required to master it differ as

*Second hole*

markedly as day and night from those required to post a decent score at Bay Hill's championship test.

Admittedly, the rustic stone-and-wood lodge at Bay Hill, while cozy, is hardly extravagant. It fits Arnie's image of what a comfortable place in the sun should look and feel like circa 1976, though guest rooms were refurbished in the late 1980s. They are now quite stylish and comfortable. The food is good, not great, and except for a few gin rummy games in the

grill, the place is dead quiet at night. But then, exceptional meals and strobe-lit clubs are far more common than championship layouts open to outside play. If you are a better-than-average golfer and a Palmer fan—black-and-white photographs of the great pro from Latrobe punching the air, hitching up his trousers, and agonizing over a missed putt decorate the grill—then Bay Hill is for you.

# GRENELEFE GOLF & TENNIS RESORT

Not only has Disney World strapped a pair of Mickey Mouse ears to the Sunshine State, turning central Florida into the world's entertainment kingdom, it has spurred resort development among the horse farms and citrus groves outside Orlando.

Grenelefe, a 1,000-acre spread located a half-hour's drive south of Cinderella's Castle, is one of the better golf resorts to have opened in the post–Disney era. Located near the sleepy agricultural community of Haines City, the resort is part of a self-contained community with its own post office, fire department, service station, and florist shop. It is also home to three golf courses, each with a different personality.

The showstopper at Grenelefe is Grenelefe West, a big-time championship layout that shatters the popular misconception that Florida courses are flat, featureless runways made difficult by the addition of sand and water. With its rolling fairways bordered by tall slash pines, the terrain is reminiscent of the North Carolina interior. Water comes into play on only three holes, while fairway bunkering is minimal. The West relies on prodigious length (a staggering 7,325 yards from the tips) and small, elevated greens to defend itself. Even from the white tees at 6,199 yards, and more especially from the light green tees at 6,898 yards, it is a formidable challenge.

While long, straight driving is imperative to good scoring, the West is primarily a second-shot golf course. High, accurate approaches are called for, though the size of the green tends to match the difficulty of the shot played to it. Regardless of size, greens throughout have narrow entrances pinched by yawning bunkers.

There are no weak holes on the West, nor does the course try to befuddle players with sneaky water, blind shots, or other sleight-of-hand tricks. Designed by Robert Trent Jones Sr. and completed in 1966 by Dave Wallace, the West is a straightforward, fire-breathing test of golf that ranks among the top courses in the state. (It is a favorite of limber-backed youths capable of launching high 1-irons.) The layout's popularity is no minor accomplishment, given the fact that Florida has nearly as many golf courses as orange trees.

If you play golf to relax and unwind, save your strokes for the East Course, an ideal test for the average player. Designed by Ed Seay and opened in 1978, the East, shorter and tighter than the West, asks for thoughtful shotmaking, not lengthy drives. The greens are not much bigger than a jumbo pizza, but most are at fairway level and accept runup shots. At several holes, golfers must contend with signature trees that were left to grow in the middle of the fairway, but for the most part the East was designed to entertain, not overwhelm. Grenelefe regulars claim that the 156-yard thirteenth hole, where the tee shot must cross a lake to find an elevated, two-tier green, is the best par three at the resort.

For nonpurists who don't shy away from the occasional gimmick, the first hole of the East can be played from an Astroturf-on-concrete abutment located on the second floor of the Resort Center a few steps from the pro shop. Although used primarily for exhibitions or dares, this stagelike tee, thirty feet above the fairway, can make for some hilarious opening salvos.

Grenelefe's South Course, opened in 1983, was intended to split the difference between the sporty East and awesome West. Designed by Ron Garl, with input from Andy Bean, the South is that rarity among resort layouts: a fun but eminently challenging course with staggered tees providing a sliding scale of difficulty. (Yardage ranges from 6,869 yards from the dark green tees to 5,174 yards from the front markers.)

Certainly the South brings together the classic ingredients of a great Florida course: large, undulating greens, traps of Saharan proportions, and lots of water. The layout opens with a straightaway par four (it is a former airstrip) guarded down its left side by a row of Oakmont-style church pew bunkers. Thereafter, the layout disappears into a subtropical forest. Lollipop pines, laurel oaks, and bay trees backdrop several of the greens. The South is Grenelefe's genuine Floridian.

The variety of holes, including doglegs that pivot around any combination of sand, water, and trees, is uncommonly good. Moreover, nearly every hole affords golfers the opportunity to chart a wide, safe route clear of trouble or plan a bolder route with a bigger payoff. Of particular note are the option-laden par fives. At the 475-yard fourth hole, golfers can steer clear of a gargantuan bunker that runs up the right side of the fairway (it is fully 200 yards long) or attempt to carry it, cutting the distance of the hole considerably. The 490-yard eighth hole is double trouble, for water must be carried on the drive and again on the approach shot.

All three courses at Grenelefe are impeccably maintained. As a result of a recent beautification program, azaleas, daisies, and flowering shrubs have been planted at various spots on the layouts, usually in places where golfers need a quick diversion from their travails.

For those seeking help with their games, the Howie Barrow Golf School offers a year-round program of four- and five-day classes. The resort is known to attract top instructors: Barrow's predecessor was David Leadbetter, who retooled Nick Faldo's swing.

There are no hotel rooms per se at Grenelefe. Guests are quartered in spacious one- or two-bedroom fairway villas. New color schemes in the rooms—lime and mahogany, strawberry and cedar, or mauve and almond—are a welcome departure from the Sunbelt pastels often found at Florida resorts. New carpets, draperies, and wall coverings, as well as tiled entryways and dome lighting in the fully equipped kitchens, are some of the recent refurbishments.

Grenelefe is not just about golf. Of the twenty tennis courts, eleven are lighted for night play. There are four swimming pools on the premises, plus a miniature golf course, rental bicycles, and miles of nature trails ideal for early morning jogging or a sunset stroll. Guided fishing excursions from

Swimming pool

a full-service marina on Lake Marion are worth joining, especially if the prospect of angling for speckled perch or largemouth bass appeals.

The names of the resort's restaurants and lounges—Camelot, Lancelot's, the Forest Pub, etc.—are a tip-off that the resort's original developers were quite enamored of King Arthur and Robin Hood. (Little John went under cover as Reynald Grenelefe to enter the Sheriff of Nottingham's service. By some inverted logic, Grenelefe is symbolic of Sherwood Forest. The West Course was first known as Arrowhead because the merry men were expert archers. It is pure coincidence that Lake Marion is close in name to Robin Hood's sweetheart, Maid Marian, though the lake *is* shaped like a chess knight.)

Grenelefe's top dining room is the Grene Heron, its interior a tasteful amalgam of rattan chairs, Audubon prints, and mirrored copper. Oysters Rockefeller, rack of lamb glazed with mustard and honey, and pork chops stuffed with bread crumbs, applesauce, raisins, and nuts are among the top selections.

Grenelefe West Course, second hole

# THE BREAKERS

*Courtyard*

The Breakers in Palm Beach is not a resort hotel in the usual sense. It's a stage set for high society, a seaside palace that reminds one and all of the fantasies available to those for whom money was no object.

The Breakers started as an inn built in 1895 by railroad magnate Henry Morrison Flagler, who not only invented Florida tourism but co-founded the Standard Oil Company with John D. Rockefeller. Destroyed by fire in 1903, the inn was soon replaced by a finer, more commodious structure and renamed The Breakers. In 1925, twelve years after Flagler's death, this second hotel burned to the ground.

The current white stucco edifice was erected in eleven-and-one-half months at a cost of more than $6 million under the aegis of William Rand Kenan, Jr., a cousin of the current owners. (The property is one of the few privately owned resorts of its class still extant and is described in the National Register of Historic Places as "culturally significant in its reflection of twentieth-century grandeur.") The architect of the hotel was Leonard Schultze, well known for his design of the Waldorf-Astoria hotel in New York. Schultze declared the oceanfront site so magnificent that it was worthy of nothing less than an Italian palace. Inside and out, The Breakers represents the most glorious architectural pillaging of Italian Renaissance design ever undertaken in America. The hotel's exterior, with its twin belvedere towers and graceful arches, calls to mind the

palatial Villa Medici in Rome. The impressive fountain in front of the hotel, its basin embraced by cherubs that are spotlit at night, is modeled after one found in the Boboli Gardens in Florence. Nearby, an Italianate courtyard called "Wheelchair Row" once sheltered aging tycoons from the Florida sun. The courtyard today, set with Ping-Pong tables, is popular with children who play hide-and-seek among the long rows of columns.

Inside, The Breakers is a time machine that whisks guests back to the Renaissance. Priceless fifteenth-century Flemish tapestries grace the walls. Colorful frescoes of fish, flora, and nudes created by a small army of Italian artisans decorate the lobby's vaulted ceiling. Enormous windows open to an interior courtyard garden of fountains and flowers inspired by the inner gardens of the Villa Sante in Rome. Travertine walls, marble floors, bronze-and-crystal Venetian chandeliers, specially woven rugs—the public rooms are in a class of their own. They are also brighter and more cheerful now than when puffy-chested scions of American industry paraded through the halls in starched formal wear. The heavy curtains that once covered the lobby's windows have been replaced by Venetian lace sheers tied back to admit light. Other improvements in the wake of a five-year, $50-million improvement program completed in 1991 (another $40 million will be spent on the hotel and its facilities through 1996) have removed all traces of dowdiness. The clientele is today younger, more down to earth. Guests no longer arrive in private railway cars with a truckload of steamer trunks and a full staff of servants.

Any final notion that The Breakers is just another fancy resort that survived the Jazz Age intact is dispelled by the dining rooms. In the skylit Circle Dining Room, scenes of Italian cities and Monte Carlo are lighted by a vast Venetian chandelier of bronze, mirrors, and crystals suspended from a circular skylight in the center of the room. It is an extraordinary room at any hour, most especially at breakfast time, when sunlight floods the chamber.

The beamed ceiling in the cavernous Florentine Room, copied from a Florentine palace, is perhaps the most impressive in the hotel. Between the ceiling, the wine list (over 500 vintages and more than 100,000 bottles in the cellar), the resident dance band's swinging tunes, and the diverting staircase that leads to an upstairs hideaway patronized during Prohibition, it's easy to overlook the fine continental cuisine. Meals in these two rooms are matched only by the Sunday champagne brunch in the Beach Club, where a harpist circulates among tables that are spaced around a room with a full view of the Atlantic Ocean. The brunch buffet spread is sybaritic: homemade pastries stacked on silver platters, raw shellfish and smoked salmon set beside ice sculptures of swans, glazed loaves of pâtés, charcuterie, and fish en croûte spread below maritime-themed tallow carvings . . . the list of delectables goes on and on. It's hard to save room for dessert, but the key lime pie is a must.

Thanks to the recent refurbishment, the hotel's 528 rooms and forty suites have been modernized. Bathrooms in most rooms remain small, but the views of the ocean and interior gardens from the bedrooms more than compensate. Interior designer Carleton Varney, who redecorated the White House for Jimmy Carter, has refurbished the lobby and loggias with new furniture, fabrics, and carpeting. The ceilings, probably the most outstanding architectural feature of the hotel, have been restored to their original splendor after years of harmful exposure to humidity. The hotel's updated arcade of shops, including a barber shop, florist, and drugstore with an old-fashioned soda fountain, were originally designed for the convenience of guests who arrived for "the season" and considered the hotel a home away from home.

Despite Flagler's characterization of golf as a passing fad, in 1897 he agreed to build a modest course with dirt greens. It is Florida's oldest eighteen-hole layout. Donald Ross stopped by in the 1920s to rework what is now called the Ocean Course to its current status as a pleasant 5,956-yard, par-70 layout. It is not quite as easy to score as it looks, especially when a breeze sweeps in off the sea. The flattish course, always within sight of the hotel's impressive facade, is landscaped in palmettos, Australian pines, and tall hedges. Populating these trees and hedges are hundreds of colorful Brazilian parrots. (The flock began as a few feral birds that interbred and flourished.) The parrots have been known to make humorous commentary about a game they've been observing for years—and seem to understand all too well.

The resort's "cottages," once occupied by Rockefellers, Astors, Morgans, Hearsts, and Carnegies, can be seen at the perimeter of the course. So can Bethesda-by-the-Sea Church, a stone house of worship that looks as if it might have been airlifted from Canterbury in England. Golfers must stroll across A1A, a major thoroughfare that bisects Palm Beach, four times during their rounds, thereby holding up for the moment the daily procession of Bentleys and Bavarian sedans through town.

A few tips for the uninitiated. The firm, slightly elevated greens of the Ocean Course do not hold—aim for the front of the green and bounce the ball to the pin. Appearances to the contrary, all putts break away from the ocean. Lastly, arrange for one of the handful of caddies who still loops at The Breakers. (Ask for Chuck Shobe, who in another life was Sonny Liston's sparring partner.) Gently testing, never overbearing, the Ocean Course is an ideal course for mixed foursomes. Ultraconvenient—the first tee is a two-minute walk from the hotel's doorstep—the layout can be played in four hours or less.

Ten miles west of the resort is Breakers West, a sister development with a more serious golf course. Designed by Willard Byrd in 1970 and recently updated by Joe Lee, Breakers West is a solid test from the white tees at 6,335 yards—and an absolute bear from the tips at 7,028 yards. Driving areas are wide, though thick rough and stands of oaks, pines, and cabbage palms border many of the fairways. Large beds of begonias, snapdragons, and impatiens beautify the layout, which serves as the centerpiece for a residential community. Greens are true and, in the winter months, quite speedy.

Perhaps the best reason to visit Breakers West is the opportunity to reenter the long, stately drive that leads to the porte-cochere of the most fabulous seaside resort hotel in America. There aren't many playgrounds of the superwealthy that have ushered themselves into the '90s with the grace and élan of this Palm Beach landmark. For palmy days and champagne nights, The Breakers is unsurpassed.

*The hotel and Ocean Course, eighteenth hole*

# PGA National Resort & Spa

Want to know where the pro at your local club goes for his midwinter fix of golf? Why, to PGA National in Palm Beach Gardens, the headquarters of the Professional Golfers Association (PGA) of America. Good value isn't the only reason the nation's pros flock to this 2,340-acre resort on PGA Boulevard at the northern tip of Palm Beach County. (PGA members receive a discount on green fees at the resort's five golf courses.) They patronize PGA National to stroll the aisles of a pro shop that resembles a small department store; hone their games at the extensive practice facilities (three driving ranges, four putting greens); and eavesdrop on videotape sessions at the resort's Jack Nicklaus–Jim Flick Golf School. But golf is work *and* play for these fellows. They need a release and usually find it at the luxurious spa with its six outdoor therapy pools, the twenty-six-acre lake with the only freshwater beach in the county, the 240-acre nature preserve (ideal for meditative walks after a discouraging round), and, in the unlikely event that golf begins to pall, the largest croquet complex in the Western Hemisphere.

But it's highly doubtful that committed golfers, pros and amateurs alike, spend too much time away from the golf courses at PGA National, especially in light of the $1.7-million makeover of the Champion Course by Jack Nicklaus in 1989–90. The original Champion had a checkered reputation as a grueling test of golf, even among the best players in the world. Site of the 1983 Ryder Cup Matches as well as the 1987 PGA Championship, the layout's convex fairways, blind water hazards, and superabundant sand traps endeared themselves to no one. So a call was placed to Nicklaus, who resides a few miles from the resort. Jack accepted the offer to remodel the course.

While retaining the original routing, Nicklaus completely revamped four holes, all for the better. The course was redesigned specifically to host the PGA Seniors Championship, which is played each spring from the gold tees at 6,742 yards. If that's your distance, this is your course. The Champion, once feared by pros and duffers alike, now offers a firm but fair challenge to discerning golfers. Aesthetically, it is one of the more attractive golf courses in southern Florida.

PGA National's other four layouts fit perfectly the description, "resort golf course." By definition, all are less rigorous than the Champion, though each has enough water and sand in play to keep players alert.

The Haig, named in honor of the legendary Walter Hagen, can play long and tight from the tips at 6,806 yards but is quite agreeable from the white tees at 6,352 yards. Fairways are tree-lined and greens are of the postage-stamp variety on this George and Tom Fazio–designed layout, the first to open at the resort. Rose bushes serve as 150-yard markers on the Haig, a reminder to harried golfers of Hagen's famous adage: "We're only here for a short visit. Don't hurry, don't worry, and be sure to smell the flowers along the way."

The Squire, nickname of mighty-mite Gene Sarazen, has been described as a thinking man's golf course. Shortest of the resort's layouts—it is a mere 6,025 yards from the white tees—the Squire demands precise shotmaking, not prodigious hitting. The Squire's par threes, all with water in play, are especially good. Unfortunately, most of the holes are routed through the backyards of homes within the extensive residential development at PGA National.

The General, named for Arnold Palmer, who for years led an army drawn to his go-for-broke style of play, is a links-style course defined by gentle moguls and swales. Wind is a factor over the open fairways of this Ed Seay–designed layout. So is water; it's in play at nearly every hole. Two of the par fives (the eighth and eighteenth) have water up both sides of the fairway and are especially challenging.

The Estate Course, located six miles west of the main resort complex, is a Karl Litten design acquired by PGA National in 1988. An open layout defined in places by tall pines and subtropical foliage, it calls for forced carries over water at several holes. (A wallop of 150 yards is required to carry the pond at the very first hole!) The Estate conjures an image of Florida long before it became the nation's fourth most populous state. Ibis, blue herons, and sand hill cranes, the last-named an endangered species, populate the lakes. So do alligators and otters. There's another plus: The residential community originally planned for the site was never built, so

*Left: General Course, eighteenth hole.*
*Photo courtesy © Creative Resources, Inc.*

*Above right: Champion Course, seventh hole*

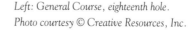

golfers play in relative tranquility far from the reminders of civilization.

Progressive in its thinking, PGA National has devised a rotation policy that keeps its golf factory running smoothly. Each day, one of the five courses is reserved exclusively for play by local members, with the remainder left open to hotel guests. It's a win-win situation: Members don't get stuck behind slowpoke golfers struggling with their games on unfamiliar terrain, and guests never feel as if speedy locals are breathing down their necks.

Accommodations at PGA National number 335 rooms (including fifty-seven suites) in the main hotel, plus ninety two-bedroom cottage suites with kitchen facilities. A major renovation program in the late 1980s restyled the guest rooms and public areas in the image of a tropical getaway, a welcome departure from its previous incarnation as a staid country club. The focal point of the refurbishment was the application of tile: French terra-cotta tile in the lobby, Mexican terra-cotta tile in the ground floor guest rooms, pink Italian tile on the verandah, and hand-painted ceramic tile framing the endless salad bar in Colonel Bogey's, the resort's casual restaurant. The hotel lobby is unusually attractive: the French tile peeks out from under hand-loomed rugs, while tall bamboo trees in terra-cotta pots create a forest effect. Large, mural-like paintings decorate the walls. At the cocktail hour, guests gather round the lobby's stylish piano bar.

Believe it or not, marinated roulade of lion, from Kenya, was once a featured dish in the Explorers dining room. Currently, the Explorers' exotic fare is drawn from the vegetable kingdom: Michigan cave-grown baby white asparagus, barely two inches long, is a typical appetizer. The room itself, cozy and low-lit, has an artist's rendering of the Milky Way on the ceiling, a large crystal globe in the center of the floor, and an antique map of the Old World on one wall.

One of the best features at PGA National, on equal footing with Nicklaus's makeover of the Champion Course, is its $5-million spa, which, combined with the health and racquet center, comprises one of the finest facilities of its kind in Florida. The centerpiece is the series of outdoor therapy pools. These include four heated flotation pools salinated with imported mineral salts, and two smaller plunge pools—one superheated and one supercooled. They make for an invigorating combination. In one of twenty-two private spa treatment rooms, guests can avail themselves of Swedish and shiatsu massages, hydrotherapy massage baths, Jacuzzis and saunas, seaweed and mud wraps, and a variety of salon treatments. In addition, the resort staff works with guests to create personal wellness programs. Those victimized by the Champion Course before Nicklaus refashioned it into one of the best resort layouts in the state would have benefited greatly from one of these customized programs.

# BOCA RATON RESORT & CLUB

SILVER MEDALIST

Around the time Blackbeard was terrorizing treasure-laden ships along the Florida coast, the entrance to Boca Raton inlet was marked on maps "Boca de Ratones." It translates from the Spanish as "mouth of the rat." Historians claim the moniker was applied because of the shape of the inlet and its sharp pointed rocks.

Aware or not of Boca Raton's checkered past and true meaning, self-taught architect and full-time eccentric Addison Mizner bought 17,500 acres of Boca Raton at the height of the Roaring Twenties to create "the greatest resort in the world—a happy combination of Venice and Heaven, Florence and Toledo, with a little Greco-Roman glory and grandeur thrown in."

Mizner built the Cloister Inn, a Mediterranean fantasy with towering beamed ceilings and beautifully landscaped grounds. The most expensive 100-room hotel of its time, the Cloister attracted tycoons, movie stars, and reigning socialites when it opened in 1926, from Harold Vanderbilt and Florenz Ziegfeld to Al Jolson and Elizabeth Arden. Said Frank Lloyd Wright of Mizner's work, "Many architects have imagination, but only Mizner has the courage to let his out of the cage."

Now as then, royal palms line Camino Real, the entrance drive to the massive pink stucco edifice and its impressive arched porte-cochere. Rare antiques from old churches and universities in Spain and Central America decorate the loggias, courtyards, gardens, and lobby. The ornate drinking fountain in the lobby would have given Caesar pause for refreshment.

As part of a recent refurbishment, original furniture has been reupholstered in leather and woven fabrics, while handmade rugs from India cover the French terra-cotta floors. Tall fishtail palms—the same as those favored by Mizner—are spaced between beveled lobby windows set in mahogany. Not only have the Cloister's rooms been updated with hand-painted wall coverings and marble bathrooms, but a new forty-eight-room concierge floor with a private parlor, called the Palm Court Club, is now open.

In addition to the charming period rooms in the Cloister, the resort also features more modern accommodations in the Tower, an imposing twenty-seven-story structure reputed to be the tallest building in Palm Beach County; in villas spaced around the golf course; and in the Boca Beach

*Tenth hole*

*The Tower and the Cloister from the water*

If there's a single criticism of the course, it has more to do with the immediate surroundings than its inherent design. Office buildings loom at the eastern perimeter of the course, while the sounds of passing traffic on Highway A1A are well within earshot on several of the front nine holes.

Resort guests may also play at the nearby Boca Golf and Tennis Club, a Joe Lee design built around real-estate pods with water in play at twelve holes. The layout was treated to a major overhaul in 1991, but the remodeled version lacks the character of the original hotel course.

Given the dining preferences of the resort's current clientele, grand, formal rooms with a full orchestra on hand have been dispensed with in favor of smaller, specialty restaurants. "Our guests want to relax, have fun, and eat good food," said Stephen Hall, Boca's food and beverage director. "We want dining at the resort to be as personal as if our guests were enjoying a meal in their own home."

Among the better dining choices is Nick's Fishmarket, a seafood restaurant that features local snapper, pompano, and dolphin as well as imported specialties; the stunning Italian-theme dining room on the top floor of the Tower; and Chauncey's Court, located near the golf pro shop, an informal café that serves everything from spicy buffalo wings to veal medallions with tiger prawns. After hours, the Patio serves after-dinner drinks, specialty coffees, and dessert to live music, while El Lago Lounge features views of the Intracoastal Waterway from its tables.

Club, located on a spit of land between the Intracoastal Waterway and the Atlantic Ocean with a half-mile of private beach at its doorstep. (A teak-decked motor yacht, *Mizner's Dream*, travels between the club and the main resort complex.) The total number of rooms at the resort is 963. For sheer variety and quality of accommodations, Boca Raton is unmatched among American resorts.

Until recently, the quality of the hotel and its staff far outstripped that of the golf course. The original resort layout was designed in 1926 by William S. Flynn, best known for his work at Merion, Shinnecock Hills, Cherry Hills, and other institutions of American golf. Boca Raton is where the legendary Tommy Armour, the most sought-after teacher of his day, instructed pupils from beneath the shade of his umbrella, gin buck in hand, from 1926 to 1955, and where Sam Snead, who participated in many a money match with hotel guests following his morning round of administrative duties, served as director of golf from 1955 to 1969. Ron Polane, a hometown friend of Snead's from Hot Springs, Virginia, who became Slammin' Sammy's assistant in 1963, has been director of golf at the resort since 1970.

Architect Joe Lee, a spiritual descendant of Flynn's (Lee learned his craft under Dick Wilson, a Flynn associate), was given the task of remodeling a course that had fallen on hard times by the mid-1980s. Lee retained twelve original hole locations and added six new holes in the makeover, reshaping three lakes in the process. He enhanced Flynn's subtly contoured greens and artful, strategic bunkers, particularly on the front nine. Lee's revision is virtually seamless—to all but the most practiced eye, the course looks to be the creation of a single author. It is a classic layout with a beckoning quality that offers fair challenge to the average player from the white tees at 6,154 yards and a firm test to better golfers from the blue tees at 6,682 yards, particularly when an ocean breeze sweeps the links.

Boca's course is always in terrific condition. Greens and tees were rebuilt and resurfaced during the facelift, while modern grass varietals carpet the gently rolling fairways.

*The Cloister*

The Spanish Terrace behind the Cloister is home to several large tropical birds kept in tall wrought-iron cages. Mizner, a notorious character who often wore silk pajamas as street wear, was reportedly seen on more than one occasion with a small monkey on one shoulder, a macaw on the other, and a pair of chows and two large monkeys in tow. He would be delighted by the collection of sharp-tongued parrots in the backyard of a hotel only he could have built.

# TURNBERRY ISLE RESORT & CLUB

## SILVER MEDALIST

Situated on an island in the Intracoastal Waterway in the Aventura district of North Miami, Turnberry Isle bears little resemblance to the exclusive yacht and country club built by developer Don Soffer for his celebrity friends in the early 1970s. The two Robert Trent Jones–designed golf courses are still there, though the famous triple green, reputedly the world's largest, has since been subdivided. The 117-slip marina still accommodates many of the world's most glamorous yachts, though one of its charter ships, *Monkey Business*, the vessel Gary Hart boarded with Donna Rice for a trip to the Bahamas that sank his presidential ambitions, has since been renamed. But the most striking change at Turnberry Isle was brought about by an $80-million expansion program completed in 1990 that culminated in the opening of the 270-room Country Club. This swanky, Mediterranean-style hotel, one of the finest new resort properties of the '90s, tripled guest capacity. It also qualified Turnberry Isle as one of Florida's toniest retreats.

Not that the resort had its head in the sand before the opening of the new hotel. Turnberry Isle, thanks to Soffer's glittery circle of friends and property owners, has always attracted celebrities and Beautiful People. This is where Jack Nicholson plays golf on vacation. Where Bill Cosby, Paul McCartney, Michael Douglas, and many others cool their heels between engagements. Where tennis stars Jimmy Connors, John McEnroe, and Ilie Nastase kept in shape at the peak of their careers, and where former Wimbledon champion Fred Stolle still reigns as director of tennis.

Turnberry Isle is also home to one of the hottest nightclubs in Miami. In fact, the attractive, designer-clad international crowd that congregates at the Monaco Lounge in the Yacht Club and, afterwards, in the Disco, is unrivaled by any other resort in golfdom.

The secluded maritime setting, coupled with a disparate collection of yachties, golfers, tennis players, sun-worshipers, spa-goers, slinky models, party animals, and conspicuous jewelry wearers of both sexes, lends the resort an ambiance altogether unique and unto itself. If you gravitate to glamour and glitter, if you like to mingle with stars of stage, screen, sports, finance, and the arts, Turnberry Isle is ground zero.

In this heady milieu of celebrities and celebrity-watchers, it's easy to overlook the golf experience. That would be a shame, because Turnberry Isle is home to a fine pair of vintage Jones layouts. Soffer, an avid golfer, personally oversees their conditioning. They are two of the best-maintained resort courses in Florida.

The main track is the South Course, former site of several LPGA events as well as the 1980 PGA Seniors Championship won by Arnold Palmer. Played from the tips at 7,003 yards, this par-72 course is a test for the best. The gold tees at 6,458 yards attract the low 80s shooter, while the whites at 6,078 yards can be enjoyed by the average player who exercises prudent course management.

With water in play at twelve holes, the primary task on the South Course is to keep your golf ball dry. Built in 1970, Jones's runway-style tees, broad fairways, and large, well-trapped greens are evident throughout. Heroic doglegs, a Jones trademark, are bordered by sculpted lagoons, their jetties frequented by sea birds. Tall palms, Norfolk pines, and dense casuarina pines line the fairways. Rising above the trees are gleaming white towers, part of Turnberry Isle's original residential community.

The back nine of the South Course offers exceptional variety and challenge. There's a double green at the eleventh hole (shared with the second hole); two heroic par threes, the thirteenth and seventeenth, where water must be negotiated; and a grand finale, the par-five eighteenth, a fishhook-shaped hole with water in play up the entire right side. The green is nearly encircled by water, so the approach must be accurate.

The shorter par-70 North Course, though watery in places, is an ideal choice for players whose swings have grown rusty over the winter. It also shapes up as a superb test for the average woman, who can reach most of the greens from the red tees at 4,991 yards.

The Country Club Hotel, convenient to both courses, was designed by a European hotel company to appeal to international sports-oriented travelers. (Twenty percent of the guests are European and South American.) Pillars, arches, and red tile roofs mark the hotel's ivory white facade, while the entryway is landscaped in palms, bougainvillea, and subtropical foliage.

Arranged in three wings—Orchid, Hibiscus, and Magnolia—the hotel offers exceedingly spacious and well-designed accommodations. Terra-cotta tile floors, Oriental area rugs, blond wood armoires, overstuffed settees, and a color scheme of almond, moss, and peach make each room a sumptuous retreat. Fresh flowers, fruit basket upon arrival, plush bathrobes, marble-topped minibars, and walk-in closets with safes and umbrellas complete the picture. The bathrooms, built mainly from Italian marble, feature sunken tubs with Jacuzzis, small color televisions, and a generous supply of fine toiletries. In addition, each room has French doors that open to flower-lined terraces with fine views of the fairways or pool gardens.

Of the resort's six restaurants, the premier dining room is found in the Country Club, at the Verandah, an elegant room done up in rich brocades and large Oriental vases. Regional Florida cuisine—fresh seafood, locally grown fruits and vegetables, and interesting preparations inspired by Miami's ethnic communities—is featured. (Where else would you get a pan-seared yellow snapper with a relish of cantaloupe, honeydew, and watermelon with smoked tangerine sauce?) The Verandah also offers a lunchtime spa menu with such items as fettuccine with clams, cilantro, and sun-dried tomatoes.

Across the pool gardens, the Grill, a casual brasserie and popular nineteenth hole overlooking the golf course, has a "golf shoe friendly" tile floor and specializes in grilled meats accompanied by fried plantain chips and chimichurri relish. The Grill also serves a traditional Japanese breakfast, for those who can handle fish first thing in the morning.

"Tea to the English is a great comforter. It loosens the tongue and encourages amity." Thus spoke a wise person in midafternoon. Afternoon tea in the Club Lounge, served daily at 3 P.M., is a well-rendered ritual. The selection of traditional English and herbal iced teas is excellent, as are the fresh local fruit tarts, miniature key lime pies, and British teacakes known as scones, served always with jam and clotted cream. The music of Chopin, Mozart, and Brahms is usually played in the lounge during afternoon tea.

*Country Club Hotel and South Course, sixth hole*

What to do after tea? Visit the spa, a combination fitness center and luxurious pampering haven where individual exercise, weight control, nutrition, massage therapy, and skin care programs are available. Incidentally, the resort's spa is not the sole province of the fair sex—45 percent of its patrons are men.

Not only can deep-sea fishing expeditions be arranged at the marina, but the resort's newest vessel, *Miss Turnberry*, the largest custom yacht ever built in the United States (it's 140 feet long and cost $12 million), is available for charter. The price? An even $12,000 per day, exclusive of food and crew. It is an amenity only Turnberry Isle offers.

*South Course, eighteenth hole*

It was the late 1950s, and postwar prosperity was in full swing. Alfred Kaskel, a masterful businessman who had amassed a fortune in the New York City real-estate market, was vacationing in Miami Beach, then America's top winter sun 'n surf destination. Kaskel, a devoted golfer, grew impatient when starting times at Miami Beach courses became difficult to obtain. He vowed to build "the finest golf resort the world had ever seen" on 2,400 acres of unpromising swampland adjacent to the Everglades in west Miami. "Kaskel's Folly," it was called. Undaunted, the farsighted developer set to work, creating first a name for the resort—an acronym of his wife's name, Doris, and his own—then hiring Dick Wilson and Robert von Hagge to design the Blue, Red, and Green courses.

The resort complex originally consisted of eight low-rise lodges fanned out on either side of the clubhouse. In many respects, it was similar to the cars produced at that time—roomy, plush, and solidly built. The following year, Kaskel persuaded the PGA Tour to schedule an event at Doral's Blue Course. He offered a total purse of $50,000, twice the size of any other Florida event. Despite immediate acceptance by the golf community, Kaskel never stopped tinkering with his creation. He installed the fountain from the 1964 New York World's Fair near the main

*The hotel*

practice putting green, built a miniature version of Versailles for a flower garden, and routinely erected bridges (or planted mature trees) on the premises overnight, mainly to shock those who had suggested these changes.

With his son, Howard, and daughters Carole and Anita still actively involved in the resort, Doral stands as a monument to Kaskel's enterprise. As the result of a $60-million refurbishment program completed in 1992, Doral has opened the door to the next generation of golfers by gutting its outdated sunburst orange-and-lime-green rooms. (Accommodations now reflect Asian and Art Deco design themes.) The club's porte-cochere, previously the scene of many logjams, has been redesigned to allow traffic to flow smoothly, and a few of the golf courses have been retooled, too. Three additional courses were added between 1965 and 1984. Doral today is not only the epitome of a modern resort, it is one of the smoothest-running golf factories in America. Yet despite its size—651 rooms, including eighty-five suites, plus the 421-room Doral Ocean Beach Resort—the staff extends a friendly, personalized welcome to each guest.

Though Doral attracts casual players and serious golfers alike, it makes its strongest appeal to golfaholics. There are ninety-nine holes of golf at

the resort; courses range in degree of difficulty from mild to killer. Guests are guaranteed the opportunity to play at least eighteen holes daily, with the option to extend to twenty-seven or thirty-six holes so long as there's daylight. When the sun sets, the spacious practice facility is lighted for night sessions, so a swing "secret" can be tested before bedtime. Management says golfers are known to tuck the packet of logo tees placed in the guest rooms under their pillows for good luck.

Doral's star attraction is the Blue Course, a.k.a. "the Blue Monster." It's a moniker that conjures the wrong image. Monsters are ugly. The Blue is a beauty. Colorful coleus plants flourish at the base of specimen trees. The superbly conditioned turfgrass follows the contour of sculpted lagoons, several of which contain coral rock atolls overgrown with palmettos and colonized by sea birds. Ranked among the best strategic layouts in the nation, the Blue Course is well worth the premium charged to play it.

Among the Blue's many outstanding holes are the two long par threes, the 216-yard fourth, which calls for a long carry over water to a peninsular green, and the uphill 228-yard thirteenth, where a cannon shot is required to find the putting surface; the twelfth, an epic par five of overnight journey proportions with water and massive sand traps signposting the way; and the infamous eighteenth, a devilish par four perennially rated by the pros as one of the toughest holes on the PGA Tour. Few finishing holes in golf can match its beauty and terror. The serpentine fairway stretches on a flat plain, with a grove of palms to the right and a lake indenting the left side of the hole. The long, narrow green, built out into the lake, rides the crest of a hill below the clubhouse, with a pair of bunkers protecting its right side. The green not only slopes from front to back, but also from right to left. Players who bail out to the right on their approach shots usually hit one of the traps—and face the prospect of a downhill bunker shot with water beyond. Most pros would rather wrestle a hungry alligator than be forced to par the eighteenth with a title on the line.

A few words of advice before waving your sword at the Blue Monster. Hire one of the caddies brought to Doral by Jim McLean, director of the resort's Learning Center, one of the top golf schools in the nation. And stick to the regular tees at 6,597 yards; the blue tees (6,939 yards) were intended for the fellows who play golf for a living. Too many golfers of limited ability tackle the tips for bragging rights, holding up play in the process.

*Blue Course, tenth hole*

Next, follow the "tame the monster" advice proffered by Peter Jacobsen, the resort's former touring pro. "It is critical to put the ball in the fairway off the tee, even if it means hitting a 3-wood or a long iron," Jacobsen said, noting that successful approach shots are next to impossible from the thick, wiry Bermuda grass rough. "Most of the greens on the Blue slope subtly from back to front, so pick a spot between the front of the green and the pin and try to keep the ball in this area. Play conservatively, play intelligently, and look at each hole on an individual basis. Don't try to make things happen at the Blue Monster. If you're impatient, you'll have many more double- and triple-bogeys than you bargained for."

Doral's Red Course, remodeled by von Hagge and reopened for play in 1991, is no longer a flat, featureless Florida resort course. It now has gently rolling fairways, contoured greens, and three holes—the sixth, seventh, and eighth—routed around a lake with a wooden embankment. However, the most significant individual hole change was made at the short par-three fifteenth, where the triple-tier, 150-foot-long, rock-encircled island green drops a total of seven feet from back to front. It's a doozie.

Similarly, the Gold Course, a watery conception (seventeen holes have lakes in play), was treated to a major facelift in 1991. It now offers

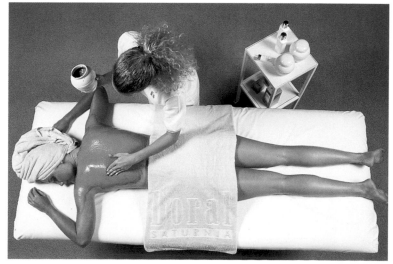

*Fango mud treatment at the Saturnia International Spa. Photo courtesy Doral Resort and Country Club*

interesting challenges, though far too many of its holes lead past the screened porches of vacation homes. The White Course sizes up as baby Blue (with smaller teeth), while the par-three Green Course, with holes ranging from ninety-seven to 159 yards, is the perfect place to fine-tune your iron game.

The Silver Course, located within a residential community a few miles from the main resort complex and opened in 1984, is a severe, neo–Scottish von Hagge–Bruce Devlin creation with an abundance of manufactured mounds and hillocky fairways. It features yet another clone of the famous island green at the TPC Stadium Course at Sawgrass (here the 141-yard fourteenth hole). The Silver has been softened of late, but it remains the toughest track at Doral. Low-handicappers with a streak of masochism claim to like it. Incidentally, the resort fishes out more than 325,000 balls each year from the lakes on its six courses. In addition to

golf balls, these lakes are also well stocked with bass, and it's not unusual to see the pros casting for largemouths at the conclusion of their rounds during the Doral Ryder Open.

Doral's 8,000-square-foot, trilevel pro shop, with annual revenues exceeding $5 million, is probably the largest (and trendiest) resort pro shop in the world. Under the direction of Carole Kaskel Schragis, the shop's exclusive line of sportswear was one of the first to turn away from the pastel polyester golf togs of the 1970s and head in the direction of fashion.

The dining rooms and lounges at Doral were recently transformed by major revisions. The resort's top room is Provare, serving contemporary northern Italian fare in a glorious room overlooking the Blue Monster. Champions is where early-to-rise golfers savor breakfast on a terrace overlooking the gardens and practice putting green, the Staggerbush Lawn

*Pools and sculptures at the Spa*

*Blue Course, eleventh hole*

Grille is a popular post-round watering hole for thirsty golfers, and the airy Sandpiper serves excellent seafood (try the stone crabs in season, served chilled with mustard sauce). Rousseau's, a large, square cocktail lounge, features a jungle motif: porcelain jaguars poised near the sound stage (there's live entertainment nightly), leopard-print bar stools, and cocktail waitresses in leopard-print outfits. Roar!

Want serious pampering with your ninety-nine holes of golf? Book into the Doral Saturnia International Spa, far and away the most opulent spa affiliated with a golf resort in America. Opened in 1987, this impressive Italianate complex is located near the Gold Course, a subtle indication that the pampering will not come cheap. (An all-inclusive week at the spa in peak season costs more than $3,000, though daily spa treatments are available à la carte to resort guests.) The spa features a four-point program of nutrition, fitness, stress management, and image-making, the last aspect designed to help both men and women improve their appearance and refine their personal style. Doral's sister spa, Terme de Saturnia in Tuscany, Italy, supplies plankton-rich fango muds (for facial and body compounds) as well as mineral waters. Exercise studios are equipped with spring-loaded floors, cascading falls are ideal for hydromassage, and the indoor climate-controlled banked track has its own sound system. The twenty-six massage rooms are painted in soothing colors, from sky blue to sea foam green. Guests are free to choose one that fits their mood.

The forty-eight suites in the Spa Villa hotel are supremely luxurious—lots of gold fixtures and marble—while the spa cuisine at Ristorante di Saturnia as well as the more formal Villa Montepaldi is excellent. Menus contain built-in calculators, enabling diners to tally calories and fat points. If it's true, as some say, that when golfers die they don't go to heaven, they go to Doral, the same can surely be said of golf widows and Saturnia.

*The Provare Restaurant.*
*Photo courtesy Doral*
*Resort and Country Club*

# INNISBROOK HILTON RESORT

SILVER MEDALIST

Like many Florida resorts, Innisbrook was conceived by a wealthy Northerner whose patience wore thin at the region's crowded golf courses. James J. Curtin, a Toledo, Ohio, marketing executive, teamed up with hometown buddy Harvey Jones to purchase 960 acres of hilly pastureland west of Tampa in 1968. Their idea was to build a private membership course with condominiums on site that could be used by the owner or rented out to resort guests, a novel concept at the time.

Illinois-based architect Lawrence Packard, known for his gently sculpted traps and free-form teeing grounds, was brought in to design the first layout, the Island Course. After routing the first few holes on flat, reclaimed swampland, its fairways flanked by lateral water hazards, Packard laid out the balance of the holes on higher ground. In fact, the Island's middle holes deliver a flurry of combinations that usually pummel most golfers into submission. As the top amateurs in the nation discovered at the 1990 NCAA Men's Division I Championship, the three-hole stretch from seven through nine can produce an alarming number of bogeys and double-bogeys. The uphill, treelined seventh, fully 536 yards (561 yards from the tips), is simply one of the most treacherous par fives in Florida. A slight dogleg left, it asks golfers to thread their shots up a narrow fairway pinched by a swamp to the left and by water to the right. The elevated green is guarded by three enormous bunkers. It is followed by the 190-yard eighth, another uphill hole calling for a precise shot to a well-bunkered green. The 388-yard ninth is a heartbreaker: a lay-up shot must be played to a fairway that ends abruptly at a lake. The hole then swings sharply to the left, where a small, well-trapped green beckons from the far side of the water. The Island's swamp-lined par-four eighteenth, with a two-tier green that slopes to a pond, is a scarier version of this hole.

"The mark of a good course is that it gives a little and takes a little," says Director of Golf Jay Overton. For the better player, the Island accurately fits that description. For the average duffer, the Island is all take, no give.

The Sandpiper, a Packard design opened in 1971, was originally intended to appeal to the high-handicapper. On the surface, its diminutive size (5,644 yards from the white tees, 6,006 yards from the blues) might suggest easy pickings. Nothing could be further from the truth. This petite par-70 layout puts a serious premium on accuracy and shotmaking. Routed on flattish land, the Sandpiper has water in play at twelve holes, often on *both sides* of the fairway! Needless to say, the careless stroke is irretrievably lost. A word of advice: Leave the driver in the bag, unless it's equipped with radar. And carry a ball retriever. Contrary to first impressions gathered from a review of the scorecard, the Sandpiper may well be the toughest 6,000-yard resort course in the nation.

Despite the excellence of the Island and Sandpiper courses, Innisbrook is known primarily for the Copperhead, a favorite of in-state golfers. Current site of the JC Penney Classic, the Copperhead was built by Packard in 1972 on rolling, pine-covered hills reminiscent of North Carolina's Sandhills region. The layout's beauty-to-challenge quotient is unmatched by any other resort course in west Florida. Unlike the Island

and Sandpiper, the Copperhead has few lateral water hazards. In point of fact, the course would be virtually impossible were it as watery as the other two. Hills, trees, and sand do a good job of defending par. Crisp, well-planned shots are rewarded throughout, though golfers are not unduly penalized by errant shots—unless, of course, they land behind a tree.

Long, tough par fours characterize the Copperhead's front nine. Two inspired strokes are required to negotiate the 397-yard third hole: There's a lake positioned in the elbow of the fairway's dogleg, while the undulating green is nearly surrounded by traps. The 426-yard sixth may be the toughest hole on the course. After guiding their drives clear of a large pine that grows in the right center of the fairway, golfers are left with a long approach from a sloping lie to an elevated green. It's the kind of shot the pros can execute without a great deal of fuss. Most everyone else plays for bogey.

In 1991, Innisbrook restored the Copperhead to its original eighteen-hole configuration (Packard had built a third nine in 1975), adding fifty yards to the first hole to bring its total yardage to nearly 7,100 yards from the tournament tees. The third nine was tacked onto the Sandpiper,

Left: Copperhead Course, fifth hole.
Photo courtesy Innisbrook Golf Resort,
© Paul Barton

Above: Copperhead Course, twelfth hole.
Photo courtesy Innisbrook Golf Resort, ©
Southern Stock Photos/M. Timothy O'Keefe

school map. For younger golfers, the Junior Golf Institute offers instruction for players aged ten to seventeen.

What to do with younger kids who don't play golf? Enroll them in the resort's Zoo Crew program. Under the direction of a trained staff, the program features playground activities, arts and crafts, games, relay races, sports clinics, story sessions, pool play, miniature golf, bowling, and movies.

though it doesn't quite fit in with the little charmer's pesky holes. A snake doesn't change its bite overnight—once a Copperhead, always a Copperhead. This third nine, rugged and rolling, shapes up as a fine end-of-the-day, predinner nine for those who still have some ammunition left from the morning round.

Not only are Innisbrook's layouts unusually varied (only two holes run parallel to each other), they are among the best-conditioned and most beautifully landscaped in the state. Flower beds are found at nearly every tee, with snapdragons, azaleas, and hibiscus in abundance. The birdlife is stupendous, mainly because the resort's wildlife preserve, located in the center of the property, provides such a favorable sanctuary for different species that frequent the Gulf Coast.

In addition to large conference groups, Innisbrook tends to attract serious golfers. Each course has a practice range with full-length mirror (so posture and address can be checked), while the Sandpiper range is lit for night sessions. In addition, the resort runs a superb instructional program called the Golf Institute. A low student-instructor ratio of 4:1, as well as a variety of classes for all types of golfers, has put the resort on the golf

The 1,000 suites at Innisbrook are housed in twenty-eight mansard-roofed lodges named for famous golf courses from around the world. In the words of one pithy observer, the decor lies "somewhere between Ivanhoe and late Frank Lloyd Wright," with massive doors, heavy furniture, and wrought-iron trimming. Overall, the accommodations are roomy and comfortable.

The resort's top dining room is Toscana, an Italian restaurant featuring Tuscan cuisine. The Sandpiper Seafood Market serves signature seafood dishes from New Orleans to New England—and farm-raised alligator, considered a delicacy by Floridians. The tail is sautéed with fresh mushrooms and a hint of wine. It tastes better than it sounds. After hours, head for the Copperhead Corral, where the drinks are served in large Mason jars and where a raucous country-and-western band entertains. The entertainment further confuses one's sense of place. It's no surprise to learn that Overton, a North Carolina native, says he never left home when he arrived at Innisbrook.

# THE RESORT AT LONGBOAT KEY CLUB

More than most barrier islands strung along the west coast of Florida, Longboat Key has had its share of notable visitors. First to step ashore in 1539 was Hernando De Soto. According to historical accounts, one of his scouts became shipwrecked in his longboat near the north end of the slender, twelve-mile-long key. Hence the name Longboat Key. Needless to say, De Soto and his men upset the quiet life of the Calusa Indians, a handsome tribe of tall natives who worshiped the sun. By the time the Indians gave up fighting the Spanish and retreated to the interior, pirates roamed the coast. Tall tales of buried treasure still circulate among the locals.

In 1910, the region was rediscovered by Chicago socialite Bertha Palmer, who claimed that Sarasota Bay was more beautiful than the Bay of Naples. Her presence attracted other wealthy patrons to the area, among them John Ringling, the circus magnate, and his wife Mable. In Sarasota (named after De Soto's daughter, Sara), Ringling built a palatial residence, called Ca'd'Zan, patterned after the Doge's Palace in Venice. He also erected a museum to house his extensive collection of Baroque art and acquired extensive real estate on the neighboring islands of St. Armands Key and Longboat Key. On Longboat, he decided in 1926 to build a grand hotel, the Ritz-Carlton, that would put all other luxurious properties in Florida in the shade, "a center of brilliance and gaiety surpassing anything of its kind in the South." He also furnished the city of Sarasota with 130 acres and spent $130,000 to build a golf course that many considered the finest layout of its day.

Alas, Florida's land boom went bust. Weeds reclaimed the six-story hotel before it ever opened. Ringling's dream of creating the world's finest resort hotel was never realized.

Flash forward to 1960. While the rest of Florida was exploding with concrete high-rises, Sarasota and environs moved slowly, maintaining their laid-back Gulf of Mexico serenity. Architect William Mitchell arrived to build the Islandside Golf Course at the south end of the key. Bordered by the Gulf of Mexico, its fairways routed among thousands of coconut palms and an all-encompassing lagoon system, the layout remains one of the best in southwest Florida. If a snorkel doesn't qualify as a fifteenth club, golfers should carry one—there's water in play *at every single hole!* In fact, water is routed up both sides of the fairway and wraps around the green of a typical Islandside par four. Landing areas are generous, but

they have to be: When a breeze sweeps in off the Gulf to play havoc with offline shots, the fairways tend to shrink. Visit in early spring when a fifteen-knot wind is blowing, and the Islandside shapes up as one of the most unforgiving BLOB (Bring Lots of Balls) courses in the nation, especially if the blue tees at 6,890 yards are chosen. Only strong single-digit handicappers should attempt them. Better to tackle this watery spread from the whites at 6,158 yards. (The course plays quite a bit longer than its measured length; tee shots receive little roll on the lush fairways.) From either set of tees, accuracy is the name of the game at the Islandside: The idea is to land the ball on the short grass at all costs. There's no recovery from the ubiquitous water or from the thick mangrove roots that rim the lagoons. Incidentally, the putting game is a joy on the Islandside.

*Tennis courts. Photo courtesy The Resort at Longboat Key Club*

The gently contoured, slightly elevated greens, most of them guarded by sand, are unusually smooth and true.

While the front nine is clustered in a tight loop near the clubhouse, the back nine stretches to the north, playing out and back in the fashion of a links. Several of the best holes—the stretch from fourteen through eighteen is particularly fine—border Gulf of Mexico Drive, which is shielded from view by tall hedges.

There's one major drawback at Longboat Key: In the peak winter season, local club members have first pick of the prime morning tee times. The same condition applies at the resort's 27-hole Harbourside Course, where guest privileges were reinstated in 1992. Visitors are advised to linger over breakfast. Better yet, spend the morning hours on the sugary white quartz sand beach stretched out with a good book on a chaise longue. Or stroll the beach in search of shells. It's not uncommon to find whelks, conchs, olives, banded tulips, and slipper shells, to name but a few. Spring, just after the water warms and the mating season has begun, is the best time for shelling. Join a guided shell walk or buy a shell identification guide and hit the beach on your own.

Shore birds are a show in themselves at Longboat Key, not surprising given the resort community's location within a wildlife sanctuary. There's the stately great blue heron, the flamingolike roseate spoonbill, the sociable white ibis, and the ever-present sandpiper, which scurries into the shallow surf to feed.

brighten the restaurant's interior. The cuisine, with the accent on local seafood, is contemporary continental, with sauces lighter than their traditional equivalents. A harpist plays after 7 P.M.

The Island House is slightly less formal but no less creative in its culinary presentations than Orchids, while Spike 'n Tees, at the golf clubhouse, and the poolside Barefoots Bar and Grille are both casual eateries.

The nearby Harbourside Moorings, one of the largest marinas on Florida's west coast, accommodates windsurfers and yachtsmen alike. Boating activities include shelling at offshore sandbars, bird-watching along mangrove habitats, and visits to islands and parks of historical interest. In addition, the offshore and inland waters of the area offer

*Islandside Course, second hole. Photo courtesy The Resort at Longboat Key Club*

Accommodations at Longboat Key are found in beautifully furnished, privately owned one- and two-bedroom suites with fully equipped kitchens, minibars, private balconies, and views of the golf course, lagoon, or beach. The complement of toiletries is creatively displayed in a large clam shell. The resort's 232 suites are situated in imposing four-to ten-story condominium towers that occupy the approximate site of Ringling's dream hotel.

Longboat Key's dining rooms are first rate. Most formal among them is Orchids, which overlooks the hotel pool and the Gulf through accordion-pleated panes of smoked glass. The windows are specially designed to admit enough light to nourish the hundreds of exotic orchids that

superb angling. Deep-sea fishing in the Gulf produces grouper, cobia, tarpon, and kingfish, while exciting light tackle fishing for trout, redfish, and snook is available in the key's bay and canals.

On the far side of the causeway linking the island to the mainland is Sarasota, the cultural capital of Florida. If your ball supply runs dry, this isn't a bad place to spend the day touring Ringling's fantastic legacy to a city that once held the promise of his dream.

# FLORIDA

## TIPS AND SIDE TRIPS

Amelia Island's main village, Fernandina Beach, was a favorite retreat of turn-of-the-century snowbirds. The town's thirty-block historic district, listed in the National Register of Historic Places, is worth exploring for its "Steamboat Gothic" and Queen Anne houses dating to the Civil War era.

In Jacksonville, an hour's drive from Ponte Vedra Beach and Sawgrass, is the Jacksonville Museum of Arts and Sciences, known for its impressive space theater and anthropological exhibits; the Jacksonville Zoo; and Fort Clinch State Park, a "living museum" where soldiers in period uniforms are known to spread the rumor that the Yanks have just burned Atlanta. Riverwalk, a wide boardwalk set along the St. Johns River, and Jacksonville Landing, a waterfront marketplace featuring more than 120 retail shops and dining establishments, are also worth a visit.

An hour's drive south of Ponte Vedra Beach is St. Augustine, the oldest (1565) permanent settlement in America. The city's landmark is Castillo de San Marco, a Spanish fort built in 1672 of coquina, a limestone formed of broken shells and coral. The town is best explored on foot: Brick-paved streets are bordered by centuries-old structures converted to curio shops and restaurants.

South of St. Augustine is Marineland of Florida, built in 1938 as an underwater movie studio. It is the state's oldest marine attraction. In addition to five porpoise shows daily, Marineland features an enormous freshwater aquarium.

Clinging to the Disney coattails in Orlando are dozens of attractions

*The Magic Kingdom. Photo courtesy © The Walt Disney Company*

that have sprouted in Orlando in the past 20 years. Shamu, the 4,500-pound killer whale, is the undisputed star at Sea World, the world's largest marine life park. At Universal Studios, the Kongfrontation ride brings visitors face to face with a giant robot version of King Kong (his breath is banana-scented). Wet 'N Wild, a water theme park, has dozens of thrilling ways to get wet. (The Corkscrew Flume and Bonzai Boggan water roller coaster are exceptional.) At Medieval Times, jousting matches and sword fights are waged in a reproduction of an eleventh-century castle event. Orlando's top nightspot is Church Street Station, a former hotel converted to a complex of saloons, cafés, and dance halls. Rosie O'Grady's Good Times Emporium, a festive, Gay '90s-type saloon at Church Street, features a Dixieland band and cancan dancers.

Not far from Grenelefe Resort in Haines City is Cypress Gardens, one of Florida's more established attractions. Tropical flowers and exotic foliage fill this gussied-up cypress swamp. There's an antebellum town, nature walks through a tropical forest, and daily water-skiing shows.

In Palm Beach, Empress Dining Cruises welcomes passengers aboard a Mississippi paddlewheeler that travels the Intracoastal Waterway through the backyards of impressive homes. However, the best way to see the palatial mansions of the super-rich is to rent a bike from The Breakers and pedal along North County Road.

An outstanding collection of nineteenth- and twentieth-century American and European art is on display at the Norton Gallery of Art in Palm Beach. Admission is free on Sundays. For a view of the Everglades, drive west to Loxahatchee Recreation Area, where guided airboat rides of the vast swamp are available.

For serious shoppers, Palm Beach is synonymous with Worth Avenue. Nearly 100 fine shops—from Cartier and Gucci to F.A.O. Schwarz and Godiva—line an attractive boulevard, their pastel storefronts and display windows shaded by awnings.

In Miami, even nongamblers thrill to see Hialeah Race Track, a National Historic Place and one of the most beautiful tracks in the world. Flamingos that live on an island in the middle of the track oval fly a circuit around the course after the seventh race.

Vizcaya, the former Miami residence of International Harvester magnate James Deering, is a colossal Venetian palazzo fronting Biscayne Bay. Artwork spanning eighteen centuries decorates its seventy rooms (thirty-four rooms are open to the public). The grand estate also has ten acres of formal gardens that contain statues, fountains, and reflecting pools.

At the Miami Metrozoo, animals roam freely on 290 acres. The viewing is ideal from the monorail that spans the plains. The zoo's re-created

*The Loxahatchee Recreation Area in the Everglades. Photo courtesy © Southern Stock Photos*

*Horse-drawn carriage on Amelia Island. Photo courtesy The Zimmerman Agency*

Broadway-style musical revues to the high-speed Python roller coaster, which makes a 360-degree loop.

Sarasota, south of Longboat Key, owes much of its cultural heritage to circus titan John Ringling, who willed his sixty-eight-acre estate to the state of Florida. On it is found his bayside palace, Ca'd'Zan (House of John in Venetian); the John and Mable Ringling Museum of Art, styled after a fifteenth-century Italian villa and containing a superb collection of Baroque art; the Asolo Theatre, a gold-and-white jewel box of an eighteenth-century Italian theater dismantled and imported to Florida by Ringling; and the Circus Galleries, featuring a fantasyland of memorabilia from the "Greatest Show on Earth."

At the southern entrance to Longboat Key is St. Armands Circle, a collection of more than 140 high-fashion boutiques, art galleries, antique stores, jewelry shops, and fine restaurants. Statues from Ringling's collection ring the circle.

African environments are especially good, as is Wings of Asia, a walk-through aviary.

At the southern tip of Miami Beach is South Beach, which in the 1930s *was* Miami Beach. Its colorful strip of time-warp Art Deco hotels along Ocean Drive is listed on the National Register of Historic Places. The Carlyle, Victor, Cardozo, Leslie, and Cavalier hotels, among others, have been beautifully restored. The Miami Design Preservation League conducts a ninety-minute walking tour of the Art Deco district on Saturdays.

A short drive from Innisbrook is the Greek fishing and sponge-diving community of Tarpon Springs. Visit the harborside shops and cafés or step aboard the St. Nicholas Boat Line sponge boat, in operation since 1924, to see how sponges are gathered.

Busch Gardens: The Dark Continent in Tampa, Florida's second most popular tourist attraction after Disney World, is a 300-acre family entertainment center where more than 3,000 animals (including a pair of rare white Bengal tigers) roam freely. Entertainment ranges from

*The Art Deco District, Miami. Photo courtesy*
*© Bill Bachmann/Southern Stock Photos*

DON'T LEAVE HOME WITHOUT...
READING THE GRAIN

The predominant grass strain cultivated on Florida greens is Bermuda grass. Unlike bent grass, the fine, thin-bladed grass that grows in cooler climes, the coarser, wider-leafed Bermuda grass thrives in the sun and is "grainy." Grain is the direction in which grass grows. Bermuda grass characteristically grows toward water or the setting sun, an important factor to consider when lining up a putt.

Here's how to read the grain on Bermuda grass greens. If the sun is bright, which it usually is in Florida, the grass will appear shiny, almost silvery in appearance when you are putting with the grain. Not only will the ball roll faster down grain than normal, it will break more than it appears. Down-grain putts demand a delicate touch with the putter. To get a softer roll, strike the ball out toward the toe of the club.

If the grass appears dark or dull, you're putting into the grain. In this instance, stroke the ball a tad firmer than normal; the resistance of the grain creates friction and slows the progress of the ball considerably. To help the ball hold its line into the grain, play the ball slightly forward in your stance to impart overspin.

On cross-grain putts, the ball will curve in the direction of the grain at normal speed. Align yourself accordingly.

Reading the grain correctly on Bermuda grass greens can also help your chipping. If you are chipping into the grain, choose a less lofted club, such as a 6- or 7-iron, to accelerate the ball along the surface of the grass. Conversely, select the most lofted club in your bag—a sand or 60-degree wedge—if you're chipping down grain, to minimize the roll of the ball.

Improved grass strains, such as Tifdwarf, have reduced the graininess of Florida greens. Also, an overseed of rye or bent grass in the winter months, when Bermuda grass is dormant, tends to minimize the effect of grain. Still, you will sink more putts and get more chip shots close to the hole if you know which way the grass grows.

BRAD DOYLE, DIRECTOR OF GOLF,
GRAND CYPRESS RESORT

# THE CAR

Not so very long ago, golf in the Caribbean was an afterthought. Glorified goat pastures and unimaginative nine-holers routed by recreation-minded hotel managers were the lot of visiting golfers until the mid-1950s. The leisurely pace and natural beauty of the islands more than compensated for the lackluster links, especially to casual players, but the Caribbean simply did not exist for serious golfers in the early Ike era.

Much has changed in the past thirty-five years. Robert Trent Jones broke the mold in 1956 on the island of Eleuthera in the Bahamas, building a course at Cotton Bay to challenge the region's first wave of jet-setters. Jones later teamed with Laurance Rockefeller in Puerto Rico, routing a magnificent pair of courses at Dorado Beach that set a high standard for golf in the tropics. (Jones returned to Puerto Rico in the early 1970s to plan a pair of layouts at Dorado's sister resort, Cerromar Beach.) Tryall, on the rugged north coast of Jamaica, not only wins the beauty prize as the prettiest course in the Caribbean, it wears the most precious crown: Each December, the resort hosts the $2.7-million Johnnie Walker World Championship of Golf, the game's richest tournament.

# IBBEAN

Despite the presence of these fine layouts, the eyes of the golf world were focused elsewhere until Pete Dye, a virtual unknown at the time, created his seaside masterpiece at Casa de Campo in the Dominican Republic in 1971. The top-ranked resort course outside the United States (among resorts, only Pebble Beach and Pinehurst No. 2 place higher on *GOLF Magazine*'s list of the 100 Greatest), the improbably named Teeth of the Dog is revered for a thrilling stretch of holes built not alongside but *into* the Caribbean Sea. "I built eleven holes and God built seven," Pete Dye once quipped.

Unlike their shaggy predecessors, these courses are well groomed year round. Not only is the climate in the islands perfect for growing turfgrass, but advances in agronomy have greatly improved playing conditions. Except for Dorado Beach and Cerromar, caddies are available at each of the Caribbean medalists.

Bring a wide-brimmed hat, a strong grade of sunscreen, and an adaptable game to cope with the tradewinds, and the same islands that Christopher Columbus bumped into on his way to Asia 500 years ago will provide at least as welcome a surprise to visiting golfers.

*Inset: The Hyatt Regency Cerromar Beach, Puerto Rico.  Large picture: Altos de Chavón, Casa de Campo, Dominican Republic*

Fine shoes and good cigars are handmade, but few golf courses share that distinction. Teeth of the Dog, the incomparable links at Casa de Campo ("house in the country") in the Dominican Republic, was indeed built by hand, though nature had a large stake in the design.

Architect Pete Dye, then in the early stage of his career, was brought in by Gulf + Western at the resort's inception in 1970 to build a golf course on a site of his choosing. Dye spent a week surveying the island's wild, rocky southeastern shore from an airplane (and later from a motorboat) to select the best locations for holes. His choice was inspired: a three-mile stretch of coast where a littoral band of mangrove and sea grape cloaked a shoreline of encrusted coral rock. Given the chance of a lifetime to create a seaside links on terrain rarely allocated for golf course development, Dye made the most of his opportunity. He and a Dominican work crew of 300 not only cleared the site with machetes, they sledgehammered the underlying rock and created topsoil from sand, dirt, and *cachaza*, a sugarcane by-product. Grass seedlings were hand-planted in this homemade soil. Later, chunks of jagged coral were used to buttress the oceanside tees. These yellowish-white building blocks resemble *dientes del perro*—teeth of the dog—which is how the course came by its unusual name.

Teeth of the Dog opens unobtrusively with four inland holes before leading golfers to the sea at the fantastic 137-yard fifth, a short downwind hole with a tiny green set on a coral shelf that juts into the surf. There is precious little room to bail out on the right side of the hole; shots that drift left are destined for Venezuela.

There is no out of bounds at Teeth of the Dog. If your ball misses the green but escapes the water, it is acceptable to wander onto the beach and play the ball from amongst the seashells, mangrove roots, and dried seaweed.

The 387-yard sixth, a slight right-to-left dogleg that follows the bend of the coastline, rewards a bold drive with a simple approach, while the 120-yard seventh (225 yards from the blue tees) calls for an all-or-nothing forced carry over a vast waste bunker built up from the

*Polo helmets*

*Terrace*

rocky shore. Near the green is a trio of island-style thatched-roof cottages built as a vacation retreat by Dye and his wife, Alice. (Alice, an exceptional golfer, was responsible for the red tee placements at Casa de Campo.) With their subtle undulations and optical illusions, the greens at Teeth of the Dog are extremely tricky. First-timers have as much chance at reading them correctly as they would deciphering hieroglyphics on the side of a pyramid. The resort's caddies, most of them consummate professionals, are worth every peso for their ability to read putts.

After a pleasant stretch of inland holes, including a few with saltwater lagoons between tee and green, Teeth of the Dog returns to the sea at the par-four fifteenth, its championship tee within shouting distance of the home of native son Oscar de la Renta, who designed the interior furnishings for the resort's casitas and villas. Rare is the golfer who can maintain his concentration from the blue tee, a coral rock platform washed by waves that offers no more comfort than a raft at sea. Across the water, a wide fairway traces the crescent shape of the bay, with a quartet of bunkers

*Teeth of the Dog Course, fifteenth hole*

positioned in the driving area down the left side of the hole. The green, protected by grassy swales, occupies a narrow neck of land that extends into the sea. It is intimidating but beautiful.

The sixteenth and seventeenth holes, both routed along the sea, must be viewed (but not necessarily played) from the blue tees to appreciate the extra amount of treachery Dye laid in store for the better player. The sixteenth, a medium-length par three, plays across a corner of the water to a large, bowling pin-shaped green that fits its peninsula as snugly as a Savile Row suit. Bunkers nearly encircle the putting surface.

The 382-yard seventeenth (435 yards from the tips) toys with a golfer's ego, tempting one and all to bite off as much of the Caribbean Sea as they dare to reach the fairway. Since the prevailing tradewinds are generally in a golfer's face on the incoming nine, discretion is the better part of valor here.

Currently ranked twenty-seventh in the world by *GOLF Magazine*, Teeth of the Dog is unquestionably the best resort course built since World War II. Kept in top condition—fairways neatly trimmed,

*The Church of St. Stanislaus, Altos de Chavón*

greens smooth and fast—the layout has an airy, unself-conscious quality about it, like a great beauty who hasn't let constant flattery go to her head. There's a single shortcoming: The blue tees at 6,888 yards present too stiff

a challenge to the 80s shooter, while the white tees at 6,057 yards are too short for the better-than-average player. An intermediate set of tees would be welcome.

The second course at Casa de Campo, the Links, was designed by Dye in 1976. Framed by patches of tall guinea grass, groves of *cajuiles* (cashew trees), and tangled sunken forests that reach down to the sea, many of the holes climb rolling hills set above the resort's polo fields, swimming pools, and tennis courts. A few border pastures where long-necked polo ponies graze contentedly. Waving fields of guinea grass eventually give way to open, freewheeling holes where a fickle wind swirls. The breeze carries the beguiling aroma of burning sugarcane, ripening fruit, horses at pasture, and the briny smell of the sea. This Dominican nosegay imprints the Links on a golfer's memory.

The 5,597-yard layout (6,461 yards from the blue tees) follows Dye's dictum that an offline shot shall come to no good. Fairways are broad, but any offline approach shot will hit the sand traps or water that guard the convoluted greens.

A third Dye course, La Romana Country Club, opened in 1990. Like the Links, it is an upcountry layout with spectacular sea views. Dye moved quite a bit of land to create conspicuous design features (particularly mounds) on this neo–Scottish layout. La Romana is private, but it can be played during the week by resort guests who request morning tee times through the pro shop.

Few resorts offer post-round cultural attractions to golfers. None are usually necessary, for a cold beer and the companionship of friends are all that is required. But at Casa de Campo, a visit should be arranged to nearby Altos de Chavón, the resort's replica of a sixteenth-century Spanish colonial village set on a cliff overlooking the muddy coils of the Chavón River.

Designed in 1978 by Roberto Copa, set designer for filmmakers Fellini and Visconti, the village was built (and "aged" to look centuries old) by Dominican stonemasons, iron workers, and carpenters. Visitors are greeted by a massive stone fountain of water-spouting dolphins and other sea creatures poised on coral thrones. Inside the gates of the village, narrow cobblestone streets lead to colorful plazas. Cafés and shops are hidden among the trees and gardens. Art galleries showcase the works of local painters and artisans. The Regional Museum of Archaeology displays pre-Columbian artifacts used by the Taino Indians who once lived along the Chavón River. As a place to stroll after a round of golf, to visit for a cocktail at sunset, or to dine at Casa del Rio high above the river gorge, Altos de Chavón is in a class of its own.

Accommodations at the resort include 277 casitas with red tile roofs and louvered shutters arranged in one- and two-story groupings. Most have views of the golf courses and gardens. All are spacious, with high-beamed ceilings. Elegant one-, two-, and three-bedroom villas, many with private swimming pools, are also available.

As a full-service resort, Casa de Campo is unmatched in the Caribbean. In addition to world-class golf, there is tennis, all water sports, trap shooting, squash, racquetball, jogging, bicycling, deep-sea and river fishing, and horseback riding. October through May is polo season.

Of the eleven restaurants and lounges on site, a favorite of golfers is El Lago Grill, an open-air, thatched-roof restaurant overlooking Teeth of the Dog and the Caribbean Sea. Its omelettes and squeezed-to-order juices get golfers off to a good start in the morning. Caribbean and Dominican dishes are features at lunch; steaks are the entrée of choice at dinner. After hours, El Lago features live entertainment and dancing. For the swivel-hipped, merengue lessons are available.

One important travel note: The drive from Santo Domingo to the resort can be long and dusty. Far better to fly to the nearby town of La Romana—or directly to the resort, which has its own airstrip.

*Left: Teeth of the Dog Course, seventh hole*

*Inset: Teeth of the Dog Course, seventeenth hole*

*Below: Teeth of the Dog Course, thirteenth hole*

"All the islands are beautiful, but this one appears to exceed all others in beauty." Thus wrote Christopher Columbus upon sighting Puerto Rico in 1493.

Another explorer of sorts, Laurance Rockefeller, happened on a remote beach west of San Juan in the 1950s. Rockefeller's stated aim was to preserve sites of great beauty and bring society's movers and shakers closer to nature. A man of style, taste, and resources, Rockefeller did not consider his own expectations apart from those of his guests. Not for him conspicuous displays of wealth. Rockefeller preferred to let nature do the talking.

Fortunately for golfers, Rockefeller was an avid (if less than accomplished) devotee of the game. When he called the USGA in the 1950s to inquire about golf course architects, he was given the name of Robert Trent Jones. A collaboration was formed that produced a handful

Lounge. Photo courtesy Hyatt Dorado Beach

of the finest golf resorts imaginable, Rockefeller turning up one superb site after another, Jones evolving new construction techniques to cope with often difficult conditions.

"Everything he did was tops," Jones said of Rockefeller's resorts. The same could be said of Jones's layouts.

Their first chance to work together came in 1958 at Dorado Beach in Puerto Rico. Jones discovered that the site's soil composition was mainly sand. A belligerent army colonel from a local club insisted that any attempt to grow grass on the site would fail. Jones disagreed. "The Scots have been growing grass on sand for 300 years," he told Rockefeller. "All you need is water and fertilizer." He was right. Today, the turf at Dorado's East and West courses is as good as it gets, especially in light of a $3-million facelift completed in 1991 and funded by Hyatt Hotels, which acquired Dorado Beach and its sister property, Cerromar, in 1985. (More than $60 million has been spent to restore these properties to their original conception.) Dorado Beach, in particular, is again every bit as special as the day Rockefeller opened it to 150 millionaires and their wives for five days of bingo, champagne, golf, and dancing in December 1958.

Dorado's East and West courses were carved from a 1,000-acre coconut and grapefruit plantation. Both layouts draw abreast of the sea, their sprawling fairways bordered by lagoons, tunneled through rain forests, and

presided over by thousands of statuesque palms. Both feature classic Trent Jones signatures: liberally contoured pedestal greens, runway-style tees, plenty of sand, and lots of water.

For overall drama, challenge, and beauty, the slight edge goes to the 6,430-yard East Course (6,985 yards from the tips), which hosts a season-ending Senior PGA Tour event each December. Its signature hole—and one of the best par fives in the world—is the 505-yard thirteenth, a diabolical Z-shaped, double-dogleg par five that can be played safely, or heroically, but never easily. Gambling long-hitters with eagle in mind must carry the corner of one lake with their drives to set up an approach shot over a second lake to a wide, shallow green. This green is not only elevated and well trapped, its rear portion slopes to the ocean barely thirty paces away. Safer options abound, but they too are fraught with difficulty: enormously tall palm trees, their cement-gray trunks culminating in lush fronds, border the lagoons and can obstruct a clear line to the green. The thirteenth is that true rarity, a golf hole that presents a fascinating array of challenges to all types of players. In the words of the designer, the hole "is demanding, but it is fair to all, and it clearly demonstrates the rewards and penalties that should be built into all great holes."

The thirteenth grabs all the attention, but the entire East Course sparkles. The 520-yard fifth, a downhill par five rated the toughest hole on the course, is framed on its left side by a forty-foot-high wall of tropical greenery. Its rolling, upland quality stands in marked contrast to the 480-yard tenth, which parallels the ocean and is swept by a fiendish crosswind that ghosts through a stand of Australian pines along the shore. The tricky 180-yard eleventh is moated by water, while the fifteenth, a medium-length par four, has enough fruit-bearing trees in the mini rain forest up its left side to consider stopping for lunch. The pause might be welcome, for the final three holes are testing par fours played into a quartering wind.

In the West Course, Jones fashioned a slightly flatter, more watery design that stretches exactly one yard farther from the white markers than the East. (The blue tees measure 6,913 yards.) The holes, many of them bent in hairpin turns around lagoons favored by egrets and pelicans, are boxed to every point on the compass, so that golfers must cope with Atlantic tradewinds from every direction. The West's foursome of par threes is ranked among the best in the Caribbean. The 165-yard

Guest room with terrace. Photo courtesy Hyatt Dorado Beach

*Twilight at the pool. Photo courtesy Hyatt Dorado Beach*

thirteenth, for example, plays to a green sited at land's end with the blue-green sea as a backcloth. Wind velocity and pin position must be carefully calculated before selecting a club.

The highest praise must be reserved for the West's fine pair of finishing holes. The 350-yard seventeenth is an extremely tight driving hole walled in by trees up both sides of the fairway. "Short, but hope for par," reads the course guide. At all costs, gear down to keep the ball in play. The 415-yard eighteenth—it plays quite a bit longer—may well be the best finishing hole in the Caribbean. It calls for high-caliber golf at a point in the round when few can produce it. A long, well-placed drive in the center of the fairway must be followed by an unerring approach to a green narrowed considerably at its entrance by deep bunkers. The wind is usually in a player's face, or slightly right to left. "A four will win," attests the guide. Every day of the week.

The director of golf operations for Hyatt Resorts Caribbean is Billy Buchanan, an agronomist who for fourteen years prepared sites for USGA

championships and PGA Tour events. Under his direction, the Dorado Beach layouts are superbly conditioned year in and year out. There's another factor in the resort's favor: The average golf employee at Dorado Beach has been on the job for more than twenty years. These staff members are skilled at welcoming golfers and putting them at ease.

Breakfast at the golf club, served on a palm-shaded terrace beside a lagoon, is supremely relaxing and complete. If mainlanders wish news of home, a newspaper is brought to the table. Place an order with the omelette or waffle chef or choose from an appetizing spread of fresh tropical fruits and home-baked muffins. If the smiling, mahogany-skinned gentleman in the straw hat at the next table looks like Chi Chi Rodriguez, it probably is. Puerto Rico's goodwill ambassador maintains a home near the eighth hole of the West Course.

The 300 rooms at Dorado Beach, substantially refurbished by Hyatt, are contained in sixteen low-rise buildings that flank two crescent beaches on either side of a central building. None of the structures exceeds the height of a palm tree. All were sited for maximum views of the ocean, pool, and fairways. Accommodations, with private balconies or patios, reflect Rockefeller's preference for simple, elegant furnishings that convey a sense of privacy and spaciousness. Rooms are cooled by ceiling fans. (Air conditioning is available, though the north coast of Puerto Rico is blessed by ocean breezes.) Fine touches include terra-cotta tile floors, marble baths, polished wood headboards, and casual furniture in soft pastels. There's peach potpourri in the bathroom, a pretty seashell for a soap dish, and an umbrella in the closet. (The Dorado area receives a good deal of rain in winter. Pack accordingly.)

There are few more elegant dining rooms in the resort world than the Surf Room, a multitiered, rectangular room faced on three sides by huge picture windows. The front of the room is angled directly to the sea, where a rock jetty breaks the ocean waves and creates a quiet lagoon for carefree swimming. At night, the breakwater and foaming surf are spotlit. Caribbean, continental, and local specialties are featured.

A short walk from the hotel is Su Casa ("your house" in Spanish), originally the plantation hacienda of a New York physician. Built to emulate a Spanish colonial mansion with twin curved staircases, an interior tiled courtyard, arched doorways, and hand-painted ceiling beams, this open-air home has been faithfully restored. Strolling guitarists and local singers and dancers entertain during dinner. Tree frogs called *coquís* fill the night with lyrical calls. Native Puerto Rican cuisine ranges from grilled shrimp served with yellow pepper chutney and sofrito sauce to charred beef carpaccio served with hearts of palm salad and mustard seed sauce. The jalapeño muffins placed on the table set the tone for the spicy entrées.

After hours, the hotel's small casino opens to gamblers (and golfers who may have failed to conquer the East's unlucky thirteenth hole). Movies are screened nightly in the salon. There is no nightclub at Dorado Beach. Rockefeller, a quiet, reserved man, did not build his resorts with party animals in mind. However, the Hyatt Regency Cerromar Beach, a sister property a mile away (the resorts are linked by shuttle bus), is home to El Coquí Club, a lively nightspot.

In the best Rockefeller tradition, nature walks are conducted by the resort's horticulture director. In addition, many of the fruit-bearing trees and flowering exotics on the property have been labeled, so that guests can explore the fantastic array of foliage on their own. Plantings are at their most dramatic in spring, summer, and fall.

Off-season package rates discounted up to 55 percent are in effect from mid-April to mid-December. For golfers anxious to tackle the inspired results of the first Rockefeller–Jones collaboration, no more incentive is necessary.

A travel tip: Automobile traffic in the capital of San Juan can be horrendous. Arrange through the travel desk for surface transportation from the airport to the resort or book a connecting flight to Dorado.

*Large picture: East Course, thirteenth hole. Inset: East Course, fifteenth hole*

# HYATT REGENCY CERROMAR BEACH

## SILVER MEDALIST

Is the world's longest swimming pool reason enough to visit a golf resort? In the case of the 1,776-foot-long serpentine extravaganza at Cerromar Beach, a pool that is longer than the Empire State Building is tall, the answer is a resounding yes.

The $3-million aquatic amusement is a series of five connected free-form pools spread over four acres between the hotel and the ocean. A swift current propels bathers past waterfalls, waterslides, flumes, ersatz grottos, peripheral Jacuzzis, and a swim-up bar where the piña coladas are nonpareil. The pool's landscaping—30,000 tropical plants and hundreds of palm trees—is exceptional. Assuming no stops are made along the way, it takes fifteen minutes to travel from the top of the river pool to its main basin. As a place to cool off after a round of golf, it has no peer.

Frankly, Cerromar's two courses haven't the style of their sister layouts at Dorado Beach a mile away. Designed by Robert Trent Jones and opened in 1972, Cerromar's courses are laid out on a flat coastal plain, not on a seaside coconut plantation fringed by a rain forest. But they are not without their virtues, especially in light of a $2-million refurbishment completed in 1990. Both layouts are ideal for the convention delegates the hotel attracts, though each gives better golfers all they can handle from the championship tees.

Wind rules the 6,298-yard South Course, which is routed behind the hotel and framed in the distance by jungled mountain ridges. The front nine plays into the prevailing sea breeze, while the back nine invites players to loft their shots on the wings of a spinnaker wind. Savvy golfers soon realize, however, that downwind shots can be difficult to control. The South is not only sandy (Jones spent fourteen traps at the 520-yard

*Above:*
*North Course,*
*seventh hole*

*Right:*
*The beach.*
*Photo courtesy*
*© Brian McCallen*

third hole alone), it is nearly as liquid as the hotel's river pool: Water comes into play on all but three holes. Beware the devilish 162-yard seventeenth: water to the right of the fairway and again behind the green nabs slicers and overclubbers.

The 6,249-yard North Course hopscotches around the property, its holes organized in three distinct sectors. Most run in an east-west direction, though the 148-yard seventh, Cerromar's showcase hole, plays directly into the teeth of the tradewinds, its huge, well-trapped green perched above the sea opposite the east wing of the hotel. The course guide description of the seventh reads as follows: "A very tough hole when the wind is blowing, *which it always is!*" While the seventh can be unsettling, most of the North's greens are not as well defended as those on the South. Also, the North's fairways are wider and its rough less taxing. If ever there was a resort course ripe for the taking, this is it.

Where the Dorado Beach property is understated and refined, the Hyatt Regency, its 504 rooms contained in a seven-story, double-Y wing configuration, is brash and bold. Rooms, most with ocean views and private balconies, were completely renovated in 1989.

The hotel's newest and most popular restaurant is Medici's, featuring northern Italian cuisine with calorically lightened sauces. Most of the

items on the menu, including pastas, seafood, and veal, are available in three portions: as appetizers, main, or side dishes. The airy, bilevel room is brightened by colorful tiles and a service staff outfitted in "Renaissance uniforms."

Cerromar's Spa Caribe, the first full-fledged spa and health club in the Caribbean, features state-of-the-art fitness equipment (Powercise machines "talk" to guests, encouraging better performance), daily aerobic and aquarobic classes, health and diet prescriptions, herbal wraps, loofah scrubs, Swedish massage, and skin care. Computers analyze individual body composition, as well as exercise and diet programs, to create a "wellness profile." Finally, spa cuisine items are offered on the resort's menus, particularly at the outdoor Swan Café near the river pool.

Cerromar is ideal for families with children. Kids over three feet tall are eligible for scuba diving and snorkeling lessons. Depending on physical coordination and a desire to learn, children can take golf lessons at age five and tennis lessons at age three. During holiday vacations and in summer, kids ages five to twelve can enroll in a complimentary camp featuring outdoor games, water sports, arts and crafts, and other activities. It should come as no surprise that nearly every child's favorite activity is splashing from one end of the river pool to the other.

# TRYALL GOLF, TENNIS & BEACH RESORT

SILVER MEDALIST

Early or late, there's a time of day when a Caribbean resort truly shines. At Tryall, a former sugar plantation twelve miles west of Montego Bay, the magic time is early morning, shortly after the fiery Jamaican sun has risen above the mountains that backdrop the 2,200-acre resort. On the open-air verandah of the Great House, a U-shaped structure built in 1834 as the plantation hub, white-jacketed waiters seat guests at tables that look far below to the Caribbean Sea. First to arrive at the table is a plate of tropical fruits: halves of grapefruit, slivers of coconut, tiny bananas, and papaya served with lime wedges. After a glass of fresh-squeezed orange juice, it's time to choose an entrée. The menu lists three types of pancakes (banana, coconut, and pineapple), all served with Jamaican rum syrup. There is homemade porridge, traditional Jamaican salt fish and akee, and a bottomless cup of Blue Mountain coffee. Also a main course called eggs Caribe.

*Bedroom in a villa. Photo courtesy Tryall Golf, Tennis & Beach Resort*

"Similar to eggs Benedict, only instead of the ham is a chunk of lobster," says the waiter in his lilting patois. "You like it, mon."

At Tryall, it's a good idea to linger over breakfast or take a dip in the spring-fed pool or loll on the resort's private beach, for morning is not the best time for golf at the resort. The hours before noon are rather muggy on Jamaica's north coast. Afternoon brings drier air and cooler sea breezes. Arrange for a tee time shortly after 1 P.M., and there'll be time after a round of golf to return to the Great House for afternoon tea, a celebrated ritual at Tryall. Afterwards, the truly ambitious can arrange to go horseback riding in the jungled hills behind the resort, the better to work up an appetite for the classic Jamaican dishes (jerk chicken, marinated conch, grilled fish) prepared by a Swiss-trained chef. After dinner, calypso bands and local entertainers perform in season.

Tryall Golf Club is, quite simply, the best course in Jamaica and one of the most beautiful in the islands. Though the layout was stretched and toughened in 1991 for the inaugural Johnnie Walker World Championship of Golf, the par-71 course remains eminently playable from the white tees at 6,346 yards. Not only are fairways generously wide, but traps are placed

*Swimming pool*

well to the left and right of the small, liberally contoured greens. Difficulty is provided by ever-present breezes and by numerous forced carries over ravines, gullies, and dry creek beds. Indeed, Tryall rewards the boldly played shot but severely penalizes timid efforts that fall short of the mark.

Designed by Texan Ralph Plummer in 1958, Tryall begins at sea level, climbs the side of the mountain, and returns to the beachfront. It's a memorable journey. There's enough golf along the way to hold anyone's attention, and enough beauty at every turn to break anyone's concentration.

Among the noteworthy holes on the front side is the uphill, par-four seventh, its tee set beside a massive, slow-turning waterwheel once used to crush sugarcane; and the 426-yard ninth, which plays from a sharply elevated tee to a narrow, canted fairway, its green sited on the far side of a

coral rock ravine. Players can cool off at the Ninth Hole Bar opposite the resort's tennis courts, where chilled ginger beer and local Red Stripe lager are the beverages of choice; either served individually or mixed in a fine combination known as a shandy or shandygaff.

Tryall's back nine transports players to the resort's rugged uplands, the holes routed up, down, and across a broad plateau and thickly vegetated land. There is precious little flat land from which to hit—awkward sidehill lies are the rule.

The 434-yard fourteenth is Tryall's postcard hole. The fairway rolls down a long, gently sloped hill toward the Caribbean, its turquoise waters flooding the horizon. The hole is beauty and beast: The fairway is not as wide in the landing area as it appears from the tee, while the second shot is usually played from a downhill lie into stiff tradewinds.

A note about Tryall's caddies: They are among the best and most knowledgeable in the Caribbean. While several of the older caddies keep alive a somewhat dubious tradition by balancing a golf bag atop their heads while they're working, most caddies merely accompany players who choose to ride in golf carts. This is especially true on hot days, when the hilly back nine can make for tough walking.

Tryall has two types of accommodation. Both offer superior comfort. The fifty-two rooms in the refurbished Great House feature Georgian-style Jamaican hardwood furniture, four-poster beds, large English porcelain tubs, and picture windows angled to the mountains or the sea. Many have private patios where room service meals can be enjoyed, and where the twinkling lights of Montego Bay or the equatorial constellations can be viewed. Stargazers can relax on these patios with a glass of pimento liqueur, an essence of allspice tasting strongly of cloves.

Scattered around the estate are forty-two two- to five-bedroom villas, each staffed with a cook, chambermaid, laundress, and gardener. The larger villas may also include a butler, bartender, and additional chambermaids. Built by a group of Texans in the late 1960s (former Governor John Connally and Senator Lloyd Bentsen were early investors), Tryall's villas, each individually decorated, are among the choicest accommodations in the West Indies. All but two feature private pools, and those chiseled into the mountainside above the Great House have unparalleled views of the sea and the golf course.

*Fourteenth hole*

# COTTON BAY CLUB

There are two speeds on the island of Eleuthera in the Bahamas: slow and full stop. Toward the south end of this narrow, 100-mile-long island is Rock Sound, where flights arrive from Nassau and the mainland. The twelve-mile drive from the airport to Cotton Bay Club, usually undertaken in a ramshackle taxi on roads that haven't been repaved since Elvis was king, is a time warp. The island hasn't changed since Juan Trippe, founder of Pan American Airways, built Cotton Bay in 1957 as a private retreat for his wealthy friends. No longer private, the club has weathered a succession of new owners and today, following $1-million makeovers in 1990 and 1992, aims to be what it once was: a Bahamian hideaway for discriminating travelers seeking relief from the hubbub and glitz of Nassau and Freeport.

Chief among the resort's assets is the mile-long crescent of pink sand that fronts Cotton Bay. (The sand is pulverized coral the consistency of talcum powder.) As a place to read a book or sunbathe while the ocean waves beat into the shore, it is unmatched. In fact, it is the finest beach attached to a golf resort in the Caribbean.

Next is the outdoor dining room. Candlelit tables are spaced under tall, floodlit palms, with a guitarist on hand to entertain. (Jackets and ties are required from December 20 to April 25.) The food is acceptable, not outstanding, though Eleuthera's pineapple is the sweetest on earth (yes,

sweeter than the Hawaiian variety), and the chilled hearts of palm soup served at lunch is a perennial favorite.

Finally, there's the golf course. Trippe called in Robert Trent Jones to route a course on 200 acres of rolling land, an unusual opportunity in the pancake-flat Bahamas. Jones not only built the best course in the Bahamas, he fashioned a resort layout that takes its place among his finest creations. Never mind that the fairways could benefit from an irrigation system or that the tees need to be rebuilt. The layout is fun, challenging, and scenic. It's also a course that can be played in several ways.

For starters, there's the safe, high-percentage route taken at low risk. (From the white tee at 6,594 yards, most of the holes epitomize Jones's "hard par, easy bogey" philosophy of design.) However, for golfers willing and able to cut the corners of traps and lagoons (there are 129 bunkers and thirteen ponds on the course), Cotton Bay rewards the bold, adventurous stroke. Then again, when the tradewinds blow strong and change direction, the careful tactician will usually beat the aggressive player.

Cotton Bay is much stronger medicine from the blue markers at 7,068 yards. When Arnold Palmer and Julius Boros squared off in a "Shell's Wonderful World of Golf" television match in 1968, neither broke the par of 72 by more than a stroke. (Both liked the layout so much they visited a second time.)

Cotton Bay hangs its hat on a pair of holes that skirt the sea. The 526-yard sixth is a sweeping left-to-right dogleg that leads to a shallow, two-tiered green set atop a jagged limestone promontory twenty feet above the Atlantic. Not only must the tee shot swing wide of trees down the right side, the second shot must be carefully placed in a bottleneck just short of the elevated green. The putting surface, like many on the course, requires careful judgment of speed and break. The view from the green of the mottled blue sea, pink sand beach, and white bungalows scattered beneath the coconut palms is a balm to three-putting, a common occurrence.

The windbreak of thick foliage beside the tee box at the 152-yard seventh has been trimmed, so that golfers now enjoy a fantastic view of Church Bay from the tee. The hole itself plays from one hilltop to another, the green set in a large hollow defended by enormous oval-shaped bunkers. A pair of sentinel palms midway between tee and green picks off stray shots. (Imagine a flapping flag framed by goal posts.) The bilevel green, nearly encased by sand, is steeply pitched. Fighting off a steady ocean breeze and the hole's claustrophobic sightlines is only half the battle—the green contours are as wavy as the rolling sea.

The layout thereafter rambles inland, its grand doglegs (many of them burly par fours) leading to pedestal greens undercut by mammoth bunkers. Golfers are brought abreast of a large yacht basin that hugs the entire left side of the short par-five sixteenth. The hole is a gambler's delight and has tempted more than

*Sixth hole*

*Seventh hole*

one player to go for the green in two shots. A miscue usually ends in disaster, for the green is tucked behind an elbow of the lagoon where bonefish, a prized sport fish, like to feed.

The director of golf at Cotton Bay is Sean O'Connor, who arrived in the mid-1960s with the intention of spending a single season at the resort. He has been in residence ever since. A nephew of Irish golfing legend Christy O'Connor, Sr., Sean, in his gentle Galway accent, can coax anyone to play better golf.

Retaining the services of a caddie at Cotton Bay enables players to stroll a course designed by Jones to be walked. Because of the limited number of accommodations (77 rooms) at the resort, tee times are not necessary. Just show up when the spirit moves you. Cotton Bay, because of its remoteness, is not a place where cruise ships disgorge passengers for their annual round of golf, thus clogging the links with duffers. A round of golf here seldom takes longer than four hours.

The remainder of the resort is ideal for those seeking escape from the workaday world. There are no phones, televisions, or radios in the rooms, which by modern lodging standards are quite modest, despite the recent makeover. The resort's single telephone is located in the lobby in a dimly lit booth. Cotton Bay attracts an early-to-bed, early-to-rise crowd. The Great Room functions as a television room and library, with board games to pass the time in the evening. Needless to say, there is no nightclub.

Cotton Bay's repeat visitors, which account for nearly 40 percent of the resort's trade, have developed a set routine. By day, nongolfers occupy seaside chaise longues, novel in hand. The book is set aside for an occasional dip in the ocean, which in these parts is crystal clear. More active guests can arrange to waterski, windsurf, or sail. The snorkeling along the breakwater around the corner from the sixth green is superb, with colorful reef dwellers as well as 200-pound groupers on hand. After lunch, more reading and beach-lounging, preferably in the shade of a wispy casuarina. At sunset, cocktails are served in the outdoor lounge overlooking the sea, followed by dinner and a stroll along a beach where, as the resort's tagline claims, "Who's Who in America goes barefoot in the Bahamas." Cotton Bay may not be the exclusive getaway it once was, but it delivers great golf and that rarest of commodities, serenity.

# THE CARIBBEAN

## TIPS AND SIDE TRIPS

*Rock cottages at Negril, Jamaica*
*Photo courtesy Southern Stock Photos, © Timothy O'Keefe*

There's little reason to stray from the all-encompassing resort complex at Casa de Campo. Altos de Chavón, an inspired re-creation of a sixteenth-century Spanish village, is well worth a half-day's visit. Guests can sail to nearby Catalina Island (visible from the seaside holes on Teeth of the Dog) aboard sailboats for a day of snorkeling. Beachgoers can arrange for transportation to fine sandy beaches at Las Minitas and Bayahibe. Deep-sea fishing charters as well as flatboat fishing in the Chavón River are also available.

Baseball is a national passion in the Dominican Republic. The village of San Pedro de Macoris near Casa de Campo has produced several major league shortstops. The professional winter season runs from October through January; the summer season is April to September. Check with one of the resort's caddies (most of whom wear the baseball caps of their favorite major league teams) for details on when and where games are played.

Old San Juan, Puerto Rico, its cobbled streets lined with some of the finest examples of Spanish colonial architecture in the Western Hemisphere, is an hour's drive east from Dorado Beach and Cerromar. The city's centerpiece is El Morro, a great fortress with moss-covered ramparts that rise 145 feet from the Atlantic. A free trolley system operates through Old San Juan's historic and shopping districts. Nightlife in San Juan features Vegas-style floor shows, cabaret revues, flashy casinos, and nightclubs. Puerto Rico's other major attractions include El Yunque, the island's 28,000-acre rain forest administered by the National Park Service (the forest receives 400 inches of rain annually and claims 250 species of trees and flowers); and Rio Camuy Cave Park, hailed by international geologists as one of the most beautiful cave systems in the

world. Visitors can view a large underground river and fantastic limestone formations during a forty-five-minute guided tour of the caverns.

At Tryall in Jamaica, twice-weekly outings are organized to nearby Miskito Cove, where resort guests have use of sailboats, windsurfers, and glass-bottom boats. Shoppers can haggle for bargains at the Montego Bay Crafts Market, while the adventurous can climb Dunn's River Falls in Ocho Rios—or arrange to float on a bamboo raft down the Martha Brae River in Falmouth, near Montego Bay. A forty-five-minute drive west of Tryall is Negril, with its gorgeous seven-mile beach and informal clifftop cafés that pulsate with reggae music.

There isn't much to do at Cotton Bay on Eleuthera, and most guests like it that way. However, a memorable picnic can be arranged through the resort to Lighthouse Point at the southern tip of the island, where the beaches run for miles without a soul in sight.

*Dunn's River Falls, Jamaica. Photo courtesy © Peter Martin Associates, New York*

Old San Juan, Puerto Rico. Photo courtesy Southern Stock Photos, © Wendell Metzen

## DON'T LEAVE HOME WITHOUT...
## A FULL SHOULDER TURN

*It's a fact of life that Caribbean golf courses are swept by tradewinds. To be successful in windy conditions, solid ball-striking is essential. The key to good contact is a full shoulder turn.*

*First, establish a solid foundation—feet shoulder-width apart, knees slightly flexed. Set the shoulders square to the target line. Start the takeaway by turning your left shoulder under your chin. This rotational move builds maximum torque in the upper body. Keep the left arm straight but not stiff and allow the wrists to hinge automatically midway in the backswing. The wrists will cock fully at the top of the swing in response to the weight and momentum of the swinging clubhead. Stay in balance and extend through impact.*

*The fuller your upper body turn, the wider your swing arc and the greater your potential clubhead speed at impact. Turning your left shoulder under your chin coils your torso like a spring, producing a powerful downswing—and longer, straighter shots that hold their line in the wind.*

JUNIOR COLÓN, HEAD PROFESSIONAL,
HYATT DORADO BEACH

# CAN

Canadians are crazy about golf. The nation's 5.1 million golfers represent 21 percent of the population, a higher participation rate than any other country in the world, including Scotland. There are more than 2,000 golf courses in Canada, most open to public play, with hundreds more under construction.

Canada's finest layouts are the legacy of Stanley Thompson, a Scottish-born Canadian who was one of the first architects to apply principles of art (notably harmony and proportion) to his strategic designs. Three of his finest efforts—Banff Springs, Jasper Park, and Cape Breton Highlands—have the added advantage of lying within national parks, forever safe from commercial encroachment.

Banff Springs, laid out in a river valley encircled by Alberta's soaring mountains, is probably the single most spectacular golf course in the world,

# ADA

while no less an authority than Alister Mackenzie, designer of Cypress Point and Augusta National, called Jasper Park to the north of Banff the finest golf course he'd ever seen. Thompson left well enough alone at Cape Breton Highlands Golf Links in Nova Scotia, its holes following the natural contours of heavily folded land.

In Quebec, "la belle province," Manoir Richelieu once had a pair of incline railways to transport rubber-legged golfers from one hilltop to another (electric golf cars are now available at this splendid resort set above the St. Lawrence River). West of the Rockies, Chateau Whistler Resort in British Columbia fits the mold of the great "railway castle" hotels built years ago by promotion-minded railroad companies. Its new Robert Trent Jones, Jr., layout was inspired by the great Stanley Thompson courses, no small irony given the fact that Thompson launched the career of Robert Trent Jones, Sr.

*Inset: Chateau Whistler Resort, British Columbia. Photo courtesy Chateau Whistler Resort*
*Large picture: Banff Springs Hotel, Alberta, Rundle nine, second hole, with elk*

# CAPE BRETON HIGHLANDS GOLF LINKS/ KELTIC LODGE

SILVER MEDALIST

Nowhere are Canadian courses more evocative of Scotland than in the Maritime Provinces. Nova Scotia (Latin for "New Scotland"), a lobster-shaped province with 4,625 miles of coastline that juts far into the Atlantic east of Maine, may have been separated at birth from the rugged interior of the Auld Sod. The Highlands Golf Links, situated within Cape Breton Highlands National Park in Ingonish Beach, could pass for the untamed wild brother of the Kings Course at Gleneagles in Scotland. Hilly and scenic, the Highlands probably is the toughest course of its size (par-71, 6,198-yards) in existence. It merits its reputation as a tiger that feasts on visiting golfers.

Designed by Stanley Thompson in 1936, the Highlands Golf Links is a natural beauty that traces the dramatic heave and toss of the land. As Thompson once explained, "Nature must always be the architect's model. The lines of bunkers and greens must not be sharp or harsh, but easy and rolling. The development of the natural features and planning the artificial work to conform to them requires a great deal of care and forethought."

Thompson did his homework at Cape Breton. In fact, he chose the very best sites for holes, irrespective of the distances that lay between greens and tees. The result is a strenuous 6½ mile nature hike interspersed with brilliant golf holes. Walks of 200 yards or more between green and tee are commonplace. (There's a shady quarter-mile stroll alongside a trout stream between the twelfth and thirteenth holes.) For those who enjoy a carefree round, these walks assure maximum enjoyment of the layout's sea, mountain, and valley setting. The Highlands is a course for deep breaths and frequent pauses, an epic links to be savored. Caddies are available in the summer months. Failing a caddie, bring a light carry bag to the Links. Otherwise, the marathon may go unfinished. An option for those who don't wish to complete the full circuit is the ten-hole "short course," consisting of holes one through five and fourteen through eighteen.

In the best Scottish tradition, holes on the Highlands Golf Links carry descriptive names that pinpoint their inherent features or pitfalls. The seemingly simple fourth hole—it measures a mere 270 yards—is called Heich O'Fash, or Heap of Trouble. It describes the hole exactly. After a well-positioned drive, golfers must play to a rakishly canted green perched atop a knoll that rejects all but the truest approaches. The massive 556-yard seventh hole is named Killiecrankie, after a famous Scottish battle waged in a long and narrow pass. The hole, rated the toughest on the course (it plays as a *par six* for women!), can massacre a scorecard. The green at the seventh,

like many on the course, is very large and severely undulating. Fairways throughout the Links are bisected by large ridges and deep swales. A slightly errant drive can kick off these slopes and bound into the tall pines and birches that border the fairways. Lichen-covered rocks and a thick blanket of moss beneath the trees render useless most searches for stray balls.

The goal at Cape Breton is not to match your handicap. The goal is to finish, for the Links serves up enough hanging lies, hit-and-hope blind shots, and triple-break putts of 100 feet or more to frazzle even the steadiest shotmaker. On a clear summer day, with the sea terns gliding overhead and the Gulf of St. Lawrence in view from the topmost holes, the Highlands Links is one of the most exhilarating golf courses in the world.

A short walk from the eighteenth green is the Keltic Lodge, a replica of an English country mansion set on a promontory between Ingonish Bay and the Atlantic Ocean. The Keltic, operated by the provincial government, offers three types of accommodations. The central edifice, a charming Victorian pastiche, has thirty-two rooms, all with ocean views. The newer White Birch Inn has forty motel-like units, while scattered on the upper portion of the hotel grounds among brambles of wild roses are eight two- and four-bedroom cottages. The cottages, with shared sitting rooms, are ideal for families and are located near marked nature trails (formerly cattle walks) that lead to the tip of the Middle Head peninsula. The stark grandeur of the rocky, wave-battered coastline can be viewed from trail's end.

For tamer scenery, there's a mile-long strand of white sandy beach along Ingonish Bay, with the broad-shouldered peak of Cape Smokey looming across the water. Even in midsummer, dips in the ocean can be bracing. A stone's throw from the ocean is a freshwater lake ringed by pine trees where the water temperature for swimming is ideal. Apple and cherry trees frame the heated saltwater swimming pool at the hotel.

The Keltic Lodge lays a fine table. The dining room, with its rows of wooden columns and painted ceiling beams, has stellar two-way views of the sea and peninsula from windowside tables. The waiters, mostly college students on summer holiday, are friendly and well trained. Many of their voices are flecked with a highland burr or Gaelic lilt, a holdover from early settlers who kept alive the mother tongue. The Keltic's seafood presentations are exceptional: The specialty of the house is local Ingonish snow crab, though the grilled salmon and lobster are superb. The generous portions are welcome to those who have worked up an appetite hiking a topsy-turvy links that turns most first-timers inside out.

*Left: The Lodge. Below: Fifth hole*

# MANOIR RICHELIEU

## SILVER MEDALIST

*The hotel*

Sheltered by the Laurentian Mountains in the beautiful Charlevoix region ninety miles northeast of Quebec City, Manoir Richelieu is eastern Canada's finest all-around resort. The complex is dominated by a massive stone manor house perched 700 feet above the St. Lawrence River. Dubbed the "Castle on the Cliff," the hotel, with its steep mansard roofs, crenellated battlements, conical towers, and ivy-covered walls, could pass for a grand chateau overlooking the Loire River.

The hotel is made all the more impressive by formal gardens and broad lawns that sweep to a precipice above the great seaway, which stretches fifteen miles across at this northern latitude.

A five-minute drive from the hotel is the golf club. "A fabulous course with intriguing obstacles," reads the hotel brochure description of the layout. It is that and more. Carved from a heavily forested mountain ledge by Herbert Strong in 1925, Manoir Richelieu is exceptionally hilly. Lord only knows how portly William Howard Taft, who drove the

first ball, made his way round the course without the assistance of a golf cart. (Caddies are available at Manoir Richelieu, but rent a cart unless you're very fit.)

Certainly the scorecard (printed in French) is deceiving: 6,110 yards from the blue tees, 5,570 yards from the middle tees, against a par of 70. Severe elevation changes and slippery plateau greens (they require the touch of a safecracker) provide the challenge. Fairways are pinched by rock ledges, ravines, and thick stands of birch and spruce trees. Mounds and knolls in the fairways can ricochet a shot in any direction. A creek meanders alongside many of the holes, while the stellar views of the river from all points on the course only serve to distract golfers.

Generally, the short holes play uphill and the long holes downhill, but there are exceptions. Most notable among them is the gargantuan eleventh, an epic par five of 580 yards. It takes its place among the most arduous holes in Canada. An accurate tee shot of 240 yards must be essayed to a plateau in order to set up a second shot across a trio of ponds stretched across the fairway. The third shot is played uphill a distance of 180 yards or more to a convoluted green with a pair of bunkers guarding its right side. Optical illusions to the contrary, all putts break away from the mountain slope and toward the water.

Following a $1-million makeover in the late 1980s, including the installation of an irrigation system, the course is in very good shape from late May through mid-October. The layout's superb condition is welcome: On a course this hilly, where the judgment of distance is difficult and the penalty for failure severe, every advantage helps. The club lacks a practice range, but its putting course is a good place to fine-tune your stroke. The attractive clubhouse, which could pass for a petit chateau in the French Alps, has a locker room, well-stocked pro shop, comfortable bar, and new steak house. The views from the clubhouse of the golf course and river are postcard material. Bring a camera and a pair of binoculars, too: Native white porpoises called *marsouins* leap and frolic in the river's tidal currents.

Make reservations well in advance for a July or August visit to Manoir Richelieu—French Canadians are golf-crazy at the moment. Better yet, visit after Labor Day, when the resort quiets down and the course is at its peak.

One caveat about visiting Quebec: The province is a bastion of French nationalism. French is the language of record. Hotel employees speak and

*Eleventh hole*

*Twelfth hole*

understand English but sometimes pretend not to. Bring a French phrase book and make every attempt to converse in the native tongue.

The five-story hotel, arranged in three wings, offers pleasing, civilized comfort in its 268 rooms and twelve suites. The resort also has six large cottages and several apartments for rent. Public rooms exude Old World charm and are especially attractive, the walls decorated with Audubon prints. The main hall is set with cozy settees and comfortable chairs arranged in conversational groupings.

The main dining room, glass-enclosed along the front wall and with a view of the river, serves meals a discerning Parisian would be hard-pressed to criticize. And while the setting of this and the other dining rooms in the hotel are formal, there is no dress code at Manoir Richelieu. (The French appreciate the traveling public's desire to dress casually on vacation.)

After hours, there are two fine lounges at the hotel: Bar Foyer and Disco Charlevoix. There's also a new pub near the disco open during the season. Summer theater productions are staged in a building adjacent to the hotel.

As for nongolf amenities, they include a heated saltwater pool, an indoor freshwater pool, horseback riding, and tennis. Lawn bowling, croquet, badminton, windsurfing, bicycling, and volleyball are also available. For golfers, there's always the temptation to return to the golf club with a firmer resolve (and a few canisters of oxygen) to conquer a truly exacting resort course.

# BANFF SPRINGS HOTEL

In the province of Alberta, the flat prairie plains erupt into spectacular mountains eighty miles west of Calgary. In a valley beyond the initial massif is Banff, a year-round sports center and cultural magnet situated within a national park, its history closely linked with that of the Canadian Pacific Railway. A bull-headed railway executive, William Cornelius Van Horne, opened the original Banff Springs Hotel in 1888 at the confluence of the Bow and Spray rivers, a site of extraordinary natural beauty. "If we can't export the scenery, we'll import the tourists!" Van Horne decided. With 250 rooms, Banff Springs was the largest hotel in the world at that time. Yet

*Sulphur nine, eighth hole*

it was dwarfed by three massive peaks, Rundle, Tunnel, and Sulphur, their battleship-gray flanks rising impressively from a cloak of bottle-green pines.

After the original hotel burned to the ground in 1926, the railroad company spared no expense in its reconstruction, importing Scottish masons and Italian stonecutters to erect an imposing rendition of a Scottish baronial castle. Guests have ranged from Theodore Roosevelt to Elizabeth Taylor, from the Prince of Wales to Marilyn Monroe (portions of *River of No Return*, starring Monroe and Robert Mitchum, were filmed in Banff).

Accommodations, done in cool shades of blue and gray, are now furnished with comfortable oak furniture, new carpeting, and marble countertops in the bathrooms. Rooms are classified as standard, superior, and deluxe depending on size and view. Deluxe rooms, with outstanding vistas of the Bow River valley framed by 10,000-foot peaks, are worth the premium.

The public rooms at Banff Springs were built on a scale rarely seen today. Gothic arches lead to enormous stone-floored halls set off by antique refectory tables, suits of armor, tapestries hung from balustraded balconies, and fireplaces large enough to park a car in. There are sixteen restaurants and pubs at the resort. Among the choices: continental cuisine with a Spanish flair at Alhambra, shabu-shabu (a form of Japanese fondue) at Samurai, and Bavarian dishes served with steins of frothy lager at Waldhaus.

The original golf course at Banff Springs was laid out by Stanley Thompson in 1928, and follows Thompson's belief that "the most beautiful courses—the ones where the greens invite your shots—are the ones which hew closely to nature." Bunkers, for example, were set into mounds that emulate the shape of the surrounding mountain peaks. Many serve as both hazard and signpost. None are placed directly in front of the greens. In addition, fairway contours echo the movement of the Bow River or mimic the rolling terrain at the base of the mountains. Driving areas are wide, but there is a preferred angle of attack at every hole. Greens range from large and undulating to small and flat. Many are raised and canted from back to front.

Because of the relatively short golf season (the course is open from early May to mid-October) and the growing demand for golf, the resort hired Geoffrey Cornish (a Thompson protégé) and Bill Robinson to construct a new nine. While the original eighteen—comprised of the Rundle and Sulphur nines—runs out and back, in the manner of a Scottish links, the new Tunnel nine, opened in 1989, was shoehorned within the perimeter of the Rundle nine. For those plotting an ideal sequence, the Sulphur is the toughest nine, Rundle the most scenic, Tunnel the most fun.

In any configuration, the 157-yard fourth on the Rundle nine is one of the finest mid-length par threes in the world. From an elevated tee, golfers play their shots over a glacial lake called the Devil's Cauldron to a tiny green set in an oval terrace and pockmarked with bunkers. The backdrop is the soaring rock face of Mount Rundle. Mountain zephyrs can play havoc with club selection. So can distance perspective. The lofty peaks can deceive the eye and create the illusion of a shorter distance than actually exists. There is the oft-told story of Gene Sarazen, who rejected his caddie's advice to play a long iron for what appeared to be a short approach shot. Fearful he would hit the ball halfway up a mountain with the caddie's suggested club, Sarazen chose his own club and advanced the ball only halfway to the green.

It is also true, however, that the ball flies farther in the thin air a mile above sea level. So two variables, perception and altitude, must be taken into consideration, especially on long approach shots.

Given stringent national park restrictions placed on the use of fertilizers and pesticides, not to mention the region's harsh winters, the course is in good condition, elk prints in the fairways notwithstanding. Banff Springs is relatively flat and may be walked, though the high altitude can tire flatlanders quickly. Most guests choose to ride in golf carts, which are included in the green fee.

Wildlife buffs should plan to visit in the fall, when elk herds descend from the mountains to initiate mating rituals. It's not unusual to see 300 elk or more on the golf course in late September. Since the resort lies within a game reserve, the animals are accustomed to the presence of humans. Nevertheless, it is not advisable to get between a bull elk and his harem.

After tackling the main track, there is opportunity to play the miniature golf course in the hotel's conference center. Twenty tons of Rundle rock were used to shape the eighteen-hole course, which features its own pro shop as well as waterfalls, rushing rivers, and miniature simulations of the big course's challenges.

Other resort amenities include bowling, a health club with two pools (the indoor pool is Olympic-size), five tennis courts, and a network of hiking trails. Mountain biking is very popular. So are the reproductions of 1929 Ford Model A roadsters the hotel makes available for rent. There is canoeing on the rivers and fishing for rainbow and Dolly Varden trout in nearby wilderness streams. Banff's great outdoors is truly great, its mountain beauty of the wild, unhinged variety. Golfers quickly discover that the Banff Springs Golf Course is by no means the tamest part of the 2,564-square-mile national park.

*The hotel and Sulphur nine, fifth hole*

# JASPER PARK LODGE

*Breakfast arrives via bicycle.*
*Photo courtesy Jasper Park Lodge*

The town of Jasper sits at the terminus of the Icefields Parkway, a two-lane road that creases an alpine wonderland. The guidebooks estimate a five-hour drive from Banff to Jasper, but very few travelers step on the pedal at the sight of ancient glaciers glued to massive peaks in the Continental Divide. The area is every kid's dream of the North Pole.

Despite its northerly location, Jasper Park Lodge is situated at a lower elevation (3,300 feet) than Banff and enjoys a longer golf season. The course, assuming the black bears are no longer reclining on its greens and asleep in its traps, is open from late April to late October. Blue skies prevail at most times of year in Alberta, which is known throughout Canada as the "Sunshine Province."

The Jasper Park Golf Course was designed by Stanley Thompson in 1925. Fifty teams of horses and 200 men spent an entire summer clearing boulders and timber to make room for the layout. As he proved here and later at Banff Springs, Thompson had a special talent for creating marvelous holes in difficult terrain.

A sprawling par-71 layout that measures 6,323 yards (6,598 yards from the blue markers), Jasper's elevated tees are invariably aligned to a distant peak. In Scotland, golfers often aim their shots to distant church steeples. At Jasper, the target is usually one of the snow-frosted mountains in the 10,000-foot range that ring the park.

The strength of the rolling, wooded layout, the holes routed in a circular clockwise direction, is its collection of par threes. One of them created quite a controversy in its day. Thompson, an ebullient, persuasive man, ran out of money during course construction and persuaded the Canadian National Railway to refinance the project. However, when he designed the fairway at the 214-yard ninth hole to resemble the voluptuous figure of Cleopatra, he ran afoul of prim railway executives. Thompson modified the curves, but the hole is still known as Cleopatra. It shares top billing with the 220-yard fourth, Cavell, named for an 11,033-foot glacier-clad pyramidal peak that backdrops the green to the south. This hole usually plays into the wind to a sloping green,

its flash-faced bunkers set well back from the green to·distort a golfer's perspective.

At the 156-yard seventh, players must fly their shots over a creek to an elevated green that slopes to a heavily wooded area on its left side. Accuracy is the order of the day. The 168-yard twelfth looks easy but plays tough: A strong left-to-right crosswind can play havoc with tee shots aimed to a well-bunkered green framed by tall pines and firs.

But the best par three of the lot may be the petite 120-yard fifteenth, called the Bad Baby. The shortest hole at Jasper, it calls for a perfectly lofted short iron shot. The tiny green is set in splendid isolation on a peninsula that juts into the jade-green waters of Lac Beauvert. The putting surface drops off sharply on all sides. Shoot for the fat part of the green, not the pin, otherwise this ornery tot will cut its teeth on your scorecard.

As for the rest of the course, golfers have a good chance of posting a decent score at Jasper if they can survive the devilish par threes. For example, three of the four par fives are well under 500 yards from the white tees. At each, the fairways are generously wide, though they do tend to narrow near the greens. As at Banff, bunkers play a key tactical role at Jasper. Their flashed faces make them appear closer to the greens than they really are, deceiving first-timers. They also seem to have magnetic appeal for golf balls. The greens, many of them elevated above fairway level, are subtly contoured and beautifully conditioned. Because tees are convenient to the greens that precede them, Jasper is an easy course to walk.

Robert Trent Jones, who apprenticed under Thompson, has written that Jasper integrates the strategic, penal, and heroic schools of golf course architecture like no other course in North America. Certainly the knockout alpine scenery tends to overshadow a layout that blends seamlessly into the terrain and calls little attention to itself. Even the hourglass figure of

*Lobby. Photo courtesy Jasper Park Lodge*

*Swimming pool and Lac Beauvert*

Cleopatra is hardly flamboyant by modern standards. Jasper exemplifies subtlety of design. Few resort layouts can claim as much. This is a course you could play every day and never get bored.

A favorite stopping point for Hollywood movie stars in the 1940s and 1950s, the resort endeared itself especially to Bing Crosby, who fell in love with the course during the 1946 filming of *The Emperor's Waltz*. He returned a year later to compete in the annual Totem Pole Golf Tournament, which he won.

Jasper's 437 accommodations are located in log cabins and cedar chalets along the shores of Lac Beauvert. Completely renovated from 1989 to 1991,

they are classified as standard, superior, deluxe, and suites. All have patios or balconies, and many have fireplaces. Beds are covered with fluffy goose down duvets. Lovely watercolors depicting Canadian woodland and mountain scenes decorate the walls.

The main lodge, set in a wide basin ringed by the eastern flank of the Canadian Rockies, dates from 1922, though much of the complex was built in the 1950s. Mock totem poles support the main beam, while bison heads are mounted above the two huge fireplaces. Decorations—native American masks and soapstone Inuit carvings—create a rustic atmosphere. Picture windows frame Lac Beauvert and snow-covered Whistlers

*Large picture: Sixteenth hole   Inset: Ninth hole   Above: Fifteenth hole*

Mountain in the distance. A harpist fills the common area with soothing melodies in the evening.

As for dining, the Beauvert Room features continental cuisine in a cavernous room that is simply too big for its own good. More intimate and appealing is the Moose's Nook, where the á la carte dishes exhibit a Canadian flair. Among the starters, there's New Brunswick fiddlehead soup, Saskatchewan rabbit jelly, and venison paté, followed by reindeer medallions stuffed with apple wedges, Yukon Arctic char in phyllo pastry, and roasted Manitoba pheasant with walnut stuffing. Canadian wines, especially the fruity varietals from British Columbia, are an excellent value. Another alternative to the Beauvert Room is the Edith Cavell Dining Room, which serves fine French cuisine with all the right touches: candlelight, tableside preparation of dishes, superb wines and desserts, and a spectacular lake-and-mountain view.

Jasper Park Lodge operates on the Modified American Plan—room prices include breakfast and dinner. Incidentally, room service is unusually prompt: Waiters dressed in gray knickers with matching caps travel from cottage to cottage on bicycles while balancing a tray on one hand.

After hours, Tent City, a 150-seat nightclub named for Jasper's first settlement, is popular with those who haven't spent all their energy hiking, horseback riding, cycling, fishing, swimming, or shopping at one of the resort's thirteen new boutiques, including Jasper Originals, which carries the handicrafts of local artisans. The Lodge also organizes Skyline Trail rides (a three-day wilderness pack trip) or white water rafting on the mighty Athabasca River.

Not content to rest on its laurels as one of the finest mountain resorts in the world, Jasper Park Lodge has proposed a ten-year, $250-million development plan pending national park approval that will add a new golf course and double the number of accommodations at the 903-acre resort. Ideally, the golf course architect hired to design the new links will draw inspiration from the original layout, a flawless conception rivaled only by Banff for mountain grandeur.

# CHATEAU
# WHISTLER RESORT

Seventy miles north of Vancouver on British Columbia's Sea to Sky Highway is Whistler Resort, a sprawling ski complex with a longer vertical drop (more than 5,000 feet) than any other ski area in North America. Cradled at the base of Blackcomb and Whistler mountains is a purpose-built village, its brick-paved central square a pedestrian mall with seventeen hotels, sixty retail outlets, and dozens of grog shops, cafés, and restaurants.

A five-minute stroll from the village over a covered footbridge is Chateau Whistler Resort, the first chateau-style hotel built in the Canadian Rockies since the turn of the century. Opened in 1989 by Canadian Pacific Hotels,

the twelve-story, 343-room property makes use of modern materials but was built along traditional lines. While its exterior is marked by a copper green gabled roof and a lone turret, the hotel interior summons a cozy, homey feel that appeals to skiers and golfers alike. The Great Hall, while a vest pocket room compared to the grand public spaces in the Banff Springs Hotel, does have a forty-foot-high ceiling and massive slabs of green slate on the floor. Hand-stenciled maple leaves decorate the walls, while original Canadian antiques—armoires, tables, chairs—fill the public rooms. Coffee tables near a double-sided fireplace hold baskets of pine cones and pieces of folk art. Picture windows in the public rooms open to the sheer vertical slopes of Blackcomb Mountain. The rooms are low-key, comfortable, and have windows that open to admit the crisp mountain air.

Restaurants at Chateau Whistler feature regional cuisine—local greens and pan-fried salmon are mainstays. Breakfast at the Wildflower Café is an early riser's dream: Buffet tables feature the repast's traditional ingredients, though many golfers opt for the All-Canadian Breakfast—Okanagan pear and apple flapjacks with Quebec maple syrup and Canadian bacon.

Thus fortified, golfers can venture out on one of two courses. The first is the Whistler Golf Course, a municipally owned layout designed by Arnold Palmer and Ed Seay in 1983 (it's a sporty meadowland layout fashioned from a peat bog). The second is the hotel's own course, built by Robert Trent Jones, Jr., and unveiled in 1992.

Built to pay homage to the great Stanley Thompson courses at Banff and Jasper, the Chateau Whistler Resort layout starts flat, traverses a broad mountain ledge along walls of exposed granite, and plays downhill at its climax. Roaring rapids in Blackcomb and Horstman creeks serenade players on the opening and closing holes. They also come into play for the unwary. Fairway bunkering was kept to a minimum, though golfers must play accurate approaches to rolling, well-defended greens. The two ski mountains—Blackcomb and Whistler—dominate sightlines from around the course, which follows a traditional out-and-back routing. Those seeking a nine-hole loop late in the day can play holes one through five, and holes fifteen through eighteen. Because of the 300-foot elevation changes, golf carts are required.

*Seventeenth hole. Photo courtesy © Henebry Photography*

After golf, there is opportunity to fish, hike, cycle, swim, windsurf, ride a horse, or play tennis. The Whistler Classical Music Festival arrives each August, while the Fall for Jazz Festival is scheduled for September. The hotel has a stylish health and fitness center (masseurs are practiced at getting out the kinks) as well as fourteen shops and boutiques. Directly outside Chateau Whistler are Blackcomb's chairlifts, which can be taken to the top of the mountain for a guided walking tour or a top-of-the-world picnic. From this perspective, with frosted peaks in the Coast Range rising in all directions, bogeys don't seem quite so bad.

*Left: Eighteenth hole. Photo courtesy © Henebry Photography.  Above: Lobby. Photo courtesy Chateau Whistler Resort*

# CANADA

## TIPS AND SIDE TRIPS

*The Bluenose II, Halifax, Nova Scotia.*
*Photo courtesy Department of Tourism, Nova Scotia*

The Keltic Lodge in Nova Scotia is the perfect jumping-off point for a counterclockwise driving tour of the Cabot Trail, a 184-mile route that leaps and plunges over some of North America's most spectacular coastline scenery. Mist-shrouded headlands, hidden coves, and deserted beaches vie with the crashing sea for attention. A sure hand at the wheel and a leisurely pace are recommended. Consider pocketing the car keys for an afternoon of hiking. Trail lengths and hiking times are listed at the entrance of each path.

On the far side of the Cabot Trail is Cheticamp, an Acadian outpost where French is still spoken. Handicraft shops carry soapstone sculptures, hooked rugs, and bolts of Scottish clan tartans. Boat tours from Cheticamp visit sea caves and unusual rock formations along the coast.

Pilot whales and rare sea birds (Atlantic puffin, razor-billed auk) can be spotted on these boat trips.

The Alexander Graham Bell Museum, in Baddeck, was the summer home of the Scottish-born inventor. Though best-known for his invention of the telephone, the museum documents Bell's pioneering work in genetics, aeronautics, and teaching systems for the handicapped.

Halifax, capital of Nova Scotia, is worth visiting for an attractive waterfront complex of restored stone warehouses called the Historic Properties. Charming shops, cafés, and seafood restaurants can be found along the district's cobblestone streets. Summer sails are available on the *Bluenose II*, a replica of a famous racing schooner docked where privateers once off-loaded booty.

Due south of Manoir Richelieu is Baie St. Paul, a lovely port and artist's colony framed by the tallest peaks in the Laurentians. The town's many galleries display Quebecois works. Horse shows, outdoor dancing, and art shows are featured each summer during the town's annual folk festival.

A two-hour drive south of the resort is Quebec City, the first French settlement in North America and one of the most charming cities on the continent. Explore the restored seventeenth- and eighteenth-century houses along cobbled streets in the Old Lower and Upper Towns (they are joined by a *funiculaire*, an enclosed elevator-cable car); stroll along cliffside Dufferin Terrace for panoramas of the St. Lawrence River far below; and visit the Citadelle, a massive fortress where Changing of the Guard ceremonies are held on summer mornings. The city's restaurants and cafés, specializing in French cuisine, are excellent.

The town of Banff has a good variety of museums, shops, restaurants, and nightspots. The Whyte Museum of the Canadian Rockies displays the works of local and national artists, while the Banff Park Museum details the region's natural history. The Banff Centre (School of Fine Arts), the town's cultural mecca, offers theatrical, musical, and visual arts programs from June through August during the Banff Festival of the Arts.

The Sulphur Mountain Gondola in Banff features a top-of-the-world panoramic observation deck as well as a charming tea house. A scenic three-hour tour of the Bow River via rubber raft can be arranged through the Banff Springs Hotel. Those who wish to experience the town's famous springs can take the plunge in the Upper Hot Springs pool near the hotel. The natural sulphur waters are very soothing (and welcome) after an active day.

Many of Alberta's finest natural attractions are found en route from Banff to Jasper along the Icefields Parkway, one of the world's great alpine roads. Glaciers, waterfalls, canyons, lakes, and scenic lookouts line the route, with occasional glimpses of moose, elk, and bighorn sheep along the way. Snowcoach and ice-walk tours are available at Columbia Icefields, the largest expanse of ice and snow in the Rockies.

The Jasper Tramway, four miles south of Jasper, whisks passengers up Whistlers Mountain to 8,084 feet. An interpretive area at the top of the lift describes life in this fragile alpine zone. At Maligne Lake, the second-largest glacial lake in the world, two-hour cruises visit Spirit Island, known for its mysterious tranquility.

*Totem poles in Stanley Park, Vancouver.*
*Photo courtesy Department of Tourism, British Columbia*

DON'T LEAVE HOME WITHOUT...
CALCULATING THE ALTITUDE

*It is important to remember when playing golf in the mountains that shots will fly farther in the thinner air. This is especially true for strong players. Hitters who don't drive the ball more than 150 yards won't notice an appreciable difference in the length of their shots at higher altitudes. However, golfers who hit the ball hard, resulting in a steep launch angle, high trajectory, and extended carry time, should figure on roughly 2 percent added distance per 1,000 feet above sea level. Club selection must be adjusted accordingly.*

*Players should spend time at a distance-marked practice range before teeing off to determine how far each club travels. At Banff, situated a mile above sea level, power hitters can subtract 10 percent from marked yardages. For example, from 150 yards, select the club you hit 135 yards. Low, boring shots played with long irons won't travel as far as lofted shots that hang longer in the air.*

*Don't trust your visual frame of reference in the mountains: Players accustomed to "eye-balling" distances on their home turf will be fooled at higher altitudes, where the air offers*

*less resistance to the ball's flight. Gauge your distance for each club on the range, and club yourself accordingly on the golf course.*

DOUG WOOD, GOLF PROFESSIONAL,
BANFF SPRINGS GOLF COURSE

Whistler is a ninety-minute drive from Vancouver, a world-class city as spectacularly sited as San Francisco. Bounded by English Bay and tall peaks in the Coast Range, it enjoys a temperate climate year round. An aerial tramway climbs to the top of 3,974-foot Grouse Mountain in North Vancouver, where picnics with a view of the city far below are popular. Vancouver's top attractions include Chinatown, known for fine Cantonese and Mandarin restaurants; Stanley Park, its gardens, putting greens, and aquarium (Canada's largest) bordered on three sides by the sea; and Gastown, where streets illuminated by gaslight fixtures and restored warehouses contain art galleries, antiques shops, cafés, and nightclubs.

Unless you're traveling directly to Scotland or Ireland, golf and golf alone is not necessarily the best reason to visit Europe. Fine as its resorts may be, the Continent's endlessly varied dialects, cuisines, fashions, architectures, and mythologies outweigh its golf challenges.

Scotland, a kingdom that has cherished and nurtured golf since the Middle Ages, needs no introduction. Everything you liked about golf in the first place is confirmed by a visit to the Auld Sod. It is a land that inhabits the senses and stays with you long after you've recovered from jet lag. The freshening breeze and inevitable rain, the shrewd appraisals of the caddies, the feel of springy turf underfoot—a trip to Scotland completes the education of a golfer. And while its resorts are scarce, no nation can match the inland splendor of Gleneagles or the seaside thrills of Turnberry.

Scotland may be the birthplace of golf, but Ireland rocked the game out of the cradle, bathed it in mother's milk (a euphemism for creamy stout), and set it loose upon the seaside dunes. There is perhaps no fiercer links in all of Europe than Waterville, where high Atlantic winds whistle through giant dunes along the shores of Ballinskelligs Bay.

Italians, a passionate people, are in the exciting first stages of a love affair with golf. Nowhere is golf in Italy more celebrated than on the Costa Smeralda of the island of Sardinia, a mecca for Europe's Beautiful People. Here Robert Trent Jones was forced by the hilly, rockbound terrain to work with one hand tied behind his back. He still managed to produce a fine layout at the Pevero Golf Club.

# OPE

Very quietly, Portugal has vaulted itself into the forefront of Europe's top golf destinations on the strength of its holdings in the Algarve, an ancient Moorish kingdom fronting the Atlantic Ocean where the weather is invariably dry and sunny. More than most resort areas, the Algarve has great topographical variety among its top venues. There are courses cut through rolling pine woodlands, refined English parkland-style layouts with fine ocean views, and one course (Penina) that is as flat as a board, with ribbons of sneaky water bisecting the fairways.

Seve Ballesteros has helped to create awareness of golf in Spain, though the Costa del Sol, its beaches fronting the Mediterranean Sea, is bursting at the seams with concrete towers. The Costa del Sol's saving grace is Torrequebrada, a thrilling test of golf with spectacular views. La Manga, at the southern tip of Spain's Costa Blanca, is an American-style spread with two fine courses and a nearby beach club.

Golf in France dates to 1857, but only recently have the French become truly enthusiastic about the game: Ground was broken on more than 250 new courses in 1990 and 1991. Golf has always been in style at Deauville, a venerable seaside resort where Parisians escape for the weekend. There's also dining, which the French do with a passion that supersedes even their newfound desire to play golf.

Europe's courses, on the whole, are not as "designed" as Stateside layouts. Natural contours, not artificial hazards, usually provide the challenge. Caddies are available at most of the resorts, as are hand trolleys. Walking is the way to go in Europe—golf carts are a relative rarity.

Avoid, if possible, the months of July and August, when Europe is overrun with tourists. Spring and fall are the best times to visit.

*Inset:  Trolleys outside the clubhouse, Estoril Palacio Golf Club, Portugal.  Large picture:  Hotel Romazzino, Costa Smeralda, Sardinia*

# THE GLENEAGLES HOTEL

AUCHTERARDER, SCOTLAND • GOLD MEDALIST

On the threshold of the Scottish Highlands an hour's drive from Edinburgh is a 830-acre estate dominated by a grand hotel that was hailed by the British press as the "Playground of the Gods" when it opened in 1924. Founded by a railroad tycoon who wished to attract titled society and moneyed travelers, the Gleneagles Hotel could very easily be a fusty shrine to prewar elegance had it not been thoroughly refurbished in the 1980s to bring it into the modern era. And while dukes and duchesses no longer arrive with their ghillies and gun dogs for months at a time, the grandeur of Gleneagles remains. The hotel's 236 rooms, including twenty suites, are unusually large and well appointed with fine Edwardian reproductions. Many have four-poster beds and exquisite views of the formal grounds and surrounding hills. Rooms in outer wings are rather a long walk from the dining rooms and lobby, but there are many joys to contemplate along the way.

Improvements to the hotel's public areas have been especially impressive. A fading dowager of a drawing room has been turned into an elegant champagne bar called Braid's. The Drawing Room, situated on the ground floor opposite the main lift, features afternoon tea and dancing nightly to a small combo. A former greenhouse

*The Gleneagles Jackie Stewart Shooting School.*
*Photo courtesy The Gleneagles Hotel*

attached to Strathearn, the main dining hall, is now an intimate à la carte restaurant called the Conservatory. Since Gleneagles lies north of Moscow, it is possible to dine in the gloaming of a near-endless summer evening in this delightful glass-walled room. The service is smooth, assured: Order an Alsatian wine to accompany the broiled halibut and turbot steaks served with sauces of rosemary and sorrel, and the correctly shaped wine glass is brought immediately to the table. Skip the full Scottish breakfast of steaming porridge, black pudding, cloutie dumplings, beef sausages, poached finnan haddock, and kippers—a breakfast substantial enough to march an army of pipers—and waiters in the Strathearn will cheerfully guide you to a buffet table laden with organic cereal ingredients, commending your choice with inimitable Scottish wit. In an effort to stay current with modern dining preferences, the Strathearn's dinner menu offers a number of vegetarian main dish alternatives to collops of wild boar with port and glazed apple, a typical hearty entrée. The rationale: "The holistic approach to well-being is increasingly recognized."

Elsewhere in the hotel, the Georgian shopping arcade has been recently expanded to include Burberry's, Harvey Nichols, and other top British manufacturers of fine merchandise. The bank and post office are still intact, as is the American Bar, a cheerful room beside a pair of mahogany swing doors at the hotel's entrance where a definitive selection of single-malt whiskies is served. At every turn, guest needs are anticipated graciously by staff members, many of them attired in the hotel's signature cream, black, and gold tartan kilts and jackets.

The resort, though closely identified with golf, has steadily broadened its appeal. The Gleneagles Jackie Stewart Shooting School, opened in 1985, was so successful it was expanded almost immediately. A rough-hewn lodge with an open hearth fireplace was built on the moors, and three new trap and skeet disciplines were added. They now include simulated bolting rabbit, settling pigeon, crossing pigeon, high pheasant, driven grouse, and rising teal. Stewart, a former auto racing champion and expert clay target marksman, is at the school on a regular basis.

The Mark Phillips Equestrian Centre, run by the ex-husband of Princess Anne and opened in 1988, is a world-class complex with covered arenas, a stable of fine horses and ponies, and superb instruction for novices and experts alike. A trail ride on the mist-covered moors in the early morning hours is not soon forgotten.

Gleneagles maintains five beats on the River Tay at Lower Scone and Almondmouth, for those who wish to angle for salmon and sea trout. Brown trout can be taken in local lochs. The hotel's guides know where the fish are.

A glass-domed health spa, Champneys, opened in 1990 at the hotel. In addition to a heated indoor swimming pool, children's pool, Jacuzzi, solaria, saunas, Turkish bath, and gymnasium, a full range of beauty and spa treatments is available. The hotel also offers croquet, lawn bowling, tennis, squash, billiards, and miles of trails for jogging or cycling.

*The hotel*

Though its amenities are as excellent and complete as those of any resort in the world, it is golf that makes Gleneagles "heich abune the heich" ("better than the best"). Among steep ridges, enclosed hollows, and elongated troughs left behind by a retreating glacier, five-time British Open champion James Braid laid out a pair of courses that to this day must be counted among the finest expressions of inland golf in the world.

The King's Course, longer and tougher of the two, circulates golfers among broom-covered slopes and flat-topped mounds on a sheltered moorland plateau 500 feet above sea level. Braid made brilliant use of the landscape's crenulations: Each hole is perfectly situated in a valley or compartment of its own. This feeling of privacy is offset by a tremendous expansiveness. Not only are fairways as broad as boulevards and greens the size of ballroom dance floors, but the forty-mile views look to the mottled-brown Ochil Hills to the east and south, the blue-tinted foothills of the Grampian Mountains to the north, and, sited on a ridge across a valley, the majestic Gleneagles Hotel, looking for all the world like a French chateau transported from the Loire Valley. The amphitheater effect created by the distant hills, the play of light on their slopes, and the layout's many elevated tees conspire to create a magical setting for golf. Closer at hand, bright yellow blossoms burst from the gorse bushes in early summer; in September, the carpets of heather turn purple. In any season, the King's is an incomparable stage for the game.

*Carriage rides travel around the estate. Photo courtesy The Gleneagles Hotel*

The routing of the course is ingenious. The first hole, a wide-open par four with the green sited atop a hill undercut by hellish bunkers, escalates golfers to a plateau on which the battle is joined for the next sixteen holes, until the grand par-five eighteenth parades players back down from the tableland.

Though it stretches to 6,815 yards for tournament play (the King's Course has been the site of the Bell's Scottish Open since 1987), the par-70 layout is best enjoyed by better players at 6,471 yards. For the less accomplished, the layout plays to a par of 68 from the forward tees at 6,125 yards.

Among the feature holes is the 374-yard third, Silver Tassie, where the blind second shot is played from a severely mounded fairway over a high, imposing ridge to a very large green set in a tassie, or cup-shaped hollow.

At the 161-yard fifth (called Het Girdle, or hot griddle), golfers mount an elevated tee sheltered by trees and play to a dangerous pulpit green, the steep slope of the green's supporting hill gouged by oblong sand pits. In a high wind, the stakes of this death-or-glory shot increase dramatically, for the green can be difficult to hold.

The best-known and most feared hole on the King's is the 448-yard thirteenth, Braid's Brawest. The drive must carry a heaving ridge pitted with two forbidding bunkers, the fairway's roller-coaster slopes often ricocheting the golf ball into unpleasant places. The long approach shot is played to a pedestal green guarded in front by a cross bunker and pinched to the left by nasty pot bunkers and a heathery downslope. The 260-yard

fourteenth, usually played downwind, can be driven by strong players, but stray shots disappear in the bracken and gorse. The green, situated in a denty den (pleasant dell), is devilishly sloped and has foiled many a long hitter with a four-putt.

Yes, the perfectly manicured turf on the King's gives the ball a flattering roll, and the broad fairways corral shots that might otherwise disappear in the broom. But when a breeze stirs, no one, not even the world's best professional, tears up the course. Then again, performance is only part of the story: Golf at Gleneagles is about reveling in the surroundings. On a fine day, with the ball flying true down fairways walled in by long sinuous ridges called eskers, and with a witty, experienced caddie at your side, the world's worries simply disappear. S.L. McKinlay, an early visitor, captured the inherent appeal of the King's Course: "At Gleneagles, the brave deserve their reward, but even the timid and incompetent cannot fail to obtain their own satisfaction."

If the King's Course is the resident Thoroughbred, the Queen's Course is its reigning beauty. Shorter and less rigorous than the King's, the Queen's encircles a number of pine-fringed lochs. Drumlins bearded with thickets of heather and gorse border the holes, many of them clever doglegs. Unlike the King's, exposed atop a plateau, the Queen's nestles on lower-lying land, its greens backdropped by tall, bottle-green firs. The layout rewards accuracy, not length, and possesses a beauty unique to itself, a beauty that disguises its challenges. The five par threes, two of them sited on the edge of Loch-an-Eerie, are superb, while the eighth and fifteenth holes, both short par fours, give big hitters a chance to reach the green with their drives. Scenic and sporty, the par 68, 5,965-yard Queen's Course (par 74 and 5,495 yards from the ladies' tees) may well be the single best venue in the world for mixed foursomes. Incidentally, the ten-minute intervals between starting times on the two courses have reduced play by 25 percent but enable guests to enjoy a more leisurely game.

Not content to rest on its laurels—according to golf professional Ian Marchbank, "If you're not moving forward in the resort business, you're sliding backwards"—Gleneagles called in Jack Nicklaus in 1989 to design a championship course to complement the King's and Queen's layouts. The existing Glendevon and Prince's courses were cannibalized for the new venue, the Monarch's Course, which opened in May 1993. Stretching to more than 7,100 yards from the tips, the par-72 layout has five sets of tees to accommodate all types of players. While James Braid had only picks and shovels, horses and carts at his disposal, Nicklaus used earthmoving equipment on stretches of flat farmland to simulate the area's glacial landforms. Holes that partake of the original Prince's Course, which shared the same topography as the King's, are exceptionally good, particularly the higher holes angled to the valley of Glendevon. Nicklaus also was asked to take into account the best vantage points for spectators—clearly the Monarch's Course was designed to host tournaments. In addition, an eleven-acre practice ground was built near the first tee and eighteenth green.

*Angling for salmon on the River Tay.
Photo courtesy The Gleneagles Hotel*

"Nicklaus took very seriously the construction of his first course in Scotland," Marchbank said of the new layout. "He was well aware of Braid's contribution and wanted to build a Scottish course (not a manufactured, American-style facility) by adapting the golf course to the terrain, not vice versa." There are, sacrilegiously, paved paths to accommodate golf carts, but early reports indicate that Jack's new creation is a superb if somewhat burlier companion to the King's and Queen's courses.

Even before the arrival of the Monarch's, Gleneagles was a fair approximation of how heaven might look to a golfer, give or take the pearly gates. The new Monarch's Course turns up the volume on the harp music.

*Queen's Course, fourteenth hole*

*Above: King's Course, fifteenth hole. Right: King's Course, sixteenth hole*

How many resort hotels in this day and age would choose to reduce their room count during a major rehabilitation to bring accommodations up to the highest standard, particularly if the hotel were not overly large to begin with and had outside its back door one of the world's finest seaside links? The answer is, very few indeed. But Turnberry, located along the Ayrshire coast in southwest Scotland not far from the birthplace of Robert Burns, is, and always has been, different.

Originally part of the Marquis of Ailsa's estate, Turnberry opened in 1906 and is recognized as the first purpose-built hotel/golf course complex ever developed. The white-faced, red-roofed Edwardian-style hotel sits

high atop a ridge, with inviting linksland at its feet and the rolling farmlands of Carrick as a backdrop. The view westward from the dining room looks past the lighthouse at the far edge of the links to ragged peaks on the distant island of Arran. Closer to shore, a granite dome known as Ailsa Crag rises from the sea, its shape appearing to rise or flatten depending on the light. On a clear day, the purple-blue coast of Northern Ireland can be sighted about seventy miles away. With a lingering sunset to admire and a glass of vintage port to accompany the Stilton cheese and homemade oatcakes served after dinner, there can be no finer window seat in all of Britain.

The mighty Ailsa Course at Turnberry, where Jack Nicklaus and Tom Watson waged their titanic struggle for the British Open title in 1977, where fighter pilots landed their planes during two world wars, and where golfers today do battle on one of the game's grandest stages, is better now than ever. The instructions to the golf staff from the resort's Japanese owners shortly after their purchase of Turnberry in 1987 were simple and to the point: "The golf course has no budget. Whatever it requires, it shall have." The mandate would be music to the ears of Scottish architect Mackenzie Ross, who revived Turnberry's Ailsa and Arran courses after World War II. (Tarmac runways are still visible in unimproved areas in the center of the links.)

Screened from the Firth of Clyde by a tall dune ridge, the 6,408-yard, par-69 Ailsa Course (6,950 yards and par 70 from the championship tees) starts off inland before sweeping to the sea at the windswept fourth hole, a difficult uphill par three of 167 yards called Woe-be-Tide. The fourth

*Ailsa Course, tenth and twelfth holes*

*Guest room. Photo courtesy Turnberry Hotel & Golf Courses*

kicks off an incomparable stretch of eight holes played along the outer perimeter of the links that have as much interest, difficulty, and beauty as any links in the world.

After negotiating the sixth hole, a well-nigh impossible par three of 222 yards (it plays like a short par four), the fairways surmount ever higher ground at the seventh and eighth holes, both colossal right-to-left doglegs, until players are brought to the cliffside ninth, a 413-yard par four named Bruce's Castle for the crumbled ruins of Robert the Bruce's ancient stronghold visible nearby. Even those playing from the shorter medal tees should summon the courage to tiptoe the narrow path that leads to the championship tee, a modest platform set atop a blackened rock pinnacle that rises from the boiling sea. "A man stands alone with his panic," is how golf commentator Henry Longhurst described a golfer's prospects from this vantage point. The tee shot must carry the better part of 175 yards to reach a hog's-back fairway marked by a stone cairn. (Hit the cairn with your drive and you owe your caddie a bottle of whisky!) The fairway, no more than thirty yards wide, rolls and tumbles along the shore to a large, bunkerless green. Gene Sarazen considered the Ailsa's ninth "the greatest par four in golf."

Ranked twentieth in the world by *GOLF Magazine* and the only resort layout to host the British Open, the Ailsa Course is a supreme test of golf. When the Firth of Clyde puffs its cheeks and exhales, it is that and more. Other courses on the British Open rota, because of their storied pasts, are more revered, but what other links employs a starter turned out in a blue blazer and rep tie who hands golfers their scorecards on the first tee and announces, when the coast is clear, "Gentlemen, play away!"?

*The hotel*

Turnberry's second layout, the par-69, 6,249-yard Arran Course, runs inland among patches of thorny gorse. Occupying flatter, more sheltered land than the Ailsa, it stresses accuracy but offers a gentle test by comparison with its big brother. It's an ideal venue for a casual second round if the weather is cooperative.

Arran or Ailsa, the day's drama can be sorted out in the hotel's cocktail bar, where the barman can discuss at length the relative merits of the more than ninety single-malt whiskies in stock. Turnberry's dining room, its bay windows bellied out onto a terrace where a lone piper in full regalia skirls his notes at day's end, serves exceptional Scottish–French cuisine. From a windowside table, one could be seated in the dining room of an ocean liner, for all one sees is water and sky. From the kitchen door filter promising scents of fresh seafood and pungent sauces used in game dishes. Nor are dinner choices restricted to dishes listed on the menu: Chef Stewart Cameron is expert at pleasing discriminating diners. Sean Connery, a frequent guest, prefers his Strinchar salmon grilled, though it's hard to improve upon the kitchen's preparation of most entrées, from Ayrshire lamb (rosettes filled with a rosemary farce and garnished with button onions, potatoes, and bacon) to pheasant, grouse, hare, and venison.

*Ailsa Course, third hole*

The hotel's public rooms, in the wake of the makeover, are especially comfortable. The Scottish country house decor is everywhere evident. For example, the walls of the hotel's elevator car are covered with the spines of leather-bound books and antique maps of Britain. Each of the day rooms, ideal for morning coffee or afternoon tea, looks to the sea beyond a pitch and putt course laid out on the beautifully landscaped grounds. Not only do primroses grace the hotel grounds, but so, incredibly, do palm trees, thanks to the warming influence of the Gulf Stream. Indeed, spring comes early and autumn late to this corner of Scotland.

The hotel, its front entrance once accessible by railway, maintains 115 accommodations (down from 134). Twenty-one of these are large suites with separate showers and Jacuzzis. All accommodations are individually and tastefully decorated. Most rooms have sea views, and each has a shiny tubular rack that warms the bath towels. The few rooms that don't face the water look to rolling hillsides dotted with grazing sheep.

Mindful of the needs of modern travelers, the resort in 1991 opened the $12-million Turnberry Country Club and Spa. The spa features sauna, steam rooms, massage, and the first hotel hydrotherapy suite in Scotland. A solarium, squash courts, a gymnasium, and an indoor swimming pool round out the complex. In addition, a new sixty-seat restaurant serves healthful spa cuisine as well as lighter international and Scottish fare. The spa facility also offers seventeen deluxe studio rooms, each with a view of the golf courses. To wake in the morning and gaze upon the majestic links, knowing that a round on the Ailsa will follow an incomparable Scottish breakfast, is enough to quicken the pace of any golfer's heart.

*Ailsa Course, eighth hole*

# WATERVILLE HOUSE & GOLF LINKS

SILVER MEDALIST

How's this for a strange pair of bedfellows? A wild and woolly links located at the tip of a rugged peninsula in southwest Ireland and a Club Med hotel that features horseback riding, Irish folk music, and games of snooker in place of windsurfing, singalongs on the beach, and costumed revues at night? Only in Ireland could such an improbable marriage work successfully.

Though a links was founded at the tip of the Iveragh Peninsula fifty miles west of Killarney shortly after the first transatlantic cable was laid at the turn of the century, the current layout, opened in 1974, was the brainchild of Jack Mulcahy, a wealthy Irish-American who spent liberally to create the sternest test of golf imaginable. With the help of Irish architect Eddie Hackett, Mulcahy routed the holes on barren, forbidding duneland routinely swept by gale-force winds. From day one, Waterville Golf Links turned the Irish golf world on its ear. Now as then, the par-72 layout stretches to 7,184 yards from the tips, an impossible distance to negotiate in high winds for all but world-class players. The medal plates at 6,549 yards are only slightly less difficult for better golfers, while the "society" tees at 6,039 yards present a fearsome test to duffers. "A beautiful monster," was how early visitor Sam Snead described the course.

Acquired in the 1980s by a consortium of Wall Street businessmen whose undisguised affection for the remote links has resulted in many changes for the better, Waterville today is fairer than its original incarnation. Certain of its incongruous touches remain, including the 100-yard-long runway-style tees and plateau greens perched atop the dunes, though many of the greenside ponds, a Mulcahy specialty, have been filled.

The front nine gets off to a mild start, though the River Inny, an estuary of the sea, flows near the second, third, and fourth holes. The green at the 362-yard third hole (all yardages are from the white tees), saved from ongoing erosion by the current owners, snuggles up to the River Inny, its devilish location suggested by PGA Tour Commissioner Deane Beman.

The 155-yard seventh, called The Island, is one of the top par threes on the course. (No less an authority than Tom Watson ranks Waterville's collection of par threes among the best in the world.) The tee shot must carry a pair of lakes that protect the front of the green. (As a joke, or maybe not, there's a life preserver ring in the water hazard.) Depending upon the breeze, club selection can range from a 3-wood to a 7-iron.

*Waterville House. Photo courtesy © Lynne Connally*

Waterville's back nine produces a sequence of stunning challenges on the wildest and most spectacular duneland south of Ballybunion. There's the 154-yard twelfth, called The Mass Hole, where the local population celebrated Mass in the vast hollow in front of the green during Cromwell's Penal Days, a time when prayer was an offense punishable by death. (The original links design called for the green to be placed in this hidden valley, but the location was changed when workmen refused to disturb the sacred ground.)

The sixteenth, a boomerang-shaped par four formerly known as Round the Bend, is nearly as storied. The hole was renamed Liam's Ace shortly after Waterville pro Liam Higgins, one of the longest hitters in Europe, aced the hole from 366 yards en route to a course record 65 in 1979.

*Sheep graze the Irish countryside*

*Fifteenth hole. Photo courtesy © Lynne Connally*

Cutting off most of the dogleg on his drive, it is said that Higgins took aim at a leprechaun holding a shamrock in the sky above the green before delivering the ball a mighty blow.

The tee at the 153-yard seventeenth, Mulcahy's Peak, occupies the flattened top of the tallest dune on the links. It's a perfect vantage point from which to view Waterville's magnificent land's-end scenery: Ballinskelligs Bay, Lough Currane, and, in the far distance, a range of peaks known as Macgillicuddy's Reeks. The challenge at hand is of a sort that whitens knuckles: A tiny green beckons from atop a small dune beyond a valley choked with vegetation.

Waterville's eighteenth hole, a huge par five of 550 yards, is formidable from start to finish. A sandy beach marks the out-of-bounds up the right side, with an abundance of heavy rough guarding the left side. The green is well bunkered. By this point in the round, the wind has whipped most players' scorecards to shreds.

Following a $7-million renovation of the former Waterville Lake Hotel, the Club Med now operates an elegant three-story hostelry with eighty double-occupancy rooms, each with telephone and television, both rare creature comforts at one of the French company's typical properties in the tropics. In addition, the hotel has six suites, each with fireplace, balcony overlooking Lough Currane, walk-in dressing room, and lounge. Visitors can also book into Waterville House, which dates to the late eighteenth century and was Jack Mulcahy's former residence. Completely renovated, Waterville House offers ten spacious suites, eight fireplaces, and access to Ireland's best salmon fishing.

Club Med's new facilities include a main dining room with a panoramic view of the lake and countryside. Meals feature French, continental, and Gaelic dishes, with flexible dining hours to suit late-to-return golfers and fishermen. Fresh salmon and trout taken locally is incomparable, especially in the hands of French chefs. There's a comfortable piano bar in the Club's lounge and a typical Irish pub, Skelligs Bar, where Irish folk singers and Guinness on tap are featured. (It should be noted that Guinness is no ordinary tipple in Ireland but a staff of life considered both drink and food.)

Club Med–Waterville also has a large indoor heated swimming pool and a fitness center with the latest in exercise equipment, ideal for the building of muscles required to prevail on the Waterville Golf Links. True to Club Med style, everything (except green fees) is included in the cost: accommodations, all meals, wine and beer with lunch and dinner, use of recreational facilities, and nightly entertainment. A typical sun 'n surf Club Med it's not. Yet the French have been crossing the English Channel en masse to test their skills on a ferocious links more difficult by far than any other in Ireland.

Take an unspoiled corner of the second-largest island in the Mediterranean Sea, let a cultivated billionaire with preservationist leanings discover it, and a glorious resort should blossom. That was the script for the development of the Costa Smeralda, a thirty-five mile stretch of untouched coastline in Sardinia, a forty-five-minute flight from Rome and an hour's drive from the airport in Olbia. Purchased by a consortium formed by the Aga Khan in the early 1960s, the Costa Smeralda (the name is derived from the striking hue of the translucent sea, which varies from emerald green to turquoise blue) was developed with exceptional care and taste. The resort's six intimate, ultra-luxurious hotels, each with its own personality, were chiseled into an arid coast of wind-sculpted rock, secluded bays, and hidden beaches. Artfully blended into the landscape, these hotels resemble weathered Sardinian fishing hamlets from another century. Their rough stucco exteriors have been allowed to discolor, while the dull red tile for their roofs was taken from old homes in the interior.

Pevero Golf Club, opened in 1972, straddles a promontory separating the sandy Bay of Pevero and Cala di Volpe—the Bay of Foxes. The course was designed by Robert Trent Jones but exhibits few of his trademarks. So unyielding was the terrain that Jones, his arm twisted by necessity, was required to follow the natural rise and fall of the land in his routing. (Jones was forced to dynamite the holes into the stony ground.) The high expense of hacking fairways from rock accounts in part for their narrowness. In fact, an inspired feat of engineering was required to construct the course.

In his book *Golf's Magnificent Challenge*, Jones addressed the construction dilemmas at Pevero. "The Aga Khan . . . called a meeting to discuss grassing the golf course. He had called in four Italian agronomists who told him that, because there was very little topsoil on the island, he had to bring in enough topsoil to spread a foot of it over the entire course, and it was going to cost millions.

"In the meantime, I had discovered that there was a lot of disintegrated granite on the property that could be crushed into dust and, with proper nutrients added, be used as soil. I said, 'Your Highness, it's your money, but if you want to take a chance on spending $35,000 for seed, I don't think you'll have to spend millions for topsoil.' Two years later they played the Italian Open there on lush grass growing in granite."

Because the fairways overlay rock, the ball tends to scoot and roll upon touchdown. Then again, a computerized irrigation system installed in 1991 is linked to a meteorological station, so that watering times are automatically adjusted to prevailing weather conditions. The course today, one of the most dramatically sited in Europe, is in superb condition.

Pevero rewards accuracy, not prodigious hitting. Alitalia's guide to Italian golf courses has this to say about the layout: "The biggest problem here is the impossibility of executing successful recovery shots off the fairway." The statement is accurate. Pevero's rough is *really* rough. Giant nuggets of fissured granite rise from lupin, lavender, and maquis, a thick, scrubby underbrush favored by wild boars. Exit the fairway at Pevero and simply bid your ball *arrivederci!*

Even Pevero's fairways aren't always safe. At the first hole, a long par four that sweeps into a valley, a trio of olive trees on the right side of the

fairway inconveniences an approach shot should your drive come to rest behind them. The 421-yard second hole (all yardages are from the men's tees at 6,799 yards, though a shorter set of markers calculated in meters is available) doglegs sharply to a green backdropped by a massive rock pile that looks borrowed from Tucson. The massive 565-yard third climbs to a high plateau green before plunging downhill at the 389-yard fourth hole, where the tee shot is played directly to the sea, with Corsica's sawtooth peaks rising in the far distance. The 188-yard seventh must take its place among Jones's best one-shotters: From a tee cut into the side of a hill bristling with vegetation, the shot is played across a lake to a shallow, well-bunkered green. Like most greens on the course, it is large and speedy, with many subtle breaks that are difficult to read.

Pevero's shorter, sportier back nine ranks among the world's most scenic. At the 400-yard thirteenth, the spectacular top-of-the-world views from the green across Cala di Volpe to rugged mountains in Sardinia's interior tend to upstage the hole's challenge. At the 201-yard fourteenth, the sea-and-mountain

*Above: Terrace overlooking the Cala di Volpe (Bay of Foxes)*

*Right: Hotel Cala di Volpe*

*Opposite above: Pier leading to Hotel Cala di Volpe*

*Opposite below: Eighteenth hole*

view from the tee is again breathtaking, the hazards posed by the rocky thickets of thorny shrubs lining the fairways seemingly diminished by the vista. Perhaps the stiffest challenge on the back nine is found at the uphill 542-yard eighteenth, where golfers climb a bottleneck fairway to a well-bunkered green located near a handsome clubhouse. Inside is a comfortable bar and a pro shop stocked with fine Italian golfwear.

Strategically, Pevero cannot be placed in Jones's pantheon of great designs. But scenically, it may have no peer among the more than 500 courses he has built. Pevero is not a course that can be assessed apart from its magnificent surroundings.

Caddies are available on request, though most players choose to pull a trolley or ride in a golf cart. The existing course may be eclipsed by a proposed twenty-seven-hole layout to be designed by Jack Nicklaus. Pending zoning approvals, the course, which will occupy a peninsula near the lavish Hotel Romazzino, has the potential to become one of the finest in Europe.

Of the six hotels available to Costa Smeralda visitors, Cala di Volpe is closest to the golf club and is perhaps the most distinctive. Designed by French architect Jacques Couelle, a self-described "artist who makes

*Lagoon and Hotel Cala di Volpe*

*Seventeenth hole*

buildings," the hotel from afar appears to be a Moorish jumble of crooked towers, rough porticoes, and rakishly angled roofs. Inside, narrow passageways honeycomb the white stucco interior, with multicolored windows—actually gobs of colored glass wedged into the plaster—admitting rainbow sunbeams. Public rooms throughout resemble a medieval Greek monastery run riotously amok. Juniper beams support the ceilings of the hotel's 123 rough-plaster rooms, each of them furnished with Sardinian arts, crafts, and antique reproductions. Cala di Volpe is by turns calculatedly eccentric and deliberately imperfect. Also very glamorous. It's a favorite getaway for European movie stars and a favorite stage set for fashion photographers.

Cala di Volpe's candlelit dining room, overlooking the bay, is formal, grandiose, and in every way exceptional. Sardinian seafood specialties—*spaghetti alla bottarga* (with mullet roe), *zuppa del pescatore* (Sardinian bouillabaisse), and pastas with sauces of *vongole* (clams), tomatoes, and basil are beyond compare. Also popular is *carta di musica* (music paper), a

parchmentlike flatbread named for the rustling its makes when eaten dry. (It plays a different melody when brushed with olive oil, sprinkled with rosemary, and heated.) *Pecorino sardo*—tangy Sardinian ewe's milk

Bar Pontile (Piano Bar), Hotel Cala di Volpe. Photo courtesy Pevero Golf Club

cheese—can be ordered in place of dessert. All dishes are accompanied by surprisingly fine regional wines, particularly the dry white Nuragus and sparkling white Vermentino di Gallura.

The hotel, which fronts one of the Costa Smeralda's most beautiful bays, has a delightful piano bar overlooking the sea and a throbbing basement disco called the Fox. Cala di Volpe's Olympic-size saltwater pool blends into the hotel's gardens, while the hotel's private beach, a secluded crescent of sand set with blue-canvas chaises and thatch umbrellas, is ten minutes away by launch. Motorboats are available for coastline tours.

The sumptuousness and rustic finery of the Costa Smeralda does not come cheap. In high season (June 20 to September 15), when a veritable navy of European aristocrats anchors its yachts at Porto Cervo, the resort area's deep-water port, double occupancy rates at Cala di Volpe or the fabulous Hotel Romazzino start at approximately $450 per night, per person (room tariffs include meals). During the less hectic periods from mid-May to mid-June and from mid-September to mid-October, rates drop by 35 percent. The weather, which can be very hot in summer, is best for golf during the cooler shoulder seasons. At most any time of year, the Costa Smeralda offers the most authentic slice of *la dolce vita* this side of a Fellini film.

Tenth hole

# PENINA GOLF HOTEL

A half-hour's flight south of Lisbon is the Algarve, an ancient kingdom fronting the Atlantic that retains a strong Moorish influence. It was to Portugal's Algarve that many Britons emigrated in the 1950s for sun and relaxation. Before long, golf courses began to sprout along the coast and in the foothills of the mountains that block the flow of cold air to the south.

Near the seaport of Portimão, its quayside cafés known for their grilled sardine lunches, is Penina, the oldest and most revered of the Algarve's golf resorts. The property was conceived by John Stilwell, an Englishman whose family is a major rice producer in the north of Portugal. It was Stilwell's farsighted notion in the mid-1960s to convert a large field of sodden rice paddies into a golf course. Pancake flat and virtually treeless, the site was planted in flowering shrubs, casuarina pines, and more than 350,000 eucalyptus trees, a tree native to Australia that grows quickly and absorbs much moisture. According to Stilwell, "Our goal was to build a course that could host major competitions but that would not be too difficult for the average resort golfer."

Though the course can be stretched to the ungodly length of 7,480 yards for tournaments (Penina is a five-time site of the Portuguese Open and hosted the 1976 World Amateur Team Championship), it measures 7,041 yards from the medal tees and a somewhat more reasonable 6,624 yards from the men's yellow tees. Ladies have all they can handle from the far forward tees at 5,822 yards, the tees British golf legend and course designer Henry Cotton played up until his death in 1987 at the age of eighty. All through his seventies, Cotton, a three-time British Open champion, played effortless golf nearly every day on the course he considered his design masterpiece.

Cotton said of Penina: "The course cannot be bullied; there are so many nominated shots to be played across water hazards or around doglegs. Play safe all the time and you can score." Cotton, however, failed to mention what number you would score by playing safe. Suffice to say that chances must be taken at Penina to gain the upper hand. It is a course for judicious gamblers and master tacticians who possess the length and imagination to skirt the hazards and plot the safest route to the green.

The relative shortness of Penina's par-35 front nine can deceive. The back side is a par 38 with four par fives, most of them requiring forced carries over watery ditches. For the first-time player, each of the long holes is a worrisome journey down an uncertain highway.

"If you don't build a certain amount of controversy into a golf course, people soon forget it. In their grumbling, they remember it," was Cotton's explanation for this water-smitten design.

Penina's signature hole is the 187-yard thirteenth (227 yards from the tips). A meandering creek, its tannin-stained water the color of oxtail soup, forms a lateral hazard down the right side of the hole, crossing in front of the green below several deep bunkers. Anything less than a perfectly stroked long iron or fairway wood scares away the white egrets that alight along the canal.

Ranked the toughest course in the Algarve, Penina still remains an "agreeable setting for the resident or visitor of more modest attainment," in the words of golf commentator Henry Longhurst. Indeed, there are no hills to climb, there is no rough immediately in front of the tees, and slopes on the large, velvety greens are comparatively gentle. At the same time, the opportunity to bury a ball in a watery grave is ever present.

The resort also offers a pair of sporty nine-hole layouts. The 2,035-yard, par-30 Quinta Course is a so-so links contained within the original eighteen; while the 3,268-yard, par-35 Monchique Course, of higher

*Swimming pool*

*Ninth hole*

quality, is located across the highway from the main resort complex. Guests are not charged a green fee to play the three courses.

From several points on the championship course, players have good views of the 200-room, Swiss-designed hotel, its three wings arranged in a crescent and set on a hill beside a large, kidney-shaped swimming pool. There is no clubhouse per se at Penina—the ground floor of the hotel contains the pro shop and locker room, so that golfers need only take the elevator downstairs from their rooms to commence their rounds. One floor up is the wood-paneled Monchique Grill, where meals are served on engraved pewter placemats. Entrées, including a selection of local fish, are cooked on an open charcoal grill. Meals usually begin with *caldo verde*, a cabbage broth flavored with *chourico*—chunks of dried smoked sausage. Menu prices are quoted in pounds sterling, not surprising given the hotel's largely British clientele. Public rooms throughout have the drawing room elegance of an English country manor.

The hotel's spacious guest rooms, beautifully appointed with polished wood furnishings, have terraces angled to cultivated fields below ferrous-orange foothills, or to violet-blue peaks in the Serra do Monchique. Each room is stocked with a complimentary half-bottle of Dow's tawny Boardroom Port, produced by Stilwell's relations in the north.

By day, a shuttle bus carries guests to nearby Alvor and its yellow sand beach, where the resort provides chaise longues and snacks. Beachgoers—and golfers seeking respite from Cotton's watery monster—often return in the evening to gamble at the Alvor Casino.

*Buffet. Photo courtesy Penina Golf Hotel*

# QUINTA DO LAGO

SILVER MEDALIST

honest, solid, straightforward test of golf, it is always kept in superb condition. Certainly the roominess of the core nines is welcome to duffers: Quinta do Lago is holiday golf at its best.

In addition to the informal Pergola restaurant, its flower-decked poolside terrace open for lunch and dinner, the resort's Casa Velha restaurant, reconstructed from a 300-year-old farmhouse, is a charming room with farm tools hung on its bleached white walls. There's a pianist on hand nightly and many fine regional seafood dishes on the menu,

Quinta do Lago ("farmhouse on the lagoon"), the most typically American of the Algarve's top golf resorts, occupies a former cattle ranch and potato farm in Almansil, fifteen miles west of the airport in Faro. (Faro is a half-hour's flight from Lisbon.) Bounded by the Atlantic Ocean and the Rio Formosa tidal inlet, an important sanctuary and staging area

*The hotel*

for migratory birds, the 1,690-acre resort is built around four lakes, one of them a large saltwater pond used for sailing, windsurfing, and other "non-polluting" sports.

The resort's three nine-hole loops, designed by American architect William Mitchell in 1974, permit eighteen-hole play in a variety of combinations. Par is 72 and the average length from the men's tees is 6,800 yards, regardless of the two nines chosen. (Reports are mixed on whether or not the resort's new fourth nine complements the original twenty-seven-hole spread.)

Quinta do Lago's B and C nines, the eighteen-hole configuration currently used to host the Portuguese Open, are very dramatic, with water in play on several of the holes and good sea views from the elevated tees. The upcountry A nine is a stunner, its fairways cut through umbrella pines that look like emerald-green lollipops stuck in the ground. Holes are backdropped by cauldron-shaped peaks in the Serra de Caldeirão. Fairways throughout are wide and rolling, the pathways clearly defined not by rough or bunkers, but by the contours of the terrain and by pine spinneys that jut into the fairways. The architecture is restrained, unadorned: The doglegs are gently angled, while the speedy greens have mild undulations.

With plenty of room to drive the ball and little fairway sand to worry about, Quinta do Lago has received high marks from European PGA Tour professionals, who praise its fairness and overall lack of gimmickry. An

*D nine, sixth hole*

including pumpkin soup with lobster (better than it sounds), prawns with Roquefort cheese, and *espadarte fumado*—smoked swordfish. Crystalized tangerines and cakes made from eggs, almonds, and sugar are popular desserts.

The 150-room Hotel Quinta do Lago, built by Saudi Arabian Prince Faisal and opened in 1988, is a dazzling white edifice with a terra-cotta tile roof set on a hill overlooking the tidal estuary. The large, airy rooms, furnished in neutral woods and pastel greens, blues, and pinks, open onto large terraces edged with tiles and hung with flowering plants. Public rooms have marble floors, wood paneling, patterned chairs, and flashy green-gold light fixtures. Restaurants at the hotel include Ca d'Oro, serving Italian cuisine, and Navegadores, its blue-and-white tiled walls depicting seafaring scenes and its menu dedicated to traditional Portuguese fare.

If horseback riding is your pleasure, pack your boots along with your spikes—Quinta do Lago has some of the best and most beautiful trails in southern Europe. The resort's Pinetrees Riding Centre has twenty horses as well as a riding ring. There's also a health club, gymnasium, sauna, heated indoor and outdoor pools, and snooker tables (the British influence) at the hotel.

The buzzwords at Quinta do Lago these days are "greenbelt" and "low density occupation," for only 7 percent of the resort's grounds have been built upon. More golf is planned, though it will have to be truly inspired to surpass the original twenty-seven-hole layout that is to the Algarve what Pinehurst is to North Carolina.

Indoor pool. *Photo courtesy Quinta do Lago*

# VILAMOURA GOLF CLUB

SILVER MEDALIST

After driving by fields of wild artichokes and bus stops plastered with bullfight posters along the Algarve's main artery, golfers arrive at Vilamoura, a well-established resort set among thick stands of umbrella pines and mimosa shrubs in sight of the sea. Built in 1969 by Frank Pennink, an English amateur champion and Walker Cup team member who turned his hand to golf course architecture when his competition days were over, the original 6,924-yard, par-73 Vilamoura layout owes much in design and concept to the Surrey heathland courses outside London. Narrow, undulating fairways plunge and dogleg through thick stands of umbrella pines, presenting a stern test of accuracy. Well-placed drives and pinpoint iron shots must be played to return a good score.

Vilamoura starts off with a few average holes set on elevated terrain. Then comes the first in a series of rigorous par threes that form the backbone of the course. A lake must be carried at the 157-yard fifth hole, its green beautifully framed by tall conifers. The 226-yard sixth hole is

relatively trouble free (which is only fair, considering its great distance), while the 153-yard tenth hole calls for a Merion-style carry over a deep ravine of parched scrub. Several of the back nine holes play to distant violet-blue peaks in the Monchique mountains, though golfers never quite escape the maritime influence. Wiggle your feet into the coarse Atlantic sand that fills the bunkers, and cockleshells will rise up around your shoelaces.

More than most Algarve resorts, Vilamoura approximates the ambiance of a private country club and attracts serious golfers with established

*Seventeenth hole*

*Vilamoura and the marina*

*Eighteenth hole and clubhouse*

handicaps, not casual holidaymakers. Like Quinta do Lago, Vilamoura is situated on a large estate with few reminders of civilization to intrude on the golf experience. There's no concrete on the course—all paths are of sand—and several of the holes have acres of sandy scrub in front of the trees, not unlike Pine Valley. Putting surfaces are relatively flat, with no "valleys of sin" or radical swales to confound players. Despite the lack of tomfoolery on the greens, however, scores can run high at Vilamoura. Nancy Lopez was medalist in the Women's World Amateur Team Championship in 1976 with a five-over-par score of 297 for seventy-two holes. (The course was played at 6,181 yards during the tournament.)

Vilamoura acquired a neighboring course, the Dom Pedro Golf Club, another Pennink design, in the mid-1980s. Renamed Vilamoura II, the course was improved and reworked by Robert Trent Jones, who authored nine new holes for the par-72, 6,920-yard layout. Relatively open, with wider, more rolling fairways than the original course, it is altogether a friendlier layout. Yet water is more of a factor. So is the steady ocean breeze on the more exposed holes. For those seeking to fine-tune their game, Vilamoura II features one of the Algarve's finest practice facilities.

The Hotel Dom Pedro, situated close by the beach, has 260 air-conditioned rooms with balconies. The resort also has villas for rent near the two layouts.

A short drive from the golf courses is the sleek 388-room Vilamoura Marinotel, which anchors the resort's busy 1,000-slip marina. Lively outdoor cafés, restaurants, and clubs line the perimeter of the marina, which is ground zero in the summer months. Vacationers stay at the Marinotel; golfers book a room nearer the golf courses, venturing to the Marinotel's Sirius Grill in the evening for its giant prawns and grouper steak with Pernod flambé.

# ESTORIL PALACIO GOLF CLUB

SILVER MEDALIST

Golfers visiting Lisbon can play several excellent resort courses in the city's fashionable suburbs of Estoril (pronounced Schto-REEL) and Cascais (Cash-KAISH). Both towns hug the mouth of the Tagus River near where it empties into the Atlantic Ocean, their courses stretched between serrated blue peaks in the Serra de Sintra and the Atlantic Ocean.

Most venerable among these courses is the Estoril Palacio Golf Club, a par-69 layout that is short at 5,742 yards but long on trouble. Site of the Portuguese Open from 1953 through 1974, the course was extended to

eighteen holes in 1938 by Scottish architect Mackenzie Ross (of Turnberry fame) from an existing nine-hole layout. Many of the holes are minor masterpieces that force even the greatest players to forfeit a shot or two.

Engraved on a forested hillside in view of Lisbon and the sea, Estoril is a beautiful course that regularly attracts Portuguese government officials who converse in a language that relies heavily on sweeping "oosh" and "dhoo" sounds. Many of these players have mastered the rolling layout's idiosyncracies. For example, the 517-yard fifth, one of two par fives on the course, plays straightaway up a slim, undulating fairway tunneled through an old forest. The double-tiered, tabletop green calls for a meticulous touch to solve its tricky breaks. Find the wrong spot on this green and three putts is a given.

The zaniest and perhaps the most thrilling hole on the course is the 171-yard ninth, where tee shots are played from a clifftop tee 150 feet above green level. The shot flies over a busy highway to the green, but only a 7- or 8-iron is required, because the elevation substantially reduces the actual distance the ball must travel. Still, a tricky crosswind can play havoc with tee shots.

Estoril's back nine is longer and tougher than the front, its challenges epitomized by the alarming 274-yard thirteenth hole, with its wall of trees

*Fifth hole*

*Dining room. Photo courtesy Estoril Palacio Golf Club, © Michael Howard*

and out-of-bounds stakes up both sides of an extremely narrow fairway. Stray hitters can empty their bag of its ball supply on this tee. Stick with the club's sporty 2,547-yard, par-34 nine-hole course if you are less than deadly accurate off the tee. The club's caddies, many of whom apprentice at the club at an early age, are first-rate.

Estoril's luxurious clubhouse, set behind the eighteenth green, is as welcoming as any in Europe, its windowed front facing the course and its second-floor terrace set above the practice putting green. The restaurant and two bars are under the management of the Hotel Palacio three miles down the road (hotel guests are made temporary members of the golf club).

The hotel, set in a garden overlooking the sea, offers 162 rooms and twenty-seven suites tastefully furnished in both traditional and contemporary styles. Handsome public rooms with marble columns, terrazzo floors, Wedgwood friezes, and high cathedral windows are lit by crystal chandeliers. The hotel exudes the kind of well-bred splendor favored by exiled aristocrats. French–Portuguese cuisine is featured in the dining room, which overlooks the gardens and swimming pool. As a place to relax and unwind after tackling the toughest little course in Europe, the Estoril Palacio is a perfect refuge for exasperated golfers.

*Grounds and pool at the hotel*

# TORREQUEBRADA

SILVER MEDALIST

Thirty years ago, Spain's Costa del Sol was little more than a string of humble fishing villages stretched along the Mediterranean Sea and backdropped by arid, hilly land dotted with whitewashed cottages. Then, sun-starved northern Europeans began to discover the region. Developers bypassed zoning codes to erect garish highrises that creep to the edge of

the sea. Golf courses sprang up, too, but by the 1980s the prospect of a six-hour round and an exorbitant green fee sent the cognoscenti elsewhere. The Costa del Sol had become the "Costa del Ripoff."

In the sad aftermath of overdevelopment, one property has retained the flavor of the region's original appeal. The Hotel Torrequebrada, located eight miles from Malaga (itself an hour's flight from Madrid), is a Vegas-style hotel that is as glitzy as any property on the Costa del Sol. However, it offers guests free green fees on a golf course that without reservation is the most spectacular layout in mainland Europe.

Designed by five-time Spanish Amateur champion José "Pepe" Gancedo in 1977, Torrequebrada is a thrilling test of golf calling for equal measures of skill, luck, and humor. Set in rolling foothills between the Mediterranean Sea and the mountains of the Sierra de Mijas, the holes

*Eleventh hole*

plunge into valleys or follow tortuous routes over heaving hills. With out of bounds to the right on fourteen holes, it's a slicer's nightmare. Landing areas are pinched throughout by trees, thick rough, and sand. Several trees have been left in front of the greens, serving both as signposts and obstacles.

At Torrequebrada, shotmaking is the golfing equivalent of bullfighting. Only the bold survive, though even a Seve Ballesteros (who loves the course) wouldn't be caught dead at Torrequebrada without a good luck charm in his pocket. Play to the wrong side of a fairway by a yard or two, and a long trickle downhill awaits. Fail to account for a fifteen-foot sidehill break on one of the large, treacherous greens, and a four-putt is the penalty. Torrequebrada is the shortest of the Costa del Sol's major tracks at 6,410 yards, but a unique brand of golf is required to conquer it.

*Tenth hole*

Matadors who can pinpoint shots with unerring accuracy do just fine. The rest soak up the glorious scenery and hope they don't run out of golf balls.

Best of all, Torrequebrada offers respite from the Costa del Sol's hubbub. The holes, one different and more breathtaking than the last, are played without intrusion from adjacent fairways. Several of the greens perch on the edge of hilly goat pastures or cozy up to one of six lakes. Only once, at the seventh green, do golfers catch a glimpse of the busy highway that pulses with traffic in high season. (Plan a trip to the Costa del Sol in the spring or fall—summer is far too hectic.)

Among Torrequebrada's feature holes is the 375-yard second, where the drive must carry a deep gorge to a narrow fairway, with the approach played to an elevated green screened in front by a grove of trees. The third is a downhill pitch of less than 100 yards to a skinny green that falls away on all sides to inescapable trouble. It calls for steady nerves and a delicate touch, a recipe for success on this most outlandish of golf courses. Triumph or disaster, the views from the course of the sea, the mountains, and the village of Benalmadena, which dates to ancient Roman times, are what bring golfers back to Torrequebrada.

The Hotel Torrequebrada, opened in 1988 and set on a 15,000-acre estate, consists of two thirteen-story towers located near the pebbly Mediterranean beach. The hotel's 350 rooms, including twenty-two suites, are stylishly appointed. All have terraces with sea views. There are four restaurants, including the elegant Café Royale, notable for its French–Basque cuisine; and five bars, one a piano bar and another set in tropical gardens beside the pool. In the seaside Aquarius spa, a health and fitness club, thalassotherapy (saltwater-and-seaweed treatment) is available.

The hotel's Fortuna nightclub, considered the liveliest on the Costa del Sol, features twice-nightly floor shows. The plush Casino Torrequebrada, reputedly the largest gaming house in Europe, offers all the usual games of chance. Roulette, baccarat, blackjack—none holds greater promise of reward than Torrequebrada's magnificent golf course.

# LA MANGA CLUB

Above: South Course, third hole. Right: North Course, ninth hole

Spain's Costa Blanca (white coast) extends along the Mediterranean Sea in the province of Alicante, an unheralded region with perhaps one-sixth the tourism of the Costa del Sol. To the north, a curtain of mountains runs parallel to the sea, descending at times to form cliffs; in the south, a vast, sandy plain of palm trees and salt deposits forms a backdrop for the beaches. Portions of the southern coast have been shamelessly exploited, but La Manga remains an isolated 1,100-acre enclave in the hills above the sea.

Built by an American millionaire in the early 1970s, La Manga (*manga* means sleeve; the resort is named for a nearby sleeve-shaped peninsula) has two fine courses. Both were designed in 1972 by Robert Dean Putnam, a former commercial artist who later established his own course design firm.

The par-72 South Course, five-time site of the Spanish Open, stretches to 6,855 yards from the tips (6,510 yards from the men's tees) and is set in a valley below kettle-shaped peaks. In many respects, it resembles an American-style course from the period: Broad, welcoming fairways lead to large, flat greens. It also could pass for a course in Palm Springs: More than 3,000 date palms define the fields of play. However, nasty barrancas crisscross the layout, some of them forbidding, twenty-yard-wide cactus-strewn trenches. Forced carries from the tee and again on approach shots are a signature feature of the layout. The most unusual hole on the course is the short par-three third, where former director of golf Gary Player suggested the building of a shallow bunker in the center of the green to strengthen the hole. It's the only mark of eccentricity on the layout.

Overall, the South Course offers solid, straightforward golf, its flat fairways ideal for walkers. But for pure pleasure, La Manga's North Course is the venue of choice.

Routed on higher ground, the 6,125-yard, par-71 North Course (6,455 yards from the back tees) ascends the foothills of the mountains, offering spectacular views of a Miami-style hotel strip on a faraway peninsula with the Mediterranean Sea on one side and a lagoon, Mar Menor, on the other. The hillier terrain makes for more interesting holes, with shots played from canted lies to greens cut into the sides of hills. The shots golfers play may be shorter than those required on the South, but accuracy is stressed on the North, especially when you consider that ice plant blooms in the rough. Both of La Manga's layouts are exceptionally well kept. Caddies are available. So are lessons from Vicente Ballesteros, Seve's younger brother.

The forty-seven rooms in the Club Hotel each have flower-decked terraces with views over the golf courses and Mar Menor. A sister property, which could pass for a Moorish castle, offers eighty three-bedroom suites. In addition, numerous villas and apartments are available for rent at La Manga.

The main restaurant in the Club Hotel is Las Mimosas, which sets a fine buffet breakfast. The prix fixe menu at lunch and dinner changes daily, though à la carte meals are also available. Flamenco shows and other live entertainments are staged nightly in the dining room.

For authentic regional cuisine, Las Parras, built to resemble an old Spanish farmhouse, serves many unusual delicacies. At each table is a wrought-iron rack hung with various types of sausage highly seasoned with spices and herbs. Arroz a banda, a rice dish with fish, chicken, rabbit, or dove accompanied by local vegetables and cooked over an open wood fire, is exceptional. Also delicious are the empanadas: open-faced pies with vegetables and salted meat or fish added. Prix fixe meals include a small jug of wine. After the meal, patrons are invited to relax with a fine brandy while a resident Spanish dancer stamps her feet and swirls her mantilla with fire and passion.

A full-service resort, La Manga also offers a pitch and putt course opposite its seven tennis courts, a gymnasium and spa, a heated swimming pool, and a beach club where sunbathing and windsurfing are popular. There's also the opportunity to ride an Andalusian horse through the Murcian hills high above the North Course.

The plaza

# DEAUVILLE
# GOLF CLUB

Claude Monet and other Impressionists journeyed to Deauville, a seaside resort town in Normandy about 125 miles west of Paris, to paint in the luminous light that suffuses the region. Artists still find their way to Deauville, but so do high-society gamblers, serious horse players, and the haut monde. Deauville is to Parisians what the Hamptons are to New Yorkers: the most select beach getaway convenient to the metropolis.

Set on spacious grounds atop Mont Canisy two miles from the center of town is the 170-room Hotel du Golf, built in a neo–Norman style of timbered walls in 1929. Inside the hotel is a time warp, its Art Deco furnishings and crystal chandeliers still intact, its bar containing murals of famous golfers and Deauville regulars (including French automobile titan André Citroën, who lost his fortune in one night at the casino). Rooms, while large and nicely furnished, are not nearly as elegant as those at the Hotel Normandy and Hotel Royal, affiliated properties located in the center of town a stone's throw from Les Planches (the boardwalk) and its

*The hotel. Photo courtesy © Brian McCallen*

*Putting green and clubhouse*

bustling seaside cafés. But neither of these fine hotels has on its doorstep one of the most scenic and enjoyable resort courses in France.

Designed in 1929 by Tom Simpson, known for his touch-up work at Ballybunion in Ireland and Muirfield in Scotland, the original Red and White nines offer a splendid test of English parkland–style golf set on rolling land that looks to the broad bay of the River Seine and the fishing village of Trouville. Closer at hand, the rolling green hills of the Pays d'Auge (where Normandy's incomparable Camembert cheese is produced) border the holes, which were designed to flatter a holidaymaker's game, not spoil it. With only ten golf carts available at the club, the course is walked by most visitors.

The opening nine, the compact 2,963-yard, par-35 Red Course, is a friendly initiation. The lush grass is flecked with tiny buttercups, the fairways are very wide, and the bunkers are posted well short of the greens.

The longer White nine is more serious stuff. The stretch of par fours from eleven through fourteen is superb, the canted fairways sloping to

apple orchards and thatched-roof cottages. There is history, too. Bordering the thirteenth tee are the ivy-covered ruins of a magnificent castle built by Louis XIV for one of his mistresses. It was razed during the French Revolution.

The White finishes in grand style. The seventeenth is a gorgeous mid-length par three, the sloping green underslung by a large bunker, while the short par-four eighteenth parades golfers past the impressive facade of the hotel.

The club's Blue nine, designed by Henry Cotton and opened in 1964, is the most challenging of the nines but perhaps not quite as charming as the original eighteen.

Hot meals are available in the golf clubhouse, which overlooks a practice putting green bordered by petunias. The hotel bar adjoins the golf course, and players are welcome to dine al fresco in fair weather. The hotel's Panoramic Restaurant is well named, its huge picture windows affording views of incoming golfers as well as glorious sunsets over the

English Channel. The dining room's specialties include turbot with langoustine sauce, and duck breast with fresh morel mushrooms. Dinner is usually polished off with Calvados, a fragrant brown brandy made from local apples.

Afterwards, there is opportunity to explore the smart shops of Deauville, a town built in 1861 by the Duc de Morny, the illegitimate half-brother of Napoleon III. Modeled after England's classic seaside resorts, Deauville has two race tracks, including the famous Hippodrome de la Touques, where the horse racing in summer is unequaled in Europe. In the Casino de Deauville, a grand gaming hall dating to 1912, chemin de fer, baccarat, and other games of chance are staged in pink marble salons ringed with columns and murals of nymphs and centaurs.

Deauville's high season is July and August. Rooms are hard to come by during that period, and the Hotel du Golf has no golf package available in those months. For golfers who don't feel the need to be in Deauville at the zenith of the season, spring and fall are the best times to visit.

*Seventeenth hole. Photo courtesy © Brian McCallen*

# EUROPE

## TIPS AND SIDE TRIPS

*Trouville, France. Photo courtesy French Government Tourist Office © Tripelon Jarry*

An hour's drive east from Gleneagles is St. Andrews, the birthplace of the game. The town's four courses are public, though advance reservations are required to play the fabled Old Course. St. Andrews itself dates to the sixth century. A walk round its lanes is a trip back in time to the Middle Ages. Must-sees: the ruins of the Cathedral; its cemetery, where Old Tom Morris and his son Young Tom are buried; St. Andrews University, founded in 1412 and the oldest center of learning in Scotland; and the St. Andrews Woolen Mill, for great buys on sweaters.

Scotland is also the home of whisky—there are more than a hundred single malts to be sampled. Tours to neighboring distilleries can be arranged through the hotel.

To tour Perthshire properly, take the road to Aberfyle, stopping along the way at Doune Castle, Scotland's finest medieval stronghold. From Aberfyle, the Duke's Road zigzags over wild hills to the Trossachs, a glorious wooded gorge that leads to a series of lochs.

In nearby Perth, the top attraction is Scone Palace, the ancient crowning place of Scottish kings, including Macbeth and Robert the Bruce. In addition to a fine collection of sixteenth-century ivories, porcelains, and *objets d'art*, the palace's pinetum is famous for many rare conifers.

Five miles from Turnberry is Culzean (pronounced CulLEAN) Castle, one of architect Robert Adam's finest creations. Set high on a bluff near the sea, the castle grounds contain some of the oldest terraced gardens in Scotland. Within the castle itself are a magnificent staircase, a round drawing room, and fine plaster ceilings. In gratitude for his role as Supreme Commander of the Allied Forces in Europe, General Dwight D. Eisenhower was given the top flat in 1946 as his Scottish residence.

From nearby Androssan, day-trippers can take the ferry across the Irish Sea to the Isle of Arran, to explore its lovely low hills, streams, glens, and lochs. The finest scenery is in the north, where the summit of Goat Fell affords one of the best panoramic views in Scotland. Potters and weavers ply their trade on the island. Serious golfers can skip the trip and arrange to play Royal Troon, Prestwick, and Western Gailes, to name three of the region's top courses.

At Waterville, in Ireland, salmon and trout fishing are available on Lough Currane. Remains of early Christian settlements, including beehive huts, stone forts, and primitive roads, are scattered around the shores of this lake.

A driving tour of the Ring of Kerry brings travelers face to face with some of Europe's most dramatic mountain-and-ocean scenery. Sheep graze pastures ribboned with old stone walls, the pastures pitching to rocky shores washed by Dingle Bay or the wide estuary of the Kenmare River. Ireland's tallest peak, Carrauntoohill (3,414 feet), is occasionally viewed (when it isn't raining) in a range of mountains called Macgillicuddy's Reeks. Ruined castles, sleepy fishing ports, and prehistoric dry-stone forts can be explored along the way.

There is very little reason to stray from Sardinia's sumptuous Costa Smeralda—nothing else on the island compares. However, golfers seeking variety can journey to the southern tip of the island to play Is Molas, a fine layout located south of Cagliari near some of the most important nuraghi (prehistoric stone towers) on the island. After the round, explore Cagliari, Sardinia's ancient capital. The city's old quarter, built atop a hill around a medieval castle, serves up fine views of the Gulf of the Angels. Operas are performed in the city's Roman amphitheater in the summer.

Portugal's Algarve is rich in post-round attractions. Due east of Penina is Portimão, a working seaport with waterfront cafés along the Arade estuary.

*Sardine fishermen in Portimão, Portugal. Photo courtesy © Brian McCallen*

West of Penina is Lagos, a former Moorish trading port girdled by thick Roman walls. Twisted alleys wind through the old quarter of town, its mosaic stone sidewalks overhung with grillwork balconies and large wrought-iron lamps. Popular attractions include the Golden Chapel, its gilded statuary, horseshoe-shaped altar, and trompe l'oeil ceiling built to honor St. Anthony; and the modest museum next door, containing folkloric and archaeological exhibits.

In Sagres, at the westernmost tip of the Algarve (and the Continent), huge rollers bash the rocks, the water churned to a milky froth as it cascades high above the cliffs near a lighthouse. It was here that Henry the Navigator assembled the finest seamen and cartographers of his day to launch the Age of Discovery in the fifteenth century. (The old observatory and school building, built by Henry, is a hostel.)

Heading east from Penina a few miles inland is Porches Pottery, a working studio and retail shop where beautiful ceramics are available at reasonable prices. The pieces are brightly painted in traditional patterns.

In the local markets of Loule, a short drive from Vilamoura and Quinta do Lago, shopping for copperware, leather goods, and polychrome earthenware is available.

The eastern outpost of the Algarve is Faro, an ancient Moorish seaport that offers two museums (one is dedicated to model ships), as well as good buys on high-fashion clothing.

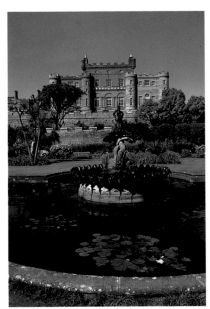

*Culzean Castle, Scotland.*
*Photo courtesy © STB Still Movies*

In Estoril, the top attraction is the glamorous casino, with its miles of marble, bright tapestries, and crystal chandeliers. Dancing and floor shows nightly.

From the Estoril Palacio, a memorable side trip can be made to Sintra, a charming summer resort nestled high in the Serra de Sintra range and referred to by Lord Byron as a "glorious Eden." Its cheerful villas give the impression of wedding cakes chiseled into the side of a mountain above the town. Sintra's two main attractions are the National Palace, a pastiche of Gothic, Manueline, and Moorish design styles dating to the fourteenth century (it was once the summer home of the kings of Portugal); and the Pena Palace, a fairy-tale castle with gilded turrets, tiled doorways, and romantic gardens.

Estoril's neighbor is Cascais, once a quaint fishing village and now a fashionable seaside getaway with fine shops, excellent seafood restaurants, and lively clubs. The Bay of Cascais is a study in contrasts: Brightly painted fishing boats rub hulls with expensive pleasure craft. Twice weekly, the town's local fair sells everything from pottery to handmade linens. On Sunday afternoons from April to October, bullfights are staged at the Praça dos Touros (the bull is not killed in a Portuguese bullfight).

Convenient to Torrequebrada on Spain's Costa del Sol is the charming seaside village of Puerto Banus, its stylish homes, restaurants, and cafés (including an Anglicized nineteenth hole called Patrick's) built around a man-made harbor where magnificent yachts are moored. The beach, framed by date palms and gardens, is one of the prettiest in the region.

Those thirsting for more adventure than Torrequebrada offers can board a ferry in Algeciras, near the Rock of Gibraltar, to visit Tangier in Morocco, one of the livelier market cities in North Africa.

A half-hour's drive from La Manga is Cartagena, an ancient seaport where good buys on shoes, ceramics, and leather goods are available. Closer to the resort, the fishing village of Cabo de Palos is well known for its tapas bars and seafood restaurants.

Across the River Touques from Deauville is Trouville, a fishing port with a time-honored seafront and harbor now lined with dozens of informal cafés and brasseries. Local specialties include crevettes (tiny shrimp), moules marinieres (marinated mussels), and saucisse de Morteau (sausages served warm with potatoes in oil and vinegar). Atop a hill with a lovely view of the Seine estuary is the Musée de Trouville. The works of Raoul Dufy and Eugène Louis Boudin (who best captured the moods of the sea in Trouville) are well represented.

On Tuesdays and Fridays in Deauville, a lively country market is held in a covered hall near the railroad station. All the makings of a perfect picnic are available.

An hour's drive from Deauville is Arromanches, where the D-Day Museum explains in detail the Normandy coast landing by the Allied Forces on June 6, 1944. Relief maps, working models, dioramas, and a stirring sound-and-light show of one of the most monumental military invasions ever staged are featured. Remnants of the artificial harbor built to receive Allied vessels are still visible at Arromanches.

---

## DON'T LEAVE HOME WITHOUT...MEASURING YOUR STANCE

In Scotland, where wind is a constant, it is vitally important to establish a firm, steady foundation before lashing away at the ball. Set up to the ball with too narrow a stance and you risk losing your balance, especially from a canted lie. A wide stance may help you stay planted in high winds, but the freedom of motion required to pivot correctly is severely restricted if the feet are too far apart. Determining how far apart to set the feet is as easy as a walk in the park.

To establish the natural, proper width of your stance, take a normal walking step forward onto your left heel. Lift your right heel off the ground and swivel to the right on your left heel and right toe. The distance between your feet is the correct width of your stance on all full-wood and long-iron shots. Narrow your stance with the shorter clubs. The weight should be distributed equally between the insides of the feet.

Since the body automatically balances itself when walking, why not tap into the biomechanics of your stride to measure the correct width of your stance? It's the best way to maintain balance in all conditions and to achieve the smooth footwork, weight shift, and pivot necessary for a sound, repeating swing.

IAN MARCHBANK, GOLF PROFESSIONAL, GLENEAGLES HOTEL GOLF COURSES

# AUSTRAL/

The far-flung group of disparate nations that falls under the heading of Austral/Asia (a.k.a the Pacific Rim) is experiencing a golf boom. Much of the new resort development in the region can be traced to the Japanese, for whom golf approaches the status of a religion (in the town of Kashiwa outside Tokyo, a Buddhist monk maintains a putting green at a Zen temple). Saddled with extraordinarily high green fees and strapped for land suitable for new development, the Japanese have invested heavily in their neighbors. In Thailand, more than sixty golf courses, many of them attached to resorts, were under construction at press time. Australia's Gold Coast, a fabulous forty-mile beachfront south of Brisbane, may be renamed the Golf Coast by the year 2000. Malaysia, Indonesia, Singapore, the Philippines, China—all are building new golf facilities, many of them laid out by top designers and underwritten by the Japanese. (It is cheaper for a Japanese golfer to fly to another country to play golf than it is for him to stay home and arrange a game.)

Traditionally, golf in Asia has been reserved for the rich and privileged. Lately, the game has become tremendously popular among a swelling middle class, much as it did in North America during the 1950s and early 1960s. The region's prosperity has ushered in a new leisure class, which has discovered golf and golf vacations.

With a few exceptions, Asia's current medalists are older, more established properties built during earlier golf booms either in the 1920s or 1960s. Japan, a small island nation devoted to perfection, has nurtured a few of the finest resorts in the world. Given the strength of the yen against most foreign currencies, golf in Japan remains a prohibitively expensive sport for most visitors. Also, a three- to six-month lead time

# ASIA

is required for hotel and tee time reservations. Finally, golfers must brace themselves for an all-day outing: At most Japanese resorts, players break for a full lunch at the turn. On the plus side, caddies in Japan (and in Thailand) are attractive, congenial young women well versed in the nuances of the game.

The environments and backdrops for golf throughout the Pacific Rim are as magnificent as any in the world. The rocky, pine-clad coast at the Kawana Hotel in Japan could pass for a stretch of 17-Mile Drive on the Monterey Peninsula, while the Phoenix Country Club in southern Japan, with its fair weather and fine beaches, resembles a suburb of San Diego. Other sites are more lush and tropical: Golfers at The Rose Garden in Thailand and Hyatt Saujana in Malaysia often hire a second caddie to carry an umbrella as a sunshade. Other resorts at higher elevations offer cool, springlike weather: Bali Handara in Indonesia and Awana Golf & Country Club in Malaysia are routed through mountain jungles where monkeys chatter in the treetops. The surrounding terrain at Wairakei in New Zealand is still being shaped by geothermal activity, while two fine Australian resorts, Sheraton Mirage Port Douglas and Hyatt Regency Sanctuary Cove, offer beachfront settings in the north and south of Queensland that rival any in the Caribbean for beauty.

As good and varied as these resorts are, Austral/Asia is a pink-faced baby awaiting future growth. The number of quality properties slated to open by the twenty-first century will create major golf destinations in this most exciting and heterogeneous part of the world.

*Inset: Caddie at Dai Hakone, Japan.   Large picture: Bali Handara, Indonesia*

# KAWANA HOTEL

The Kawana Hotel, located two hours by express train southwest of Tokyo in the suburbs of Ito City, is sited on the Izu Peninsula on terrain that could have floated across the Pacific Ocean from the Monterey Peninsula. The resort complex is the result of one man's vision—and flexibility.

The hotel was founded as a modest eight-room, Western-style hostelry in the 1920s by the late Baron Kishichiro Okura, one of Japan's best-known businessmen and a tourism pioneer. Okura, who traveled extensively throughout Europe and America, built many fine hotels in Japan, notably the Imperial Hotel in Tokyo and Kyoto Hotel in Kyoto. Curiously, Okura had intended to create a country estate similar to the ones he had seen while studying in England. He chose a tract of land beyond the fishing village of Kawana as his site, but when he visited the property a year later, he found that the man in charge of construction had started to build a golf course. The baron was informed that the land lay atop porous lava rock, the perfect foundation for a golf course. He shelved his dream of a formal, woodsy retreat and decided to leave well enough alone.

In 1928, the resort opened the 5,711-yard, par-70 Oshima Course, named for the spectacular views from its holes of Oshima Island, from which rises Mount Mihara, an active volcano. Six years later, work began on the present red-roofed, white-faced hotel facility, which now has 140 rooms. Okura, an art collector, decorated the public rooms with pieces from his own collection. The hotel strives to offer what it calls the "exotic atmosphere of southern Europe," and with its French-trained chefs and year-round balmy weather, it comes very close.

*Fuji Course, sixth hole*

*Swimming pools*

In 1936, British architect Charles H. Alison arrived to build Kawana's second layout, the Fuji Course. Named for the majestic frosted cone of 12,388-foot Mount Fuji, which dominates all sightlines from the course, the 6,187-yard, par-72 course (6,691 yards from the tips) is a thorough test of skill, strategy, and course management. Routed on exceptionally hilly land, its steeply pitched fairways rising and plunging through dense pine forests, the Fuji Course has nary a flat lie. Compounding its difficulties, the fairways serve as corridors for the often-strong sea breezes. The many uphill holes, combined with the heavy Pacific air, require the use of more rather than less club. Bunkers are strategically positioned and steep-faced, an Alison trademark. As on an authentic Scottish links, many of these bunkers are not visible from the tees or fairways (this is especially true of the more cavernous pits). Most of the holes lie astride a sliver of land that tumbles to the sea, but a few holes, notably the 397-yard second and 415-yard fifteenth, trace the curve of the dramatic, rockbound coast, a coast that could have been separated at birth from Big Sur.

Arguably the most difficult course in Japan when a strong breeze sweeps in off the Pacific, the Fuji Course, ranked ninety-fifth in the world by *GOLF Magazine*, is Japan's Pebble Beach. Only here the terrain is steeper and the fairways narrower than those at Pebble Beach. Accuracy and control are necessities.

The shorter, sportier Oshima Course is not without its delights. Though far less taxing than the main track, a few of the holes (all have names) are notorious. The fourth hole, a 351-yard right-to-left dogleg that parallels the sea, is affectionately called "Good-bye," because that is the appropriate comment for anyone who hooks the ball from the tee. As on the first five holes, the green is backdropped by the Pacific Ocean. The Oshima turns inland thereafter, its challenges slightly tamer away from the sea. There are several blind approach shots to be negotiated on both courses, but the caddies are very good about walking ahead to indicate the proper line to the green. Caddies at Kawana (and throughout Japan) are young women who cover their heads with lampshadelike hats and large white kerchiefs. Most are consummate professionals who grew up near the resort, play the

game themselves, and know its subtleties. Most of them have mastered enough English to communicate the distances to the greens and the direction and speed of the putts.

Both layouts are kept in superb condition. Like many of the older, established layouts in Japan, the Oshima and Fuji courses feature two greens at each hole, to ensure top playing conditions throughout the year. The bent grass greens are used in cool weather, while the alternative greens are planted in korai grass, the hardy Korean varietal that thrives in the heat. These are employed in the warm-weather months. Putts on korai grass greens must be stroked firmly—the thick-bladed grass offers quite a bit of resistance to a rolling golf ball.

Kawana's halfway houses are delightful. Hot towels, cold soft drinks, and hot sake are provided. And while many clubs in Japan require golfers to stop after nine holes for a full lunch, a round of golf at Kawana can be played continuously.

Meals at the hotel are served in three restaurants. French-inspired entrées are featured in the main dining room, while the grill room features everything from a Kawana Coast Lunch—abalone steak, lobster Nantua gratin, and grilled turbot—to the sirloin Birdie Steak. "Taste the delightful birdie steak to enable you to make birdie score," the menu reads. The Inakayi, a 350-year-old Japanese farmhouse transported from the moun-

*Inayaki Restaurant. Photo courtesy Kawana Hotel*

tains to the resort, serves authentic Japanese fare in a cozy wood-walled room. Meals throughout are superbly prepared and presented.

The resort provides all the amenities necessary for a restful vacation. There are three swimming pools, tennis courts, billiard room, card room, game room, and an observation tower from which the hotel grounds and surrounding area may be viewed. Nearly 5,000 cherry trees sprout pink blossoms from January to May at Kawana. Unlike other parts of the country, where *sakura* (cherry blossoms) can be seen only for a week or so, at Kawana the trees bloom from winter through spring. Moreover, the Izu Peninsula is blessed with clement weather. Golf is a four-season affair here. If there is one drawback (besides the high tariff) to the Kawana Hotel, it is the advance notice required. Bookings must be made three to six months prior to arrival to secure a room and a tee time.

*Large picture: Fuji Course, sixteenth hole. Inset: The hotel*

*West Red Course, first hole*

Two hours by rapid train northwest of Tokyo is Karuizawa, a highland resort revered as much for its winter sports as for golf. But with seven full-size eighteen-hole courses, the resort has established itself as Asia's largest golf factory, the Pinehurst of Japan. The site of a modest town during the feudal period, Karuizawa was first developed as a place of rest for travelers who had to climb the steep mountain pass nearby to reach the highlands of Shinano Province (present-day Nagano Prefecture).

In 1886, British missionary Alexander Shaw, who was teaching in the city of Nagano, happened to stay in one of Karuizawa's inns. He fell in love with the region's pristine larch and pine forests, which reminded him of his homeland, and decided to establish a summer retreat for his family. Soon other missionaries as well as doctors and teachers joined the Shaw family, which had converted an old inn into a summer home. They were

followed by princes and princesses, poets and artists. Then as now, the beauty of the mountain forest provides peace and inspiration.

Today Karuizawa retains many of the features of those early times. There are Victorian period houses in town; the inn where Shaw first stayed still stands at the end of the main street. The same photo studio that memorialized travelers in period dress now sells antique snapshots. Despite the greatly expanded facilities of the modern-day resort, it's a place that hasn't lost its charm or appeal. Karuizawa continues to function as an elite vacation getaway for Tokyo's prominent families.

The resort itself, surrounded by a thick forest, is backdropped by broad-shouldered Mount Asama, an active volcano. At 8,400 feet, it is one of the highest mountains in the region. Smoke often billows from its crater. Developed by Yoshiaki Tsutsumi, a high-powered Japanese businessman who created the first multilevel driving range in Tokyo, the Karuizawa golf complex offers eight golf courses, or 144 holes. The facility, largest of its kind in Japan, is located five minutes away from the resort's accommodations. Seven courses radiate from a single clubhouse while the eighth, the Karuizawa Prince Hotel Course, is located right on the beautifully landscaped grounds. Needless to say, the operation runs like clockwork.

Seven of Karuizawa's courses are the handiwork of Robert Trent Jones, Sr., and Jr. The fifty-four holes of the West Course (Gold, Blue, and Silver) were designed by Jones, Sr., and date to the early 1970s. The fifty-four holes of the East Course (Iriyama, Takaiwa, and Oshitate) as well as the

*Mount Fuji seen across the water. Photo courtesy © Hakone Prince Hotel*

newest course, the West Red Course (opened in 1988), were designed by Jones, Jr. Unlike the resort's preceding six layouts, all of which offer a firm challenge (the Japanese like their golf courses to put up a sturdy defense of par), the Red Course is a fun test of golf, with lots of water and sand, but not in the wrong places. There's also a good mix of doglegs.

All of the Karuizawa courses are exquisitely maintained. Alternative greens are not used. Each course uses the one-green concept, because the bent grass that surfaces them flourishes in the cool mountain climate. They are exceptionally true.

The toughest course? Many consider Jones, Jr.'s Gold Course, which can stretch to 7,137 yards, the most difficult test, though Jones, Sr.'s Iriyama and Takaiwa layouts, played from the tips, are nearly as scrappy.

*Driving range*

The Karuizawa layouts are relatively flat and, therefore, easy to walk. The resort's female caddies use trolley carts that handle up to four bags. These caddies are unusually attentive: They arrive at the green ahead of time to fix ball marks before golfers have a chance to find them. They read putts, clean balls, tend the pins—they do everything but play the shot for you.

The clubhouse and other structures at the golf course complex are made from logs imported from Finland. The halfway house at the ninth hole of the Red Course, for example, is a gorgeous log building with a glass front situated near the tenth tee. From the lounge, golfers have a beautiful view of the ninth and tenth holes.

The Karuizawa Prince Hotels pioneered the concept of a large-scale resort in Japan. In addition to the East, West, and South hotels, nearly 600 Finnish log cabins are nestled among the trees and set around the golf courses. Understated and comfortable, many of these cabins can accommodate up to eight people.

The 108-room Prince Hotel South, situated in a quiet corner of the resort's gardens, offers magnificent views of Mount Fuji from the windows of its guest rooms. Its best restaurant is the Beaux Sejours Dining Room, where each of the brick-walled box seats is set on a different level, and where the service and cuisine are designed to put one in mind of a multistarred gourmet dining establishment in Paris. Instead of the Eiffel Tower, Mount Asama is in view at any point in the room through the floor-to-ceiling windows. After dinner, patrons are invited to relax in the British-style Windsor Bar. Afternoon tea, a ritual elevated to the status of art in Japan, can be enjoyed in the hotel's Rindo Lounge facing the beautiful courtyard.

At the smaller, seventy-two-room Prince Hotel East, which harmonizes beautifully with its surroundings, the color schemes of the roomy, comfortable accommodations reflect the shades and hues of the countryside. A large picture window offers a view of the highland greenery, with the Finnish log Prince cottages dotting the countryside. The main dining

*Above: Gold Course, seventeenth hole. Right: Prince Hotel Course, tenth hole*

room in the Hotel East is a large restaurant with glass walls on two sides that admit sunlight. It offers Japanese, Western, and Chinese cuisine in a pleasant environment. The Porto Restaurant is informal, while the Shinano Japanese Restaurant features typical native dishes, including sukiyaki and shabu shabu, both made with thin slices of beef. Also popular is yakitori, grilled morsels of chicken on bamboo skewers, and teppan-yaki, a hot plate consisting of meat and seafood. The hotel's main bar boasts a collection of spirits and liqueurs from all over the world. (By day, the main bar functions as a tea room.) The hotel also features several fine specialty shops.

Business and conference groups generally book into the 188-room Prince Hotel West, its guest rooms convenient to large exhibition and banquet halls.

All told, there are seventeen different room floor plans available at Karuizawa. The choices are nearly as overwhelming as those posed by the myriad array of golf courses.

With a climate comparable to that found in the Middle Atlantic states, the resort is open from late April through early November. Cherry trees bloom in late April, followed by magnolias with brilliant yellow blossoms. In autumn, the larch trees turn a fiery orange before their small needles fall. The resort area is known for both its fresh air and fresh water. (Karuizawa is reputed to have an optimum balance of ozone in the air, which accounts for the many summer camps in the area. Water for the resort comes from mountain springs.) Nearby farms produce excellent vegetables, especially lettuce and cabbage, and a wide variety of fruits are grown on the nearby mountain slopes.

In addition to a golf course for every day of the week, cycling, hiking, and horseback riding are available at the resort. Cycling lanes have been laid out along the area's major roads, while marked hiking trails trace interesting routes. The most popular hiking trail starts at Shiraito Falls, where the Yu River falls over a broad ledge of rock, creating a waterfall that resembles a curtain of fine silk thread. The trail leads past bubbling hot springs before concluding at the Old Mikasa Hotel, built in 1905 and the first Western-style building in Karuizawa to be designed by a Japanese architect. For those who wish to take a refreshment break, coffee and tea shops are found along the paths.

Karuizawa is situated within a large wildlife preserve. Foxes, *tanuki* (Japanese raccoons), weasels, and squirrels frequent the woods. High in the mountains roam *kamoshika*, a type of antelope unique to Japan. Karuizawa is also known as a bird sanctuary. During the summer months, bird-watching walks are scheduled twice daily. At dawn and dusk, a chorus of wrens, thrushes, and cuckoos fills the air with song.

# HAKONE PRINCE RESORT

SILVER MEDALIST

*Escalator from the fifteenth
to the sixteenth hole*

Nestled on the shores of Lake Ashi near Fuji-Hakone-Izu National Park some ninety minutes west of Tokyo by car or rail, the 2,250-acre Hakone Prince Resort offers two fine courses and a complex that typifies Japanese reverence for the environment.

The resort's prime appeal is found in its wide variety of accommodations, which span every taste and need. The centerpiece of the complex is the elegant Hakone Prince Hotel, designed by the renowned architect Togo Murano, its interior shape lending each of the ninety-six guest rooms a different view. At the Ryuguden Annex, traditional Japanese accommodations are contained in buildings with asymmetrical pagoda-style roofs set beside Lake Ashi. Within the Fuyo-tei Annex, a sedate hideaway built of cedar, traditional Japanese rooms are covered with finely woven rice mats (tatami) and partitioned by paper screens. Attention is directed from the interior to the exterior, a hallmark of Japanese architecture. In both annexes, two meals daily (included in the room tariff) are served in the guest quarters. The timbered Prince chalet, designed to resemble an alpine Swiss chalet, has twelve rooms, each with a different decor. The fifty-room Lakeside Lodge offers more modern accommodations beside the lake, while the resort's 142 cottages, crafted from Finnish logs, offer understated comfort and privacy in a forested landscape.

Le Trianon, the main dining room at the Hakone Prince, is perhaps the finest restaurant found at any of Japan's resorts. Named for the Trianon palaces of Versailles, the curved room features high ceilings, sand-colored walls, and free-form chandeliers. Superb continental cuisine is featured, often with a Japanese twist. For example, the sautéed veal is served with Odawara plum sauce, while the breast of duckling is prepared with a wild peach sauce.

*Above: Le Trianon Restaurant.
Photo courtesy © Hakone Prince Hotel*

Breakfast is available in the Yamaboshi Coffee House, where a fireplace warms the room on cool mornings. The room opens to a terrace on warm, sunny days.

The resort's main golf course, Dai-Hakone, was designed in 1954 by a Japanese Buddhist monk who had spent time in Europe, became interested in golf, and was later asked to design the facility. The monk wished golfers a long, happy journey: The par-74 course stretches to 7,307 yards from the tips (6,744 yards from the white tees), though the holes are exceptionally wide. Bring your graphite-shafted driver to Dai-Hakone: Length, not accuracy, is the order of business. And while golfers must negotiate a few forced carries over small creeks and fairway bunkers, placement can be readily sacrificed for distance. However, players must beware of out of bounds at a few holes. Also, the relatively small, well-bunkered greens can cause fits. Strategically placed fairway bunkers and grassy mounds can also play havoc with stray shots on this flat floor-of-the-valley course, though the imaginatively conceived holes entertain more than they bedevil

golfers. Dai-Hakone sports two sets of greens, one sown with bent grass, the other planted in hardy korai grass for summer use. The layout is situated near a sister property, the ninety-six-room Hakone Sengokuhara Prince Hotel.

The resort's second course, Hakone-En, is located near the Lakeside Lodge and offers a far gentler challenge than the original track. It's a pleasant warm-up course, nothing more.

In addition to the two courses, the resort features a pair of swimming pools, fourteen tennis courts (four lighted for night play), a driving range, an aquarium, and opportunities for fishing and boating. The entire resort complex is in view of Mount Fuji, Japan's tallest peak and one of the most beautiful and symmetrical cones in the world.

*Left: Japanese-style room in the Ryuguden Annex. Photo courtesy © Hakone Prince Hotels*

*Below: Dai-Hakone Course, Eighth hole*

# PHOENIX HOTELS & RESORT

—◆❖◆—

## SILVER MEDALIST

At the southern end of Kyushu Island in the popular vacation area of Miyazaki is Japan's version of San Diego. Here the flowers bloom year round, the sun invariably shines, and the temperature is always clement. Snowbirds flock to Miyazaki from November through April to escape the chilly winters up north—and to play golf when their friends back home are clearing snow from their driveways.

The Phoenix Country Club, carved from a thick black pine forest that lines the Pacific coast, offers challenging play on three distinctive nines: the Sumiyoshi, Takachiho, and Nichinan courses. Annual site of the Dunlop Phoenix Tournament, which attracts many of the world's top players, the relatively flat, gently rolling course was designed by Gohkichi and Sadakichi Ohashi. Their stated goal was to design a resort golf course that made full use of the natural environment, yet would have enough championship character to test the world's best shotmakers.

For starters, fairway bunkers were eschewed in favor of the strategic use of pine spinneys, particularly at the dogleg holes. And while many of the pines on the course are more than 200 years old and have been twisted into odd shapes by the wind, many more were of inconsequential height when the twenty-seven-hole complex opened in 1971. Initially, these small pines could be negotiated without trouble from tee to green. Today, they have matured to the point where they present major obstacles to good scoring—especially to those prone to errant tee shots.

Like most Japanese courses, the Phoenix nines are lengthy: 3,500 yards from the back tees of the Sumiyoshi nine, 3,616 yards at the Takachiho nine, and 3,402 yards at the Nichinan nine. (The yardages from the regular men's tees are 3,153, 3,315, and 3,092 yards, respectively.) And while fairway bunkers are virtually absent from the design, small, generously contoured greens protected by deep bunkers place a premium on accurate approaches. The sand for the bunkers is taken from the nearby seashore, which is of volcanic origin. The sand is dark, nearly black, and is heavy-textured. It also retains water quite well, which means that an incoming shot, even one with a high trajectory, rarely plugs.

Miyazaki's climate prompted the architects to opt for the two-green concept at the club. One is planted in bent grass, the other in a new strain of Bermuda grass that is less coarse and grainy than korai grass.

*Halfway House*

As is true throughout most of Japan, there are no golf carts at the Phoenix Country Club. Female caddies pull from two to four bags on trolleys. Players should prepare themselves for a one-hour lunch break between nines (a six-hour round of golf is customary at the resort). Hotel guests are given priority for tee times, though a three-month advance reservation is suggested in this golf-happy region.

The resort offers guests a pair of stark white, ten-story hotels: the 296-room Sun Hotel Phoenix and the 196-room Seaside Hotel Phoenix. Both are convenient to the country club and the beach. The Sun Hotel features Japanese-style rooms (floor seating on tatami mats, rooms separated by sliding screens, a futon mattress laid on the floor) as well as Western-style accommodations. Regardless of style, a cotton robe (*yukata*) and a kimono are placed in each room. All of the Sun Hotel's rooms command a fine view of the Pacific Ocean.

In its restaurants, local seafood delicacies are featured, including a favorite summer dish, *hiyajiru*, a mixture of miso (bean paste) and fish served on rice. French cuisine is available at the Jukai restaurant, while à la carte sushi is served at the Kaboocha restaurant. All the dining rooms have fine views of the golf courses and the sea. There's also a lively nightclub at the hotel. The venturesome can sample *shochu*, a locally produced liquor distilled from barley and spring water.

Other amenities at the property include outdoor swimming pools, six tennis courts, a driving range, a thirty-six-lane bowling alley, an amusement park, and the Phoenix Natural Zoo, where re-created environments

*Takachiho nine, first hole*

hold over 1,500 animals of seventy-six species. But for golfers eager to discover for themselves the difficulties confronting the pros each November during the Dunlop Phoenix Tournament, there is only one place to be in the San Diego of Japan.

*Sumiyoshi nine, second hole*

# THE ROSE GARDEN

SILVER MEDALIST

There are lively hill-tribe and rhythmic bamboo dances, with accompaniment on ancient Thai musical instruments. The joyful ritual of a traditional Thai wedding is reenacted, as is the ceremony of ordination into the Buddhist monkhood. There are displays of Thai-style boxing and sword-fighting. But the highlights of the show are the large Asian elephants adorned in colorful fabrics that perform the pachyderms' version of precision dancing.

Before or after the show, artisans demonstrate silk-weaving, fruit-carving, umbrella-painting, garland-making, rice-pounding, and pottery-

*Lily pond*

An hour's drive southwest of Bangkok, one of Asia's most vibrant cities, is a resort complex set within landscaped tropical gardens where Thailand's reputation as the "land of smiles" is renewed daily. Built in the early 1960s by a family of horticulturists who supplied roses to Bangkok, one of the resort's chief attractions is its cultural show, which is staged every afternoon in an area of the resort built to resemble a typical Thai village. The hour-long exhibition is presented by a 150-member troupe of local performers, many of whom work at The Rose Garden in other capacities.

*Women caddies on the first hole*

*The hotel*

making. A majestic Chinese pavilion houses an extensive collection of antique Chinese furniture and *objets d'art*, while aviaries contain hundreds of exotic birds. Tropical flowers, plants, and shrubs bloom in profusion in the nurseries. On the recreation side, the resort features cycling, tennis, tree-shaded swimming pools, an eight-acre lake for paddle-boating, elephant rides, and rice-barge trips on the river. In sum, The Rose Garden encapsulates everything that is enchanting about Thailand.

Guests are quartered in the Rose Garden Hotel, each of its eighty rooms and suites featuring a private balcony overlooking the gently flowing Nakhon Chaisri River with its ever-changing procession of floating markets. Antique wooden Thai-style houses are also available to guests. In addition to open-air barbecues held several times each week, the resort's dining rooms (including a floating restaurant) are exceptional. Several feature the inimitable Thai cuisine, its flavor counterpoints of hot chillies and spicy curries balanced by mild herbs and coconut-milk sauces.

Five minutes from the resort complex is the Rose Garden Golf Club, one of Asia's most attractive settings for the game. A long, flattish layout bordered by a profusion of flowering shrubs and trees, the par-72 course, former site of the Thailand Open, is a tropical garden spliced with golf holes. Stretching to 7,085 yards from the tips (to be played by low-handicappers only—the verdant fairways give little roll), the regular men's tees at 6,435 yards offer challenge enough to most players. Characterized by slightly raised, well-bunkered greens planted in thatchy Bermuda grass (they putt sluggishly), the Rose Garden's strongest defense against low scoring is its network of man-made lakes and canals, which crisscross half the holes. Should you hit into the water, a local "klong boy" will dive in and retrieve your ball for a small fee.

The backbone of the course is its par fives, each of which rewards strong, accurate play. The 530-yard fifth and 510-yard seventh holes, for example, are both narrow, with tightly guarded greens that can play tough when a breeze sweeps in off the Gulf of Thailand. The 500-yard eleventh is a superb double-dogleg that pivots twice to the left, with trouble up the right side (slicers beware), though a watery ditch and out of bounds up the left side foil hookers, too.

The best-laid plans for a handsome score are usually undone by the monstrous 530-yard eighteenth. The "klong boys" do their best business here. After a testing tee shot played over a lake, the second shot must carry a canal that bisects the fairway. A large lake guarding the right side of the green must be avoided before golfers can stroke their final putts and avail themselves of the palacelike clubhouse. It commands a fine view of the course and rivals any in Asia for comfort.

The Rose Garden's caddies are something special: more than 400 Thai girls, most of them teenagers attired in yellow smocks and red coolie hats who are expert at guiding visiting players around the course. When they smile their disarmingly friendly smiles, it's simply not possible to dwell on a foozled shot.

# HYATT SAUJANA GOLF & COUNTRY CLUB

## SILVER MEDALIST

Wherever the British Empire spread its influence, a legacy of golf was established. Malaysia, a former British colony, not only welcomes visitors to great private clubs like Royal Selangor, it also has a number of fine resorts. One of the newest and best is the Hyatt Saujana, which opened in 1987 and is conveniently located fifteen miles from the capital city of Kuala Lumpur and a five-minute drive from Subang International Airport.

Saujana's two courses, designed by Californian Ronald Fream, were carved from a hilly oil-palm plantation. The resident firebreather is the Palm Course, current site of the Malaysian Open. Nicknamed the Cobra

is a corps of 200 of them) don't advise players to look too long for a stray ball—king cobras make their home among the oil palms.

A few of the holes on the Palm Course have become the stuff of legend. The 180-yard second (214 yards from the tips) has garnered a reputation as one of the most dreaded holes in southeast Asia. From an elevated tee hacked from the jungle, players must fly their tee shots over a palm-studded ravine to an enormous, elevated green undercut by several deep sand pits. The multitiered green, sharply tilted from back to front, rivals any on the Old Course at St. Andrews for size and undulation. Small wonder the Palm's second is the best known (and most notorious) hole in Malaysia.

The 375-yard eighth hole provides more thrills and chills. Nicknamed the Stadium, this sharp right-to-left dogleg is defined by a hill on one side and a deep ravine and valley on the other. The fairway bottlenecks near the green, which is well protected by pot bunkers. Even the caddies have problems reading the subtle breaks on this green.

The Palm's back nine flattens out considerably, presenting more standard parkland-style challenges. But so much damage is done by the rigorous front that the playing of the incoming nine is often nothing more than a carefree formality.

Saujana's shorter Bunga Raya Course, named for Malaysia's national flower, crosses a railway line and draws close enough to Subang Airport

*Palm Course, first hole*

for its deadly array of challenges, the Palm is marked by medium-wide fairways cut through dense stands of squat palms that lead to large, convoluted greens. Muddy creeks meander through the course, while grassy hillocks and swales define landing areas and green sites. Fairways are planted in paspalum grass, a sturdy variety not often seen in the Far East. The ball sits up nicely on this dense, wiry grass. Depart the fairway, and the ball lodges in heavy rough or comes to rest among the palms. Saujana's caddies (there

that the tails of the parked giant 747s can be seen outside their hangars. From the topmost holes, a broken line of jungle ridges and steam-filled valleys looms into view. (The name Saujana is derived from an old Malay expression meaning "as far as the eye can see.") As on the Palm Course, a timid or misplayed shot comes to ruin on the Bunga Raya, though its challenges overall are slightly milder. Its par threes, however, can be ferocious. The 159-yard third hole plays across a gully, though a bail-out area to the

*Clubhouse*

courts, an Olympic-size swimming pool, and a billiard room. Ti Chen, the club's Chinese restaurant, serves superb Cantonese cuisine at lunch and dinner.

The Hyatt, a grouping of low-rise, rectangular-shaped buildings, is joined by covered walkways and surrounded by landscaped gardens, pools, and man-made lakes. The interior of the hotel reflects the colorful Malaysian culture, with wood carvings, handblocked batik, and paintings by local artists decorating the walls.

Designed to appeal to international businessmen (there are extensive meeting facilities at the hotel), the Hyatt's 230 rooms feature individually-controlled air-conditioning (a must in the tropics), Telex, and direct dial phones. There's also a modern fitness center and spa.

The resort's restaurants are varied and superb. The newest is Senja (translated as "dusk"), which is built on stilts above a man-made lake that

*Palm Course, second hole*

right of the green rescues a miscue. The most picturesque hole on the course is the 172-yard seventh, where a mid- to long-iron is played across a ravine to an L-shaped green cut into the base of a hill. The saving grace of the well-bunkered green is its relative flatness. Like most holes at Saujana, the seventh is a scenic delight but is merciless to offline shots.

Facilities at Saujana's low-rise, open-air clubhouse, perched on a hill overlooking the two courses, include indoor squash and outdoor tennis

divides the hotel from the country club. A bar, dining room, and night-club rolled into one, Senja was constructed with glass walls, timbered floors, and a boardwalk, for romantic dining. The chef's specialties, especially exotic local seafood, are displayed nightly: parrotfish, stingray, salmon imported from New Zealand, and large tiger prawns, bred in local rivers. Spicy Malaysian preparations of meat dishes are also featured. About the only item missing from the menu is loin of king cobra.

# AWANA GOLF & COUNTRY CLUB

## SILVER MEDALIST

*Clubhouse*

At 3,100 feet above sea level, the Awana Golf & Country Club in central Malaysia scrapes the clouds. The golf course, set on a rugged plateau, with several holes terraced into the side of a mountain, was redesigned by Ronald Fream in 1984 from an earlier Japanese routing that eroded badly and proved to be unplayable. Even in its reincarnation, the layout is exceptionally hilly and challenging. Not only do most of the holes climb up or plunge down steep hills, they are generally narrow, with lakes, out-of-bounds stakes, and stone-lined irrigation ditches guarding the fairways. Bamboo forests, tall trees, and ferns the size of houses hem in the holes, particularly on the back nine. Monkeys chatter in the recesses of the jungle. Occasionally, a wild boar tears through the underbrush. Awana is no ordinary golf course—it's a billy-goat track designed to test a player's legs, patience, and ability to factor elevation changes into distance judgment. The straight ball is everything at Awana. The course isn't long (6,560

*Fourth hole*

yards from the tips), but it is extremely unkind to offline shots. Far from Malaysia's steamy coast, Awana's weather is cool and springlike much of the year. (Avoid the period from November to January, when monsoons carry rain and fog to the mountains.) Fairways are covered in local cowgrass, a bristly, coarse-bladed strain similar to crabgrass. However, the bent-grass greens are smooth and fast.

Awana's best and most scenic holes are its par threes. At the fourth, golfers play from an elevated tee across a pond to an enormous, four-tiered green backdropped by a canyon. Simply reload if you hit short or long. At the long fifteenth (it stretches to 238 yards from the back tees), lush greenery defines the hole between tee and green, with a small pond snaring shots that fall short and to the left. A few of the holes, especially the zigzag par-five twelfth, can be adventurous or exasperating, depending upon the length and direction of your tee shot. The twelfth, among others, would not find a place in most modern designs. But then, mountain jungle courses attached to a full-service resort are few and far between.

Awana's clubhouse is integrated into a six-story condominium complex that offers superb lodgings for visiting golfers. Awana's 160 rooms feature Jacuzzis, kitchenettes, large living rooms, and balconies decked with bougainvillea and set above Japanese gardens. Amenities include a gymnasium, two heated outdoor swimming pools, and a children's playroom. The club's open-air cocktail bar and dining room serve up spectacular views of the golf course and distant hilly jungles. (The topiary animals placed behind the ninth green can be viewed from the dining room.) There are five tennis courts (three lighted for night play) and squash courts in the sports complex, as well as saunas and steam baths. There's also a practice putting green and a triple-tier driving range. For those whose legs are rubbery after climbing Awana's hills, a masseur is available. A bicycle track and a walking trail lead out into the countryside.

At the very top of the mountain, about 2,000 feet higher than the golf course, is the Genting Highlands resort, which offers Malaysia's only casino gambling. The Chinese, inveterate gamblers, pack the casino twenty-four hours a day. The resort's three modern hotels offer 1,070 rooms (none exceed Awana's accommodations for convenience or quality). Malaysia's version of a Las Vegas floor show is staged nightly in the 1,200-seat Genting Theater Restaurant, which features sumptuous Chinese cuisine. Genting and Awana are linked by Malaysia's longest cable car system, a system that could have (and should have) been extended to the golf course.

*The hotel*

# BALI HANDARA COUNTRY CLUB

SILVER MEDALIST

leafy banana trees, to the emerald green of the cemaralilin trees, to the brilliant sheen of the Kentucky bluegrass fairways. Because of its volcanic origin and lush vegetation, many visitors draw similarities between Bali Handara and Hawaii's upland courses—until they hear Hindu prayer chants emanating from the temples of Pancasari.

It's almost foolhardy to single out feature holes on a course blessed with such overpowering beauty. But Bali Handara's exquisite setting tends to mask a first-class test of golf that stretches to a daunting 7,010 yards from the championship tees. (It's more manageable from the regular tees at 6,372 yards.) The course gets off to a quick start: The number-one handicap hole is the 405-yard third, a narrow left-to-right dogleg with a fairway divided by a stream. (The entire layout is crisscrossed by mountain brooks.) The second shot is a forced carry over water to one of the smaller and more undulating greens on the course.

On the incoming nine, the 483-yard, par-five fifteenth hole is distinguished by a bunker in the center of the fairway modeled after the notorious Principal's Nose bunker on the sixteenth hole of the Old Course at St. Andrews. (Thomson won the 1955 British Open at St. Andrews and often incorporates strategic elements of the storied links in his designs—even in places as far removed from Scotland as Bali.) The 402-yard sixteenth, second in difficulty only to the third hole, brings into play a menacing fairway trap to the left and a pond to the right, the fairway bottlenecked between the two hazards.

In addition to an attractive golf clubhouse and modern accommodations in the main lodge, rustic Balinese-style bungalows are available at the resort. There is no air-conditioning or heating system in these cottages, though a fire in the living room fireplace is welcome on cool evenings. The cottages serve up spectacular views of the volcanic mountains, jungles, and the first hole.

Meals are served in the Kamandalu restaurant, where *bebek tutu* (Balinese duck), *nasi goreng* (fried rice), and *mie goreng* (fried noodles) are among the featured dishes. Light snacks and refreshments (including Bintang, the Indonesian beer of choice) are served at Segara Madu, a more casual eatery. Nightlife is nonexistent at Bali Handara. This is a place where guests gather to watch the sunset's reflection in quiet Lake Buyan, and where the lights are turned out early, the better to rise fully refreshed to play the Miss Universe of golf courses.

The reigning beauty queen of exotic golf courses is Bali Handara, a fantastic layout contained within the bowl of an extinct volcano at the edge of a rain forest. Indeed, Bali Handara ("beautiful valley") could double for the Garden of Eden in any golfer's dream of heaven. Located 4,000 feet above sea level in the highlands of central Bali ninety minutes by car from the steamy coastal city of Denpasar, the course was designed by Peter Thomson, John Harris, Michael Wolveridge, and Ronald Fream in 1975. However, it was *built* by 1,500 Balinese, many of them women.

It is said that nearly everyone on this enchanted island 500 miles south of the Equator is an artist. The rice planter is also a dancer, the carpenter a carver of ceremonial masks, the tailor a maker of batik fabrics. Under the direction of an expatriate British golf professional, villagers shaped the course by hand, integrating the fairways into the surrounding greenery of the crater floor. Holes are framed by a dazzling tapestry of flowering shrubs and broad-leafed plants that can distract even the most single-minded golfer. Raised tees, buttressed by moss-covered rocks, are landscaped with scarlet flowers and purple hedges. Greens are beautifully framed by jungle-covered mountain ridges often shrouded in mist. Despite the riot of colorful vegetation, the color green predominates, from the bright green of the

*Left: Sixteenth hole*

*Right: Traditional Balinese gateway*

*Opposite: Eighteenth hole*

# WAIRAKEI INTERNATIONAL GOLF COURSE

SILVER MEDALIST

It's not exactly around the corner for Americans, but New Zealand is worth finding on the strength of Wairakei alone. Located in an area of geothermal activity on North Island midway between Wellington and Auckland, the course was created in the early 1970s to help develop the area near Lake Taupo (famed for its trout fishing). On a high plateau marked by smoking fumaroles, spouting geysers, and burping mud pits, designer John Harris created a splendid layout on pumice and volcanic cinder.

Wairakei's most infamous hole is the long (608 yards from the tips) par-five fourteenth, nicknamed The Rogue for the rogue borehole that sheared off the top of a conical hill and once belched sulphurous steam.

Harris built a giant horseshoe-shaped green at the base of the exploded hill, protecting its entrances with bunkers and hollows. Out in the fairway, a giant pine tree deflects shots that aren't aimed far enough to the left or right of its branches. Deep fairway traps snare errant tee shots and wayward second shots. This brutal test of length and accuracy is hands down the most formidable hole in New Zealand.

It doesn't stand alone, however. At the 413-yard sixteenth, where a small pond guards the left side of the green, a sign cautions golfers who've hooked their approach shots into the hazard to use a ball retriever. The reason: extremely hot thermal water.

Wairakei's accommodations are relatively modest. The government-operated hotel has ninety rooms, including fifteen villa suites. A buffet breakfast and lunch are available in the Graham Room, which also serves à la carte dinners. In addition, the Fairway Grill features an à la carte bistro. World-class accommodations (and meals) are available at nearby Huka Lodge, set on seventeen acres alongside the Waikato River and featuring superb accommodations for thirty-four guests. The lodge's six-course meals, including local seafood, game, and surprisingly good New Zealand wines, are nonpareil.

While golf is played year round in New Zealand, October through April (late spring through early fall in the Southern Hemisphere) is the best time to visit.

*Above:*
*Thirteenth hole*

*Left:*
*Tenth hole*

*Far left:*
*Sixteenth hole*

*All photos courtesy*
*New Zealand*
*Tourism Office,*
*© Leonard Cobb*

# SHERATON MIRAGE AT PORT DOUGLAS

SILVER MEDALIST

The Great Barrier Reef, the world's largest living organism, is also the backdrop for Australia's splashiest new resort. In fact, the closest mainland point to the reef's immense coral patchwork is found on Queensland's far north coast at the Mirage Resort at Port Douglas. In Australia's equivalent of the Caribbean—the climate here is decidedly tropical—pristine Four Mile Beach fronts the Coral Sea at a 300-acre complex anchored by the Sheraton Mirage at Port Douglas. This is no ordinary Sheraton. Designed with characteristic Queensland latticing, the creamy white, low-rise hotel provides 300 rooms and suites in detached wings connected to the central

edifice by covered walkways. Each wing has its own butler service. The rooms, done in soft coral shades, each contain a private balcony and marble bathroom with spa tub. Guests can also choose to rent a secluded two-, three-, or four-bedroom villa with the same services (day care center, valet parking, etc.) available at the hotel. Hotel rooms and villas alike look out on tropical gardens and saltwater lagoons edged by man-made beaches.

A two-minute drive from the hotel is the Mirage Country Club, where the Peter Thomson–Mike Wolveridge duo fashioned a course with a Jekyll-and-Hyde personality. The front nine (called the Reef Nine) was built on sandy soil along Four Mile Beach and serves up stunning views of the Coral Sea. A few of the tees and greens back into a dense rain forest, while two of the nine's par fives, the third and seventh holes, parallel the ocean from tee to green. It's a thrilling, windswept test of golf.

The back, or Mountain Nine, was constructed over mangrove swamps and looks to the majestic Mossman River Gorge and distant tableland rain forests. The mangroves were bulldozed inward and covered with topsoil to create the land for this nine, which offers greater challenge than the front. The Mountain Nine is known for the par-four twelfth, which confronts golfers with a monstrous bunker up its left side called the Sahara Desert; and the 190-yard thirteenth, where an island green beckons from a lagoon frequented by saltwater crocodiles. According to *GOLF Magazine* correspondent Tom Ramsey, "These crocodiles, unlike the Florida alligator, are not to be trifled with. They have been known to grab a horse or a cow by the nose and pull them underwater." Play safely.

Despite its split personality, the Mirage exhibits good balance: There are three par threes, fours, and fives on each nine, the architects bending the shape of the holes to fit the two elongated parcels of land set aside for the layout in 1988. Plans are afoot to sculpt a third nine out of the mangroves and attach it to the existing Mountain Nine. The Reef Nine would then be reserved for more casual play by those who welcome the chance to play a jungly links.

The Mirage invites players to warm up before the round at a driving range that fronts a lagoon. Golfers hit floating balls (they feel solid at impact but lose zip after 100 yards or so) into the water. The splash is satisfying when it doesn't spell disaster. The balls are later directed by an artificial current to the far end of the range, where they are retrieved and recycled.

In addition to fine meals served at the Country Club restaurant and terrace, the Sheraton offers a good range of dining options. Macrossans offers exceptional continental cuisine indoors or on a terrace, while exotic cocktails (and afternoon tea) are served in the Daintree Lounge, which overlooks the lagoons and the sea.

By day, the hotel's freshwater swimming pool features a swim-up bar at one end and snorkeling and scuba diving classes at the other. The resort's 125-slip marina has craft available for game fishing, sailing, scuba diving—or for picnicking on one of the many tiny, secluded islands rising from one of the world's greatest natural wonders.

*Opposite: Twelfth hole*

*Above: Swimming pool. Photo courtesy Sheraton Mirage Resort at Port Douglas*

*Left: Waterfall*

# HYATT REGENCY SANCTUARY COVE

## SILVER MEDALIST

An hour's drive south of Brisbane—or an even shorter drive from a settlement called Surfers Paradise—is a $375-million resort that has set the standard for development along Queensland's Gold Coast. Situated on Hope Island in the Coomera River, the resort got off to a rousing start in 1988 when Frank Sinatra was paid $1 million to sing twenty-four songs on opening night.

The Palms, opened in 1986, is a sporty test stretching to 6,574 yards (6,015 yards from the regular tees). Most important, the drainage problems that had plagued the layout's fairways in years past have been solved. Woven through old groves of cabbage palms, the Palms has water in play at thirteen holes to bedevil careless players. However, its main purpose is to provide a carefree, scenic round of golf for middle to high-handicappers who can elect to ride in golf carts, though most Australians prefer to walk. The Palms functions as a daily fee course that is open to the public.

Sanctuary Cove's second layout, the Pines, is a horse of a different color. Designed by Arnold Palmer and Ed Seay, the Pines has been rated the most challenging and difficult in the land by the Australian Golf Union. It plays monstrously tough from the tips at 7,300 yards, although staggered tees give everyone a fighting chance.

Routed through a thick pine forest and dotted with lakes, the Pines could pass for a firebreather in northern Florida—the TPC at Sawgrass without the railroad ties, for instance. The layout's bent grass greens are exceptionally slick, though threading the ball through the pines and over the lakes presents the major obstacle to good scoring. The Pines is reserved exclusively for club members and guests of the Hyatt Regency Sanctuary Cove.

The clubhouse at Sanctuary Cove, the equal of any private club in America, would make a Hollywood mogul feel at home. There's a luxuriously appointed spa, Italian marble flooring, and other opulent touches. For example, the "wallpaper" in the men's card room is cashmere.

The 247-room Hyatt Regency Sanctuary Cove, inspired by a colonial Australian home, compares favorably to the country club in quality. The hotel's Great House is distinguished by stained-glass windows, polished Australian red cedar walls, and parquet floors. Guests receive complimentary continental breakfast each morning as well as canapés and cocktails each evening in the hotel's Regency Club, an exclusive section of the hotel consisting of five low-rise lodges.

Rooms and suites, all furnished with balconies, follow an Australian country theme (it's a variation of Ralph Lauren/Polo Down Under): cedar armoires, cedar washstands in the bathrooms, and fine toiletries.

The Hyatt's top dining room is The Grange. The more casual Cove Café overlooks the marina, but the best view is found at Michael's Bar, a comfortable saloon favored by club members and resort guests alike. It's a favorite nineteenth hole of golfers who like to congregate by its curved Queensland bay window to enjoy a lingering sunset over the Coomera River.

*Large picture: Palms Course, seventh hole*
*Inset above: Country Club and lagoon pool*
*Inset below: At dusk. All photos courtesy Sanctuary Cove Resort*

# AUSTRAL/ASIA

## TIPS AND SIDE TRIPS

Greenmount Beach, Queensland, Australia. Photo courtesy
© Queensland Tourist and Travel Corp.

Not far from the Phoenix Hotel & Resort, sports and recreation can be pursued in Miyazaki's Prefectural Sports Park, which serves as the spring training grounds of the Tokyo Yomiuri Giants baseball team. The Miyazaki Science Center boasts the world's largest planetarium dome, while the Peace Tower in Heiwadai Park serves up a fine panorama. In a pine grove near the tower is the Haniwa Doll Garden, where clay doll replicas of those found during excavation of burial grounds in Miyazaki Prefecture are on display.

The Rose Garden in Thailand is conveniently located between Bangkok and the beach resorts of Hua Hin and Cha-am. Other nearby attractions include the famous Bridge over the River Kwai, the still unspoiled floating market at Damnoen Saduak, and the world's highest chedi (temple) at Nakhon Pathom. In Bangkok, arrange to tour the klongs, or canals, in one of the city's sleek, long-tailed boats, preferably one with a sunshade. It's the best way to see the teeming city and avoid its often gridlocked streets.

Convenient to the Kawana Hotel is the scenic Jogasaki coast and its many spa towns. Sushi and sashimi dishes available in seaside restaurants along the coast are among the best available in Japan. Izu Seaside Park and its maritime exhibits is a short drive south from the resort. *Hanami*—cherry blossom viewing parties—are held throughout peak blossom time. Merry-makers pack picnic lunches and sing, dance, eat, and drink under the canopy of the flowering trees. Some of these trees are illuminated, enabling the festivities to continue into the night.

In the Karuizawa area, a number of picturesque villages along Japan's old feudal highway are still intact. One of these former *shukuba* is Miyota, home of Ocean Whiskey's pure malt Karuizawa and blended Asama brands of Scotch whiskey. Both are prepared in copper stills with peat-dried malt and barley from Scotland and aged for fifteen to twenty years in oak barrels. Komoro, once the site of an important castle, is known for its lovely park and cherry trees. Karuizawa's main landmark is the still-active volcano of Mount Asama, which is best viewed from Usui Pass. The Onioshidashi rocks (Japanese for "pushed out by demons"), formed in 1783 by the mountain's last great eruption, rank among the world's most remarkable lava deposits. Located nearby are the Asama Museum and Asama Pasture (where fresh milk is served).

Hakone is well known for its hot springs, mountain scenery, and historic spots. In this region of deep glens and ravines, the aerial cablecar and funicular railway are the main modes of transportation. Gora, a spa developed on the slope of Mount Sounzan, is the terminal of the railways. Nearby is the Open Air Museum, a park with indoor and outdoor sculpture exhibits. Other points of interest include the Hakone Shrine, said to have been founded in 757; Owakudani and Kowakidani valleys, where sulphurous fumes rise from crevices in the rock; and Old Hakone Check-Point, where a replica of the original Check-Point House dating to 1618 can be viewed.

Mount Agung, Bali. Photo courtesy © Tibor Boguar/The Stock Market

The Hyatt Saujana Hotel & Country Club is very convenient to Kuala Lumpur, a model Asian city where British colonial buildings, Moorish mosques, and Chinese shops nestle among new skyscrapers. Top attractions include Masjid Negara (National Mosque); National Museum and Art Gallery; the Selangor Pewter Demonstration Centre (Malaysia is known for its fine pewter); and the National Zoo. The city's night market attracts Burmese and Nepalese traders who sell beaded necklaces, semiprecious stones, antique tea caddies, hand-carved wooden masks, and other novelties.

Genting Highlands, above the Awana Golf & Country Club, is a remote, all-inclusive mountaintop resort with nothing around it except jungle-covered hills. Kuala Lumpur is about an hour's drive from the resort.

In Bali, the most appealing scenery and villages are found well away from the island's major tourist centers. A drive round Mount Agung, a volcano that destroyed much of eastern Bali in 1963, leads through tiny settlements where lush ferns hang down from the cliffs. Bali Barat National Park, off the island's north coast, offers superb snorkeling. Rafting trips on the Ayung river in the center of the island are popular. Ubud is known for its terraced rice fields and international artist's colony, while nearly all of Bali is marked by Hindu and Buddhist temples, several of them ancient. Yeh Pulu, for example, features a rock wall of intricate reliefs dating back 600 years. Balinese paintings, wood carvings, and batik fabric (Indonesia's national handicraft) are the items most in demand by shoppers.

*Replica of a pirate ship on Lake Ashino, Hakone, with Mount Fuji. Photo courtesy © The Stock Market*

Not far from Wairakei in New Zealand, near the town of Te Kuiti, are the Waitomo Caves, famous for the Glow Worm Grotto. Underground boat tours travel through limestone caves lit from above by the insects' luminescent bodies. Scenic preserves along Lake Taupo, the nation's largest lake, can be visited by boat or explored via footpath. The Tongariro River, which flows into the lake near Turangi, is world famous for its trout fishing (four-pounders are considered average). To the west of Lake Taupo, Pureora Forest Park is one of the last strongholds of the sweet-voiced kokako, a member of the wattle-bird family. In nearby Rotorua, travelers can view spouting geysers and boiling mud pools, while spent golfers can soak in the steaming, sulphur-enriched waters of the pumice-bottomed Polynesian Hot Pools.

The Great Barrier Reef is the main attraction along Australia's northeast coast near Port Douglas. Day trips can be planned to Lizard Island, known for its spectacular coral formations and abundant marine life; Dunk Island, famous for its lush rain forest; or Great Keppel Island, home to seventeen white sandy beaches and several popular nightclubs. Deep-sea fishing charters originate in nearby Cairns, a staging point for some of the world's finest black marlin fishing, while nature lovers can journey to the Daintree Forest and Cape Tribulation for a look at an untouched rain forest.

Sanctuary Cove is convenient to Seaworld, Australia's largest marine attraction; Dreamworld, a family theme park; and Koala Town, where koala bears can be seen. Much of the Gold Coast is unashamedly commercial and is reminiscent of southern California in the 1960s. Surfers Paradise is known for its trendy boutiques, while gamblers usually gravitate to Jupiters Casino. For passive entertainment, visit Kirra and Burleigh Heads south of Sanctuary Cove to watch some of the best surfers in the world ride near-perfect waves into shore.

## DON'T LEAVE HOME WITHOUT...A KNOCKDOWN SHOT

*The eastern shore of Australia along the Gold Coast is subject to strong winds off the South Pacific Ocean. Local golfers have become adept at manufacturing knockdown shots to better control the ball in the breeze. So should you.*

*The secret to a low, piercing shot that penetrates the wind is a solid hit and a low follow-through. The setup for a knockdown shot is all-important: Align yourself square to the target, spread your feet slightly wider than shoulder width, and place between 60 and 70 percent of your weight on the left foot. Play the ball farther back in your stance than normal and set your hands at least two inches ahead of the clubface. Grip pressure should be firm, particularly with the left hand. This setup encourages a descending blow designed to launch the ball on a low trajectory.*

*The swing itself should be rhythmic but compact. Sweep the clubhead back primarily with the arms to minimize wrist cock. (Choking down slightly on the grip reduces both the action of the wrists and the arc of the clubhead, promoting a lower shot.) A three-quarter backswing is sufficient in most situations: The idea is to maintain balance and control of the club. On the downswing, extend fully through the ball with the left hand leading the shot. Finish low, with your arms and the club pointing to the target. A properly executed knockdown shot will bore into a headwind and hold its line in a crosswind.*

PHIL CURD, DIRECTOR OF GOLF,
SANCTUARY COVE RESORT

# DIRECTORY

Amelia Island Plantation
Amelia Island, FL 32034

The American Club
Highland Drive
Kohler, WI 53044

Arizona Biltmore
24th Street & Missouri
Phoenix, AZ 85016

Awana Golf & Country Club
8th Mile
Genting Highlands
69000 Genting Highlands
Malaysia

Bali Handara Country Club
P. O. Box 324 Denpasar
Pancasari, Bali
Indonesia

The Balsams
Dixville Notch, NH 03576

Banff Springs Hotel
P.O. Box 960
Spray Avenue
Banff, Alberta
Canada TOL OCO

Barton Creek
8212 Barton Club Drive
Austin, TX 78735

Bay Hill Club & Lodge
9000 Bay Hill Boulevard
Orlando, FL 32819

Black Butte Ranch
P. O. Box 8000
Black Butte Ranch, OR 97759

Boca Raton Resort & Club
501 East Camino Real
Boca Raton, FL 33432

The Boulders
P. O. Box 2090
34631 North Tom Darlington Drive
Carefree, AZ 85377

Boyne Highlands
Harbor Springs, MI 49740

The Breakers
One South County Road
Palm Beach, FL 33480

The Broadmoor
1 Lake Avenue
Colorado Springs, CO 80906

Callaway Gardens
Pine Mountain, GA 31822

Cape Breton Highlands Golf Links/
Keltic Lodge
Ingonish Beach, Nova Scotia
Canada B0C 1L0

Casa de Campo
La Romana
Dominican Republic

Chateau Whistler Resort
4599 Chateau Boulevard
P.O. Box 100
Whistler, B.C.
Canada VON 1BO

The Cloister/Sea Island
Golf Club
Sea Island, GA 31561

The Coeur d'Alene Resort
On the Lake
Coeur d'Alene, ID 83814

Cotton Bay Club
P.O. Box 28
Rock Sound, Eleuthera, Bahamas

Deauville Golf Club
14800 Deauville
France

Walt Disney World
P.O. Box 10,000
Lake Buena Vista, FL 32830

Doral Resort and Country Club
4400 Northwest 87 Avenue
Miami, FL 33178

Estoril Palacio Golf Club
Parque do Estoril
2765 Estoril, Portugal

The Equinox
Route 7A
Manchester Village, VT 05254

Four Seasons Resort and Club/
TPC at Las Colinas
4150 North MacArthur Boulevard
Irving, TX 75038

The Gleneagles Hotel
Auchterarder, Perthshire
Scotland PH3 1NF

Grand Cypress Resort
60 Grand Cypress Boulevard
Orlando, FL 32836

Grand Traverse Resort
6300 U.S. 31 North
Grand Traverse Village, MI 49610

The Greenbrier
White Sulphur Springs, WV 24986

Grenelefe Resort
3200 State Road 546
Grenelefe, FL 33844

Hakone Prince Resort
144 Motohakone, Hakone-machi
Ashigarashimo-gun, Kanagawa
250-05
Japan

The Hotel Hershey
Hotel Road
Hershey, PA 17033

The Homestead
Hot Springs, VA 24445

Horseshoe Bay Country Club
Resort
Box 7766
Horseshoe Bay, TX 78654

Hyatt Dorado Beach
Dorado, Puerto Rico 00646

Hyatt Grand Champions Resort
*see* Indian Wells

Hyatt Regency Cerromar Beach
Dorado, Puerto Rico 00646

Hyatt Regency Hilton Head
P.O. Box 6167
Hilton Head Island, SC 29938

Hyatt Regency Sanctuary Cove
Hope Island
Queensland 4212
Australia

Hyatt Saujana Golf &
Country Club
Subang International Airport
Highway
P.O. Box 111
46710 Petaling Jaya
Malaysia

Indian Wells Golf Resort/
Hyatt Grand Champions
44-500 Indian Wells Lane
Indian Wells, CA 92210

The Inn and Links at Spanish Bay
17 Mile Drive
Pebble Beach, CA 93953

Innisbrook Hilton Resort
P.O. Drawer 1088
Tarpon Springs, FL 34688

Jasper Park Lodge
P.O. Box 40
Jasper, Alberta
Canada T0E 1E0

Kapalua Bay Hotel & Villas
One Bay Drive
Kapalua, Maui
Lahaina, HI 96761

Karuizawa
Karuizawa, Karuizawa-machi
Kitasaku-gun, Nagano 389-01
Japan

Kauai Lagoons Golf &
Racquet Club
P.O. Box 3330
Kalapaki Beach
Lihue, HI 96766

Kawana Hotel
1459 Kawana
Ito, Shizuoka Prefecture
Japan

Kiawah Island Inn and Villas
P.O. Box 12357
Charleston, SC 29412

Kingsmill Resort
1010 Kingsmill Road
Williamsburg, VA 23185

La Costa Resort and Spa
Costa del Mar Road
Carlsbad, CA 92009

La Manga Club
Los Belones
Cartagena, Murcia, Spain

La Quinta Hotel Golf &
Tennis Resort
P.O. Box 69
49-499 Eisenhower Drive
La Quinta, CA 92253

Linville Golf Club / Eseeola Lodge
P.O. Box 98
Linville, NC 28646

The Lodge at Pebble Beach
17 Mile Drive
Pebble Beach, CA 93953

Loews Ventana Canyon Resort
7000 North Resort Drive
Tucson, AZ 85715

Manoir Richelieu
181 rue Richelieu
Pointe-au-Pic
Charlevoix, Quebec
Canada G0T 1M0

Marriott at Sawgrass
1000 TPC Boulevard
Ponte Vedra Beach, FL 32082

Mariott's Grand Hotel & Resort
Point Clear, AL 36564

Marriott's Seaview Resort
401 South New York Road
Absecon, NJ 08201

Mauna Kea Beach Hotel
One Mauna Kea Beach Drive
Kohala Coast, HI 96743

Mauna Lani Resort
P.O. Box 4959
Kohala Coast, HI 96743

Ojai Valley Inn & Country Club
Country Club Road
Ojai, CA 93023

Palmetto Dunes Resort
P.O. Box 5628
Hilton Head Island, SC 29938

Penina Golf Hotel
P.O. Box 146 Penina
8502 Portimão Codex
Algarve, Portugal

Pevero Golf Club
07020 Porto Cervo,
Costa Smeralda
Sardinia, Italy

PGA National Resort & Spa
400 Avenue of the Champions
Palm Beach Gardens, FL 33418

The Phoenician
6000 East Camelback Road
Scottsdale, AZ 85251

Phoenix Hotels & Resort
3083 Hamayama, Shioji
Miyazaki 880-01
Japan

Pinehurst Resort and Country Club
P.O. Box 4000
Pinehurst, NC 28374

Port Ludlow Golf & Meeting
Retreat
9483 Oak Bay Road
Port Ludlow, WA 98365

Port Royal Golf & Racquet Club
P.O. Drawer 7229
Hilton Head Island, SC 29938

Princeville Resort
P.O. Box 3040
Princeville, Kauai, HI 96722

Quail Lodge Resort & Golf Club
8205 Valley Greens Drive
Carmel, CA 93923

Quinta do Lago
Almansil 8100 Loule
Algarve, Portugal

The Resort at Longboat Key Club
301 Gulf of Mexico Drive
Longboat Key, FL 33548

The Resort Semiahmoo
9565 Semiahmoo Parkway
Blaine, WA 98230

The Rose Garden
4/8 Sukhumvit Soi 3
Bangkok 10110
Thailand

The Sagamore
110 Sagamore Road
Bolton Landing, NY 12814

Sheraton Mirage Port Douglas
P.O. Box 172
Port Douglas, Queensland 4871
Australia

Silverado Country Club & Resort
1600 Atlas Peak Road
Napa, CA 94558

Sunriver Lodge & Resort
P.O. Box 3609
Sunriver, OR 97707

Torrequebrada
P.O. Box 67
29630 Benalmadena
Costa Del Sol, Spain

Tryall Golf, Tennis & Beach Resort
Box 1206
Montego Bay, Jamaica, West Indies

Turnberry Hotel & Golf Courses
Turnberry, Ayrshire
Scotland KA26 9LT

Turnberry Isle Resort & Club
19999 West Country Club Drive
Aventura, FL 33180

Ventana Canyon Golf &
Racquet Club
6200 North Clubhouse Lane
Tucson, AZ 85715

Vilamoura Golf Club
Vilamoura 8125 Quarteira
Algarve, Portugal

Waikoloa Beach Resort/
Hyatt Regency Waikoloa
HC02 Box 5455
Waikoloa, HI 96743

Wairakei International
Golf Course
Wairakei Hotel
Taupo, New Zealand

Waterville House and Golf Links
Waterville, Ring of Kerry
Ireland

Westin Hilton Head
135 South Port Royal Drive
Hilton Head Island, SC 29928

Westin Kauai
Kalapaki Beach
Lihue, HI 96766

Westin La Paloma
3800 East Sunrise Drive
Tucson, AZ 85718

The Wigwam Resort
Litchfield Park, AZ 85340

The Williamsburg Inn/
Golden Horseshoe Golf Courses
P.O. Box C
Williamsburg, VA 23187

Wintergreen
P.O. Box 706
Wintergreen, VA 22958